RAPE AND
SEXUAL ASSAULT
II

Garland Reference Library
of Social Science (Vol. 361)

RAPE AND SEXUAL ASSAULT II

Ann Wolbert Burgess

Garland Publishing, Inc.
New York & London 1988

Library of Congress Cataloging-in-Publication Data

Rape and sexual assault II.

    (Garland reference library of social science ; vol. 361)
    Includes bibliographies.
    1. Rape—United States. 2. Rape victims—United States. 3. Child molesting—United States.
I. Burgess, Ann Wolbert. II. Series: Garland reference library of social science ; v. 361.
HV6561.R368 1988   362.8'83'0973   87-23624
ISBN 0-8240-8528-0 (alk. paper)

Printed on acid-free, 250-year-paper

Manufactured in the United States of America

CONTENTS

Part 1. The Victims of Rape and Sexual Assault

Contributors   xi
List of Figures   xiii
List of Tables   xv
Preface   xix

√ **Chapter 1.** Hidden Rape: Sexual Aggression and
   Victimization in a National Sample in Higher
   Education   **3**
           Mary P. Koss
                 Previous Research   4
                 Methods   5
                 Results   10
                 Discussion   20
                 References   24

Chapter 2. Victims of Violence and
   Psychiatric Illness   **27**
           Elaine (Hilberman) Carmen, Patricia
           Perri Rieker, and Trudy Mills
                 Abuse and Psychiatric Illness   27
                 Methods   29
                 Results   30
                 Discussion   35
                 Conclusions   37
                 References   38

Chapter 3. Histories of Violence in an Outpatient
Population: An Exploratory Study   **41**
     Judith Lewis Herman
               Methods   42
               Results   43
               Discussion   47
               References   48

Chapter 4. Sexual Trauma, Dysfunction, and
Preference Associated with Alcohol and Drug
Dependency in Nurses   **51**
     Eleanor J. Sullivan
               Methods   53
               Results   54
               Discussion   57
               References   59

Chapter 5. Sexual Harassment of Students by
Teachers: The Case of Students in Science   **61**
     Arlene McCormack
               Study Description   63
               Sexual Harassment Experiences   66
               Summary and Discussion   68
               Notes   70
               References   71

Chapter 6. Compounding Factors in the Rape of
Street Prostitutes   **75**
     Mimi H. Silbert
               Methods   77
               Results   79
               Summary and Conclusions   87
               References   88

Chapter 7. The Sexual Abuse of Boys: Childhood
Victimizations Reported by a National Sample   **91**
     Leslie I. Risin and Mary P. Koss
          Methods   93
          Results   97
          Discussion   101
          References   104

Chapter 8. Victim Response Strategies in
Sexual Assault   **105**
     *Daniel L. Carter, Robert Alan Prentky, and
     Ann Wolbert Burgess*
          Methods   108
          Results   114
          Discussion of Findings   116
          Clinical Observations of Victim Response 118
          Notes   128
          References   129

Chapter 9. Sexualized Therapy: Causes and
Consequences   **133**
     Roberta Apfel and Bennett Simon
          Causes of Therapist-Patient Sexual
              Contact   134
          Consequences of Therapist-Patient
              Sexual Contact   144
          Consultation and Evaluation   146
          References   149

Chapter 10. Self-Blame in Recovery from Rape:
Help or Hindrance?   **151**
     Bonnie L. Katz and Martha R. Burt
          Previous Research   152
          Methods   155
          Results   160
          Discussion   164
          References   167

Chapter 11. Responding to the Needs of Rape Victims:
Research Findings   **169**
  Linda E. Ledray
      Previous Research   170
      Study Goals   172
      Methods   173
      Results   177
      Discussion   187
      References   189

Part 2.   The Social Context of Rape and Sexual Assault

Chapter 12. Sexual Socialization and Attitudes
toward Rape   **193**
  Ilsa L. Lottes
      Etiology of Rape   194
      Attitudes toward Rape   203
      References   214

Chapter 13. Vulnerability to Sexual Assault   **221**
  Suzanne S. Ageton
      Conceptualization of Vulnerability   223
      Research Design   226
      Study Sample   226
      Analysis Procedures   229
      Victim and Control-Group Comparisons   230
      Uniqueness of Sexual-Assault Victims   240
      Notes   241
      References   242

Chapter 14. Adolescents and Their Perceptions
of Sexual Interactions **245**
Jacqueline D. Goodchilds, Gail L. Zellman,
Paula B. Johnson, and Roseann Giarrusso
Perceptions of Responsibility for "Dating"
Outcomes 246
Cues and Signals Concerning Sexuality 252
Expectations for Dating Relationships 256
Application of the Label *Rape* to
Nonconsensual Sex between
Acquaintances 264
Notes 269
References 269

√**Chapter 15.** Rape-Law Reform: An Analysis **271**
Mary Ann Largen
Rape: The Common-Law Tradition 271
Rape-Law Reform: Origins and Goals 273
Legislative Success: Significant Change,
Pastiche of New Laws 275
A Postreform Analysis 278
References and Bibliography 290

Chapter 16. The Impact of Crime on Urban Women **293**
Stephanie Riger and Margaret T. Gordon
Victimization of Urban Women 295
Women's Responses to Urban Crime 300
Precautionary Strategies 302
Mitigating Circumstances 305
Crime and Quality of Life for Women 307
Understanding the Impact of Crime on
Women 309
References 312

Chapter 17. An Analysis of Pornography Research   **317**
           Gail Dines-Levy
                    Limitations of Pornography Studies   318
                    An Alternative Method for Studying
                        Pornography   320
                    References   322
Index   325

CONTRIBUTORS

Suzanne S. Ageton, Ph.D.
J.D. Candidate
School of Law
University of Colorado
Boulder, Colo.

Roberta Apfel, M.D., M.P.H.
Assistant Professor of Psychiatry
Harvard Medical School,
    Cambridge Hospital
Cambridge, Mass.

Ann Wolbert Burgess, R.N.,
    D.N.Sc.
Van Ameringen Professor of
    Psychiatric Nursing
University of Pennsylvania
    School of Nursing
Philadelphia, Pa.

Martha R. Burt, Ph.D.
Director of Social Services
    Research Program
The Urban Institute
Washington, D.C.

Elaine (Hilberman) Carmen, M.D.
Professor of Psychiatry
Boston University School of
    Medicine
Boston, Mass.

Daniel L. Carter, B.A.
Research Project Coordinator
Massachusetts Treatment Center
Bridgewater, Mass.

Marieanne L. Clark, M.S.
Editor
Hinsdale, Mass.

Gail Dines-Levy
Ph.D. Candidate, Lecturer in
    Sociology
Wheelock College
Boston, Mass.

Roseann Giarrusso, M.A.
Graduate Student
Department of Sociology
University of California, Los
    Angeles
Los Angeles, Calif.

Jacqueline D. Goodchilds, Ph.D.
Adjunct Associate Professor
Department of Psychology
University of California, Los
    Angeles
Los Angeles, Calif.

Margaret T. Gordon, Ph.D.
Director of Center for Urban
    Affairs and Policy Research
Northwestern University
Evanston, Ill.

Judith Lewis Herman, M.D.
Assistant Clinical Professor of
    Psychiatry
Harvard Medical School,
    Cambridge Hospital
Cambridge, Mass.

Paula B. Johnson, Ph.D.
Core Faculty
California School of Professional
    Psychology, Los Angeles
Los Angeles, Calif.

Bonnie L. Katz
Ph.D. Candidate, Research
    Consultant
The Urban Institute
Washington, D.C.

Mary P. Koss, Ph.D.
Professor
Department of Psychology
Kent State University
Kent, Ohio

Mary Ann Largen
Program Associate
Stone Center for Developmental
    Services and Studies
Wellesley College
Wellesley, Mass.

Linda E. Ledray, R.N., Ph.D.
Director of Sexual Assault
    Resource Service
Hennepin County Medical Center
Minneapolis, Minn.

Ilsa L. Lottes, Ph.D.
Graduate School of Education
University of Pennsylvania
Philadelphia, Pa.

Arlene McCormack, Ph.D.
Assistant Professor of Sociology
University of Lowell
Lowell, Mass.

Trudy Mills, Ph.D.
Assistant Professor
Department of Sociology
University of Arizona
Tucson, Ariz.

Robert Alan Prentky, Ph.D.
Director of Research
Massachusetts Treatment Center
Bridgewater, Mass.

Patricia Perri Rieker, Ph.D.
Director of Psychosocial
    Research
Dana-Farber Cancer Institute
Boston, Mass.

Stephanie Riger, Ph.D.
Associate Professor of
    Psychology
Lake Forest College
Lake Forest, Ill.

Leslie I. Risin, M.A.
Graduate Student
Ohio University
Athens, Ohio

Mimi H. Silbert, Ph.D.
President, C.E.O.
Delancey Street Foundation
San Francisco, Calif.

Bennett Simon, M.D.
Clinical Associate Professor of
    Psychiatry
Harvard Medical School, Beth
    Israel Hospital
Boston, Mass.

Eleanor J. Sullivan, R.N., Ph.D.
Associate Dean, Associate
    Professor
School of Nursing
University of Minnesota
Minneapolis, Minn.

Gail L. Zellman, Ph.D.
Research Scientist
The Rand Corporation
Santa Monica, Calif.

FIGURES

8.1   Victim Response Strategies   123

10.1   Distribution of Amount of Blame for Rape Attributed to Self   161

11.1   Beck Depression Inventory Scores by Four Treatment Conditions   178

11.2   Beck Depression Inventory Scores by Two Treatment Conditions   179

11.3   Symptom Checklist Depression-Scale Scores by Four Treatment Conditions   180

11.4   Symptom Checklist Phobic-Anxiety-Scale Scores by Four Treatment Conditions   182

11.5   Symptom Checklist Anxiety-Scale Scores by Four Treatment Conditions   183

11.6   Behavioral Outcome by Four Treatment Conditions   184

11.7   Behavioral Outcome by Two Treatment Conditions   184

TABLES

1.1 Frequencies of Individual Sexual Experiences
Reported by Postsecondary Student: Prevalence
since Age 14   8

1.2 Prevalence Rates for Five Levels of Sexual
Aggression and Sexual Victimization   11

1.3 Frequencies of Individual Sexual Experiences
Reported by Postsecondary Student: One-Year
Incidence   13

1.4 Descriptive Characteristics of Sexual Victimizations
Reported by Women: Continuous Criterion
Variables   15

1.5 Descriptive Characteristics of Sexual Victimizations
Reported by Women: Dichotomous
Variables   16

1.6 Descriptive Characteristics of Sexually Aggressive
Acts Reported by Men: Continuous Criterion
Variables   18

1.7 Descriptive Characteristics of Sexually Aggressive
Acts Reported by Men: Dichotomous Variables   19

2.1 Social History and Admission Behaviors of Abused
and Nonabused Psychiatric Patients   32

2.2 Social History and Admission Behaviors of Abused
and Nonabused Male and Female Psychiatric
Patients   34

2.3 Anger/Aggression Coping Behaviors of Abused and
Nonabused Male and Female Psychiatric Patients   34

3.1 Demographic Characteristics of 190 Consecutive
     Outpatients   44

3.2 Diagnoses of 190 Consecutive Outpatients   44

3.3 Histories of Violence of 190 Consecutive
     Outpatients   45

3.4 Type of Victimization of 190 Consecutive
     Outpatients   45

3.5 Type of Offense of 190 Consecutive Outpatients   45

3.6 Victimization History and Diagnosis of Females in
     190 Consecutive Outpatients   46

3.7 Offender History and Diagnosis of Males in 190
     Consecutive Outpatients   46

4.1 Analysis of Sexuality and Sexual Problems
     Associated with Alcohol and Drug Dependency
     in Nurses   55

4.2 Sexual Trauma and Sexual Problems of Male and
     Female Alcoholic/Drug-Dependent Nurses   56

5.1 Level of Schooling, Field of Study, and Gender of
     Student Participants   63

5.2 Sexual Harassment and Student Gender   65

5.3 Experiences of Sexual Harassment and Level of
     Schooling   65

6.1 Attitudes of Prostitutes after Rape   82

6.2 Perceptions of Prostitutes after Rape   87

7.1 Situational Characteristics among Three Levels of
     Severity of Childhood Sexual Abuse   99

8.1 Victim Characteristics   109

8.2 Victim Response Associated with Expressive
     Aggression before or during Offense   115

8.3 Victim Response Associated with Expressive
     Aggression after Sexual Act   115

8.4   Victim Response Associated with Physical Injury   116

10.1   Correlations of Self-Blame with Other Variables   163

11.1   Frequency Distribution of Beck Depression
       Inventory Scores by Treatment Group at Three
       Weeks   178

11.2   Beck Depression Inventory Sample Size by
       Treatment Group   179

11.3   Correlation of Beck Depression Inventory Scores
       and Symptom Checklist Depression Scores at
       Contact Points for Treatment Groups   180

11.4   Summary of Findings: Analysis of Variance   185

11.5   Summary of Findings: Repeated-Measures
       Contrasts   185

13.1   Significant Mean ($\overline{X}$) Differences between Victims
       and Controls on Self-Report Delinquency and
       Victimization Scales, 1978   231

13.2   Significant Mean ($\overline{X}$) Differences between Victims
       and Controls on Attitudinal and Behavioral
       Scales, 1979   232

13.3   Significant Mean ($\overline{X}$) Differences between Victims
       and Controls on Attitudinal and Behavioral
       Scales, 1980   235

13.4   Mean Differences between Future Sexual-Assault
       Victims (V) and Controls (C) on Selected
       Attitudinal Scales   238

14.1   Responsibility for Outcome: All Vignettes   248

14.2   Responsibility for Outcome: "Rape" Vignettes   248

14.3   Responsibility for Outcome: ANOVA F Values   250

14.4   Situational Cues   253

14.5   Behavioral Cues   254

14.6   Circumstances Legitimizing Force   255

14.7   Perceptions of Attire as a Signal for Sex   259

14.8   Perceptions of Location as a Signal for Sex   261

14.9   Perceptions of Behavior as a Signal for Sex   263

14.10 Overall Application of Rape Label   266

14.11 Application of Rape Label by Level of Force,
       Relationship, and Setting   267

14.12 Application of Rape Label by Levels of Force
       and Relationship   267

16.1   Victimization Rates in the U.S., 1978   296

16.2   Feelings of Personal Safety When Out Alone in
       Neighborhood at Night   301

16.3   Demographic Distribution of Frequent Use of
       Precautionary Behavior   303

PREFACE

This second volume of research on rape and sexual assault addresses a wide range of topical issues focusing on two major areas: victim populations and the social context of rape. With the continuing increase in reported rapes and identification of new victim groups comes the need for an expanded understanding of the impact of sexual assault. The chapters in this book provide a basis for new insights into both the effect of rape on its victims and the social constructs that support and promote rape in our culture.

PART 1: THE VICTIMS OF RAPE AND SEXUAL ASSAULT

In chapter 1, "Hidden Rape: Sexual Aggression and Victimization in a National Sample of College Students," Mary P. Koss presents her findings from a study involving 6,159 women and men enrolled in 32 U.S. institutions of higher education. Women's reports of experiencing and men's reports of perpetrating rape, attempted rape, sexual coercion, and sexual contact provided data for prevalence rates, incidence rates, and descriptive characteristics. The results reinforce recent suggestions that the methods currently used to measure sexual assault in national crime statistics and criminal victimization studies are inadequate. The study demonstrates that sexual assault consists of a small number of identified cases and a much larger number of hidden cases of rape. Descriptive profiles of sexual aggression and victimization are presented, and study implications for clinical work, research, and rape-education/prevention programming are suggested.

Various studies have advanced our knowledge of rape's impact on victims by investigating possible linkages between prior sexual victimization and subsequent life difficulties. In chapter 2, "Victims of Violence and Psychiatric Illness," Elaine (Hilberman) Carmen, Patricia Perri Rieker, and Trudy Mills investigate the relationship between physical and sexual abuse and psychiatric illness. The life (experiences of 188 male and female psychiatric patients were reconstructed through an in-depth examination of psychiatric inpatient records. Almost half of the patients had histories of physical and/or sexual abuse; 90% of the abused patients' responses to chronic victimization included difficulty in coping with anger and aggression, impaired self-esteem, and inability to trust. The authors compare male and female victims and discuss the clinical implications of abuse.

Exploring this theme in another population, Judith Lewis Herman evaluated diagnostic summaries of 190 consecutive outpatients in an urban teaching hospital's psychiatric clinic. Chapter 3, "Histories of Violence in an Outpatient Population: An Exploratory Study," describes the findings of her review of the patients' experiences of physical and sexual violence. Approximately one-third (32%) of the female patients had been victimized and 29% of the male patients had been abusive to others. The majority of the violence was intrafamilial. Diagnoses of borderline personality disorder and substance abuse were associated with a history of victimization in female patients. The author suggests that on the basis of these findings, systematic questioning of all patients regarding their experiences of violence appears warranted.

Sexual trauma, sexual functioning, and sexual preference were compared with the occurrence of alcoholism and drug dependency in a national survey of 661 registered nurses. In chapter 4, "Sexual Trauma, Dysfunction, and Preference Associated with Alcohol and Drug Dependency in Nurses," Eleanor J. Sullivan reports on this study, which found that alcoholic and drug-dependent nurses had a significantly higher incidence of sexual abuse, sexual dysfunction, pregnancy problems, and homosexuality than their nondependent colleagues. Although more male than female nurses were homosexual, female homosexual nurses were more often victims of incest than their male counterparts. Other study findings are also discussed, and the author poses questions requiring further investigation.

In chapter 5, "Sexual Harassment of Students by Teachers: The Case of Students in Science," Arlene McCormack reports the findings of a study of self-reported incidents of sexual harassment by teachers of students in four scientific fields. Of the 1,178 students who responded to survey questions, 2% of the men and 17% of the women reported being sexually harassed by their teachers. The results of cross-tabular analysis indicate that of the 101 written descriptions of sexual harassment, 38 occurred at or before college. However, a systematic analysis of these written descriptions indicates that there was no one type of sexual harassment experience typical of any given level of schooling. The results suggest that as women continue their educations, their chances of encountering sexual harassment from teachers are likely to increase. Also included in the chapter is a discussion of the conflict and confusion surrounding sex roles and professional roles.

Mimi H. Silbert presents findings from a study of 200 women street prostitutes in chapter 6, "Compounding Factors in the Rape of Street Prostitutes." The author documents the serious problem of rapes unrelated to the victims' prostitution: nearly three-fourths of the prostitutes interviewed were raped, in most cases by total strangers, with significant force involved. Virtually every victim reported physical injuries and extremely negative emotional attitudinal impacts from the rape, yet very few reported the rape or sought help. Their emotional trauma was compounded by several factors: the code of the street prostitute precluded emotional display, the helplessness from the victimization was exacerbated by a general feeling of powerlessness in life, and the justice and intervention systems were perceived as unresponsive and even harmful. The study's findings demonstrate the urgent need to provide specially tailored services for prostitutes who are rape victims.

Because child sexual abuse is a problem that is often concealed, studies of reported cases of sexual abuse of boys represent only a fraction of the total cases that actually occur. The goal of the study reported by Leslie I. Risin and Mary P. Koss in chapter 7, "The Sexual Abuse of Boys: Childhood Victimizations Reported by a National Sample," was to extend this previous work to a national basis. Self-reports of childhood sexual experiences were obtained from 2,972 men in an approximately representative national sample of students in higher education. In the sample, 7.3% of the men reported a childhood experience that met at least one of three criteria for sexual abuse. The descriptive characteristics of the abusive incidents are reviewed, and those characteristics that differentiated among three levels of sexual abuse (exhibition, fondling, and penetration) are presented. The authors also discuss operational definitions of sexual abuse and the behavioral specificity of sexual abuse screening questions for use in future research on men and boys.

In chapter 8, "Victim Response Strategies in Sexual Assault," Daniel L. Carter, Robert Alan Prentky, and Ann Wolbert Burgess report on a study of 108 convicted, incarcerated rapists and their 389 victims. The authors' first goal was to examine empirically the hypothesized interaction of differentiated subgroups of rapists with combative and noncombative victim responses. If such an interaction does exist, it is imperative to understand its implications for potential victims of sexual assault. Consequently, the authors' second goal was to address that issue by setting forth clinically derived recommendations for alternative resistance strategies geared to four subgroups of rapists. Although relatively abstract suggestions are made about behavior in a highly traumatic situation, knowledge may be the victim's only weapon. As such, knowledge can provide the victim with a sense of power as well as the confidence necessary to take action.

In chapter 9, "Sexualized Therapy: Causes and Consequences," Roberta Apfel and Bennett Simon outline within a psychoanalytic framework considerations in the treatment of patients sexually abused by psychotherapists. Theories concerning the abusive actions of psychotherapists are discussed, and case examples illustrate the impact of such behavior on the victimized patients. Patient issues center around problems of trust, anxiety, and guilt concerning the sexual contact. For the therapist (either the consultant or the long-term therapist), problems include finding the best way to evaluate and understand the patient's account, the need to avoid repeating in some new and disguised form the previous therapist's problems, and finally, the question of whether it is therapeutic for the patient to report and press charges against the previous therapist.

Recently, several advancements have been made in understanding important issues in the recovery of rape victims. In chapter 10, "Self-Blame in Recovery from Rape: Help or Hindrance?," Bonnie L. Katz and Martha R. Burt present new data on self-blame from rape victims themselves. The authors discuss self-blame as an adaptive mechanism and suggest that, contrary to some contemporary theories, self-blame is experienced by rape victims as negative and distressing, rather than as comforting or helpful to recovery. Because 68% of the respondents did blame themselves at least in part for the rape, the authors recommend that intervention efforts be geared to consider the effects of self-blame.

In chapter 11, "Responding to the Needs of Rape Victims: Research Findings," Linda E. Ledray reports on her study evaluating the impact of rape and the relative efficacy of two methods for treating rape victims. The data indicated that rape had a significant negative impact on the victims studied, with considerable depression anxiety, and phobic anxiety found on initial assessment. However, these responses appear time limited, especially with treatment. Both treatment methods, supportive counseling and guide to goals, were found to be effective in reducing symptomatology in rape victims, although guide to goals was found to be somewhat more so.

PART 2: THE SOCIAL CONTEXT OF RAPE AND SEXUAL ASSAULT

The social-science literature on the sociocultural etiology of rape and on attitudes toward rape is reviewed by Ilsa L. Lottes in chapter 12, "Sexual Socialization and Attitudes toward Rape." The author observes that recent research has supported the views that widely accepted attitudes about rape not only help sexually coercive/assaultive men to justify and deny the negative effects of their behavior, but also severely hinder both the reporting of rape and the recovery of rape victims. Examples of the following callous attitudes toward rape victims are discussed: (1) women enjoy sexual violence, (2) sex is the primary motivation for rape, (3) women are responsible for rape prevention, (4) rape happens only to certain kinds of women, (5) women falsely report many rape claims, (6) women are less desirable after they have been raped, and (7) rape is justified in some situations.

The adolescent population is particularly important to the study of rape and sexual assault. In chapter 13, "Vulnerability to Sexual Assault," Suzanne S. Ageton uses a national probability sample of adolescents to test some generally stated ideas about vulnerability to sexual assault. The availability of a representative sample of adolescents, which contained a subsample of sexual-assault victims, offered a unique opportunity to study the issue of vulnerability. Ageton compares the victims to a control group on several factors believed related to vulnerability to sexual assault (race, social class, sex-role attitude, and deviant lifestyle) in order to better understand the concept of differential risk.

Jacqueline D. Goodchilds, Gail L. Zellman, Paula B. Johnson, and Roseann Giarrusso discuss male and female adolescents' attitudes about gender roles in dating relationships in chapter 14, "Adolescents and Their Perceptions of Sexual Interactions." Four substudies of a major project are reported; these substudies address adolescents' perceptions of responsibility for dating outcomes, adolescents' cues and signals concerning sex and assault, expectations for dating relationships, and teenagers' application of the rape label to nonconsensual sex between acquaintances. The authors also discuss what the results of these substudies tell us about contemporary social attitudes toward sexual relationships.

Recent developments in rape-law reform are examined by author Mary Ann Largen in chapter 15. "Rape-Law Reform: An Analysis" provides a historical review of rape laws and their reform before presenting the findings of a three-state study of the impact of reform in light of original intent. Prosecutors, judges, victim counselors, defense attorneys, and police officers were surveyed concerning such issues as impact of changes in reporting, changes in jury behavior, victims' experiences in the criminal-justice system, changes in case characteristics, and various reform features.

Authors Stephanie Riger and Margaret T. Gordon, in "The Impact of Crime on Urban Women," contend that women's reactions to crime are shaped by a number of factors residing both in themselves and in their environments. It is not simply rates of victimization that generate women's fear, but also the nature and perceived likelihood of that victimization. Chapter 16 delineates the unique nature of crime against women and describes women's attitudinal and behavioral reactions to crime. The authors review a variety of sociopsychological and community-related factors that affect women's responses to crime and discuss some implications of these responses for the quality of women's lives.

Gail Dines-Levy extends the debate concerning the relationship between pornography and rape in chapter 17, "An Analysis of Pornography Research." She argues that the short-term, limited-exposure studies of pornography do not adequately address the issue of the long-term effects of repeated exposure to pornographic themes found in the general mass media. Using an example from the mass media, the author illustrates how one type of study examines pornography. An alternative method of study that uses message-system analysis and investigation of subjects' perceptions also is discussed.

PART 1

The Victims of Rape and Sexual Assault

CHAPTER
1

HIDDEN RAPE

Sexual Aggression and Victimization in a National Sample of Students in Higher Education

MARY P. KOSS
Kent State University

"You better not never tell nobody but God. It'd kill your mammy."
(Walker 1982, 1)

Officially, 87,340 rapes occurred in 1985 (Federal Bureau of Investigation [FBI] 1986). However, this number greatly underestimates the true scope of rape since it includes only instances that were reported to the police. Because many victims never tell even their closest friends and family about their rape (Koss 1985), it is unrealistic to expect that they would report the crime to the police. Government estimates suggest that for every rape reported to police, 3-10 rapes are not reported (Law Enforcement Assistance Administration [LEAA] 1975).

Victimization studies such as the annual National Crime Survey (NCS) are the major avenue through which the full extent of crime is estimated (e.g., Bureau of Justice Statistics [BJS] 1984). In these studies, the residents of a standard sampling area are asked to indicate those crimes of which they or any other household members have been victims during the previous six months. The survey results are then compared to the number of reported crimes in the area, and the rate of unreported crime is estimated. On the basis of such research, the authors of the NCS have observed rape is an infrequent crime (LEAA 1974, 12) and is the most rare of NCS measured violent offenses (BJS 1984, 5). Women's chances of being raped have been described as a small fraction of 1% (Katz and Mazur 1979).

Portions of this chapter are scheduled to appear in the *Journal of Clinical Psychology* 55, 1987.

However, the accuracy of these conclusions and the validity of the research on which they are based must be examined closely, as the perceived severity of rape influences the social and economic priority it is accorded.

Several features of the NCS approach (e.g., BJS 1984) may lead to underreporting of rape, including the use of a screening question that requires the subject to infer the focus of inquiry, the use of questions about rape that are embedded in a context of violent crime, and the assumption that the term *rape* is used by victims of sexual assault to conceptualize their experiences.

In an effort to extend previous research on rape (e.g., Koss and Oros 1982; Koss 1985) to a national sample, the *Ms.* Magazine Project on Campus Sexual Assault was undertaken. Because the FBI definition of rape (used in victimization studies such as the NCS) limits the crime to female victims (BJS 1984) and because women represent virtually 100% of reported rape victims (LEAA 1975), the project focused on women victims and male perpetrators.

PREVIOUS RESEARCH

Several recently reported estimates of the prevalence of sexual victimization have been reported that were based on studies designed specifically to gauge the extent of sexual assault. Kilpatrick and colleagues (Kilpatrick, Veronen, and Best 1984; Kilpatrick et al. 1985) conducted a victimization survey via telephone of 2,004 randomly selected female residents of Charleston County, South Carolina. In their sample, 14.5% of the women disclosed one or more attempted or completed sexual assault experiences, including 5% who had been victims of rape and 4% who had been victims of attempted rape. Of the women who had been raped, only 29% reported their assault to police. Russell found that 24% of a probability sample of 930 adult women residents of San Francisco described experiences that involved "forced intercourse or intercourse obtained by physical threat(s) or intercourse completed when the woman was drugged, unconscious, asleep, or otherwise totally helpless and unable to consent" (Russell 1984, 35). Only 9.5% of these women reported their experience to police.

Many studies of the prevalence of rape and lesser forms of sexual aggression have involved college students however. There are scientific as well as pragmatic reasons to study this group. College students are a high risk group for rape because they are in the same age range as the bulk of rape victims and offenders. The victimization rate for females peaks in the 16-19 year age group, and the second highest rate occurs in the 20-24 year age group. These rates are approximately four times higher than the mean for all women (BJS 1984). In addition, 47% of all alleged rapists who are arrested are individuals under age 25 (FBI 1985). Approximately 25% of all persons age 18-24 are attending school (U.S. Bureau of Census 1980). Finally, a substantial proportion of rape prevention efforts take place under the auspices of educational institutions and are targeted at students.

Kanin and his associates (Kanin 1957; Kirkpatrick and Kanin 1957; Kanin and Parcell 1977) found that 20-25% of college women reported forceful attempts by their dates at sexual intercourse during which the women ended up screaming, fighting, crying, or pleading and that 26% of college men reported making a forceful attempt at sexual intercourse that caused observable distress and offense in the woman. Rapaport and Burkhart (1984) reported that 15% of a sample of college men acknowledged that they had obtained sexual intercourse against their dates' will. Koss and colleagues (Koss 1985; Koss and Oros 1982; Koss et al. 1985) administered the self-report sexual experiences survey to a sample of 2,016 female and 1,846 male Midwestern university students. They found that 13% of the women experienced a victimization that involved sexual intercourse as a result of actual force or threat of harm; and 4.6% of the men admitted perpetrating an act of sexual aggression that met legal definitions of rape.

All of these prevalence studies suggest that rape is far more extensive than reported in official statistics. However, reported prevalence rates for rape vary from 5% (Kilpatrick et al. 1985) to 20-25% (Kanin 1957; Russell 1984). Unfortunately these different figures are not easy to reconcile as the studies involved both relatively small and geographically diverse samples and different data collection techniques.

METHODS

The *Ms.* Magazine Project on Campus Sexual Assault involved administration of a self-report questionnaire to a sample of 6,159 students enrolled in 32 institutions of higher education across the United States. The following is an overview of the project's methodology, described more fully elsewhere (Koss, Gidycz, and Wisniewski 1987).

SAMPLING PROCEDURES

The sampling goals of the project were to represent the universe of the U.S. college student population. No sample design could be expected to result in a purely random or representative sample, as the subject of rape is sufficiently controversial that some schools targeted by a systematic sampling plan can be expected to refuse to participate.

On the basis of enrollment-characteristics data maintained by the U.S. Department of Education (Office of Civil Rights 1980), the nation's 3,269 higher education institutions were sorted by location into ten regions (i.e., Alaska, Hawaii, New England, Mideast, Great Lakes, Plains states, Southeast, Southwest, Rocky Mountain, and West). Within each region, institutions were placed into homogeneous clusters according to five criteria: (1) location inside or outside a standard metropolitan statistical area (SMSA) of certain sizes; (2) enrollment of minority students above or below the national mean percentage; (3) control of the institution by private secular, private religious, or public authority; (4) type of institution, including university, other four-year college, two-year junior college, and technical/vocational institution; and (5) total enrollment within three levels. Every xth cluster was sampled according to the proportion of total enrollment accounted for by the region. Replacements were sought from among other schools in the homogeneous cluster if the original school proved uncooperative.

The amount of time required to obtain a sample of cooperating institutions was extended; some schools required 15 months to arrive at a final decision. During that period, 93 schools were contacted and 32 institutional participants were obtained. Of the institutions, 19 were first choices; the remaining 13 were solicitated from among 43 replacements. The institutional participants were guaranteed anonymity.

A random selection process based on each institution's catalogue of course offerings was used to choose target classes and alternates. The questionnaire was administered in classroom settings by one of eight postmaster's level psychologists: the two men and six women used a prepared script and were trained to handle potential untoward effects of participation. The anonymous questionnaire was accompanied by a cover sheet that contained all the elements of informed consent. Only 91 persons (1.5%) indicated that they did not wish to participate.

SUBJECTS

The final sample consisted of 6,159 students: 3,187 females and 2,972 males. The female participants were characterized as follows: mean age = 21.4 years; 85% single, 11% married, and 4% divorced; 86% white, 7% black, 3% Hispanic, 3% Asian, and 1% native American; and 39% Catholic, 38% Protestant, 4% Jewish, and 20% other or no religion. The male participants were characterized as follows: mean age = 21.0 years; 90% single, 9% married, 1% divorced; 86% white, 6% black, 3% Hispanic, 4% Asian, and 1% native American; and 40% Catholic, 34% Protestant, 5% Jewish, and 22% other or no religion.

Because of the assumptions on which the sampling plan was based and the hesitancy of many institutions to participate, the sample is not completely representative. Four variables were examined to determine the sample's representativeness: (1) institution location, (2) institution region, (3) subject ethnicity, and (4) subject income. Region in which the institutions were located was the only variable on which significant discrepancy was noted. The regional disproportion is unimportant in many respects, as even without extensive sampling in the West, the individual participants in the sample were still reflective of national enrollment in terms of ethnicity and family income. Nevertheless, for purposes of calculating prevalence data, weighting factors were used.

SURVEY INSTRUMENT

The data on the incidence and prevalence of sexual aggression were obtained through the use of the ten-item sexual experiences survey (Koss and Oros 1982; Koss and Gidycz 1985). This survey is a self-report instrument designed to reflect various degrees of sexual aggression and victimization. During survey administration, separate wordings were used for women and for men. The text of all ten items (female wording) can be found in table 1.1. Descriptive data were obtained through the use of closed-ended questions administered subsequent to the survey. The survey booklet instructed all respondents who described any level of experience with sexual aggression or victimization to turn to a section of questions about the characteristics of the most serious incident in which they were involved.

Many investigators have questioned the validity of self-reported sexual behavior. The accuracy and truthfulness of self-reports on the sexual experiences survey have been investigated (Koss and Gidycz 1985), and significant correlations were found between a woman's level of victimization based on self-report and her level of victimization based on responses related to an interviewer several months later ($r = .73, p < .001$). Most importantly, only 3% of the women (2/68) who reported experiences that met legal definitions of rape were judged to have misinterpreted questions or to have given answers that appeared to be false. Men's levels of aggression as described on self-report and reported to an interviewer were also significantly correlated ($r = .61, p < .001$).

A further validity study was conducted in conjunction with the Ms. project. Because previous work had raised more questions about the validity of males' responses than about females' reponses, male students

TABLE 1.1
FREQUENCIES OF INDIVIDUAL SEXUAL EXPERIENCES REPORTED BY POSTSECONDARY
STUDENT: PREVALENCE SINCE AGE 14

Sexual Behavior	Women			Men		
	%	M	SD	%	M	SD
1. Have you given in to sex play (fondling, kissing, or petting, but not intercourse) when you didn't want to because you were overwhelmed by a man's continual arguments and pressure?	44	3.2	1.5	19	2.9	1.5
2. Have you had sex play (fondling, kissing, or petting, but not intercourse) when you didn't want to because a man used his position of authority (boss, teacher, camp counselor, supervisor) to make you?	5	2.7	1.7	1	2.5	1.5
3. Have you had sex play (fondling, kissing, or petting, but not intercourse) when you didn't want to because a man threatened or used some degree of physical force (twisting your arm, holding you down, etc.) to make you?	13	2.1	1.5	2	2.3	1.5
4. Have you had a man attempt sexual intercourse (get on top, attempt to insert his penis) when you didn't want to by threatening or using some degree of force (twisting your arm, holding you down, etc.), but intercourse *did not* occur?	15	2.0	1.4	2	2.0	1.2
5. Have you had a man attempt sexual intercourse (get on top, attempt to insert his penis) when you didn't want to by giving you alcohol or drugs, but intercourse *did not* occur?	12	2.0	1.4	5	2.2	1.4
6. Have you given into sexual intercourse when you didn't want to because you were overwhelmed by a man's continual arguments and pressure?	25	2.9	1.6	10	2.4	1.4
7. Have you had sexual intercourse when you didn't want to because a man used his position of authority (boss, teacher, camp counselor, supervisor) to make you?	2	2.5	1.7	1	2.0	1.4
8. Have you had sexual intercourse when you didn't want to because a man gave you alcohol or drugs?	8	2.2	1.5	4	2.5	1.5
9. Have you had sexual intercourse when you didn't want to because a man threatened or used some degree of physical force (twisting your arm, holding you down, etc.) to make you?	9	2.2	1.5	1	2.3	1.5
10. Have you had sexual acts (anal or oral intercourse or penetration by objects other than the penis) when you didn't want to because a man threatened or used some degree of physical force (twisting your arm, holding you down, etc.) to make you?	6	2.2	1.6	1	2.5	1.5

Notes: The sample size was 3,187 women and 2,972 men. All questions were prefaced with instructions to refer to experiences "from age 14 on." Sexual intercourse was defined as "penetration of a woman's vagina, no matter how slightly, by a man's penis. Ejaculation is not required."

were selected as subjects. The sexual experiences survey items were administered both by self-report and by one-to-one interview on the same occasion and in one setting. The interviewer was a fully trained, licensed, and experienced male Ph.D. clinical psychologist. Subjects were 15 male volunteers, identified by first name only, recruited through newspaper advertisements on the campus of a major university. Participants gave their self-reports first and then were interviewed individually. The results indicated that 14 of the participants (93%) gave the same responses to the survey items on self-report and in the interviews.

SCORING PROCEDURES

The groups labeled rape ("yes" responses to items 8, 9, and/or 10 and any lower-numbered items) and attempted rape ("yes" responses to items 4 and/or 5 but not to any higher-numbered items) included individuals whose experiences met broad legal definitions of these crimes. The legal definition of rape in Ohio (Ohio Revised Code 1980, 2907.01A, 2907.02), similar to many states, is the following: .

Vaginal intercourse between male and female, and anal intercourse, fellatio, and cunnilingus between persons regardless of sex. Penetration, however slight, is sufficient to complete vaginal or anal intercourse. . . . No person shall engage in sexual conduct with another person . . . when any of the following apply: (1) the offender purposely compels the other person to submit by force or threat of force, (2) for the purpose of preventing resistance the offender substantially impairs the other person's judgment or control by administering any drug or intoxicant to the other person.

The group labeled sexual coercion ("yes" responses to items 6 and/or 7 but not to any higher-numbered items) included subjects who engaged in/ experienced sexual intercourse subsequent to the use of menacing verbal pressure or misuse of authority. No threats of force or direct physical force were used. The group labeled sexual contact ("yes" responses to items 1, 2, and/or 3 but not to any higher-numbered items) consisted of individuals who had engaged in/experienced sexual behavior (such as fondling or kissing) that did not involve attempted penetration, subsequent to the use of menacing verbal pressure, misuse of authority, threats of harm, or actual physical force.

RESULTS

PREVALENCE OF SEXUAL AGGRESSION/VICTIMIZATION

Prevalence rates indicate the total number of persons who report experiences with sexual aggression or victimization during a specified time period, which in this study was since the age of 14. The unweighted response frequencies for each item of the Sexual Experiences Survey are presented in table 1.1. The frequencies of victimization ranged from 44% (women who reported having experienced unwanted sexual contact subsequent to coercion) to 2% (women who reported having experienced unwanted sexual intercourse subsequent to the offender's misuse of authority). The frequency with which men reported having perpetrated each form of sexual aggression ranged from the 19% who said that they had obtained sexual contact through the use of coercion to the 1% who indicated that they had obtained oral or anal penetration through the use of force. Those respondents who had engaged in/experienced sexually aggressive acts indicated that each act had occurred a mean of 2.0–3.2 times since age 14.

However, the data on the individual sexually aggressive acts are difficult to interpret, because persons may have engaged in/experienced several different sexually aggressive acts. Therefore, respondents were classified according to the highest degree of sexual victimization/aggression they reported (see table 1.2). With weighted data correcting for regional disproportions, 46.3% of women respondents revealed no experiences whatsoever with sexual victimization, while 53.7% of women repondents indicated some form of sexual victimization. The most serious sexual victimization ever experienced was sexual contact for 14.4% of the women, sexual coercion for 11.9% of the women, attempted rape for 12.1% of the women, and rape for 15.4% of the women. Weighted data for males indicated that 74.8% of men had engaged in no forms of sexual aggression, whereas 25.1% of the men revealed involvement in some form of sexual aggression. The most extreme level of sexual aggression perpetrated was sexual contact for 10.2% of the men, sexual coercion for 7.2% of the men, attempted rape for 3.3% of the men, and rape for 4.4% of the men. Examination of these figures reveals that the effect of weighting was minimal and tended to reduce slightly the prevalence of the most serious acts of sexual aggression.

TABLE 1.2

PREVALENCE RATES FOR FIVE LEVELS OF SEXUAL AGGRESSION AND SEXUAL
VICTIMIZATION

| Sexual Aggression/Victimization (Highest Level Reported) | Sex | | | |
| | Women (%) | | Men (%) | |
	Weighted	Unweighted	Weighted	Unweighted
No sexual aggression/victimization	46.3	45.6	74.8	75.6
Sexual contact	14.4	14.9	10.2	9.8
Sexual coercion	11.9	11.6	7.2	6.9
Attempted rape	12.1	12.1	3.3	3.2
Rape	15.4	15.8	4.4	4.6

Notes: The sample size was 3,187 women and 2,972 men. Prevalence rates include sexual experiences since age 14.

The relationship of prevalence rates to the institutional parameters used to design the sample was examined via chi-square and analysis of variance (ANOVA). Due to the large sample size, differences that have no real practical significance could reach statistical significance. Therefore, effect sizes were calculated using Cohen's method (w for chi-square and f for F) to gauge the importance of any significant differences (1977). Cohen's guidelines for interpretation of effect sizes are the following: a w or f of .1 indicates a small effect, a w of .3 or an f of .25 indicates a medium effect, and a w of .5 and an f of .4 indicates a large effect. The prevalence of sexual victimization as reported by women did not differ according to the size of the city where the institution of higher education was located [X^2 (8, $N = 2728$) = 5.55, $p < .697$, $w = .05$], the size of the institution [X^2 (8, $N = 2728$) = 6.35, $p < .608$, $w = .05$], the type of institution [X^2 (8, $N = 3086$) = 10.37, $p < .240$, $w = .05$], or whether the minority enrollment of the institution was above or below the national mean [X^2 (4, $N = 2728$) = 4.03, $p < .401$, $w = .04$]. However, rates of sexual victimization did vary by region [X^2 (28, $N = 3086$) = 63.00, $p < .001$, $w = .14$] and by the governance of the institution, [X^2 (8, $N = 3086$) = 22.93, $p < .003$, $w = .09$. The rate at which women reported having been raped was twice as high in private colleges (14%) and major universities (17%) as it was at religiously affiliated institutions (7%). Victimization rates were also slightly higher in the Great Lakes and Plains states than in other regions.

The prevalence of reported sexual aggression by men also did not differ according to city size [X^2 (8, N = 2641) = 6.41, p < .600, w = .05], institution size [X^2 (8, N = 2641) = 3.76, p < .878, w = .04], minority enrollment [X^2 (4, N = 2641) = 4.84, p < .303, w = .04], governance [X^2(8, N = 2875) = 13.66, p < .091, w = .07], and type of institution, [X^2(8, N = 2875) = 3.99, p < .858, w = .04. However, the percent of men who admitted perpetrating sexual aggression did vary according to the region of the country in which they attended school [X^2 (28, N = 2875) = 56.25, p < .001, w = .14]. Men in the Southeast admitted rape twice as often (6%) as in the Plains states (3%) and three times as often as in the West (2%).

Finally, the relationships between the prevalence rates and individual subject demographic variables were also studied and included income, religion, and ethnicity. The rate at which women reported experiences of sexual victimization did not vary according to subject's family income [F (4, 3010) = .31, p < .871, f = .06] or religion [X^2 (16, N = 3077) = 17.86, p < .332, w = .08]. The prevalence rates of victimization did vary according to ethnicity [X^2 (16, N = 3075) = 37.05, p < .002, w = .11]. For example, rape was reported by 16% of white women (N = 2655), 10% of black women (N = 215), 12% of Hispanic women (N = 106), 7% of Asian women (N = 79), and 40% of native American women (N = 20).

The number of men who admitted acts of sexual aggression did not vary according to subject's religion [X^2 (16, N = 2856) = 20.98, p < .179, w = .09] or family income [F (3, 2821) = .08, p < .987)]. However, the number of men who reported acts of sexual aggression did differ by ethnic group [X^2 (16, N = 2861) = 55.55, p < .001, w = .14]. For example, rape was reported by 4% of white men (N = 2484), 10% of black men (N = 162), 7% of Hispanic men (N = 93), 2% of Asian men (N = 106), and 0% of native American men (N = 16).

INCIDENCE OF SEXUAL AGGRESSION/VICTIMIZATION

Incidence rates indicate how many new episodes of an event occurred during a specific time period. In this study, respondents were asked to indicate how many times during the previous year they had engaged in/ experienced each item listed in the survey. To improve recall, the question referred to the previous academic year from September to September, time boundaries that are meaningful to students. Some subjects reported multiple episodes of sexual aggression/victimization during the previous year. Therefore, the incidence of sexual aggression/victimization was calculated two ways. First, the number of people who reported one or more episodes during the year was determined. Second, the total number of sexually aggressive incidents that were reported by women and by men was calculated.

The incidence rate for rape during a 12-month period was found to be 353 rapes involving 207 different women in a population of 3,187 women. Comparable figures for the other levels of sexual victimization were 533 attempted rapes (323 victims), 837 episodes of sexual coercion (366 victims), and 2,024 experiences of unwanted sexual contact (886 victims). The incidence data for the individual items used to calculate these rates are found in table 1.3.

TABLE 1.3

FREQUENCIES OF INDIVIDUAL SEXUAL EXPERIENCES REPORTED BY POSTSECONDARY
STUDENT: ONE-YEAR INCIDENCE

| Sexual Experience | Sex | | | |
| | Women | | Men | |
	Victims	Incidents	Perpetrators	Incidents
Sexual contact by verbal coercion	725	1716	321	732
Sexual contact by misuse of authority	50	97	23	55
Sexual contact by threat or force	111	211	30	67
Attempted intercourse by force	180	297	33	52
Attempted intercourse by alcohol/drugs	143	236	72	115
Intercourse by verbal coercion	353	816	156	291
Intercourse by misuse of authority	13	21	11	20
Intercourse by alcohol/drugs	91	159	57	103
Intercourse by threat or force	63	98	20	36
Oral/anal penetration by threat or force	53	96	19	48

Note: The sample size was 3,187 women and 2,972 men.

Incidence rates for the sexual aggression admitted by men also were calculated. Responses to the three items that characterize rape for the 12-month period preceding the survey indicate that 187 rapes were perpetrated by 96 different men. Comparable incidence rates during a 12-month period for the other levels of sexual aggression were 167 attempted rapes

(105 perpetrators), 854 episodes of unwanted sexual contact (374 perpetrators), and 311 situations of sexual coercion (167 perpetrators). The incidence data for the individual items that were used to calculate these rates also are presented in table 1.3.

From these data, victimization rates can be calculated. If the total number of all the women who during the previous year reported a sexual experience that met legal definitions of rape and attempted rape is divided by two (to obtain a six-month basis) and set to a base of number of 1,000 women (instead of the 3,187 women actually surveyed), the victimization rate for the surveyed population of women was 83/1,000 women during a six-month period. However, the FBI definition of rape (i.e., forcible vaginal intercourse with a female against consent by force or threat of force, including attempts) on which the NCS is based is narrower than the state laws (i.e., oral, anal, or vaginal intercourse or penetration by objects against consent through threat, force, or intentional incapacitation of the victim via drugs) on which the groupings in this study were based (BJS 1984). Therefore, the victimization rate was also calculated in conformance with the FBI definition. Elimination of all incidents except those that involved actual or attempted vaginal sexual intercourse through force or threat of harm resulted in a victimization rate of 38/1,000 women during a six-month period.

Perpetration rates were also determined using data from the male subjects. When all unwanted oral, anal, and vaginal intercourse attempts and completions were included in the calculations, a perpetration rate of 34/1,000 men was obtained. Use of the FBI definition resulted in a perpetration rate of 9/1,000 college men during a six-month period.

DESCRIPTIVE PROFILE OF
SEXUAL AGGRESSION/VICTIMIZATION

To develop a profile of the sexual aggression/victimization experiences that were reported by postsecondary students, researchers used inferential statistics descriptively.

WOMEN'S VANTAGE POINT   Women were asked detailed questions about the most serious victimization, if any, that they had experienced since the age of 14. These criterion variables were analyzed by chi-square analysis for dichotomous data and ANOVA for continuous data by the five levels of the sexual victimization factor. The results of the ANOVAs with calculated effect sizes are reported in table 1.4 and the results of the chi-square analyses with calculated effect sizes are reported in table 1.5.

TABLE 1.4
DESCRIPTIVE CHARACTERISTICS OF SEXUAL VICTIMIZATIONS REPORTED BY WOMEN:
CONTINUOUS CRITERION VARIABLES

Variable	Level of Sexual Victimization (Mean Response)				F	p	f
	Sexual Contact	Sexual Coercion	Attempted Rape	Rape			
How well known	3.40$_a$	3.88$_{abc}$	3.29$_b$	3.19$_c$	25.67	.000	.05
How many times	2.05$_a$	2.50$_{abc}$	1.70$_b$	2.02$_{ac}$	17.49	.000	.03
Age at assault	17.27$_{ab}$	19.00$_{bc}$	17.92$_c$	18.51$_a$	15.89	.000	.03
How long ago	3.79$_a$	3.87$_b$	3.81$_c$	4.28$_{abc}$	9.66	.000	.02
Prior intimacy	2.71$_{ada}$	4.06$_{abc}$	3.30$_{bd}$	3.52$_a$	29.23	.000	.06
Clarity nonconsent	3.93$_a$	3.52$_{abc}$	4.07$_b$	4.05$_c$	16.15	.000	.03
Perceived violence	3.11$_a$	3.10$_b$	3.31$_c$	3.88$_{abc}$	48.86	.000	.09
Degree of resistance	3.43$_{ab}$	3.12$_{ace}$	3.79$_{be}$	3.80$_{ae}$	31.49	.000	.06
Impact of resistance	2.06$_{ad}$	2.46$_{ada}$	1.86$_{ab}$	2.99$_{abe}$	108.98	.000	.19
Emotions: scared	2.80$_a$	2.73$_b$	2.99$_c$	3.66$_{abc}$	40.01	.000	.08
Emotions: angry	3.08$_{ad}$	3.17$_{abc}$	3.47$_{ad}$	3.97$_{abe}$	36.07	.000	.07
Emotions: depressed	3.14$_{ad}$	3.33$_{bd}$	3.19$_c$	3.93$_{abc}$	36.49	.000	.07
Responsible: woman	2.76	3.27	2.78$_b$	2.80$_c$	14.75	.000	.03
Responsible: man	3.86$_a$	3.90$_b$	4.03$_c$	4.29$_{abc}$	15.51	.000	.03
Family reaction	4.09$_a$	4.07	3.97	3.70$_a$	3.84	.010	.02
Police reaction	1.02	1.01	1.01	1.02	.37	.776	.00
Campus reaction	3.60	4.50	3.50	4.00	.34	.777	.05

Note: Means are significantly different from any other means that share a common subscript ($p < .05$).

From the data in these tables, the following profile of the rapes reported by women students emerge. (All items were scored on a 1 [not at all] to 5 [very much] scale unless otherwise indicated.) The victimizations happened 1–2 years ago when the women were 18-19 years old ($M = 18.5$); 95% of the assaults involved one offender only; 84% involved an offender who was known to the victim; 57% of offenders were dates. The rapes happened primarily off campus (86%), equally as often in the man's house or car as in the woman's house or car. Most offenders (73%) were thought to be drinking or using drugs at the time of the assault, while the victim admitted using intoxicants in 55% of the episodes. Prior mutual intimacy had occurred with the offender to the level of petting above the waist ($M = 3.52$ on a 1–6 scale). However, the victims believed that they had made their nonconsent to have sexual intercourse "quite" clear ($M = 4.05$). Typically, the victim perceived that the offender used "quite a bit" of force ($M = 3.88$), which involved twisting her arm or holding her down. Only 9% of the rapes involved hitting or beating, and only 5% involved weapons. Women rated their amount of resistance as moderate ($M = 3.80$). Forms of resistance used by many rape victims included reasoning (84%) and physically struggling (70%). Many women (41%) were virgins at the

TABLE 1.5
DESCRIPTIVE CHARACTERISTICS OF SEXUAL VICTIMIZATIONS REPORTED BY WOMEN:
DICHOTOMOUS VARIABLES

	Level of Sexual Victimization % Responding "Yes"								
Variable	Sexual Contact	Sexual Coercion	Attempted Rape	Rape	X^2	N	df	p	w
One man involved	99	99	97	95	19.95	1485	6	.003	.12
Perpetrator was date	71	86	70	57	132.42	1484	12	.000	.30
Party or group context	42	40	48	55	68.68	1475	9	.000	.22
Happened on male turf	52	52	53	50	35.50	1464	6	.001	.16
Happened off campus	84	86	82	86	3.33	1455	3	.344	.05
Man lives apt/home	53	64	54	73	100.59	3079	9	.000	.18
Man alcohol/drugs	35	64	54	73	138.56	1471	6	.000	.31
Woman alcohol/drugs	29	31	58	55	100.23	1476	6	.000	.26
Force used: held down	8	9	41	64	292.52	1449	3	.000	.45
Force used: hit	2	1	2	9	88.77	1407	3	.000	.25
Force used: weapon	1	0	1	5	29.56	1396	3	.000	.15
Resistance: reason	65	71	81	84	44.95	1378	3	.000	.18
Resistance: struggle	33	26	52	70	162.50	1288	3	.000	.36
Woman was virgin	79	43	60	41	130.95	1466	3	.000	.30
Told anyone	47	42	58	58	28.49	1456	3	.000	.14
Visited a crisis center	1	2	3	8	18.05	800	3	.000	.15
Reported to police	2	1	3	8	17.68	794	3	.000	.15
Used a campus agency	2	0	1	2	3.49	1229	3	.000	.05
Sex with man since	37	48	35	42	13.77	1448	3	.003	.10
Ended relationship	79	73	82	87	24.87	1363	3	.000	.14
Expect it again	36	33	37	41	5.12	1415	3	.163	.06
It was definitely rape	1	3	3	27	285.00	1434	9	.00	.45

time of their rape. During the rape, victims felt scared (M = 3.66), angry (M = 3.97), and depressed (M = 3.93). Rape victims felt somewhat responsible (M = 2.80) for what had happened, but believed that the man was much more responsible (M = 4.29).

Almost half of victimized women (42%) told no one about their assault. Just 8% of the victims who told anyone reported to police (equivalent to 5% of all rape victims), and only 8% of the victims who told anyone visited a crisis center (again equivalent to 5% of all rape victims). Those who reported to police rated the reaction they received as "not at all supportive" (M = 1.02). On the other hand, family (M = 3.70) and campus agency (M = 4.00) reaction were seen as supportive.

Surprisingly, 42% of the women indicated that they had sex again with the offender on a later occasion, but it is not known if this was forced or voluntary; most relationships (87%) did eventually break up subsequent to the victimization. Many rape victims (41%) stated that they expected a similar assault to happen again in the future, and only 27% of the women whose experience met legal definitions of rape labeled themselves as rape victims.

Although these analyses demonstrated statistically significant differences between the situational characteristics of the rapes reported by women compared with the lesser degrees of sexual victimization, the effect sizes of these differences were generally small. Thus, the descriptive profile of the rapes reported by college women is applicable to a great extent to the lesser degrees of sexual victimization as well. With the effect sizes for guidance, the following large and important differences between rapes and other forms of sexual victimization can be noted. Rapes were less likely to involve dating partners than other forms of sexual victimization. While 70-86% of lesser forms of victimization involved dating couples, only 57% of the rapes did. Men who raped were perceived by the victims as more often drinking (73%) than men who engaged in lesser degrees of sexual aggression (35-64%). Rapes, as well as attempted rapes, were more violent. More than half of rape victims (64%) and attempted rape victims (41%) reported that the offender used actual violence, such as holding them down, while fewer than 10% of other victims reported actual force. Likewise, the use of physical resistance was reported by many more victims of rape (70%) and attempted rape (52%) than by victims of lesser degrees of sexual assault (26-33%). Finally, rape victims (27%) were much more likely than any other group (1-3%) to see their experience as a rape.

MEN'S VANTAGE POINT   Men were asked detailed questions about the most serious sexual aggression, if any, that they had perpetrated since the age of 14. These criterion variables also were analyzed by chi-square analysis for dichotomous data and ANOVA for continuous data by the five levels of the sexual aggression factor. The results of the ANOVAs with post hoc tests and calculated effect sizes are reported in table 1.6, and the results of the chi-square analyses with calculated effect sizes are reported in table 1.7.

With these data, characteristics of the rapes perpetrated by college men can be determined. The rapes happened one to two years ago when the men were 18-19 years old ($M = 18.5$); 84% of the assaults involved one offender only; 84% involved an offender who was known to the victim; 61% of offenders were dates. The rapes happened primarily off campus (86%), equally as often in the man's house or car as in the woman's house or car. Most men who raped (74%) said they were drinking or using drugs at the time of the assault, and most (75%) perceived that their victims were using intoxicants as well. Men believed that mutual intimacy had occurred with the victim to the level of petting below the waist ($M = 4.37$), and they felt that the victims' nonconsent to have sexual intercourse was "not at all" clear ($M = 1.80$).

TABLE 1.6
DESCRIPTIVE CHARACTERISTICS OF SEXUALLY AGGRESSIVE ACTS REPORTED BY MEN: CONTINUOUS CRITERION VARIABLES

Variable	Level of Sexual Aggression (Mean Response)				F	p	f
	Sexual Contact	Sexual Coercion	Attempted Rape	Rape			
How well known	3.67_a	3.69_b	3.27	3.20_{ab}	7.03	.001	.17
How many times	2.20	2.29	1.90	2.29	1.54	.203	.10
Age at assault	17.87	18.70	18.36	18.49	2.50	.058	.10
How long ago	4.06	3.78	3.85	3.69	1.20	.310	.10
Prior intimacy	3.51_a	4.18_{ab}	3.56_a	4.37_{b}	8.15	.000	.20
Clarity nonconsent	2.25_a	2.15	2.06	1.80_a	4.30	.005	.14
Perceived violence	2.45_a	2.59	2.84	2.85_a	4.52	.004	.14
Degree of resistance	2.01	1.87	2.11	1.83	2.17	.091	.10
Impact of resistance	2.21_a	2.34_a	1.92_{ab}	2.59_{b}	7.93	.000	.20
Emotions: scared	1.56	1.51	1.44	1.52	.34	.794	.20
Emotions: angry	1.40	1.39	1.53	1.45	.51	.673	.00
Emotions: depressed	1.79	1.72	1.71	1.59	.78	.506	.00
Emotions: proud	1.76_a	1.83_b	1.97	2.27_{ab}	4.10	.007	.14
Responsible: woman	2.56	2.92	3.00	2.85	3.71	.012	.14
Responsible: man	2.81	2.94_a	2.76	2.43_a	3.90	.009	.15
Partners since	1.56_a	2.32_b	2.01	2.53_{ab}	10.24	.000	.23

Note: Means are significantly different from any other means that share a common subscript ($p < .05$).

Typically, men who raped perceived that they were "somewhat" forceful ($M = 2.85$) and admitted twisting the victim's arm or holding her down. Only 3% of the perpetrators of rape said that they hit or beat the victim, and only 4% used weapons. They perceived victims' resistance as minimal ($M = 1.83$). Forms of resistance that assailants observed included reasoning, which was used by 36% of the rape victims, and physically struggling, which was used by 12%. Few men (12%) were virgins at the time they forced a woman to have sexual intercourse.

During the assault, offenders felt minimal negative emotions, including feeling scared ($M = 1.52$), angry ($M = 1.45$), or depressed ($M = 1.59$). Instead, perpetrators of rape were more likely to feel proud ($M = 2.27$). Although they felt mildly responsible ($M = 2.43$) for what had happened, rapists believed that the woman was equally or more responsible ($M = 2.85$). Half of the men who reported an act that met legal definitions of rape (54%) told no one at all about their assault, and only 2% of them were reported to police by the victim. Among the men, 55% indicated that after the assault they had had sex with the victim again, but it is not known if this was forced or voluntary. A substantial number of men who raped (47%) stated that they expected to engage in a similar assault at some

TABLE 1.7
DESCRIPTIVE CHARACTERISTICS OF SEXUALLY AGGRESSIVE ACTS REPORTED BY
MEN: DICHOTOMOUS VARIABLES

Variable	Level of Sexual Aggression % Responding "Yes"				X^2	N	df	p	w
	Sexual Contact	Sexual Coercion	Attempted Rape	Rape					
One man involved	92	95	90	84	19.43	608	9	.022	.18
Victim was date	71	77	63	61	38.35	599	12	.001	.25
Party or group context	46	39	39	49	28.68	587	9	.000	.22
Happened on male turf	39	54	41	41	21.92	588	6	.039	.19
Happened off campus	86	86	77	86	4.41	580	3	.220	.09
Man lives apt/home	62	72	58	69	26.75	2868	9	.008	.10
Man alcohol/drugs	33	35	67	74	75.65	590	6	.000	.36
Woman alcohol/drugs	31	35	65	75	82.21	591	6	.000	.37
Force used: held down	7	1	12	17	27.86	582	3	.000	.22
Force used: hit	0	1	0	3	11.26	573	3	.000	.14
Force used: weapon	0	1	0	4	15.23	572	3	.000	.16
Resistance: reason	42	35	44	36	2.91	526	3	.405	.08
Resistance: struggle	4	1	15	12	23.46	498	3	.000	.22
Man was virgin	48	24	33	12	34.01	588	3	.001	.24
Told anyone	34	37	47	46	6.78	588	3	.079	.11
Reported to police	2	1	1	2	.16	555	3	.983	.02
Sex with woman since	37	64	32	55	38.64	563	3	.000	.27
Expect it again	28	29	38	47	14.46	549	3	.002	.16
Definitely was *not* rape	96	94	90	88	15.04	566	9	.089	.16

point. Most men (88%) who reported an assault that met legal definitions of rape were adamant that their behavior was definitely not rape.

Although these analyses demonstrated statistically significant differences between the assault characteristics reported by men who raped compared with men who perpetrated lesser degrees of sexual aggression, the effect sizes of these differences were generally small. Thus, the descriptive profile of the rapes reported by male college students generally is applicable to the lesser degrees of sexual aggression as well. With the effect sizes for guidance, the following large and important differences between rapes and other forms of sexual aggression can be noted. Men who raped were more often drinking (74%) than men who engaged in lesser degrees of sexual aggression (33–67%). They perceived that the victim was more often drinking (75%) than was perceived by men who perpetrated lesser degrees of sexual aggression (31–65%). Men who reported behavior that met legal definitions of rape were less likely to be virgins at the time of their assault (12%) than other sexually aggressive men (24–48%). Men who perpetrated rape and sexual coercion were more likely to have sex with the victim again (64% and 55% respectively) than other perpetrators (32–37%). In addition, men who raped reported sexual intercourse with a larger number of partners since the assaultive episode than was reported by less sexually aggressive men.

DISCUSSION

In this study, behaviorally specific items regarding rape and lesser forms of sexual aggression/victimization were presented in a noncrime context to an approximately representative national sample of college students. The results indicate that 15.4% of women reported experiencing and 4.4% of men reported perpetrating, since the age of 14, an act that met legal definitions of rape. Because virtually none of these victims or perpetrators had been involved in the criminal justice system, their experiences qualify as "hidden rape," which is not reflected in official crime statistics such as the *Uniform Crime Reports* (e.g., FBI 1985).

As mentioned earlier, a victimization rate for women of 38/1,000 was calculated. This rate is 10–15 times greater than rates based on the NCS (BJS 1984), which are 3.9/1,000 for women age 16–19 and 2.5/1,000 for women age 20–24. Even men's rate of admitting to raping (9/1,000) is two to three times greater than NCS estimates of the high risk of rape for women between the ages of 16–24. At least among students in higher education, it appears that official surveys (such as the NCS) fail to describe the full extent of sexual victimization.

However, NCS rates are based on representative samples of all persons in the U.S. in the 16–24-year-old group, whereas the present sample represents only the 25% of persons age 18–24 who attend college. Using other available data for guidance, one can speculate how the victimization rates among postsecondary students might compare with the rates among nonstudents in the same age group. Although the data do not suggest a direct relationship between level of education and rape victimization rates, the rates are related to family income. Thus, nonstudents, who are likely to come from poorer families than students enrolled in higher education, might show even higher incidence rates than those found in the study sample. However, only when empirical data on young persons not attending school become available can the victimization rates reported in the NCS for persons age 18–24 be fully analyzed.

The characteristics of the rapes described by study respondents differ from the characteristics of rapes described by official statistics (e.g., BJS 1984). For example, 60–75% of the rapes reported in the NCS by women age 16–24 involved strangers, and 27% involved multiple offenders (i.e., group rapes). Study respondents, most of whom were between the ages of 18–24, did report stranger rapes (16%) and group rapes (5%), but the vast majority of incidents were individual assaults (95%) that involved close acquaintances or dates (84%).

The differences between the kinds of rape described in official reports and in this study suggest that it is episodes of intimate violence that differentiate between the results. Either the wording of screening questions or the overall crime context-questioning of the NCS may fail to elicit from respondents the large number of sexual victimizations that involve close acquaintances.

The findings of this study demonstrate that men do not admit enough sexual aggression to account for the number of victimizations reported by women. Specifically, 54% of women claimed to be sexually victimized, but only 25% of men admitted any degree of sexually aggressive behavior. However, the number of times that men admitted perpetrating each aggressive act is virtually identical to the number of times women reported experiencing each act. Thus, the results fail to support notions that a few sexually active men could account for the victimization of a sizable number of women. Clearly, some of the victimizations reported by college women occurred in earlier years and were not perpetrated by the men who were surveyed. In addition, some recent victimizations may have involved community members who were not attending college. Future research must determine the extent to which these explanations account for the sizable difference in rates.

The data on validity suggest that those sexual experiences reported by the women did, in fact, occur, while additional relevant sexual experiences may not have been reported by men. Men may not be intentionally withholding information, but rather may be perceiving and conceptualizing potentially relevant sexual experiences in a way that was not elicited by the wording of the sexual experiences survey. Scully and Marolla (1982) studied incarcerated rapists who denied that the incident for which they were convicted was a rape. Many of these men, although they used physical force and injured their victims, saw their behavior as congruent with consensual sexual activity. It may be that some men fail to perceive accurately the degree of force and coerciveness that was involved in a particular sexual encounter or to interpret correctly a woman's consent or resistance.

This hypothesis is supported by the descriptive differences between men's and women's perceptions of the rape incidents. Although there were many points of agreement between men and women (e.g., the proportion of incidents that involved alcohol and the relationship of victim and offender), victims saw their nonconsent as clearer and occurring after less consensual intimacy than offenders. Victims perceived their own resistance and the man's violence as much more extreme than the offenders did. Future research might compare consent, violence, and resistance attributions among sexually aggressive and sexually nonaggressive men. If differences were found, the line of inquiry would lead to a new focus for rape prevention programs—educating vulnerable men to perceive accurately and communicate clearly.

The results of the study have additional implications for clinical treatment and research. The extent of sexual victimization uncovered by the national survey suggests that clinicians should consider including questions about unwanted sexual activity in routine intake interviewing of women clients and that they more frequently should consider sexual victimization among the possible etiological factors that could be linked to presenting symptoms. Of course, the study sample consisted of students, whereas many psychotherapy seekers are adults. However, it is not unusual for symptoms of post-traumatic stress disorder, which victims of rape may experience, to emerge months or even years after the trauma (American Psychiatric Association 1980).

For researchers, these results in combination with the work of others begin to describe the full extent of rape and suggest how reported statistics on rape reflect only those rapes reported to police (i.e., 5%), rapes acknowledged as rape by the victim (i.e., 27%), and those for which victim assistance services are sought (i.e., 5%), rather than reflecting rapes that have not been revealed (i.e., 42%). Future research must address the traumatic cognitive and symptomatic impact of rape on victims who do not report, confide in significant others, seek services, or even identify as victims. It is possible that the quality of many women's lives is reduced by the effects of encapsulated, hidden sexual victimization and the victims' subsequent accommodation to the experience through beliefs and behavior (Koss and Burkhart 1986).

Statistically significant regional and ethnic differences in the prevalence of sexual aggression/victimization were found. Unfortunately, the meaning of these results cannot be fully interpreted, as ethnicity and region were confounded (i.e., minority students are not distributed randomly across the regions of the country). However, effect sizes calculated on the variables of region and ethnicity indicate that their impact on prevalence rates is small. In the future, researchers will need to analyze the effect of ethnicity by controlling for region (and vice versa). As a result, other data available on the subjects, including personality characteristics, values, beliefs, and current behavior, can be used to attempt to account for any remaining differences.

Overall, the prevalence rates for sexual victimization/aggression were robust and did not vary extensively from large to small schools; across types of institutions; or among urban areas, medium-sized cities, and rural areas. The ubiquity of sexual aggression and victimization supports Johnson's observation that "the locus of violence rests squarely in the middle of what our culture defines as 'normal' interaction between men and women" (Johnson 1980, 146). As the editors of the *Morbidity and Mortality Weekly Report*, issued by the Centers for Disease Control in Atlanta, have noted, there is an ". . . increasing awareness in the public health community that violence is a serious public health problem and that nonfatal interpersonal violence has far-reaching consequences in terms of morbidity and quality of life" (Centers for Disease Control 1985, 739). Future research needs to devote attention to the preconditions that foster sexual violence.

Within the rape epidemiology literature are studies that have differed in methodology and have reported varying prevalence rates. Although the Ms. project involved a set of self-report questions whose validity and reliability have been evaluated, each data-collection method has advantages and disadvantages and cannot be fully assessed without reference to the special requirements of the topic of inquiry, the target population, and practical and financial limitations. Future epidemiological research must define how much variation in rates is due to the method of data collection or the screening question format and how much is due to sample differences. Nevertheless, the most important conclusion suggested by this entire line of research is that rape is much more prevalent than official statistics suggest.

This research was supported by a grant to the author from the Antisocial and Criminal Behavior Branch of the National Institute of Mental Health, MH-31618. To protect the anonymity of the participating institutions, the author cannot thank by name the people across the country who made the study possible; nevertheless, she expresses her appreciation. The author also acknowledges the assistance of Mary Harvey, who stimulated development of the study; Ellen Sweet of the *Ms.* Foundation for Education and Communication, who aided in the administration of the project and lent prestige to the work by allowing the use of the *Ms.* identity on survey materials; Hugh Clark of Clark/Jones, Inc., who supervised the sampling procedures; Ann Maney of the National Institutes of Mental Health, who gave technical advice; Thomas Dinero, who provided statistical consultation; and Chris Gidycz and Nadine Wisniewski, who performed data analyses.

REFERENCES

American Psychiatric Association. 1980. *Diagnostic and statistical manual of mental disorders*. 3d ed. Washington, D.C.: American Psychiatric Association.

Bureau of Justice Statistics. 1984. *Criminal victimization in the United States, 1982*. Washington, D.C.: U.S. Department of Justice.

Centers for Disease Control. 1985. Adolescent sex offenders—Vermont, 1984. *Morbidity and Mortality Weekly Report* 34: 738–741.

Cohen, J. 1977. *Statistical power analysis for the behavioral sciences*. rev. ed. New York: Academic Press.

Federal Bureau of Investigation. 1986. *Uniform crime reports*. Washington, D.C.: U.S. Department of Justice.

Johnson, A.G. 1980. On the prevalence of rape in the United States. *Signs: Journal of Women in Culture and Society* 6: 136–46.

Kanin, E.J. 1957. Male aggression in dating-courtship relations. *American Journal of Sociology* 63: 197–204.

Kanin, E.J., and S.R. Parcell. 1977. Sexual aggression: A second look at the offended female. *Archives of Sexual Behavior* 6: 67–76.

Katz, S., and M.A. Mazur. 1979. *Understanding the rape victim: A synthesis of research findings*. New York: John Wiley and Sons, Inc.

Kilpatrick, D.G., L.J. Veronen, and C.L. Best. 1984. Factors predicting psychological distress among rape victims. In *Trauma and its wake: The study and treatment of post-traumatic stress disorder*, ed. C.R. Figley, 113–41. New York: Brunner/Mazel.

Kilpatrick, D.G., et al. 1985. Mental health correlates of criminal victimization: A random community survey. *Journal of Consulting and Clinical Psychology* 53: 866–73.

Kirkpatrick, C., and E.J Kanin. 1957. Male sexual aggression on a university campus. *American Sociological Review* 22: 52–58.

Koss, M.P. 1985. The hidden rape victim: Personality, attitudinal, and situational characteristics. *Psychology of Women Quarterly* 9: 193–212.

Koss, M.P., and B.R. Burkhart. 1986. Clinical treatment of rape. Under review.

Koss, M.P., and C.A. Gidycz. 1985. Sexual Experiences Survey: Reliability and validity. *Journal of Consulting and Clinical Psychology* 53: 422–23.

Koss, M.P., and C.J. Oros. 1982. Sexual Experiences Survey: A research instrument investigating sexual aggression and victimization. *Journal of Consulting and Clinical Psychology* 50: 455–57.

Koss, M.P., C.J. Gidycz, and N. Wisniewski. 1987. The score of rape: Sexual aggression and victimization in a national sample of students in higher education. *Journal of Consulting and Clinical Psychology* 55. Forthcoming.

Koss, M.P., et al. 1985. Nonstranger sexual aggression: A discriminant analysis of the psychological characteristics of undetected offenders. *Sex Roles* 12: 981–92.

Law Enforcement Assistance Administration. 1974. *Crimes and victims: A report on the Dayton–San Jose pilot survey of victimization.* Washington, D.C.: National Criminal Justice Information and Statistics Service.

————. 1975. *Criminal victimization surveys in 13 American Cities.* Washington, D.C.: U.S. Government Printing Office.

Office of Civil Rights. 1980. *Fall enrollment and compliance report of institutions of higher education.* Washington, D.C.: U.S. Department of Education.

Ohio Revised Code. 1980. 2907.01A, 2907.02.

Rapaport, K., and B.R. Burkhart. 1984. Personality and attitudinal characteristics of sexually coercive college males. *Journal of Abnormal Psychology* 93: 216–221.

Russell, D.E.H. 1984. *Sexual exploitation: Rape, child sexual abuse, and sexual harassment.* Beverly Hills, Calif.: Sage Publications.

Scully, D., and J. Marolla. 1982. Convicted rapists' construction of reality: The denial of rape. Paper presented at meeting of American Sociological Association, September, San Francisco.

U.S. Bureau of Census. 1980. *Current population reports 1980–1981.* Washington, D.C.: U.S. Government Printing Office.

Walker, A. 1982. *The Color Purple.* New York: Harcourt Brace Jovanovich.

VICTIMS OF VIOLENCE AND PSYCHIATRIC ILLNESS

ELAINE (HILBERMAN) CARMEN
Boston University School of Medicine

PATRICIA PERRI RIEKER
Dana-Farber Cancer Institute

TRUDY MILLS
University of Arizona

The growing body of knowledge about victims of violence strongly suggests that physical and sexual abuse may be frequent, if not inevitable, life experiences for many people. However, psychological and social conditions that link such victimization to subsequent psychiatric illness have only recently been identified as subjects for clinical investigation. As a result, the importance of the victim-to-patient process is neither appreciated by clinicians nor adequately conceptualized by researchers. This lack of recognition persists in spite of extensive, but unsynthesized, literature on the psychosocial consequences of child abuse, spouse abuse, rape, and incest. As a way of addressing this gap in our knowledge, this chapter reports the results of an investigation into the relationship between physical and sexual abuse and psychiatric illness in a psychiatric inpatient population.

ABUSE AND PSYCHIATRIC ILLNESS
Only in the last decade have mental health professionals begun to examine the extent to which victims are represented in a variety of clinical settings.

Reprinted, with changes, from American Journal of Psychiatry 141:378–83, 1984.
Copyright 1984, the American Psychiatric Association. Reprinted by permission.

For example, Rounsaville and Weissman (1977–78) reported that 3.8% of the women presenting to an emergency trauma service and 3.4% of the women presenting to an emergency psychiatric service had been battered by men with whom they were intimate. However, when Stark and associates (1979) analyzed new data from the same emergency trauma service, they concluded that "where physicians saw 1 out of 35 of their patients as battered, a more accurate approximation is 1 in 4; where they acknowledged that 1 injury out of 20 resulted from domestic abuse, the actual figure approached 1 in 4. What they described as a rare occurrence was in reality an event of epidemic proportions" (Stark, Flitcraft, and Frazier 1979, 467).

Rosenfeld (1979), in a review of all his female psychotherapy patients seen in a group practice setting over one year, found that six of the 18 women were incest victims, only one of whom offered this information spontaneously. The underreporting of victims in psychiatric samples is consistent with the finding of Hilberman and Munson (1977–78) that half of all women referred for psychiatric consultation in a rural medical clinic were in battering relationships. Post and associates (1980), in a preliminary report on the prevalence of domestic violence among psychiatric inpatients, further substantiated the relationship of abuse and psychological disorder. Of the 60 patients (38 women and 22 men), 48% gave histories of a battering relationship: 50% of the women had been battered, and 21% reported abusing their partners; 14% of the men had been battered and 27% reported abusing their partners. Other forms of abuse were not discussed.

Several studies (Stark, Flitcraft, and Frazier 1979; Green 1978; Herman 1981; Hilberman 1980) provide evidence of the profoundly self-destructive behaviors that emerge after victimization. These are the behaviors that demonstrate a clear link between abuse experiences and psychiatric illness. Green (1978) compared 59 abused and neglected children with 29 neglected children and 30 children who were neither abused nor neglected. Self-destructive behaviors (biting, cutting, burning, head banging, suicide attempts) were exhibited by 40.6% of the abused children, 17.2% of the neglected children, and 6.7% of the controls. Green concluded that "the abused child's sense of worthlessness, badness, and self-hatred as a consequence of parental assault, rejection, and scapegoating formed the nucleus for subsequent self-destructive behavior" (1978, 581). The new research on violence against women not only corroborates this pattern, but also provides a vivid psychological portrait of female victims of incest, spouse abuse, and rape (Herman 1981; Hilberman 1980; Dobash and Dobash 1979; Burgess and Holmstrom 1974; Symonds 1976).

METHODS

To explore the relationship between violence and psychiatric disorder, we reconstructed the life experiences of patients through an indepth examination of psychiatric inpatient records. It was necessary to compare male and female patients as well as to compare abused and nonabused patients in order to clarify this relationship.

The nonrandom sample for this retrospective study included all patients discharged over 18 months (January 1980 through June 1981) from one of three adult psychiatric inpatient units in a university teaching hospital. The final sample consisted of 188 adult and adolescent male and female patients. Multiple discharges were treated as one case. A comparison of the demographic characteristics of this sample with those of inpatients from all wards during the previous two years confirmed that the study sample was representative in terms of race and sex.

A standardized coding instrument developed by the research team (two psychiatrists, two sociologists, and one social worker) was used to analyze the following content of the discharge summary and other patient records: demographic information; social, medical, and psychiatric histories; behavior before and during hospitalization; and details about the type and extent of violence. Clinicians were interviewed to verify ambiguous details or to supply missing data.

Violence was defined as any form of serious physical or sexual abuse described in the discharge summary or in the record. These abuse events included child abuse, incest, marital violence, and assault or rape occurring outside of the family. Instances in which abuse was suspected but not confirmed in the records were not coded as violence. Decisions about what behaviors constituted abuse were conservative, and ambiguous cases were discussed until the research team reached a consensus. In this way, a high degree of intercoder consistency was achieved. We collected data about the type of abuse, the severity and duration of the abuse, and the relationship of the patient to the abuser. Similar data were collected for those patients who were abusers. In addition, a scale was constructed for measuring the patient's ability to cope with anger and aggression during the hospitalization.

Cross-tabulation and multivariate techniques were used to analyze the data. Chi-square analyses were used to compare the abused and non-abused patients. We used the .05 level of significance to point out important differences between groups. Because this was an exploratory study with a nonrandom sample, the chi-square values are presented as descriptive statistics and not as statistical tests conducted to retain or reject null hypotheses. Additional analyses of these data have been reported elsewhere (Mills, Rieker, and Carmen 1985).

RESULTS

SAMPLE DESCRIPTION

The patients in the study were a diverse group: 80% were white and 20% were black; 65% were female and 35% were male. Their ages ranged from 12 to 88 years. Adolescents made up 15% of the sample, and the elderly made up 4%. Only 25% of the patients were married; 47% had never been married. Educational and occupational data showed that 26% had not graduated from high school (some were students) and that 18% were college graduates; 21% were professionals, and 33% worked in clerical, sales, craft, or unskilled jobs. Fifty-two percent had annual incomes of less than $10,000. The low incomes of the patients may reflect the substantial percentage (35%) who were disabled or unemployed before hospitalization. However, the income data were less accurate than the educational and occupational data and should be interpreted cautiously. Half of the patients had affective disorders, and the other half was divided among psychoses (18%), personality disorders (13%), adjustment reactions (11%), substance abuse (5%), and psychosomatic disorders (2%).

EXTENT OF ABUSE

Given our conservative coding of abuse, the prevalence appears high. Of the 188 patients, 80 (43%) had histories of physical and/or sexual abuse. Abuse was suspected but not confirmed in the records of an additional 7%. Of the 80 abused patients, 53% ($N = 42$) had been physically abused, 19% ($N = 15$) had been sexually abused, and 29% ($N = 23$) had been both physically and sexually abused. The majority of sexual abuse (71%) had occurred more than a year before admission, compared with 40% of physical abuse. Of the abused patients, 41% had been abused by more than one person.

Ninety percent ($N = 72$) of the abused patients had been abused by family members. Fifty-one percent had been abused by husbands or former husbands, 40% by fathers or stepfathers, and 23% by mothers or stepmothers. Of those patients who had been sexually abused, 66% ($N = 25$) had been abused by family members. The largest group of sexually abused patients had been abused by fathers (34%); siblings accounted for 16% of sexual abuse cases and strangers for 29%.

Female patients were much more likely than males to have histories of abuse. Fifty-three percent ($N = 65$) of the females and 23% ($N = 15$) of the males had been abused. There were also differences between sexes in the patterns of abuse. Males (mainly teenagers) were most frequently abused by parents during childhood and adolescence, whereas females were abused by parents, spouses, and strangers. For the females, abuse started in childhood and continued through adulthood. Only 4 of the 38 patients who had been sexually abused were males, as were their assailants. Teenagers were much more likely than adults to have been abused. Seventy-five percent of the 28 teenagers had been abused, compared with 39% of the adults. Black patients were slightly more likely than the white patients to have been victims of abuse (50% compared with 41%), but this reflects the fact that black patients in this sample were predominantly female (85%) and the females were more likely than the males to have histories of abuse.

COMPARISONS OF ABUSED AND NONABUSED PATIENTS

Can abused patients be differentiated from nonabused patients in a clinical setting? To answer this question, we made comparisons on the basis of social history data, behaviors at the time of admission, behaviors during hospitalization, and diagnoses. In the analysis, diagnoses did not differentiate between abused and nonabused patients.

One significant family characteristic of the abused patients was the excessive use of alcohol by parents. Of the abused patients, 31% had alcoholic fathers, compared with 13% of the nonabused patients. The figures for alcoholic mothers were 13% and 5%, respectively. Table 2.1 provides a further comparison of social history characteristics of abused and nonabused patients. We found that abused patients were more likely than nonabused patients to have past histories of suicidal and assaultive behaviors and criminal-justice system involvement.

The patients displayed a wide range of behaviors and symptoms at the time of admission to the hospital. As table 2.1 indicates, these behaviors did not differentiate abused from nonabused patients. At the time of admission, precipitants for hospitalization were equally likely to include suicidal behavior, aggressiveness, depression, drug abuse, disordered conduct, anxiety, and psychosomatic symptoms. The patients differed only with respect to organic symptoms. However, this may be a spurious finding that derives from limitations in the data.

Two important differences emerged when we examined various behaviors during the hospitalization. First, abused patients tended to remain in the hospital longer than the nonabused group. Of the abused group, 26% were hospitalized longer than 90 days, whereas only 9% of the nonabused group were hospitalized for that length of time. The average stay for nonabused patients was 43 days, and for the abused patients it was 58 days.

TABLE 2.1
SOCIAL HISTORY OF ADMISSION BEHAVIORS OF ABUSED AND
NONABUSED PSYCHIATRIC PATIENTS

Behavior	Abused Patients ($N = 80$)		Nonabused Patients ($N = 80$)		
	N	%*	N	%*	X^2
Social History					
Abuse of alcohol	17	21	38	35	3.665
Abuse of illicit drugs	14	18	26	24	0.826
Suicide attempt(s)	36	45	32	30	4.061*
Criminial-justice					
involvement	12	15	5	5	4.814*
Abuse of others	20	25	14	13	3.719*
Admission					
Suicidal	35	44	45	42	0.019
Aggressive/destructive	20	25	20	19	0.798
Depressive symptoms	49	61	66	61	0.000
Substance abuse	19	24	25	23	0.000
Organic symptoms/					
confusion	2	3	15	14	5.929*
Conduct disorder	12	15	9	8	1.441
Anxiety/agitation	25	31	33	31	0.000
Psychosomatic	13	16	13	12	0.377
Psychotic	19	24	41	38	3.643

*Percentages do not total 100% because some patients exhibited more than one behavior.
*$p<.05$.

Second, abused and nonabused patients differed in how they dealt with
anger and aggression during their hospitalization. This is especially
pertinent to our study, as anger is an expected response to abusive events.
Thus we developed a measure of the inpatients' aggression-coping behavior. This measure focused on whether the anger was mainly directed
inward or outward and whether behavioral control of aggressive impulses
was maintained. Four categories were used to measure this aspect of
hospital behavior.

Category 1 describes a behavior pattern in which the anger was directed
inward in a passive, overcontrolled manner. These generally depressed,
frightened, and withdrawn patients felt worthless, hopeless, and undeserving but were not actively suicidal. Although these passive patients
were not behavioral problems on the ward, their passivity frustrated
clinicians' attempts to establish therapeutic relationships.

Category 2 patients directed their anger inward, but in a more overt,
active fashion. This coping style was characterized by active suicidal
intent and/or savage self-hatred, with loss of control reflected in a variety
of self-destructive and self-mutilating behaviors. At times, some of these

patients alarmed even experienced clinicians with their uncontrollable self-mutilation and their resolutely maintained unempathic attitude toward themselves.

Category 3 patients directed their anger outward in a controlled manner. Some of these patients expressed anger appropriately, while others displaced and projected their anger and hostility elsewhere (most prominently toward hospital staff). In all cases, however, control of aggressive impulses remained intact.

Category 4 patients directed their anger outward, with aggressive and sometimes violent behaviors toward others. Such loss of control was reflected in outbursts of barely contained murderous rage, threats to harm others, and actual assaults.

The four behavior patterns were not mutually exclusive, and some patients displayed aspects of more than one type of coping behavior. For some patients, the information available was insufficient for classification.

A higher percentage of abused patients (20%) than of nonabused patients (10%) displayed the behavior pattern of category 2, that is, they directed their anger inward in an actively self-destructive fashion. This finding is explored further in our discussion of sex differences.

COMPARISON OF ABUSED MALES AND FEMALES

As noted earlier, abused patients were more likely to be female: 65 females and 15 males were abused. The majority of abused males were teenagers (60%), and the majority of abused females were adults (81%).

There were other differences between male and female abused patients. First, they presented themselves differently at the time of hospitalization (see table 2.2). The behavior of the abused females resembled that of the other females at the time of hospitalization (i.e., they were equally likely to be suicidal, depressed, etc.).

Abused males, however, differed from the other males, as shown in table 2.2. The small number of abused males in the study decreased the likelihood that the findings would be statistically significant. Nevertheless, three of the relationships were statistically significant, and three of the remaining comparisons showed substantial differences between percentages of abused and nonabused males. The abused males were less likely to appear depressed, suicidal, or psychotic at the time of hospitalization. They were more likely than nonabused males to be aggressive or to have disordered conduct or psychosomatic symptoms. Because the majority of abused males were teenagers, the increase in disordered conduct reflected age as well as abuse.

TABLE 2.2
Social History and Admission Behaviors of Abused and Nonabused Male and Female Psychiatric Patients

Behavior	Males Abused ($N = 15$)[a]		Nonabused ($N = 50$)			Females Abused ($N = 65$)		Nonabused ($N = 58$)		
	N	%	N	%	X^2	N	%	N	%	X^2
Social History										
Abuse of alcohol	4	27	27	54	2.447	13	20	11	19	0.000
Abuse of illicit drugs	4	27	17	34	0.047	10	15	9	16	0.000
Suicide attempts	8	53	14	28	2.272	28	43	18	31	1.419
Criminial-justice involvement	6	40	3	6	8.513*	6	9	2	3	0.869
Abuse of others	9	60	11	22	6.139*	11	17	3	5	3.111
Admission										
Suicidal	4	27	21	42	0.589	31	48	24	41	0.272
Aggressive/destructive	6	40	10	20	1.526	14	22	10	17	0.139
Depressive symptoms	4	27	30	60	3.889*	45	69	36	62	0.417
Substance abuse	4	27	15	30	0.000	15	23	10	17	0.334
Organic symptoms/ confusion	0	0	4	8	0.269	2	3	11	19	6.591*
Conduct disorder	6	40	3	6	8.513*	6	9	6	10	0.000
Anxiety/agitation	3	20	16	32	0.328	22	34	17	29	0.119
Psychosomatic	4	27	7	14	0.569	9	14	6	10	0.100
Psychotic	0	0	18	36	5.778*	19	29	23	40	1.054

[a]These columns should be interpreted with caution since the number of abused males was small.
*$p < .05$.

TABLE 2.3
Anger/Aggression Coping Behaviors of Abused and Nonabused Male and Female Psychiatric Patients

Anger/Aggression Coping Behavior	Males Abused ($N = 15$)[a]		Nonabused ($N = 50$)		Females Abused ($N = 65$)		Nonabused ($N = 58$)	
	N	%	N	%	N	%	N	%
Directed inward								
Controlled (category 1)	2	13	17	34	27	42	21	36
Uncontrolled (category 2)	1	7	6	12	15	24	5	9
Directed outward								
Controlled (category 3)	0	0	2	4	7	11	5	9
Uncontrolled (category 4)	5	33	9	18	9	14	7	12
Directed both inward and outward	4	27	10	20	5	8	9	16
None of the categories	3	20	6	12	2	4	11	19

Other differences between the abused males and females emerged when behaviors before hospitalization were examined. Table 2.2 shows that the abused males were much more likely than the abused females (and other males) to have abused others. Of the abused males, 60% had been violent toward others, while only 17% of the abused females had been violent. Abused males were also more likely than abused females (and other males) to have had criminal-justice system involvement.

Perhaps the most important characteristic that distinguished the behavior of the abused males and females was that the males had become more aggressive while the females had become more passive. In some ways, the sex-role stereotypes seemed to be exaggerated in this sample. This was evident in the way that the abused males and females coped with anger (see table 2.3). Thirty-three percent of the abused males coped with anger by directing it aggressively toward others (category 4), but only 14% of the abused females did so. The majority of abused females (66%) directed their anger inward (categories 1 and 2), compared with only 20% of the abused males. Abused males, more than nonabused males, coped with anger by aggressively directing it toward others, while abused females were more likely than other females to turn their anger inward. For example, 24% of the abused females, compared with 9% of the nonabused females, were actively self-destructive during hospitalization.

DISCUSSION

Our finding that almost half of the psychiatric inpatients in this sample had histories of physical and/or sexual abuse should not come as a surprise, given the prevalence of violence in the general population. As this study demonstrates, most of the abuse occurred in the context of the family. Although families are usually viewed as providing the primary support networks for individuals, our data confirm the findings of other researchers that female adults and children of both sexes are at highest risk for violence within the family (Herman 1981; Dobash and Dobash 1979; Carmen, Russo, and Miller 1981; Gelles and Straus 1975). In a retrospective study, reported in *Clinical Psychiatry News* (1982), Putnam found that of 40 patients with multiple personality disorder, 80% had been severely abused by family members during childhood. It is important to bear in mind that victims of family violence might be overrepresented in any psychiatric sample because violent family systems may produce a population at risk for chronic abuse as well as for psychiatric illness.

Victims of physical and sexual abuse are faced with an extraordinary task of conflict resolution as they look for a context in which bodily harm and threats to life can be understood. When the assailant is an intimate or a family member, this process is immeasurably complicated by the profound betrayal of trust. Such victims must also cope with ongoing vulnerability to physical and psychological danger when the abuser has continuing access to the victim. It was not uncommon, in our sample, for a patient to have experienced multiple kinds of abuse. There were numerous cases of women who were physically or sexually abused as children and subsequently raped or abused by spouses and others in adulthood. This pattern of increased vulnerability of female victims to other kinds of abuse was also described in Herman's study of incest victims (1981) and Hilberman's review of research on battered women (1980). Since the number of males was small and the majority were adolescents, it is unclear if such vulnerability to multiple abuse is the same among men with histories of victimization.

What is clear from the inpatient summaries and our clinical experiences is that the psychological and behavioral manifestations of chronic abuse reflect extraordinary damage to the self, which then becomes the object of the victim's hatred and aggression. While there are psychodynamic issues specific to each kind of abuse, our observations indicate a common pattern of responses to chronic victimization. Although these psychosocial responses may have different behavioral manifestations in abused males and females, the psychic trauma is similar. These victims have extreme difficulties with anger and aggression, self-image, and trust.

In contrast to the outrage and disgust experienced by others hearing of the abuse, victims do not usually acknowledge their anger toward their abusers, in part because their rage is perceived as dangerous and potentially uncontrollable and in part because of the complex relationship between victim and abuser. After years of abuse, victims blame themselves as they come to believe that the abuse can be explained only by their essential "badness."

In our sample, the abused females directed their hatred and aggression against themselves in both overt and covert ways. These behaviors formed a continuum from quiet resignation and depression to repeated episodes of self-mutilation and suicide attempts. Self-destructive behaviors were related to feelings of worthlessness, hopelessness, shame, and guilt. These affects escalated when anger threatened to surface and, at such times, often culminated in impulsive self-destructive episodes. Markedly impaired self-esteem was prominent among these patients, as they conveyed a sense that they were undeserving of any empathic understanding or help from clinicians.

In comparison, the mainly adolescent male victims, although experiencing many of the same feelings of self-hatred, more often directed their aggression toward others. It is likely that these outward displays of aggression were defenses against intolerable feelings of helplessness and vulnerability. In the hospital, this internal dynamic was reflected in alternating expressions of anguish and despair, followed by threatening "macho" behavior and displays of physical prowess. Patterns of sex role socialization obviously shape the differential responses to abuse of males and females.

The social histories and inpatient process notes provide impressive evidence of the abused patients' lack of trust and the way in which inability to trust complicates the evaluative and treatment processes. Herman (1981) reported the same finding in her study of father-daughter incest, in which she described a dual pattern of inability to feel trust when this would be appropriate and to protect oneself when trust is inappropriate. In our sample, expectations of abandonment and exploitation by the clinician were prominent; hence, victims did not spontaneously reveal the abuse or easily form therapeutic alliances.

In the absence of direct information about past or current abuse, our data suggest that abused patients are not easily distinguished from nonabused patients at the time of admission to the hospital. Rather, the significant differences between abused and nonabused patients emerged during the course of hospitalization and were reflected both in the treatment difficulties and the greater length of time that abused patients remained in the hospital. These outcomes may be the end result of victims' (1) inability to trust, which delays or prevents the development of a therapeutic liaison, (2) impaired self-esteem, whereby abused patients judge themselves as undeserving of treatment, and (3) difficulty in coping with aggression, whereby anger is destructively directed toward the damaged self or others.

CONCLUSIONS

Clinicians generally ask patients about abuse experiences if they have some reason to suspect abuse. However, these suspicions are often based on unfounded stereotypes about victims and violent families. Increasing awareness of the extent of violence in society leads us to suspect that psychiatric patients are more likely to have experienced physical and/or sexual violence than to hear voices, yet clinicians are systematic in their inquiries about hallucinations while overlooking the reality and importance of violent assaults. Our research underscores the discrepancy between the alarming numbers of people who are physically and sexually abused and the relative lack of attention that is given to these topics by clinicians in taking routine psychiatric histories.

Clinicians are largely unaware of the psychosocial consequences of abuse because the victim-to-patient process is an area of clinical research that has been underconceptualized. Thus, even when abuse is identified, clinicians' confusion about the role of abuse in psychiatric illness leaves them unprepared to implement special treatment approaches for what appears to be a large proportion of psychiatric patients. (A separate paper presents a theoretical model that captures the complexity of the victim-to-patient process and its implications for treatment [Rieker and Carmen 1986].) From our perspective, a major focus of treatment must be to help victims become survivors. This transformation is contingent on recognizing how chronic abuse constructs the individual's social identity as a victim and how the survival strategies employed by victims interfere not only with emotional development, but with the therapeutic alliance and process.

Because the theoretical understanding of the victim-to-patient process lags behind clinical experiences with victims, our research raises more questions than it answers about the effects of abuse and the conditions that leave some, but not all, victims vulnerable to psychiatric illness. We believe we have provided a realistic description of the lives of chronically abused females whose self-destructive behaviors and silence make them difficult to identify and treat. However, because most of the abused males in our population were adolescents, we can only conjecture about their fates as adult men. It may be that, if the behavioral response pattern of the abused adolescent males seen in our population continues into adulthood, they become inmates in other structured environments, such as state mental hospitals and prisons. It is possible that these men are coerced into treatment only after they have become dangerous and assaultive; hence, the treatment focus is on their abusive behaviors while their histories of victimization go unrecognized. The large population of Viet Nam veterans in prisons and psychiatric hospitals would provide a relevant sample of adult male victims for further study.

The authors thank Jean Gross, A.C.S.W., and Leonora Stephens, M.D., for their contributions to the research.

REFERENCES

Abused child, multiple personality tied. 1982. *Clinical Psychiatry News*, September, 2.

Burgess A.W., and L.L. Holmstrom. 1974. *Rape: Victims of crisis*. Bowie, Md.: Robert J. Brady Co.

Carmen, E.(H.), N.F. Russo, and J.B. Miller. 1981. Inequality and women's mental health: An overview. *American Journal of Psychiatry* 138: 1319–30.

Dobash R.E., and R. Dobash. 1979. *Violence against wives: A case against the patriarchy*. New York: Free Press.

Gelles, R.J., and M.A. Straus. 1975. Family experience and public support of the death penalty. *American Journal of Orthopsychiatry* 45: 596–613.

Green, A.H. 1978. Self-destructive behavior in battered children. *American Journal of Psychiatry* 135: 579–82.

Herman, J.L. 1981. *Father-daughter incest*. Cambridge, Mass.: Harvard University Press, 1981.

Hilberman, E. 1980. Overview: The "wife-beater's wife" reconsidered. *American Journal of Psychiatry* 137: 1336-47.

Hilberman, E., and K. Munson. 1977–78. Sixty battered women. *Victimology: An International Journal* 2: 460–71.

Mills, T., P.P. Rieker, and E.(H.) Carmen. 1985 Hospitalization experiences of victims of abuse. *Victimology: An International Journal* 9: 436–49.

Post, R.D., et al. 1980. A preliminary report on the prevalence of domestic violence among psychiatric inpatients. *American Journal of Psychiatry* 137: 974–75.

Rieker, P.P., and E.(H.) Carmen. 1986. The victim-to-patient process: The disconfirmation and transformation of abuse. *American Journal of Orthopsychiatry* 56: 360–70.

Rosenfeld, A.A. 1979. Incidence of a history of incest among 18 female psychiatric patients. *American Journal of Psychiatry* 136: 791–95.

Rounsaville, B., and M.M. Weissman. 1977–78. Battered women: A medical problem requiring detection. *International Journal of Psychiatry in Medicine* 8: 191–202.

Stark, E., A. Flitcraft, and W. Frazier. 1979. Medicine and patriarchal violence: The social construction of a "private" event. *International Journal of Health Services* 9: 461–93.

Symonds, M. The rape victim: Psychological patterns of response. *American Journal of Psychoanalysis* 36: 27–34.

HISTORIES OF VIOLENCE IN AN OUTPATIENT POPULATION

An Exploratory Study

JUDITH LEWIS HERMAN
Harvard Medical School

Within the last decade, a large body of new research has demonstrated that sexual and domestic violence are social problems of major importance. Large-scale survey data from nonclinical populations indicate that for girls, the risk of sexual abuse is greater than one in three, and that for adult women, the risk of rape is about one in four (Russell 1984). Boys also face appreciable, though lesser, risk of childhood sexual abuse (Finkelhor 1979). Estimates of domestic physical abuse are less accurate; however, it is clear that children of both sexes are at considerable risk for physical abuse by parents and that adult women remain at high risk for physical abuse by their spouses (Pagelow 1984).

The consequences of physical and sexual violence in terms of psychiatric morbidity are only beginning to be appreciated. Recent studies indicate that the sequelae of both acute and chronic trauma may be severe and long lasting. Follow-up studies of adult women who were raped (Becker, Skinner, and Abel 1983; Burgess and Holmstrom 1979; Nadelson et al. 1982) or battered (Hilberman 1980) and of children who were physically (Green 1983; Lynch and Roberta 1982) or sexually (Gelinas 1983; Goodwin 1982; Herman 1981) abused reveal both catastrophic acute reactions and persistent chronic disability in a significant proportion of victims. For example, Terr (1983) found that 100% of 26 kidnapped children continued to show symptoms of post-traumatic stress disorder four years after the event. Some specific psychiatric syndromes, such as multiple personality disorder, have been etiologically related to severe childhood trauma (Sachs, Goodwin, and Braun 1986).

Victims of domestic and sexual violence frequently present as psychiatric patients. For example, a retrospective survey of 180 psychiatric inpatients found that 43% had histories of physical and/or sexual abuse, in most cases at the hands of family members (Carmen, Rieker, and Mills 1984). Post and colleagues (1980) found that 48% of a sample of 60 adult inpatients gave histories of a battering relationship. Emslie and Rosenfeld (1983), in a study of 65 hospitalized children and adolescents, reported that 35% of the girls and 8% of the boys had a history of sexual abuse. In an analysis of psychiatric emergency room visits, Stark, Flitcraft, and Frazier (1979) estimated that 25% of the female patients were battered.

Our study was undertaken to explore further the connection between experiences of violence and psychiatric patient status. Though this connection has been documented in inpatient and emergency room populations, no corresponding study has been done of an outpatient population, a group that might be considered more diverse and less severely disturbed. Moreover, though previous studies have demonstrated the existence of a large proportion of victims in a psychiatric patient population, the possibility that many patients might also be perpetrators of sexual or domestic violence has not been explored.

Three hypotheses were considered: (1) that a significant proportion of an outpatient population would report experiences of serious violence, either as victims, as offenders, or both; (2) that marked sex differences would be observed in experiences of violence; and (3) that histories of violence might be especially common in patients who fall into particular diagnostic categories. Such associations, if they could be identified, might shed some light on the process by which traumatic experiences are linked to the development of psychopathology.

METHODS

Diagnostic summaries were reviewed on all new outpatients evaluated by an interdisciplinary team at the psychiatry department of Cambridge Hospital, an urban teaching hospital, during a two-year period (July 1982–June 1984). The investigator participated as the team's staff psychiatrist in most of the case evaluations during this period.

The following data were recorded for each patient: demographic information, diagnoses on axes I and II of the American Psychiatric Association's Diagnostic and Statistical Manual III (DSM-III), and presence or absence of violence in the patient's history. Violence was defined as any experience of physical or sexual assault or abuse. Experiences of ordinary corporal punishment or consensual playful fighting among peers were not included, and ambiguous situations were recorded as negative. The patient's role as victim and/or offender as well as the type of violence were recorded. Interviewers had not been specifically instructed to gather data on the patients' experiences of violence; thus, only the information elicited in the course of routine clinical evaluation was recorded.

Male and female patients were compared on demographic indices, on major diagnostic categories, and on their experiences of violence. Comparisons were also made between victim/nonvictim and offender/nonoffender patient populations. Data analysis was conducted by means of cross-tabulation and chi-square computation.

RESULTS

One hundred and ninety patients were included in the sample: 105 women and 85 men. The majority were single people in their 20s and 30s. In class and ethnic background, they were representative of the city of Cambridge, the majority being white, working-class people, with a minority from the more privileged university community (see table 3.1). Diagnostically, the patient group was diverse, ranging from persons with high levels of adaptive functioning who were experiencing transient situational reactions to persons with chronic mental illness and severely impaired functioning. The frequencies and sex ratios of the major diagnoses were consistent with those reported in field trials of DSM-III (Williams and Spitzer 1983) (see table 3.2).

Forty-two patients, or 22% of the total, reported at least one experience in which they were victims of physical or sexual violence. Thirty-one patients, or 16% of the total, acknowledged having been physically or sexually abusive to others. Sex differences were pronounced: the majority of identified offenders (81%) were male, while the majority of identified victims (81%) were female ($p < 0.005$). Approximately one-third of the female outpatient population reported at least one experience of victimization. Of the male outpatient population, 29% had been abusive to others (see table 3.3).

The majority of the reported violence was intrafamilial: 86% of the victims reported that they were abused by family members, and 61% of the offenders abused relatives. The type of abuse most commonly reported by victims was physical abuse in childhood. The second most common type was wife beating. Of those patients who had ever been married, 23% of the women had been beaten by their husbands, and 20% of the men had assaulted their wives. Histories of sexual victimization were elicited from 13% of the women and none of the men; however, 10% of the men had

TABLE 3.1
DEMOGRAPHIC CHARACTERISTICS OF 190 CONSECUTIVE OUTPATIENTS

Characteristic	Male Patients	Female Patients	Total
Age			
20 or under	3	4	7
21–30	26	46	72
31–40	29	29	58
41–50	17	12	29
51–60	6	10	16
over 60	4	4	8
Total	85	105	190
Marital status			
Single	46	52	98
Married	16	25	41
Separated/divorced/			
widowed	23	28	51
Total	85	105	190
Occupation			
Unemployed	40	34	74
Working class	27	25	52
Factory/service	16	6	22
Office	4	12	16
Skilled/			
technical trade	7	7	14
Student	7	14	21
Professional/manager/			
small-business owner	7	5	12
Housewife	0	20	20
Data not available	6	5	11
Total	85	105	190

TABLE 3.2
DIAGNOSES OF 190 CONSECUTIVE OUTPATIENTS

Diagnosis	Male Patients ($N = 85$)	Female Patients ($N = 105$)	Total ($N = 190$)	Male:Female Ratio
Personality disorder	46	27	73	2:1
Substance abuse	39	19	58	2:1
Adjustment disorder	13	28	41	1:2
Depressive disorder	12	28	40	1:2
Psychotic disorder	18	20	38	1:1
Psychosomatic disorder	4	6	10	1:1
Organic mental disorder	4	5	9	1:1

TABLE 3.3
Histories of Violence of 190 Consecutive Outpatients

Violence History	Male Patients	Female Patients	Total
Victim history[a]			
Victims	8	34	42
Nonvictims	77	71	148
Total	85	105	190
Offender history[b]			
Offender	25	6	31
Nonoffender	60	99	159
Total	85	105	190

[a]$X^2 = 15.4; df = 1; p < 0.005.$ [b]$X^2 = 18.8; df = 1; p < 0.005.$

TABLE 3.4
Type of Victimization of 190 Consecutive Outpatients

Victimization	Male Patients ($N = 8$)	Female Patients ($N = 34$)	Total ($N = 42$)
Physical child abuse	6	16	22
Spouse abuse	0	12	12
Sexual child abuse	0	9	9
Rape	0	8	8
Assault	2	1	3
Total	8	46	54

TABLE 3.5
Type of Offenses of 190 Consecutive Outpatients

Offense	Male Patients ($N = 25$)	Female Patients ($N = 6$)	Total ($N = 31$)
Assault	13	6	19
Spouse abuse	8	0	8
Sexual assault	6	0	6
Sexual abuse of child	5	0	5
Physical abuse of child	2	0	2
Murder	1	0	1
Total	35	6	41

committed serious sexual offenses ranging from child molestation to rape (see tables 3.4 and 3.5). Almost half of these offenses had not come to the attention of legal authorities.

TABLE 3.6
Victimization History and Diagnosis of Females
in 190 Consecutive Outpatients

Diagnosis	Victims (N = 34)	Nonvictims (N = 71)	Total (N = 105)
Borderline personality	8 (23.5%)	4 (5.6%)	12 (11.5%)[a]
Substance abuse	10 (29.4%)	9 (12.7%)	19 (18.1%)[b]
Dysthymic disorder	9 (26.5%)	9 (12.7%)	18 (17.1%)
Adjustment disorder	9 (26.5%)	19 (26.7%)	28 (26.7%)
Psychotic disorder	7 (20.6%)	13 (18.3%)	20 (19.0%)
Eating disorder	3 (8.8%)	0 (0%)	3 (2.8%)
Suspected temporal lobe epilepsy	3 (8.8%)	0 (0%)	3 (2.8%)

[a] $X^2 = 6.8$; $df = 1$; $p < 0.01$.   [b] $X^2 = 4.8$; $df = 1$; $p < 0.05$.

Diagnoses of borderline-personality disorder and substance-abuse disorder were particularly common in women with a history of victimization (see table 3.6). Of the 12 women in this study who received the diagnosis of borderline-personality disorder, 8 had been abused in childhood or adolescence. Of the 19 women with substance-abuse diagnoses, 10 had a history of victimization. Women with a history of victimization were four times as likely to be given a diagnosis of borderline personality ($p < 0.01$) and twice as likely to be given a substance-abuse diagnosis ($p < 0.05$) as those who had not been victimized.

The only diagnosis found to be characteristic of male patients who had been abusive to others was antisocial-personality disorder (see table 3.7). Eleven of the 25 male offenders were given this diagnosis. Substance abuse and psychosis were not significantly associated with violence toward others in the male patient population.

TABLE 3.7
Offender History and Diagnosis of Males
in 190 Consecutive Outpatients

Diagnosis	Offenders (N = 25)	Nonoffenders (N = 60)	Total (N = 85)
Antisocial personality	11(44%)	3 (5%)	14 (16%)[a]
Substance abuse	9 (36%)	30 (50%)	39 (46%)
Psychosis	6 (24%)	12 (20%)	18 (21%)
Adjustment disorder	5 (20%)	8 (13%)	13 (15%)
Depressive disorder	2 (8%)	10 (17%)	12 (14%)

[a] $X^2 = 20.4$; $df = 1$; $p < 0.001$.

By contrast, all 6 of the female patients who had been violent toward others had psychotic disorders, severe alcoholism, or both. Histories of victimization were somewhat more common in patients who were violent toward others; however, the majority of patient offenders had not themselves been victimized.

DISCUSSION

Whether as victims, as offenders, or as both, a substantial proportion of this outpatient population reported experiences of serious violence. These results must be considered minimum estimates, because data on histories of violence were not obtained by a systematic interviewing protocol or by specifically trained interviewers. In fact, when these results are compared with data gathered systematically from large, nonclinical populations, the estimates of physical and sexual victimization are low for the women patients and even lower for the men. It seems reasonable to infer from these discrepancies that the interviewers often failed to obtain histories of victimization, especially from male patients. This oversight cannot be ascribed to inexperience among the interviewers; most probably, it reflects a generally low level of awareness, even among sophisticated clinicians, of the prevalence and significance of violence. Male patients may have been particularly reticent about experiences of victimization, and clinicians may have had difficulty in asking about them, since such experiences conflict with social expectations that men be strong, invulnerable, and uncomplaining.

The findings of major sex differences in violent behavior are consistent with previous reports (Carmen, Rieker, and Mills 1984; Pagelow 1984; Russell 1984). Female patients were much more commonly victims of violence; male patients were much more commonly offenders. Even without systematic interviewing, 10% of the males were found to be sex offenders. Such a high estimate has not been reported previously. Since reliable prevalence estimates from the general population are not available for comparison, there is no way to determine whether these results represent unusually deviant behavior attributable to psychopathology in a patient population.

In general, the available diagnostic categories did not offer a meaningful way of distinguishing between men who were violent toward others and those who were not. Psychotic illness and/or substance abuse were clearly implicated when female patients became assaultive, but did not generally account for the assaultive behavior of male patients. The one diagnostic correlate of violence toward others was antisocial personality, but since a history of abusiveness toward others is one of the major factors in determining the diagnosis, this association is not particularly illuminating. These negative results are consistent with the views of many social theorists who argue that a great deal of sexual and domestic violence falls within the range of normative social expectations for men and cannot be explained easily by concepts of deviance or psychopathology (Dobash and Dobash 1979; Herman 1981; Pagelow 1984; Russell 1984; Schechter 1982).

In female patients, however, clear connections were observed between experiences of victimization and the development of particular types of psychopathology. Diagnoses of borderline-personality disorder and substance abuse were unusually common in women who had been victims of violence. These results, which must be validated by more methodologically rigorous research, are consistent with a growing body of literature documenting the long-term psychological sequelae of physical and sexual abuse (Carmen, Rieker, and Mills 1984; Gelinas 1983; Goodwin 1982; Herman 1981).

The reality of sexual and domestic violence has not yet been integrated into ordinary clinical teaching or practice. On the basis of even the minimal prevalence figures reported in this study, it would seem reasonable to incorporate basic information about sexual and domestic violence into the core curriculum for mental health professionals and to include questions about experiences of domestic and sexual violence in protocols for routine evaluation of all patients. A careful exploration of a history of violence should include questioning about patients' experiences as victims and as perpetrators. Because these matters are severely stigmatized, particular training will usually be necessary to help clinicians overcome their own discomfort as well as the reticence of patients. However, as in the case of other sensitive subjects (such as suicide or substance abuse), patients can be expected to respond positively to careful and sympathetic questioning and, in fact, may express relief if offered the opportunity to share experiences that have been borne as oppressive secrets.

REFERENCES

Becker, J., L. Skinner, and G. Abel. 1983. Sequelae of sexual assault: The survivor's perspective. In *The sexual aggressor: Current perspectives on treatment*, ed. J. Greer and I. Stuart. New York: Van Nostrand Reinhold.

Burgess, A., and L. Holmstrom. 1979. Adaptive strategies and recovery from rape. *American Journal of Psychiatry* 136: 1278–82.

Carmen, E., P. Rieker, and T. Mills. 1984. Victims of violence and psychiatric illness. *American Journal of Psychiatry* 141: 378–83.

Dobash, R.E., and R. Dobash. 1979. *Violence against wives: A case against the patriarchy.* New York: Free Press.

Emslie, G., and A. Rosenfeld. 1983. Incest reported by children and adolescents hospitalized for severe psychiatric problems. *American Journal of Psychiatry* 140: 708–10.

Finkelhor, D. 1979. *Sexually victimized children.* New York: Free Press.

Gelinas, D. 1983. The persisting negative effects of incest. *Psychiatry* 46: 312–32.

Goodwin, J. 1982. *Sexual abuse: Incest victims and their families.* Boston: John Wright.

Green, A. 1983. Child abuse: Dimensions of psychological trauma in abused children. *Journal of the American Academy of Child Psychiatry* 22: 231–37.

Herman, J.L. 1981. *Father-daughter incest.* Cambridge, Mass.: Harvard University Press.

Hilberman, E. 1980. Overview: The "wife-beater's wife" reconsidered. *American Journal of Psychiatry* 137: 1336–47.

Lynch, M., and J. Roberta. 1982. *Consequences of child abuse.* London: Academic Press.

Nadelson, C., et al. 1982. A follow-up study of rape victims. *American Journal of Psychiatry* 139: 1266–70.

Pagelow, M. 1984. *Family violence.* New York: Praeger.

Post, R., et al. 1980. A preliminary report on the prevalence of domestic violence among psychiatric inpatients. *American Journal of Psychiatry* 137: 974–75.

Russell, D. 1984. *Sexual exploitation: Rape, child sexual abuse, and sexual harassment.* Beverly Hills: Sage Publications.

Sachs, R., J. Goodwin, and B. Braun. 1986. The role of childhood abuse in the development of multiple personality. In *Multiple personality and dissociation,* ed. B. Braun and R. Kluft. New York: Guilford.

Schechter, S. 1982. *Women and male violence.* Boston: South End Press.

Stark, E., A. Flitcraft, and W. Frazier. 1979. Medicine and patriarchal violence: The social construction of a "private" event. *International Journal of Health Services* 9: 461–93.

Terr, L. 1983. Chowchilla revisited: The effects of psychic trauma four years after a school-bus kidnapping. *American Journal of Psychiatry* 140: 1543–50.

Williams, J., and R. Spitzer. 1983. The issue of sex bias in DSM-III. *American Psychologist* 38: 793–98.

SEXUAL TRAUMA, DYSFUNCTION, AND PREFERENCE ASSOCIATED WITH ALCOHOL AND DRUG DEPENDENCY IN NURSES

ELEANOR J. SULLIVAN
University of Minnesota

The association between dependency on alcohol and/or drugs and sexual problems has been reported in numerous studies. Sexual abuse has been linked with alcoholism and/or drug addiction of the victim (Cohen and Densen-Gerber 1982; Covington and Kohen 1984; Beckman 1979). Cohen and Densen-Gerber (1982) found that sexual abuse had occurred for 35% of female patients in treatment for alcohol and drug dependency in the United States and Australia. In another study, the majority of subjects in alcohol treatment had been raped as children or adults (Murphy et al. 1980). Covington and Kohen (1984) studied matched pairs of alcoholic and nonalcoholic females and found that 74% of the alcoholic females had experienced sexual abuse, while only 50% of the nonalcoholic females had been abused. Parental alcohol or drug abuse has been associated with incest in several studies (Sanchez-Dirks 1979; Server and Janzen 1982). Carmen, Rieker, and Mills (1984) studied 188 physically and/or sexually abused and nonabused psychiatric patients and found that the only significant family characteristic distinguishing the abused and nonabused patients was parental alcoholism.

Although sexual dysfunction in male alcoholics has been reported (Carpenter and Armenti 1971), similar problems have only recently been noted for female alcoholics (Wilsnack and Beckman 1984). Instead, female sexual functioning has been studied primarily as it relates to effects on the outcome of pregnancy (fetal alcohol syndrome). However, Covington and Kohen's study of matched pairs of alcoholic and nonalcoholic females indicates that alcoholic females experienced sexual dysfunction both prior to and concurrent with alcoholism (Covington and Kohen 1984).

Sexual preference has been linked with alcoholism in males, but Nardi (1982) suggests that few studies have addressed the relationship between alcoholism and male homosexuality. However, female homosexuals were studied by Lewis and colleagues in 1982; the researchers compared 57 homosexual females with 43 heterosexual females. Their findings suggest that heavy and problem drinking occurred significantly more often in the homosexual sample, and this difference was not explained by a history of frequenting bars or by a family history of alcoholism.

Nurses' problems with alcoholism and drug dependency have only recently been reported in the literature, with the incidence of such disorders estimated to be higher than in the general public (Bissell and Haberman 1984; Sullivan 1985). Socialization into the nursing profession encourages traditionally feminine behavior in both male and female nurses. Such behavior is primarily passive, with direct action not expected or rewarded. Heavy drinking, drug taking, and active sexual pursuit are behaviors similarly discouraged by feminine socialization. It might be expected, then, that the incidence of alcoholism or drug dependency would be lower in both male and female nurses.

The purpose of the study reported in this chapter was to examine nurses' reports of sexual trauma, dysfunction, and sexual preference and to explore associations of sexual problems with alcohol or drug dependency. Although sexual problems are associated with alcoholism in the general population, nurses' experiences of sexual abuse, dysfunction, and preference have not been addressed. The literature on sexual trauma suggests, however, that for those nurses who become alcoholic or drug dependent, a number of them will report experiencing sexual abuse, problems of sexual functioning, and same-sex preference.

METHODS

A national survey was conducted of two target populations: (1) registered nurses recovering from alcohol and drug dependency (*dependent* nurses) and (2) registered nurses not identified as alcoholic or drug dependent (*nondependent* nurses). A sample from each population was obtained.

Access to any population of dependent nurses is difficult, as this group is reluctant to be identified because of the threat of loss of nursing license. Taking the sensitive nature of the problem into consideration, the study's investigator contacted state nursing associations with organized programs of assistance for dependent nurses. Additional access to the dependent nurse population was gained through notices placed in national publications and posted at national meetings, requesting the assistance of individuals with access to recovering dependent nurses. It was determined that access to dependent nurses actively taking drugs or alcohol would be nearly impossible, as they probably would not be willing to be identified.

There are 1.7 million registered nurses in the United States, with thousands of licensees in most states. In addition, many nurses are licensed in more than one state because nurses usually retain their licenses when they move from state to state. In an attempt to access a representative sample of this huge population, the investigator contacted 20 state boards of nursing representing all regions of the country. Six state boards had the facilities to provide a random sample of 300 state-licensed registered nurses for a minimum cost. The participating states were Maine, Tennessee, Missouri, Nevada, Idaho, and Maryland.

An extensive questionnaire requesting information on biographic and professional variables was distributed to the two samples. Associations between alcoholism/drug dependency and sexual trauma, functioning, and preference were examined, with the two groups compared via chi-square analysis. Descriptive data also were reported.

The CAGE questionnaire (Ewing and Rouse 1970) was modified for inclusion of drug use as Ewing (1984) suggests may be done to fit the clinical population. (CAGE stands for a person's attempt to Cut down on drinking, Annoyance with others' interference with drinking, Guilty feelings about drinking, and use of an Eye-opener drink in the morning.) Four questions were included in the survey instrument to screen for alcohol and drug dependency in the sample of nurses not identified as dependent. If nondependent nurse subjects answered any of the four questions in the affirmative, they were excluded from the study.

Distribution of the instrument to the population of dependent nurses who agreed to participate was conducted by individuals with access to the population. Persons from 24 states distributed questionnaires. All

responses were anonymous; the only identification tabulated was the state
of origin as designated by postmark. In this way, the researcher did not
have access to the names of the respondents, and members of peer
assistance committees and other individuals who distributed the instrument to recovering nurses did not have access to subjects' responses.

Responses were received from 139 nurses who identified themselves as
alcoholic or drug dependent. These nurses resided in a total of 19 states.
The response rate was not known because the number of questionnaires
distributed to the population was unknown.

Surveys were sent to 1,800 nurses licensed in a total of six states, but 18
states of residence were represented. Responses received from the
nondependent nurse sample totaled 522, with a response rate of 30%.

RESULTS

The sample consisted of 661 registered nurses, 139 recovering from
alcohol and drug dependency and 522 identified as not alcohol and/or drug
dependent. However, of the 522 nondependent nurses who responded to
the survey, 384 (73%) answered "no" to all the alcoholism screening
questions, 92 (18%) answered "yes" to one or more of these questions; and
46 (9%) did not respond to the screening questions. Only nondependent
nurse subjects with negative responses to the screening questions were
included in the study. Thus, the adjusted sample consisted of: 139
dependent nurses and 384 nondependent nurses.

COMPARISON OF DEPENDENT AND
NONDEPENDENT NURSES

Comparison of the dependent and nondependent nurses revealed no
significant differences in ages; the majority of nurses in both groups were
between 26 and 40 years of age. Significant differences between the
groups were found in regard to gender, with males accounting for 12% of
the dependent-nurse sample but only 2% of the nondependent-nurse
sample. In the dependent-nurse sample, 62% reported an alcoholic parent,
while only 28% of the nondependent-nurse sample reported parental
alcoholism.

Subjects were asked to report problems related to sexuality, sexual
abuse, and sexual functioning (table 4.1). Differences between the groups
were found. The majority (54%) of the dependent nurses reported both
sexual trauma and other problems, while less than one-fourth of the
nondependent nurses stated that sexual problems had occurred in their

TABLE 4.1
ANALYSIS OF SEXUALITY AND SEXUAL PROBLEMS ASSOCIATED WITH ALCOHOL AND
DRUG DEPENDENCY IN NURSES

Problem	Alcoholic/Drug Dependent Nurses ($N = 139$)		Nondependent Nurses ($N = 384$)		X^2	df^a	p
Parental alcoholism	86	61	108	28	50.990	2	.0001
Reported sex problems	75	54	79	20	53.153	1	.0001
Molestation	25	18	35	9	58.330	2	.0001
Incest	15	10	8	2	58.528	2	.0001
Out-of-wedlock pregnancy	11	8	20	5	58.223	2	.0001
Abortion	19	13	13	3	58.619	2	.0001
Miscarriage	16	11	18	4	54.809	2	.0001
Sexual dysfunction	24	17	5	1	75.985	2	.0001
Body image affected by illness/surgery	17	12	15	4	55.153	2	.0001
Homosexuality	18	12	6	1	64.825	2	.0001

^{a}Degrees of freedom for specific problems includes category of "not applicable" for those reporting no sexual problems.

lives. Subjects also were asked to identify the nature of their sexual problems. Of the two groups of nurses, dependent nurses reported more difficulties in each category (incest, sexual molestation, out-of-wedlock pregnancy, miscarriage, abortion, illness or surgery affecting body image, and problems with sexual dysfunction) than the nondependent nurses. In addition, a significantly higher number of dependent nurses (13%) reported homosexual preferences than the nondependent nurses (2%). Given the extensive nature of sexual trauma reported by the sample of dependent nurses, additional analyses of their responses were conducted.

SEXUAL PROBLEMS OF DEPENDENT NURSES

The responses of dependent nurses ($N = 40$) who reported being sexually abused indicate that 12 subjects were victims of incest and the remainder were molested and/or raped by persons outside the family. The victim's age at the time of abuse was asked, and 23 (58%) reported they were under age 14 at the time of the first abusive incident. Several subjects volunteered the information that the abuse continued for several years.

Subjects' responses of illness or surgery that affected body image or life goals included hysterectomy, mastectomy, obesity, and infection. One nurse related the following poignant experience: "I had an emergency hysterectomy at age 25 after a physician ruptured my uterus with an intrauterine device. His reponse was that the world was a better place because I was an addict and now barren."

Sexual dysfunction was described by respondents as a lack of interest in sex, as a result of a rape at age 15, and as a result of a partner's problems with sexual identity that interfered with the nurse's own sexuality. One female homosexual respondent stated that dysfunction occurred when she attempted a heterosexual marriage. Several female heterosexuals stated that they had sexual problems after a boyfriend or husband announced his homosexual preference.

TABLE 4.2
SEXUAL TRAUMA AND SEXUAL PROBLEMS OF MALE AND FEMALE ALCOHOLIC / DRUG-DEPENDENT NURSES

Problem	Male (N = 17)		Female (N = 122)	
	N	%	N	%
Reported sexual problems	13	76	62	51
Molestation	2	12	23	19
Incest	2	12	13	11
Sexual dysfunction	4	24	20	16
Body image affected by illness/surgery	3	18	14	11
Homosexuality	9	53	9	7

Male and female dependent nurses are compared in table 4.2. Victimization and dysfunction were reported by both males and females. The only significant difference between the two groups was the incidence of homosexuality. Over half of the sample of male dependent nurses reported homosexuality, while only 7% of the female dependent nurses reported same-sex preferences ($p = .001$).

Sexual trauma (molestation or incest) was compared with sexual preference and dysfunction, and only one significant association was found. Incest and homosexuality were significantly associated ($p = .008$). Seven of the nine female homosexual nurses were sexually abused by a parent and one of the nine homosexual males was a victim of incest. Another male respondent wrote that he was a victim of emotional incest that was not acted out by the mother.

Incidence of sexual trauma was compared to parental alcoholism, and no significant associations were found. Dependent nurses who were sexually abused by a family member or others did not have an alcoholic mother or father more often than the dependent nurses with histories of abuse. Additionally, those with alcoholic parents were no more likely to experience out-of-wedlock pregnancy, abortion, sexual dysfunction, or homosexuality than nurses with alcoholic parents.

DISCUSSION

The high incidence of sexual trauma and sexual difficulties reported by the dependent-nurse sample when compared with nondependent nurses is congruent with studies of alcoholism and drug dependency in the general population (Cohen and Densen-Gerber 1982; Covington and Kohen 1984; Murphy et al. 1980). Carmen and colleagues (1984) found that abuse and alcoholism of the parent were associated, but in this sample of alcohol- and drug-dependent nurses, neither incest nor other sexual abuse was related to parental alcoholism at a statistically significant level. Female sexual dysfunction and dependency have been associated in studies by Wilsnack and Beckman (1984), and the results of this study concur. Four of the 17 male subjects who reported sexual problems also reported experiencing sexual dysfunction, and although this number is too small for generalization, it is consistent with prior studies (Carpenter and Armenti 1971).

An additional, unexpected finding of this study was that 18% of the group presumed to be nonalcohol and drug dependent responded positively to questions that could indicate a present or potential problem with alcohol or drugs. An additional 8% did not respond to the screening questions, although they did complete the questionnaire. The possible incidence in this sample of nurses seems high and should be investigated further.

The incidence of males in the sample of recovering dependent nurses is higher than the incidence of males in the nursing population would suggest (2%–3%) and as confirmed by the nondependent sample, but it is consistent with previous smaller studies of nurses who are alcohol and drug dependent (Bush 1983). It should be noted that all the dependent nurses reported in this study are recovering from their addictions. Do more male nurses (as males in the general public) more often become dependent on alcohol or drugs, or does the male nurse more often recover from dependency? These questions should be addressed in future studies.

The incidence of homosexuality in both male and female dependent nurses may reflect the higher incidence of homosexuality found in some studies of alcoholism and homosexuality (Carpenter and Armenti 1971; Nardi 1982). Half of the dependent male nurses reported that they were homosexual. Most of the female homosexual dependent nurses were also victims of incest. These findings raise more questions than they answer. What are the relationships, if any, among incest, homosexuality, and alcohol or drug abuse? Is a female victim of incest more likely to become homosexual or alcohol or drug dependent and to choose a helping profession such as nursing? Are males who choose nursing more likely to be homosexual, alcohol/drug dependent, or both?

Results of this study should be considered cautiously. A convenient, purposive sample of alcohol- and drug-dependent nurses was utilized; selection and distribution were not controlled by the investigator. The response rate was not known because the number of subjects who received the survey was unknown. The sample was self-selected by response. More importantly, the alcohol- and drug-dependent nurses were recovering from their disease; nurses who were active users of alcohol or drugs were not included.

Although the selection of the nondependent nurse sample was random, only six state boards of nursing were able to provide access to subjects at a reasonable cost. Thus, the sample may have reflected a regional bias unknown to the researcher. Additionally, the low response rate in this sample reflects a positive bias inherent in mailed survey research.

In this study, both parental alcoholism and sexual abuse occurred more frequently in the histories of nurses who were alcohol or drug dependent. It might be suggested that either historical event put the nurse at risk for developing a dependency on alcohol or drugs. Additionally, nurses who became alcohol or drug dependent reported a continuing history of sexually related problems, including miscarriage, abortion, out-of-wedlock pregnancy, sexual dysfunction, and alterations in body image.

Questions must be raised about the possibility that the nursing profession may put nurses at risk for addictive disease. The stress nurses experience in caring for ill and dying patients is known. Nurses have access to a variety of powerful mood-altering drugs and are accustomed to seeing patients' positive responses to such medications. Alcohol or other drugs could be used for coping, and for some, addiction might develop.

The high incidence of possible alcohol or drug dependency in the sample of nondependent subjects is of concern. These nurses are practicing professionals. If they are or become alcoholic or drug dependent, patients in their care may be put at risk. Possibly the willingness of the nondependent sample to participate in the study reflects some concern about their own drinking or drug problems. Again, the effect of these factors is unknown and bears additional investigation.

The findings of this exploratory study should be investigated further. Longitudinal studies of alcohol- and drug-dependent nurses, such as those being conducted by Bissell and Haberman (1984), should continue, and a more controlled study comparing alcoholic/drug-dependent nurses with nondependent nurses would result in more conclusive findings. The health of the practitioners in one of the nations's largest professional groups and the safety of their patients mandate further attention to this serious problem.

This research was supported in part by a grant from the Improved Research Quality Fund, University of Missouri. The author thanks Virginia Luetje, R.N., M.S.N., St. Louis University, for her sensitivity to these problems in patients and her suggestion to include this content in the study.

REFERENCES

Beckman, L.J. 1979. Reported effects of alcohol on the sexual feelings and behavior of women alcoholics and non-alcoholics. *Journal of Studies on Alcohol* 40: 272–82.

Bissell, L., and P.W. Haberman. 1984. *Alcoholism in the professions.* New York: Oxford University Press.

Bush, C. 1983. A review of research: The impaired nurse. Paper presented at 1st National Symposium on the Impaired Nurse, Emory University, Atlanta.

Carmen, E., P.P. Rieker, and T. Mills. 1984. Victims of violence and psychiatric illness. *American Journal of Psychiatry* 141: 378–83.

Carpenter, J.A., and N.P. Armenti. 1971. Some effects of ethanol on human sexual and aggressive behavior. In *The biology of alcoholism*, ed. B. Kissan and H. Begletter, 509–43. New York: Plenum Press.

Cohen, F.S., and J. Densen-Gerber. 1982. A study of the relationship between child abuse and drug addiction in 178 patients: Preliminary results. *Child Abuse and Neglect* 6: 383–87.

Covington, S.S., and J. Kohen. 1984. Women, alcohol, and sexuality. In *Cultural and sociological aspects of alcoholism and substance abuse*, ed. B. Stimmel, 41–56. New York: Haworth Press.

Ewing, J.A. 1984. Detecting alcoholism: The CAGE questionnaire. *Journal of the American Medical Association* 252: 1905–07.

Ewing, J.A., and B.A. Rouse. 1970. Identifying the hidden alcoholic. Paper presented at 29th International Congress on Alcohol and Drug Dependence, Sydney, Australia.

Lewis, C.E., M.T. Saghir, and E. Robbins. 1982. Drinking patterns in homosexual and heterosexual women. *Journal of Clinical Psychiatry* 43: 277–79.

Murphy, W.D., et al. 1980. Sexual dysfunction and treatment in alcoholic women. *Sexuality and Disability* 3: 240–55.

Nardi, P.M. 1982. Alcoholism and homosexuality: A theoretical perspective. *Journal of Homosexuality* 7: 9–25.

Sanchez-Dirks, R. 1979. Reflections on family violence. *Alcohol Health and Research World* 4: 12–16.

Server, C.J., and C. Janzen. 1982. Contraindications to reconstitution of sexually abusive families. *Child Welfare* 61: 279–88.

Sullivan, E.J. 1985. Characteristics of recovery in chemically dependent nurses. Paper presented at 34th International Congress on Alcoholism and Drug Dependency, August, Calgary, Canada.

Wilsnack, S.C., and L.J. Beckman. 1984. *Alcohol problems in women: antecedents, consequences, and intervention.* New York: Guilford Press.

CHAPTER

5

SEXUAL HARASSMENT
OF STUDENTS
BY TEACHERS

The Case of Students in Science

ARLENE McCORMACK
University of Lowell

> [He] went to bed with a few students (male and female) who were
> taking his course. He approached me often; I refused. Conse-
> quently, I failed the course—definitely did not deserve to! I was
> close to the assistant principal—he couldn't do anything about
> the teacher, but he changed my grade on the records and gave me
> my diploma. (From pretest questionnaire 10)

It is often stated that educational institutions, rather than being forerunners
of change, are institutions that reflect reality in the greater society and that
their primary function is the socialization of children and young adults to
fulfill the expectations that have become custom or tradition (Stockard
1980). Such statements are made by those who view educational institutions as microcosms of the greater society. They argue that the socialization process in our schools includes patterns, established in our culture, of
interaction between men and women as well as those between superiors
and subordinates. The situation between teachers and students is one in
which both of these traditional patterns of interaction converge.

Benson and Thomson (1982) see the initiation of sexual demands upon
the student, regardless of whether a threat or an exchange for a favor, as

Reprinted, with changes, from *Sex Roles* 13: 21–32, 1985, by permission.

a situation that results in the creation of an intimidating environment for the student. Because teachers have positions of authority from which they evaluate the performance of the student, the initiating of sexual demands can leave the student unsure of the teacher's reaction to a refusal. All such initiation is viewed as sexual harassment on the part of the teacher.

Other researchers claim that this view is incorrect. Taylor (1981) argues that the modern university cannot be thought of as a kind of microcosm because the interpersonal relationships found within the university are much more free and joyous than those found on the outside. In a discussion of such free relationships, Taylor focuses on the intense intersexual relations among the members of this community and highlights sexual relations between students and teachers. According to Taylor, university characteristics that foster this intense situation include: (1) a sophisticated faculty, well read, widely traveled, and original and independent in its thinking, (2) a substantial number of female undergraduates who are psychologically and otherwise more mature than their male counterparts, and (3) a university administration that prefers to be kept uninformed of the sexual relationships within its community.

Explicit propositions that offer favors and grades in exchange for sexual relations do not, in Taylor's view, constitute acts of sexual harassment. Only when an explicit threat is made or a retaliatory act taken, does such an act constitute a problem. Further, it is Taylor's opinion that what is commonly referred to as an "A for a lay" is a situation that is accepted without question or noticeable comment by most members of the university community.

The opposing positions taken by Benson and Thomson and by Taylor are indicative of the confusion that surrounds sex roles and professional roles in today's educational institutions. This confusion, which produces anxiety and discomfort in both students and teachers, is finally being addressed. Indeed, a refutation of Taylor's position is supported by the growing interest in, discussion of, and policy decisions concerning the sexual harassment of students by their teachers (Maihoff and Forrest 1983; Metha and Nigg 1983; Stokes 1983; Blanshan 1983; Simon and Forrest 1983; Meek and Lynch 1983; Kaufman and Wylie 1983).

Beginning with a survey conducted in 1976 (Safran), reports of sexual harassment of working women by their employers became more frequent (Silverman 1977; Bularzik 1978; Farley 1978; Laurence and Klos 1978; Mackinnon 1979). More slowly, findings of sexual harassment of students by their teachers began to emerge in popular sources (Field 1981; Zehner 1982), in educational literature (Fields 1979; Vance 1981), in national reports (Till 1980), and in dissertations (Myers 1981; McCormack 1983). Yet, while there is an increasing literature concerned with the sexual harassment of students, surprisingly few reports in social science journals have addressed this topic. Further, these reports are focused mainly on establishing the presence and extent of sexual harassment in various educational institutions or on attempts by various institutions to prevent or control such harassment. Little assessment is made of how students describe such experiences, of which students are likely to encounter such experiences, and of whether such incidents vary by the level of schooling or length of educational career.

Policy solutions to the problem of sexual harassment cannot be effective until there is a fuller understanding of the phenomenon of sexual harassment. This chapter presents study findings and discussion in an effort to add further to that understanding.

TABLE 5.1
LEVEL OF SCHOOLING, FIELD OF STUDY, AND GENDER OF STUDENT PARTICIPANTS

Gender and Schooling Level	Field of Study				
	Physics	Chemistry	Economics	Sociology	N
Men					
Undergraduates	86	99	78	26	289
Graduates	127	117	61	53	358
Women					
Undergraduates	35	89	86	61	271
Graduates	32	88	49	76	245
Totals	280	393	274	216	1163

STUDY DESCRIPTION

SAMPLING DESIGN

This chapter reports the findings of a study of the sexual harassment of students in four fields of science (physics, chemistry, economics, and sociology) at 16 northeastern universities.[1,2] Lists of students majoring in each field were provided by the universities, and students were randomly sampled by the use of a table of random numbers. Volunteer study participants numbered 1,178 students. Table 5.1 presents the level of schooling and field of study for men and women students.

All the data used for analysis were derived from undergraduate and graduate questionnaires administered at each study site. The survey instrument was developed and refined using the results of indepth interviewing of 36 graduate students in the New England area. Interviews with several faculty members were also useful in broadening understanding of the phenomenon of sexual harassment.

METHODOLOGY AND ANALYSIS

Analysis of the survey data was centered on both closed- and open-ended questions. Cross-tabular analysis, tests of mean differences, and systematic analysis of answers to open-ended questionnaire items were used to assess the presence and extent of sexual harassment, whether sexual harassment is likely to increase as women continue their academic careers, and whether family background characteristics influence the likelihood of such experiences. The written descriptions of experiences of sexual harassment are directly quoted from the questionnaires and were analyzed to provide a fuller understanding of the sexual harassment experience.

While formal definitions of what exactly constitutes sexual harassment vary to some degree, all such definitions refer to sexually oriented practices that are unwelcomed by the student. Such practices are viewed as creating an intimidating academic environment, interfering with academic performance, and/or preventing the recipient's full and equal enjoyment of educational opportunities (Volpe and Day 1981; Storrie and Dykstra 1982). The definition used in this study is one adopted by the Council of Graduate Departments of Psychology (Council of Graduate Education 1980). Students were presented with the following definition:

> Sexual harassment is defined as the use of one's authority to coerce another individual into sexual relations or to punish the other person for his/her refusal. Sexual harassment also includes any deliberate, repeated, unsolicited oral or written comment, statement, anecdote, gesture, or physical contact of a sexual nature that is offensive and unwelcomed.

Students were then asked the following:

> Have you ever experienced sexual harassment from any of the teachers that you have come into contact with? If yes, indicate when (high school, etc.) and briefly describe the experience.

RESULTS

Of the 1,178 students who answered the question concerning sexual harassment, 9% claimed that they had been harassed. As expected, men were much less likely than women to encounter this experience. Only 2% of the 655 men reported such harassment. Of the 523 women who answered this question, 17% reported sexual harassment by a teacher (see table 5.2).

Of the 89 women who reported sexual harassment, 12% reported such experiences on more than one educational level. Given that these women

TABLE 5.2
SEXUAL HARASSMENT AND STUDENT GENDER

Student Gender	Sexual Harassment		
	Harassed (%)	Not Harassed (%)	N
Men	2	98	655
Women	17	83	523
Total students	9	91	1178

Note:X^2 = 86.100; $p < .0001$.

were at different points in their educational careers and that such a difference was likely to influence the frequency of such experiences occurring, sexual harassment was classified for analysis by the number of experiences rather than by the individuals who experienced them. This type of classification allows a clearer understanding of when (i.e., on which levels of schooling) women students are likely to encounter such experiences.

The results of a systematic analysis of open-ended questionnaire items indicate that the 89 women reported 105 episodes of sexual harassment. An analysis of only those episodes in which an educational level was specified (101 episodes) shows that of the 39 experiences reported by undergraduates, 24 occurred before college and 15 occurred at the college level (see table 5.3). The results also show that graduate women encounter more experiences of sexual harassment by the time they finish their undergraduate studies (31 experiences) than they encounter in high school (15 experiences).

A recent study found that students with lower-class backgrounds were likely to report devaluating experiences with their teachers (McCormack 1983). To determine whether the family background characteristics of the 89 women who reported harassment differed from those of women who did not report such incidents, the study compared these two groups based on father's and mother's education, family income, and prestige of father's occupation. The results of a series of difference-of-means tests

TABLE 5.3
EXPERIENCES OF SEXUAL HARASSMENT AND LEVEL OF SCHOOLING

Schooling Level	Sexual Harassment			
	Before College	College	Graduate School	N
Undergraduate Women	24	15	0	39
Graduate Women	15	31	17	63

indicate that there were no significant differences between the two groups of women when family background characteristics were taken into account.

SEXUAL HARASSMENT EXPERIENCES

Most students at all levels of schooling provided descriptions of their experiences of sexual harassment. Students who did not claim sexual harassment also provided comments helpful in understanding this problem.

An analysis of the experiences shows that there is no specific type of experience that is more common to one level of schooling than to another. On all levels, the experiences ranged from an approach for a kiss, to a hand on the knee, to an invitation to pose for pornographic pictures, to outright coercion into a brief sexual relationship.

A common experience was the comments made to the students and the ways that teachers looked at these women. Student descriptions often depicted the teacher's actions as overly friendly. A sampling of student descriptions of this common experience includes the following:

> [My professor made] constant embarrassing comments (precise suggestions) and [gave me] undressing looks.

> [I was the recipient of] unsolicited comments and statements as well as occasional gestures and stares to undress.

> [My teacher was] constantly commenting on my dress, touching my hair, calling me on the phone and dropping by my home.

> [The teacher] began calling me on the phone, asking me out, offering me rides home from school, etc.

Often, these students were aware that they were not the only focus of the teacher's affections:

> [My teacher] used to proposition lots of women. He used to bother me in the library, ask why I was ignoring him, etc. He tried to get me to go to his apartment. The chairman found out and fired him.

> Constant comments, statements, anecdotes, etc. [were directed at me], gestures and physical contact more rarely. [There was] no outright coercion, although I've seen teachers coerce other students.

> [My teacher] kept me after school many unnecessary times "just to talk" and made advances toward me and several of my friends.

> [My professor was] in the habit of approaching girls. I had reprimands and requests for resignation set in motion—the motion was successful.

Some students mentioned teachers who explicitly offer grades in return for sexual relations. Atlhough most of the students who rejected such offers did not suffer for their refusal, others did.

> One full professor of sociology offered to "solve" the Ph.D. granting problem in exchange for sex.

> [The professor] made repeated oral statements and physical gestures toward me. [He] gave me a D in the course (when I did not respond), which I brought before the department. The grade was reversed.

Noticeable in these descriptions is that many women found a way to handle the situation. While some went to the principals of their schools and others went to the heads of their departments, still others found relief by talking to the teacher directly:

> A sexist professor who criticised women and made offensive comments . . . made a pass. This was a very tense situation until I got up the nerve to sit down and discuss the whole thing with him. He then left me alone and did not lower any grades of mine.

> [My professor] kept making unwanted advances, mostly when he had been drinking at parties. He'd stick his hand up my rear, make lewd comments, etc. There was never any threat of reprisal involved, however, so I went and talked to him. He has stopped his behavior.

Other students reported experiences which involve outright sexual propositions. However, not all of those who received these propositions, or who engaged in actual sexual relations with the teacher claimed sexual harassment.

> [I] had a sexual relationship with one of my graduate school professors. While it has been/was somewhat exploitive, I think that was mostly due to the nature of our personalities and the relationship and not related to my academic standing. I would not class it as sexual harassment.

> I had a year-long affair with a teacher in high school and was propositioned by another. I think in the particular environment I was in there was absolutely no coercion involved.

While it cannot be ascertained what that "particular environment" was, the idea that harassment can occur even when consent is given was expressed by another student:

> I had an affair with my high-school teacher. [It was] sexual harassment of a different kind [because it involved] a naive young person. I disagree with what "unwelcomed" is.

SUMMARY AND DISCUSSION

The results of this investigation of sexual harassment of students indicate that approximately one in every six women, regardless of family background, will be likely to experience sexual harassment from teachers. This finding is consistent with that of a 1979–80 nationwide study conducted by the National Advisory Council on Women's Education Programs that claims that 10-20% of women students experience sexual harassment. However, it is lower than Benson and Thomson's finding that 30% of the undergraduate women at the University of California, Berkeley, had been sexually harassed during their four years of study (Benson and Thomson 1982). Such discrepancy may have occurred due to the difference in the number of institutions investigated.

As women continue their educations, their chances for victimization are likely to increase. However, no specific type of sexual harassment was found to be associated more with one level of schooling than with another. Embarrassing comments, undressing looks, physical contact, and coerced sexual relations occurred on all levels. Several women took action to stop such behavior by bringing the matter to a person in authority, while other women approached the teacher directly. However, such action was not apparent in the majority of descriptions.

The study findings support the contention that sexual harassment, when it occurs, is not an isolated incident. It is widespread, not discussed, and appears to be an accepted part of the academic environment.

Articles investigating the academic environment and including discussions about the interpersonal relations between teachers and female students rarely, if ever, acknowledge sexual harassment as a common phenomenon. One explanation for the lack of indepth discussions of sexual harassment may involve the nature of the topic. In the first stage of this study, when the experiences of graduate students were being related to the interviewer face to face, the subject often made the student appear uncomfortable and reticent to talk. Turning off the tape recorder did not remedy the situation. One reason for this may be that students, as well as teachers, often confuse sexual harassment with sexual activity.

As a preliminary to the study, I had the opportunity to discuss sexual harassment with several male professors at various institutions in the Northeast. One professor pointed out that in the 1960s, when he first began teaching, there was no distinction drawn between sexual harassment and other forms of sexual activity between teachers and students. Any sexual activity was equally condemned as immoral behavior on the part of the instructor. As sexual mores became more liberal, such activities became tolerated, but still no distinction was drawn. Perhaps this lack of differentiation may account for the fact that sexual harassment was not defined as a social concept until the past decade. Until 1976, there was no term to express sexual harassment; thus, it was literally unspeakable, which made a generalized, shared, and social definition of it inaccessible (MacKinnon 1979).

Other male teachers, upon being made aware of the topic of the study, related stories of at least one woman student who sexually harassed *them* or one of their friends. These students offered to have sexual relations with the professors, sometimes in return for passing a course or thesis project. While the fact that students instigate sexual propositions for a favor or for pleasure cannot be denied, the question is whether such propositions can be termed sexual harassment. The answer lies in an awareness of the unequal power relationship between teacher and student.

The degree of power a teacher holds over a student increases with the student's desire to attain a goal mediated by the teacher and decreases with the student's possibility of reaching this goal outside of the relationship. Given the current nature of the colleague system, teachers rarely interfere with decisions and actions imposed on students by other teachers. Most vulnerable to the abuse of power, therefore, are students to whom academic goals are most important. Given the uneven power relationship between teacher and student, assertions that students sexually harass teachers attribute power to the powerless.

To speak about sexual harassment is, of course, to speak mainly about the oppression of women. As Lerner (1973) points out, most men find it difficult to take the oppression and exploitation of women seriously because to do so would raise fundamental questions about their sexual and social relations. Discussions of sexual harassment as a specific form of exploitation cause discomfort because they call those sexual relations directly into question. Because sexual feelings and sexual activities are not comfortable topics of conversation in our society, the confusion that surrounds distinctions between sexual activity and sexual harassment is not surprising.

It is to be expected that in any environment in which men and women interact, sexual feelings exist and, depending on societal customs, are expressed in various behaviors. Just as many faculty members discuss with one another the physical attributes and assumed sexual capabilities of students, many students discuss teachers in a like manner. Such behaviors occur regardless of the gender of the teacher or student. It is also acknowledged, although not widely discussed, that some teachers and students do have sexual relationships. While such experiences can muddy academic distance, these experiences are not necessarily a form of harassment. When the students' physical attributes and assumed sexual capabilities are made the basis for evaluation and reward, however, there results a situation that Adler (1976) terms sexploitation. In these cases, the personal worth of the students are reduced, and a situation of devaluation in interaction occurs. When the students are aware of such devaluation, they may come to doubt the basis for their achievements. Such experiences can lead to the lowered self-concept of the student.

Many teachers are aware that such situations occur, and that awareness has often been made responsible for the tension that exists in opposite-sex student/teacher interaction. Male teachers who react to this awareness in an extreme way often distance themselves from women students altogether, thereby imposing limitations on students whose academic success often counts on developing a close working relationship with their instructors. While some male professors react to the awareness of the conflict between sex roles and professional roles by refusing to interact with women students, others use this awareness as a point of understanding in their relationships with female students. However, most probably interact in a tension-filled environment, not quite understanding why a woman might be upset about receiving what they may view as a compliment (Adler 1976).

As the proportion of women students in academic settings increases, as women continue to enter areas of learning and work that were once considered male strongholds, and as sex-role stereotypes are increasingly challenged, concern over the misuse of institutional power as a barrier to that development will grow. Understanding the phenomenon of sexual harassment is one step in responding to that concern.

The author acknowledges the assistance of Evelyn Glenn and Michael Useem in providing comments and encouragement and John Wilkes for providing access to the data.

NOTES

1. Northeastern universities with first-rank (1–30 nationally) or second-rank (adequate ranking) departments in physics, chemistry, economics,

or sociology served as study sites. Such ranking resulted from the analysis of 7,500 evaluations of graduate departments made by faculty members. Departments in 130 institutions nationwide were ranked on the criteria of: (1) the quality of the graduate faculty, (2) the effectiveness of the doctoral program, and (3) the estimate of recent changes in the quality of graduate education (Roose and Anderson 1970).

2. The sampling design of the study was originally chosen by the investigators of a larger, ongoing study, funded by the National Science Foundation, into which the present study was incorporated. The larger study required this design in order to take advantage of existing information about the distribution of cognitive styles among academic scientists. A previous study (Wilkes 1977) had produced information about the cognitive styles of faculty members in these same fields and institutions.

3. The educational level of the fathers of the women in this sample ranged from sixth grade to the doctoral level, with a mean and median grade level of 16 years of schooling. The educational level of the mothers of the women in this sample ranged from sixth grade to graduate school, with a mean and median grade level of 15 years of schooling. The 1960 Hodge-Siegel-Rossi prestige scores were used as measures of the occupational prestige of father's occupation. These scores ranged from 17 to 82, with a mean and median score of 58. An assessment of family incomes for the year 1981 indicated that the family income of women in this sample ranged from less than $5,000 to $100,000 and over, with an average family income of between $30,000 and $39,000 per year.

REFERENCES

Adler, N.E. 1976. Women students. In *Scholars in the making*, ed. J. Katz and R. Hartnett. Cambridge, Mass.: Ballinger Publishing Co.

Benson, D.J., and G.E. Thomson. 1982. Sexual harassment on a university campus: The confluence of authority relations, sexual interest and gender stratification. *Social Problems* 29: 236–51.

Blanshan, S.A. 1983. Activism, research, and policy: Sexual harassment. *Journal of the National Association for Women Deans, Administrators, and Counselors* 46: 16–22.

Bularzik, M. 1978. Sexual harassment at the workplace: Historical notes. *Radical American* 12: 25–43.

Council of Graduate Education. 1980. Annual meeting of American Psychological Association, Toronto, Canada.

Farley, L. 1978. *Sexual shakedown: The sexual harassment of women on the job.* New York: McGraw-Hill.

Field, A. 1981. Harassment on campus: Sex in a tenured position? *Ms.* 15: 68–73.

Fields, C.M. 1979. One-fourth of women psychologists in survey report sexual contacts with their professors. *Chronicle of Higher Education* 11: 1, 15.

Kaufman, S., and M.L.Wylie. 1983. One-session workshop on sexual harassment. *Journal of the National Association for Women Deans, Administrators, and Counselors* 46: 39–42.

Lawrence, K., and K.A. Klos. 1978. *Sex discrimination in the workplace.* Germantown, Md.: Aspen Systems.

Lerner, M.P. 1973. *The new socialist revolution.* New York: Dell Publishing Co., Inc.

MacKinnon, C. 1979. Sexual harassment of working women. New Haven, Conn.: Yale University Press.

Maihoff, N., and L. Forrest. 1983. Sexual harassment in higher education: An assessment study. *Journal of the National Association for Women Deans, Administrators, and Counselors* 46: 3–8.

McCormack, A. 1983. Harassment sexual or otherwise: The role of devaluaton in student/teacher interaction. Ph.D. diss. Boston University.

Meek, P.M., and A.Q. Lynch. 1983. Establishing an informal grievance procedure for cases of sexual harassment of students. *Journal of the National Association for Women Deans, Administrators, and Counselors* 46: 30–33.

Metha, A., and J. Nigg. 1983. Sexual harassment on campus: An institutional response. *Journal of the National Association for Women Deans, Administrators, and Counselors* 46: 9–15.

Myers, C.L. 1981. Sexual harassment in higher education: A perceptual study of academic women in a state university system. Ph.D. diss. Florida State University.

Roose, K.S., and C.J. Anderson. 1970. *A rating of graduate programs.* Washington, D.C.: American Council of Education.

Safran, C. 1976. What men do to women on the job: A shocking look at sexual harassment. *Redbook,* November, 158–69.

Silverman, D. 1977. Sexual harassment: Working women's dilemma. *Quest: A Feminist Quarterly* 3: 15–24.

Simon, L.A.K., and L. Forrest. 1983. Implementing a sexual harassment policy at a large university. *Journal of the National Association for Women Deans, Administrators, and Counselors* 46: 23–29.

Stockard, J. 1980. Sex iniquities in the experiences of students. In *Sex equity in education,* ed. J. Stockard et al. New York: Academic Press.

Stokes, J. 1983. Effective training programs: One institutional response to sexual harassment. *Journal of the Association for Women Deans, Administrators, and Counselors* 46: 34–38.

Storrie, K., and P. Dykstra. 1982. Bibliography on sexual harassment. *Resources for Feminist Research* 15: 15–20.

Taylor, R. 1981. Within the halls of ivy—The sexual revolution comes of age. *Change* 13: 22–29.

Till, F.J. 1980. *Sexual harassment, a report on the sexual harassment of students.* Washington, D.C.: Department of Health, Education, and Welfare.

Vance, T. 1981. Sexual harassment of women students. *New Directions for Higher Education* 33: 29–40.

Volpe, R., and A.E. Day. 1981. Preliminary report: Toward the establishment of sexual harassment at Ryerson. Typescript.

Wilkes, J. 1977. Scientific styles and disciplinary emphasis. Paper presented at annual meeting, Society for the Social Study of Science, Harvard University, Cambridge, Mass.

Zehner, H. 1982. Love and lust on faculty row. *Cosmopolitan*, April, 269–72.

COMPOUNDING FACTORS IN THE RAPE OF STREET PROSTITUTES

MIMI H. SILBERT

Delancey Street Foundation

The past decade has witnessed an increased awareness of the problems of rape and sexual assault. The influence of the women's movement has heightened consciousness and given visibility to the subject as well as provided impetus to increased rape research, reporting, prevention, and treatment services. The present-day body of literature on the topic is large and steadily expanding. However, except for brief references or some clinical discussions, prostitutes are generally not included among the subjects of recent studies.

Amir (1971), who in his study of rape examined a number of victimization-related variables, makes only a passing reference to the problems attendant to street prostitutes, noting that "The risk of rape for lower-class women in low-status occupations is greater than the risk for middle-class women." MacKellar (1975) extends this brief, broad comment to explore, as a peripheral point, different types of high-risk populations (e.g., women with bad reputations, hippies, and prostitutes) and notes the complicating problems of such populations in terms of society's lack of full support. Her work, apparently based primarily on Amir's research, does not document either the rapes of these high-risk populations or the complicating problems to which she refers.

There are other commentaries on the compounded difficulties of victims who are socially and legally marginal. A case in Denver, reported by

MacDonald (1971), involved a 20-year-old woman known to be sexually promiscuous who was abducted and raped by a group of school boys. The woman was charged with contributing to the delinquency of minors.

This issue of "respectability" of victims has been examined in two studies. Jones and Aronson (1973) found that, according to 234 students who recommended punishments and rated victim fault for six case accounts, married victims or single virgins were faulted more for rapes than divorced women. However, these researchers also found that the mean sentences for rapists who raped "respectable married" women should be longer than the mean sentences for rapists who raped divorcees. They conclude that "injuring a highly respectable person can be viewed as a more serious outcome than injuring a less respectable person" (Jones and Aronson 1973, 417).

Feldman-Summers and Lindner (1976) conducted a study to determine the extent to which irrelevant characteristics of the victim (her marital status, sexual experience, and profession) influence judgment about her responsibility for the rape and the psychological impact of the rape on her. They specifically included the prostitute as one of the five types of victims (married women, single virgins, single nonvirgins, divorced women, and prostitutes). Their findings indicate that as the respectability of the victim decreased, her perceived responsibility for the rape increased. The prostitute was seen as most responsible for her own victimization: "All individual comparisons between the prostitute and the other victims yielded significant differences ($p < .005$) in the same direction (i.e., the psychological impact of the assault on the prostitute was perceived as being less than the psychological impact on any other victims)" (Feldman-Summers and Linder 1976, 143).

Burgess and Holmstrom's chapter (1976) "The Prostitute" states that the prostitute is exploited in two ways: (1) by rape, and (2) by sex-stress situations that include nonpayment and perversion. The authors stress the extreme vulnerability of prostitutes to these two forms of exploitation and provide excerpts from several case illustrations of prostitutes seen in the hospital immediately following a sexual assault. They note that prostitutes respond to such victimization with "a variety of feelings" (Burgess and Holmstrom 1976, 268) and cite anger, desire for revenge, and a need to ventilate. They recommend that clinicians not jump to conclusions about prostitutes, listen carefully to them, encourage dialogue and ventilation of feelings, and encourage them to remain under close medical supervision. While no data are included, this clinical literature is an important first step in examining the effects of sexual assault on prostitutes.

The literature on prostitutes is primarily limited to discussing women's motivations for entering prostitution, ethnographic studies of the lifestyle, and legal issues surrounding prostitution. Sexual assault on prostitutes is generally excluded. What few references there are discuss primarily the sexual exploitation of juvenile prostitutes prior to their becoming prostitutes and do not report on sexual assault of prostitutes since their entering the occupation (e.g., James 1977, 1978, 1979; Silbert 1982a; Silbert and Pines 1981, 1982a, 1982b, 1983; Silbert et al. 1982). This chapter represents the first major attempt to study rape of prostitutes as prostitutes.

METHODS

DEFINITIONS

For the purpose of the study, *prostitution* was defined as the exchange of sex for money, excluding the exchange of sex for commodities. A *prostitute* was identified, by self-definition, as one who exchanges sex for money on a regular, full-time basis. Because of conflicting public opinions about the ability of prostitutes to be raped ("it is a professional hazard") and their involvement in the rape ("they were asking for it"), the most restrictive definition of rape was used. *Rape of prostitutes* was defined as forced penetration unrelated and outside the prostitute-customer interaction. Information about job-related sexual abuse, such as rape by customers, was also collected and reported under a separate category (Silbert and Pines 1982c).

SUBJECTS

Two hundred juvenile and adult street prostitutes in the San Francisco Bay area served as subjects in the study. The mean age of the subjects was 22. The youngest one was 10, the oldest 46. Of the prostitutes, 70% were under 21 and 60% were 16 and under; many were 10, 11, or 12 years old.

Of the women interviewed, 78% reported starting prostitution as juveniles. In addition, 69% of them were white, 18% black; 11% Hispanic, 2% American Indian, and 1% Asian. Marital status was reported as follows: 68% were single and never married; 22% were divorced, separated, or widowed. Only 10% were either married or living under common law marriages. Despite the fact that two-thirds of the sample came from families of middle or higher incomes, the average financial situation of the women interviewed was described as "just making it." A high percentage (88% of the total sample and 92% of the juveniles) described themselves as either "very poor" or "just making it."

INTERVIEWERS

The interviewers in the study were members of the Delancey Street Foundation, a self-help residential facility nationally known for its successful treatment of prostitutes, criminals, and drug addicts (Silbert 1980a). The interviewers themselves were representative of the target population: all had been juvenile and/or adult prostitutes and had been victims of sexual assault. Given the sensitivity of the subject matter as well as the general lack of trust in the target population, the credibility of the interviewers was of critical importance. The fact that the interviewers had themselves been members of the target population maximized their credibility as well as their understanding of the prostitute's jargon and lifestyle and added an immediacy of rapport necessary to create an atmosphere conducive to sharing painful emotions and experiences. All interviewers participated in three weeks of intensive training that covered interviewing techniques and the basics of research methodology. Uniformity of presentation, common usage and definition of terms, uniformity of scoring, and sensitivity to the needs of the subjects all were stressed.

INSTRUMENT

A special instrument developed for purposes of the study (Silbert 1980b) had four parts: (1) background information, (2) history of sexual assault, (3) history of juvenile sexual exploitation, and (4) plans for the future. The second part included job-related sexual assault and sexual assault that was not job related (i.e., rape). For each rape, a series of questions was asked, including situation descriptions of the event (e.g., age at the time of the rape, rape reporting), description of the rapist (e.g., his approximate age, race, and size relative to victim), description of the rape (when did it occur, where, and what physical force was used), and rape impact (physical, emotional, and attitudinal). The whole series of rape questions was repeated for each rape incident.

PROCEDURE

The questionnaire was administered to 200 street prostitutes. Questions posed by the interviewers were coded directly into categories on the questionnaire during the course of the interview; responses were also tape-recorded and transcribed. Interviews lasted an average of four hours, depending on the number of rapes reported by the subject.

RESULTS

The study found that 73% of the subjects had been raped, for a total of 193 rapes unrelated to the women's work as prostitutes. Of these, 71% occurred since the women entered prostitution. Sexual exploitation prior to the women's becoming prostitutes was also high (Silbert 1982a; Silbert and Pines 1981, 1983).

RAPE DESCRIPTION

In 84% of the cases, the rapist was a stranger to the victim; in 3%, he was wearing a mask and she could not see him; 4% were former husbands or boyfriends; 1% were family members; 2% were former customers). In 27% of the rape cases, more than one person assaulted the woman. Of the multiple assailants, the average number of assailants was four.

The average age of the rapist was in the late twenties; most were black (44%), with 38% white, 14% Hispanic, 2% Asian, and 2% American Indian. Most (93%) of the rapists were much larger (60%) or larger (33%) than their victims. Nearly half (44%) of the rapes involved the use of some weapon. In those cases in which a weapon was used, in 37% of the cases it was a gun, in 51% a knife, and in 13% some other weapon (such as a chain or a club). In 90% of the rapes, the victim believed that the rapist was drinking and/or using some type of drug.

Most of the rapes (47%) occurred at night between 8:00 p.m. and 2:00 a.m.; 26% occurred in the evening (2:01 p.m. to 8:00 p.m.); 24% occurred in the early morning hours (2:01 a.m. to 8:00 a.m.); only 4% occurred during the day (8:01 a.m. to 2:00 p.m.).

Approximately one-third (34%) of the rapes occurred in the assailant's home or vehicle; 18% occurred in the victim's home or car; 14% occurred in a hotel or similar place; 14% of the rapes occurred in a secluded place. On the average, the rapes occurred 11 miles away from the victim's house and 6 miles away from her work. She got there by being dragged (36%), forced into the rapist's car (45%), or forced into using her own car (2%). In most of the remaining 18% of the cases, the rape occurred after the victim was already at the location of the rape.

Of the rapes, 90% involved vaginal penetration with penis, 3% involved penetration with objects, 28% involved fellatio, 21% involved anal penetration with penis, 1% involved anal penetration with object, and 7% involved cunnilingus. Multiple assailants were involved in 45% of the rapes.

In 19% of the cases, there were witnesses to the rape. However, in 90% of the cases, no one came to the victim's aid.

In 91% of the rapes, the assailant used some type of physical force. Every woman raped reported at least one incident involving physical force. In 78% of the rapes, the woman was held down, in 59% she was beaten or hit, in 40% her arms were twisted, in 23% she was choked, in 18% she was threatened with a gun, in 17% the victim was threatened with a knife, in 7% the woman was drugged, and in 15% she was tied up. On the average, the rapes involved three types of force. Every victim reported that threats were used.

Almost every rape involved extreme levels of violence. Indeed, both the statistics and the open-ended comments gathered in the study suggest that the first compounding factor in the rape of street prostitutes is reflected in the fact that there was more violence involved in the rape when the woman disclosed that she was a prostitute.

In 19% of the rape cases, the victims tried to stop the violence by telling the assailant that they were prostitutes (e.g., "Calm down. I'm a hooker. Relax, and I'll turn you a free trick without all this fighting."). Rather than assuage the violence, this assertion only exacerbated the problem: the assailant increased the amount of violence in every single case. Assailants became furious at hearing the victim say she was a prostitute, and most started screaming, demanding that the woman retract what she had said, and insisting on taking her by force. In order to reassert their own control, the assailants then became extremely violent. In all the cases in which the victims told the rapist they were prostitutes, the victims sustained even more serious injuries that those women who did not disclose that they were prostitutes.

In 12% of the 193 cases, the victims who told the rapists that they were prostitutes not only were subjected to more violence than those who didn't tell, but also elicited from the assailants overt comments related to pornography. (In most of the remaining cases in which victims told the rapist they were prostitutes, indirect references were made to pornography.) An analysis of this 12% revealed a pattern of response by the assailants to the disclosure. On hearing that their victims were prostitutes, the assailants responded in a manner characterized by the following four elements: (1) their language became more abusive; (2) they became significantly more violent, beating and punching the women excessively, often using weapons they had shown the women; (3) they mentioned having seen prostitutes in pornographic films, the majority of them mentioning specific pornographic literature; and (4) after completing the forced vaginal penetration, they continued to assault the women sexually in ways they claimed they had seen prostitutes enjoy in the pornographic literature they cited. One woman described what happened:

> After I told him I'd turn him a free trick if only he'd calm down and stop hurting me, then he just really blew his mind. He started calling me all kinds of [names] and sounded like a wailing animal. Instead of just slapping me to keep quiet, he really went crazy and began punching me all over.... Then he told me he had seen whores just like me in [three pornographic films mentioned by name] and told me he knew how to do it to whores like me. He knew what whores like me wanted.... After he finished raping me, he started beating me with his gun all over. Then he said, "You were in that movie. You were in that movie. You know you wanted to die after you were raped. That's what you want; you want me to kill you after this rape just like [specific pornography film] did."

This particular woman suffered, in addition to forced vaginal penetration, forced anal penetration with a gun and excessive bodily injuries, including several broken bones. For a period of time, the rapist held a loaded pistol at her vagina and threatened to shoot her, insisting this was the way she had died in the film he had seen. He did not, in fact shoot the victim (Silbert and Pines 1984; Silbert 1986).

Women responded to the rape, when it was occurring, by both verbal and physical attempts to stop it. Verbal responses included: trying to reason with the rapist (47%), pleading with him (42%), screaming or crying for help (44%), and threatening physical force (16%). All these are active responses. In addition, there were many passive responses, indicative of the women's despair and helplessness: 17% kept quiet, 15% turned "cold," and 40% cried.

Physical responses most often included kicking (39%), hitting (31%), scratching (27%), tearing clothes (9%), biting (14%), running away (9%), and using a weapon (1%). Because of the extreme physical violence involved, in many of the rapes the victims could not move.

PHYSICAL IMPACT

In most of the cases, the victims sustained some physical injury: 69% sustained injuries on the face or body, 38% sustained injuries in the genital area; 13% had broken bones, 22% suffered shock. On the average, in each rape case the victim sustained 2.4 different kinds of injuries.

In 50% of the rapes, the women sought medical help, although the majority did not acknowledge that they had been raped. In 42% of the cases, they required medication. In 11%, they required surgery, and in 36% of the cases, they required medical follow-up.

In 18% of the rape cases, the woman contracted a venereal disease and in 28% a vaginal infection. In 2% of the rape cases, the victim became pregnant as a result of the rape.

Following 69% of the rapes, the victim experienced a significant increase in such physical problems as sleeping, menstrual, and eating difficulties. The average number of physical problems mentioned was 2.3, but some women mentioned as many as 4, 5, and 6 physical problems.

EMOTIONAL IMPACT

In almost all the rapes, the woman was afraid for her life (81%) and felt helpless (79%). In over half the cases (59%), the victim experienced hatred and rage; in over half (51%), she also experienced hurt, disgust, and shame. In 46%, she experienced responsibility for the rape and blamed herself. Many women experienced shock (43%), depression (26%), and relief to be alive (32%). Some of the emotional trauma of the rape was evident even at the time of the interview, which in some cases occurred years after the rape. When one looks at the women who were raped rather than at the rape incidents as the units of analysis, one can see that every rape victim experienced, at least once, fear, helplessness, guilt, rage, shock, hurt, depression, and relief to be alive.

In 20% of the rapes, the victims increased their use of tranquilizers following the rape; 17% increased their use of alcohol; 24% started smoking heavily. Increased use of illegal drugs occurred after 51% of the rapes.

TABLE 6.1
ATTITUDES OF PROSTITUTES AFTER RAPE

Extent rape affected attitudes toward:	At Time of Rape (%)						At Time of Interview (%)					
	X̄	1 Strong Negative	2 Moderate Negative	3 No Effect	4 Moderate Positive	5 Strong Positive	X̄	1 Strong Negative	2 Moderate Negative	3 No Effect	4 Moderate Positive	5 Strong Positive
Men	1.5	70	13	17	0	0	2.0	39	28	32	1	0
Self	1.7	51	27	19	2	1	2.5	21	25	42	9	4
Sexuality	1.9	48	14	36	2	0	2.5	22	17	55	5	1
Emotional relationships	2.0	44	16	37	2	2	2.7	12	14	64	8	2
Friendships	2.3	36	10	47	5	2	2.8	11	8	70	8	3

The rape also had an extremely negative impact on the attitudes of the rape victims, especially toward men and sexuality (see table 6.1). Some of that impact was still evident long after the rape, at the time of the interview. The rape also had a negative and long-lasting impact on the victim's perception of herself, on her emotional relationships, and on her friendships.

In 84% of the cases, the respondents claimed that the rape experience had no positive effects whatsoever. The remainder stated that it made them smarter and more experienced about people, more careful, or more mature.

DISCLOSURE

Despite the violence involved and the highly traumatic impact of the rape on the victims, only in one-third of the cases did the victim discuss the rape with someone after it happened. Results show that 19% told police, 6% told a sexual assault center, 4% told a hospital, 6.5% told a physician, 0.5% told other prostitutes, and 0.5% told a stranger. It usually was the same woman who told not only the police but also a boyfriend, a friend, or someone else. The majority of victims never talked to anyone about the rape.

Of those who disclosed the rape, 39% did so immediately, 6% discussed it the same day, 5% on the following day, 2% within a week, 0.5% within a month, and 0.5% within a year. The remaining victims who disclosed told someone only after several years.

VICTIM INTERVENTION

Most research acknowledges the importance of intervention services to meet the physical and mental health needs of rape victims. Primary medical care is seen as the first measure of assistance for victims who require it. Similarly, early psychological assistance is recognized as important for successful recovery (Symonds 1980). Researchers agree that people who experience victimization without adequate emotional support run a high risk of suffering from long-term disability (Stein 1980). It is seen as critical that the victim be given a sense of power as one of the early antidotes to the feelings of helplessness and powerlessness that accrue from the assault. A sense of control along with compassion from those who come in contact with the victim are critically important to the psychological recovery of the victim.

Unfortunately, the study revealed that the negative impact from the violent rape was compounded by numerous factors related to disclosure and intervention. The prostitute victims generally did not discuss the rape incident, and when they did, many did not receive compassionate or supportive responses. The majority did not utilize intervention services. Also compounding the problem were their perceptions that they must remain stoic, isolated, and strong, along with a perceived lack of understanding by the medical and justice system.

When the results of this study are compared to the results reported in other studies (e.g., Approach Associates 1975; Ford and Ford 1975; Queen's Bench Foundation 1975), it appears that prostitutes were less likely to report their victimization to the police, were less likely to use any other professional services, and when treated were likely to receive worse treatment than rape victims who were not prostitutes. Most of the women in the Approach Associates study noted shock in realizing that someone would willfully attempt to harm them. They were "stunned," "dumbfounded," and "incredulous" to find out that "it can happen to me." For many, a sense of personal well-being was shattered. Their world no longer seemed secure and benign. In contrast, the prostitutes accepted their vulnerability and total helplessness, as well as the knowledge that the world is cruel and vicious, as part of life. The rape only underscored their cynical viewpoints.

The emotional trauma experienced by rape victims in general (Factor 1954; Halleck 1965; Sutherland and Scherl 1970; Symonds 1975) appears to be compounded by several factors in the case of street prostitutes. The informal code of the street prostitute precludes a display of hurt or emotional upset or the leaning on personal or societal supports for assistance in emotional trauma. Most of the prostitutes felt they could not break that code and, therefore, dealt with their feelings alone and/or suppressed them.

In 63% of the rape cases, the women never discussed the rapes or the traumatic impacts until the interview. These feelings did not emerge until the women were in a safe setting removed from the streets. Research reveals that after any severe stress or trauma such as rape, most persons recover only gradually and that special care and close personal and societal supports are often needed (Leighton 1959; Dunham 1961; Mischler and Scotch 1963; Lowenthal and Havens 1968; Nuckolls, Cassel, and Kaplan 1972). Not leaning on others for support and suppressing painful emotions would tend to compound the impact of rape on prostitutes.

A need for the rape victim to ventilate has been noted by many authors (Halleck 1965; Brodyaga et al. 1975). Burgess and Holmstrom (1974, 1976) in particular emphasize this emotional need of the rape victim. Along with the usual rape trauma syndrome they describe, Burgess and Holmstrom (1974) distinguish two pathological variations: (1) the compounded reaction in which previous psychological disabilities exacerbate the impact of the rape trauma; and (2) the psychic upset through anxiety, hostility, loss of self-confidence, paranoia, or agitation.

The need for ventilation, particularly of anger, is stressed also by Nadelson and Notman (1976), who detail some of the psychodynamics of the rape's impact upon the victim. One important dynamic they explore is the tendency in the rape victim toward repressing anger. A ventilation and redirection of anger outwardly toward appropriate targets is seen as an important process in readjustment. The general despair and isolation of the prostitutes is exacerbated by the fact that the majority never ventilated their emotions about the rapes.

The victim's reluctance to talk about the rape may seem justified when one reviews the way people responded to those who did discuss the rape with someone. In 72% of the rape cases that were disclosed, the woman's telling about the rape had either a mixed effect or a bad effect on her relationship with the person told about the rape. In half of the cases disclosed, the person who was told about the rape was neither protective nor supportive. In almost half of the cases (47%), he/she seemed ashamed and disappointed in the rape victim. In almost half the cases (49%), the victim had some bad feelings about him/her. In almost three-fourths of the cases involving a boyfriend, the victim felt that after sharing the experience with him, their sexual activity was not as good as it should be. In 38% of the cases, the person who was told was not at all helpful to the victim in recovering from the rape, and in 49% of the cases, the person blamed the victim to some extent for her own victimization.

Only 6% of the rape victims sought psychological help: 1% saw the helping professional one more time, 1% saw the person two more times, and 4% saw the counselor three more times. Additionally, 3% of the victims sought help from an agency or a group, such as Women Against Rape. In most cases, the women felt they were treated positively. Only 37% said they were treated negatively or indifferently, although 47% felt that being a prostitute affected the way they were treated.

The vast majority of prostitutes did not seek help of any kind, and they explained this was the case for several reasons: because of fear at being identified as a prostitute (21%), because of embarrassment over a prostitute being raped (32%), because they did not know whom to consult (15%), because of feelings that services would not help (11%), because of lack of information (13%), because they felt there was no need (6%), and because of cost (2%). The lack of social supports and assistance in working through the rape trauma left prostitutes isolated with long-term, unresolved problems.

Another factor compounding the negative impact of rape on prostitutes was their general sense of powerlessness. The helplessness usually experienced as a result of rape (Brownmiller 1975) is exacerbated in the case of street prostitutes by their pervasive feelings of impotence in life. The strongest sense of power these women experience derives from their sense of control over their sexual activities. The majority of the street prostitutes interviewed were poor and unskilled. With no options or control over other areas of their lives, they placed a disproportionate amount of importance on their lifestyle and toughness as prostitutes and on their ability to control sexual activity. The impact of rape was thus compounded by the fact that the rape took this one sense of control away from them. It left them in a complete state of psychological paralysis: hopeless, helpless, debilitated, and trapped in a pattern of victimization that they felt unable to change.

If one looks at reporting the rape to police as a way of taking action and regaining some control over the situation, the prostitute's powerlessness was again compounded by her lack of reporting. In this sample, 81% did not report the rape. Of those 19% who did report to police, 72% stated that the police were negative or indifferent in their responses; 28% perceived the police as positive or helpful. Their negative experiences with law enforcement compounded the sense of hopelessness they felt.

Only 8% of the rapists were ever found or identified by law enforcement officers. In 1% of the cases, the rapist confessed or was found guilty of rape; in 4% of the cases, the rapist was found guilty of a lesser offense; in 3% of the cases, the charges against the rapist were dropped or he was found not guilty.

In the majority of cases in which the victims decided not to report the rape to police, the reasons given were: police would not take rape of a prostitute seriously (35%), embarrassment over admitting they were prostitutes who could be raped (44%), it was not worth it because of low apprehension and conviction rates (15%), negative prior experiences with police (11%), fear of reprisal by the rapist (13%), lack of evidence (7%), outstanding warrant (6%), and cost in time (1%).

Additionally, prostitutes did not avail themselves of mental health, medical, or criminal-justice systems because of their perceptions that these systems would not respond as positively to the rape of a prostitute as they would to the rape of a more "legitimate" victim. When asked how doctors, police, district attorneys, and judges were apt to respond to the rape of a prostitute, as compared with the rape of a woman who is not a prostitute, over 90% responded that the reaction was likely to be much more negative toward the prostitute (see table 6.2).

TABLE 6.2
PERCEPTIONS OF PROSTITUTES AFTER RAPE

Official	Response	$\bar{X}$	Much Less Likely 1	2	Equally Likely 3	4	Much More Likely 5	Don't Know 6
Doctor	Concerned treatment	1.3	84	7	7	0	1	2
Police	Take a report	1.1	96	2	1	0	0	2
District attorney	Prosecute	1.3	92	2	3	0	0	3
Jury	Convict	1.3	90	2	2	2	2	3

SUMMARY AND CONCLUSIONS

The results of indepth interviews with 200 street prostitutes reveal an overwhelming amount of sexual assault, with almost three-fourths of the prostitutes (73%) reporting being raped. This figure represents only completed rapes and does not include forced intercourse by customers, attempted rapes, or other sexual abuses. Over three-fourths of the rapes occurred after the women became prostitutes but had nothing to do with the women's being prostitutes. Instead, the rapes were associated with the victims' vulnerability as women living in high-crime areas of the city and working during high-crime hours. In those cases in which the victim told the rapist that she was a prostitute, the rapist often went berserk, saying the act was a rape and not a trick. In every instance, those rapes ended up being even more violent, with the victims sustaining even more serious injuries, than the rapes in which the victims did not disclose that they were prostitutes.

All the rapes in the study (193 cases), especially those occurring after the subjects entered prostitution, involved more rapists who were strangers, more use of force, and more serious injury to the victim than rapes of women who were not prostitutes (as described in published research on rape). Yet the prostitutes were less likely to report the rape to police and less likely to request any other sort of professional or agency-based help. Despite the fact that almost all the victims reported serious physical injuries and extremely negative emotional impacts, only 9% of the victims sought out services or any kind of assistance, support, counseling, or advocacy. The majority of the rapes were never discussed with anyone prior to the interviews, despite the short-term and long-term negative impacts.

The general literature on rape describes rape victims responding to rape by feeling stunned that such a thing could happen to them and by feeling that their beliefs in the world as a secure place and in people as trustworthy were shattered. For the prostitute victims, the general response was of a different nature. The majority of them experienced a final, devastating awareness that there was no aspect of life over which they could exert control. This final lesson served as one more advancement in development of the victims' psychological paralysis, characterized by immobility, acceptance of victimization, feeling trapped and hopeless, and the inability to take the opportunity to change (Silbert 1982b, 1982c, 1984).

All the results of this study document the urgent need for intervention services especially designed for prostitutes who are victims of sexual abuse. In the last part of the questionnaire, subjects were asked directly what they would recommend for prostitutes who are rape victims: 98% suggested a 24-hour switchboard, 97% selected group counseling, 99% percent chose individual counseling, 98% requested social supports and advocacy, 97% recommended "rap" groups and prevention techniques, and 98% selected legal services. Content analysis of the open-ended responses confirmed the data from the forced-choice questions and emphasized as well the importance of establishing services provided by women who are former prostitutes and who are experienced in both street life and victimization and the importance of formulating ways to cope successfully with the problem.

This research was sponsored through the Delancey Street Foundation by the National Center for the Prevention and Control of Rape, National Institute of Mental Health, grant no. RO1 MH 327.82. The author would like to thank Ayala Pines for supervising the research design and Teri Lynch, Auristela Frias, JoAnn Mancuso, Charlotte Martin, and Alice Watson for their assistance in collecting the data.

REFERENCES

Amir, M. 1971. *Pattern of forcible rape*. Chicago: University of Chicago Press.

Approach Associates. 1975. *Sexual assault: Improving the institutional response*. Report no. 2, August. Oakland, Calif.

Brodyaga, L., et al. 1975. *Rape and its victims: A report for citizens, health facilities, and criminal justice agencies*. Washington D.C.: National Institute of Law Enforcement and Criminal Justice.

Brownmiller, S. 1975. *Against our will: Men, women, and rape*. New York: Simon and Schuster.

Burgess, A., and L. Holmstrom. 1974. Rape trauma syndrome. *American Journal of Psychiatry* 131: 981–85.

———. 1976. The prostitute. In *Community mental health: Target populations*, ed. A.W. Burgess and A. Lazare, 264–72. Englewood Cliffs, N.J.: Prentice-Hall.

Dunham, J.N. 1961. Social structures and mental disorders: Competing hypotheses of explanation. *Milband Memorial Fund Quarterly* 39: 259–310.

Factor, M. 1954. Women's psychological reaction to attempted rape. *Psychoanalytic Quarterly* 23: 243-44.

Feldman-Summers, S., and K. Lindner. 1976. Perceptions of victims and defendants in criminal assault cases. *Criminal Justice and Behavior* 3 (June): 143.

Ford, K., and R. Ford. 1975. Reported rape in Palo Alto (1971–1974). Typescript.

Halleck, S. 1965. Emotional effects of victimization. In *Sexual behavior and the law*, ed. R. Slovenko. Springfield, Ill.: Charles C. Thomas.

James, J. 1977. Women as sexual criminals and victims. In *Sexual scripts*, ed. J. Laws and P. Schwartz, 179. Hinsdale, Ill.: Dryden Press.

———. 1978. Juvenile female prostitutions: Final report. University of Washington. Typescript.

———. 1979. *Entrance into juvenile prostitution*. Progress report to the Department of Health, Education and Welfare. Seattle: University of Washington.

Jones, C., and E. Aronson. 1973. Attribution of fault to a rape victim as a function of the respectabiity of the rape victim. *Journal of Personality and Social Psychology* 26: 415–19.

Leighton, A.H. 1959. *My name is legion*. New York: Basic Books.

Lowenthal, M., and C. Havens. 1968. Interaction and adaptation: Intimacy as a critical variable. *American Sociological Review* 33: 20–30.

MacDonald, J. 1971. *Rape: Offenders and their victims*. Springfield, Ill.: Charles C. Thomas.

MacKellar, J. 1975. *Rape: The bait and the trap*. New York: Crown Publishers, Inc.

Mischler, E.G., and N.A. Scotch. 1963. Sociocultural factors in the epidemiology of schizophrenia: A review. *Psychiatry* 26: 315–51.

Nadelson, C., and M. Notman. 1976. The rape victim: Psychodynamic considerations. *American Journal of Psychiatry* 133: 408–13.

Nuckolls, K.B., J. Cassel, and B.H. Kamplan. 1972. Psycho-social assets, life crisis and the prognosis of pregnancy. *American Journal of Epidemiology* 95: 431–41.

Queen's Bench Foundation. 1975. *Rape victimization study*. San Francisco: Office of Criminal Justice Planning.

Silbert, M. 1980a. A process of mutual restitution. In *Mental Health and the self-help revolution*. ed. A. Gartner and F. Reissman. New York: Human Science Press.

――――. 1980b. Sexual assault of prostitutes: Phase I final report. Typescript.

――――. 1982a. Prostitution and sexual assault: A summary of findings. *Biosocial: The International Journal for Research* 3: 69–71.

――――. 1982b. Sexual assault of prostitutes: Phase II final report. Typescript.

――――. 1982c. Sexual assault of prostitutes: Summary final report. Typescript.

――――. 1984. Treatment of prostitute victims of sexual assault. In *Victims of sexual aggression: Treatment of children, women, and men*, ed. I. Stuart and J. Greer, 25–85. New York: Van Nostrand Reinhold Co.

――――. 1986. *The effects on juveniles of being used for prostitution and pornography*. Report prepared for Surgeon General's Workshop on Pornography and Public Health. Washington, D.C.

Silbert, M., and A. Pines. 1981. Sexual child abuse as an antecedent to prostitution. *Child Abuse and Neglect* 5: 407–11.

――――. 1982a. The endless cycle of victimization. *International Journal of Victimology* 7: 122–33.

――――. 1982b. Entrance into prostitution. *Youth and Society* 13: 471–500.

――――. 1982c. Occupational hazards of street prostitutes. *Criminal Justice and Behavior* 8.

――――. 1983. Early sexual exploitation as an influence in prostitution. *Social Work* 28: 285–89.

――――. 1984. Pornography and the sexual abuse of women. *Sex Roles* 10: 857–68.

Silbert, M., et al. 1982. Substance abuse and prostitution. *Journal of Psychoactive Drugs* 14: 193–97.

Stein, J. 1980. Better services for crime victims: A prescriptive package. *Evaluation and Change*, special issue, 103.

Sutherland, S., and D. Scherl. 1970. Patterns of response among victims of rape. *American Journal of Orthopsychiatry* 40: 503–22.

Symonds, M. 1975. Victims of violence. *American Journal of Psychoanalysis* 35: 19–26.

――――. 1980. The second injury. *Evaluation and Change*, special issue, 36.

CHAPTER 7

THE SEXUAL ABUSE OF BOYS

Childhood Victimizations Reported by a National Sample

LESLIE I. RISIN
Kent State University

MARY P. KOSS
Kent State University

Recent reports from treatment programs reveal that a substantial proportion of referrals involve boys. For example, 25% of the sexual-abuse victims at the Children's Hospital in Washington, D.C., are male (Rogers 1979). The National Study of the Incidence and Severity of Child Abuse and Neglect, an investigation of cases of child abuse reported by professionals, estimated that there were approximately 7,600 cases of sexual abuse of boys in 1979 (Burgdorf 1980). Yet because child sexual abuse is a problem that is often concealed, studies of reported cases reflect only a small fraction of actual cases.

Empirical studies of unreported sexual abuse among nonclinical populations also suggest the existence of a sizable number of male victims. For example, Finkelhor (1979) administered a self-report survey to 796 college students at six New England colleges and universities. Child sexual experiences were defined as abuse if they occurred with a person at least 5 years older in the case of boys under 12, and 10 years older in the case of boys age 13–16. Of the 266 men surveyed, 8.6% reported an experience that met the criteria for sexual abuse. Later, as part of a study on parents' attitudes and responses to sexual abuse, Finkelhor (1984) conducted a self-report survey in the Boston area that included 185 adult

This chapter has been accepted for publication in the *Journal of Interpersonal Violence*.

male respondents. Among this group, 6% of the men reported an abusive childhood sexual experience. In their study of homosexuality, Bell and Weinberg (1978) included a San Francisco-area probability sample of heterosexuals to compare with their homosexual subjects. Private interviews were conducted with each of the 284 men. Results indicated that 2.5% of the heterosexuals and 4.9% of the homosexuals had a prepubertal experience with an adult male involving physical contact.

Among the major methodological considerations in child sexual abuse research is the operational definition used to guide case identification. A number of alternative criteria have been developed. For example, Finkelhor (1979) focused on the age discrepancy between victim and perpetrator. Russell (1983) placed emphasis on the exploitative nature of the sexual experience. Gold (1986) used the presence of either age discrepancy or physical force. However, certain sexual experiences may have the potential to be abusive where forms of coercion other than actual physical force are used and regardless of whether there is or is not an age discrepancy between the child and the perpetrator. Thus, Finkelhor and Hotaling (1984) have recommended that criteria for sexual abuse include "sexual contact that occurs to a child as a result of force, threat, deceit, while unconscious, or through exploitation of an authority relationship, no matter what the age of the partner" (31).

A further methodological limitation in existing studies of unreported/ nonclinically identified cases of sexual abuse among general populations is that they are based on small samples of restricted generalizability. As a result, the number of index cases identified often is too small to form a reliable data base. For example, beginning with a survey sample of 796, Finkelhor (1979) identified only 23 male victims for use in his analyses of sexual abuse of boys.

Our study was undertaken to expand the available data base on the sexual abuse of boys to a large, approximately representative national sample of 2,972 male students in higher education. Although results based on a sample of college students are still restricted in generalizability to other students, this group represents 26% of all persons in the U.S. age 18–24 (U.S. Bureau of Census 1980). In addition, there are both pragmatic and scientific advantages for the use of postsecondary students in this research. College students are relatively accessible for research and can participate on the basis of their own informed consent. A representative sample of younger persons is difficult to obtain because the sensitive nature of the topic increases both institutional and parental resistance to involvement. Finally, as compared with adult men, postsecondary students have a shorter recall period since the abusive episode, which lessens somewhat the problem of memory decay.

In our study, a broad and inclusive set of criteria, based on the recommendations of Finkelhor and Hotaling (1984), were developed to define child sexual abuse. A childhood sexual experience was defined as abusive if it was characterized by any one of the following three criteria: (1) there was a significant age discrepancy between the child and the other person (i.e., 5 or more years older for boys under 12, 8 or more years older for boys 13 or older), (2) some form of coercion was used to obtain the participation of the victim (i.e., gifts, candy or money, threats to hurt or punish, use of power over victim, or actual physical force), and/or (3) the other person was a caregiver or an authority figure (i.e., babysitter, uncle, aunt, grandparent, stepparent, or parent).

All subjects who reported any childhood sexual experience were asked a series of follow-up questions. The responses to these questions were used to determine the prevalence among boys of abusive childhood sexual experiences as defined by the objective criteria cited above. These data were also used to present a brief overview of the descriptive characteristics of those incidents that qualified as sexually abusive and to determine whether three levels of childhood sexual abuse (exhibition, fondling, and penetration) could be differentiated.

METHODS

The data for the study were collected via a self-report questionnaire of 6,159 students in 32 U.S. institutions of higher education during a nationwide survey of sexual assault experiences. (Data from women respondents are not reported here.) The methods of sample design, institutional recruitment, questionnaire construction, validity and reliability checks, and administration procedure have been described in detail elsewhere (Koss, Gidycz, and Wisniewski forthcoming). Procedures and results of this nationwide study are also discussed in chapter 1.

SAMPLING PROCEDURES

The sampling goals of the project were to represent the universe of the U.S. higher-education student population in all its diversity. No sample design could be expected to result in a purely random or representative sample, however, because the subject matter is sufficiently controversial that some schools targeted by a systematic sampling method could be expected to refuse to participate. The U.S. Department of Education (Office of Civil Rights 1980) maintains records of the enrollment characteristics from 3,269 institutions of higher education. The data for 1980 (the latest available at the time of sample design) were provided to the survey consultants.

On the basis of these data, the institutions were sorted by location into the ten U.S. Department of Education regions. Within each region, institutions were placed into homogeneous clusters according to five criteria: (1) location inside or outside of a standard metropolitan statistical area (SMSA) of certain sizes; (2) enrollment above or below the national mean-percentage enrollment of minority students; (3) control of the institution by private secular, private religious, or public authority; (4) type of institution (university, four-year college, two-year junior college, and technical/vocational school); and (5) total enrollment within three levels. Every xth cluster was sampled according to the proportion of total enrollment accounted for by the region. Replacements were sought from among other schools in the homogeneous cluster if the original target school proved uncooperative.

The amount of time required to obtain institutional cooperation was extended; some schools required 15 months to arrive at a final decision. During that period, 93 schools were contacted and 32 institutional participants were obtained. Of the institutions, 19 were first choices; the remaining 13 were solicited from among 43 replacements. The actual institutional participants cannot be listed because they were guaranteed anonymity.

The questionnaires were administered to students during regularly scheduled classes. A random selection process based on the entire catalogue of course offerings from each institution was used to choose target classes and alternates. The questionnaire was administered by one of eight post-master's level clinical psychologists (two men and six women) who used a prepared script and were trained in standard procedures to handle potential untoward effects of participation. Participation was completely anonymous, but the cover sheet of the questionnaire included all the elements of informed consent. The participation rate among students asked to respond was 98.5%.

STUDY SUBJECTS

The final sample consisted of 6,159 persons, including 2,972 men. The men were characterized as follows: M age = 21.0; 91% single, 9% married, 1% divorced; 86% white, 6% black, 3% Hispanic, 4% Asian, and 1% native American; and 40% Catholic, 34% Protestant, 5% Jewish, and 22 % with other or no religious affiliation. Four variables were examined to determine the extent to which this sample was representative of the U.S. higher-education enrollment: institution location within or outside of an SMSA and a region, subject ethnicity, and income. Region in which the institutions were located was the only variable on which a significant discrepancy was noted, as the sample underrepresented students in the West and overrepresented students in New England and the Southwest. In previous research (Koss, Gidycz, and Wisniewski forthcoming) weighting factors were used to correct for regional disproportion. However, comparison of weighted and unweighted data among men revealed that the impact of correction for disproportion was minimal (i.e., 7.8% unweighted versus 7.7% weighted prevalence among men of reports of perpetrating behavior that would legally qualify as rape or attempted rape). Because this chapter is primarily descriptive and because the impact of the weighting factors in previous research was minimal, no weighting factors were used in the analyses reported below.

QUESTIONNAIRE FORMAT

All data were obtained via a self-report questionnaire entitled "National Survey of Intergender Relationships." This title was chosen so that participants would not prejudge the content before explanations were given. However, the oral and written description of the study explained the content explicitly.

The questionnaire consisted of 330 questions divided into seven sections with a branching format. The content covered included participant demographics, sexual experiences before the age of 14, sexual experiences after the age of 14, situational characteristics of child sexual experiences and adult sexual aggression, family and social history, current social behaviors, and psychological characteristics. Only the data on prevalence and situational characteristics of sexual experiences before the age of 14 are reported here.

The items used to elicit childhood sexual experiences were those developed by Finkelhor (1979), with minor editorial changes to increase appropriateness for the sample population and to be consistent with other sections of the questionnaire. The text asked the following: Did you have any of these experiences before age 14?

1. Another person showed his/her sex organs to you
2. A request by someone older than you to do something sexual
3. You showed your sex organs to another person at his/her request
4. Another person fondled you in a sexual way
5. Another person touched or stroked your sex organs
6. You touched or stroked another person's sex organs at his/her request
7. Attempted intercourse (got on top of you, attempted to insert penis, but penetration did not occur)

8. Intercourse (oral, anal, or vaginal) with any amount of penetration (ejaculation not necessary)

The introductory instructions included the following text: "Many people have sexual experiences as children, either with friends or with people older than themselves. The following questions ask about any experiences you may have had before you were 14." Inquiry into childhood sexual experiences was limited to the years before age 14 to prevent interference with the primary focus of the funded study, which was sexual victimization and aggression after age 14. However, because Finkelhor (1979) reported a breakdown of sexual abuse prevalence by age, rates for boys age 13 or younger could be obtained from his work for purposes of comparison with the result of our study. Follow-up questions were used to elicit detailed information about the most severe (i.e., highest numbered) sexual-abuse episode the subject had experienced. In cases when the respondent had experienced multiple incidents of an experience, he was instructed to refer to the experience he remembered the best.

Many investigators have questioned the validity of self-reported sexual behavior. To explore this issue, we administered the questionnaire to male subjects both by self-report and by one-to-one interview on the same occasion. The interviewer was a fully trained, licensed, and experienced male Ph.D. clinical psychologist. Subjects were 15 male volunteers, identified by first name only, recruited through newspaper advertisements on the campus of another major university. Participants gave their self-reports first and then were interviewed individually, with interview questions focusing on the participants' sexual history both before and after the age of 14. The intent was to match the participants' verbal responses with their questionnaire responses. The results indicated that in the judgment of the interviewer, 14 of the participants (93%) gave the same responses to sexual experiences both on self-report and in the interviews.

SCORING PROCEDURES

The childhood sexual experiences reported by the men were identified as abusive if examination of the follow-up items revealed that they met one of the three criteria presented earlier (i.e., the other person was a caregiver or authority figure, there was an age discrepancy between participants, and/or some form of coercion was used to obtain the involvement of the victim). Respondents who reported sexually abusive experiences were then classified according to the most serious incident they had experienced. Three mutually exclusive classes of sexual abuse were developed: *exhibition* ("yes" response to items 1, 2, or 3 but not to any higher-numbered items), *fondling* ("yes" responses to items 4, 5, or 6 and any lower-numbered items but not to any higher numbered items), and *penetration*, including attempts ("yes" to items 7 or 9 and any lower-numbered items.

RESULTS

PREVALENCE OF SEXUAL ABUSE

Application of the operational criteria for sexual abuse to subjects' responses to Finkelhor's (1979) items resulted in the identification of 216 men (7.3%) who reported an abusive sexual experience before the age of 14. Exhibition was the most serious incident ever experienced for 34.7% of the men, fondling the most serious incident for an additional 34.7% of the men, and penetration, including attempts, was the most serious incident for 30.7% of the men.

DESCRIPTIVE CHARACTERISTICS OF SEXUAL ABUSE

The average age of victims at the time the sexual abuse first occurred was 9.8 years, and the median age was 10. Most victims reported that only one person other than themselves was involved (82.4%). Although the majority of victims reported that the sexual abuse happened only once (53.1%), 19.7% of the victims indicated that the abuse occurred five or more times. Most perpetrators were acquaintances of the victims; only 15.3% were strangers. The greatest proportion of victims were abused by an older person they knew, such as a neighbor, teacher, or friend of their parents (25%); many boys reported victimization by a babysitter (23.1%); and the remainder of boys were abused by a friend of their brother or sister (8.8%), their mother or father (7.4%), an aunt, uncle, or grandparent (6.9%), a brother or sister (6%), a same-age peer (5.6%), or a stepfather or stepmother (1.9%). Thus a total of 22.2% of the boys were sexually abused by a family member.

The average age of offenders was between 18 and 20 years. Offenders were just slightly more often male (53.3%) than female (42.7%). A small proportion of the victimizations involved both a male and a female perpetrator (4.2%). Almost half (47.8%) of the females designated as the other person involved in the sexual behavior were babysitters between 14 and 17 years old. Among the 36.6% of victims who reported that the offender utilized some form of coercion to make them participate, just 9.9% reported actual physical force or threats of harm. Many men indicated that the primary reason they participated in the sexual activity was because they were curious (30.7%). The vast majority of men told no one about the sexual abuse (81.2%). Many, but not all, of the men (61.9%) felt at least somewhat victimized by the experience.

DIFFERENTIATION OF LEVELS
OF SEXUAL ABUSE

To determine if the situational characteristics of exhibition, fondling, and penetration differed, we conducted chi-square analyses. To evaluate the extent to which obtained differences reflected important effects, we calculated effect-size estimates for chi-square using the method presented by Cohen (1977). The effect size for chi-square, known as w, was calculated by taking the square root of X^2/N. Cohen's guidelines for interpretation suggest that a w of .1 indicates a small effect, a w of .25 indicates a medium effect, and a w of .4 indicates a large effect. The variables on which exhibition, fondling, and penetration were compared; the percentage of "yes" responses for each variable calculated within level of sexual abuse; and the chi-square, probability level, and effect size of the comparison are presented in table 7.1.

FREQUENCY AND DURATION   Exhibition, fondling, and penetration experiences were significantly different with respect to the number of times the abuse occurred [$X^2(8, N = 201) = 27.01; p < .001$]. Many boys experienced exhibition and fondling only once (67.1% and 55.1% respectively), but over a third of boys (35.5%) who reported acts of penetration indicated five or more occurrences. The levels of sexual abuse also differed in the duration of the abuse [$X^2 (10, N = 195) = 30.74; p < .001$]. Fewer penetration reports involved experiences of one day or less (30.7%) compared with exhibition and fondling (85.5% and 69.6% respectively).

CHARACTERISTICS OF OFFENDERS   The levels of sexual abuse differed in the number of others involved in the experience [$X^2(8, N = 200) = 15.80; p < .05$]. Exhibition (14.9%) and penetration (12.9%) were more likely than fondling (2.9%) to involve two or more offenders. The levels of sexual abuse differed in the relationship between victim and offender [$X^2 (16, N = 202) = 28.76; p < .05$]. Exhibition more often involved parents or stepparents (12.9%) than did fondling or penetration (5.7% and 0% respectively). The groups did not differ in the age or sex of the other person involved in the sexually abusive incident.

REASONS FOR PARTICIPATING   The levels of sexual abuse differed in the reason given by the victim for participating [$X^2 (14, N = 190) = 32.42; p < .01$]. More fondling (9%) than exhibition or penetration incidents (both

TABLE 7.1

SITUATIONAL CHARACTERISTICS AMONG
THREE LEVELS OF SEVERITY OF CHILDHOOD SEXUAL ABUSE

Variable	Severity Level (%)			X^2	p	w
	Exhibition	Fondling	Penetration			
Times happened						
One	67.1	55.1	37.1			
Two	20.0	14.5	12.9			
Three	4.3	4.3	11.3			
Four	0.0	7.2	3.2			
Five or more	8.6	18.8	35.5			
				27.01	.001	.37
Duration						
1 day or less	85.5	69.6	45.6			
2–14 days	5.8	8.7	12.3			
2–4 weeks	2.9	1.4	10.5			
1–6 months	0.0	7.2	5.3			
6 months–1 year	1.4	7.2	17.5			
Over 1 year	4.3	5.8	8.8			
				30.74	.001	.40
Number of others involved						
Only one	71.6	92.8	82.3			
Two others	14.9	2.9	12.9			
Three or more	1.5	4.3	4.8			
				15.80	.045	.28
Relationship to other person						
Stranger	17.1	17.1	11.3			
Known older person	25.7	27.1	24.2			
Friend of brother/sister	4.3	8.6	16.1			
Brother or sister	5.7	5.7	4.8			
Same-age peer	11.4	2.9	1.6			
Babysitter	17.1	22.9	33.9			
Uncle/aunt/grandparent	5.7	8.6	4.8			
Stepfather/stepmother	0	1.4	3.2			
Father/mother	12.9	5.7	0			
				28.76	.026	.38
Sex of other person						
Male	49.3	60.9	46.8			
Female	44.9	37.7	48.8			
Both	5.8	1.4	4.8			
				6.03	.419	
Partner age						
Under 10	11.4	1.4	1.6			
10–11	2.9	4.3	6.5			
12–13	7.1	11.6	8.1			
14–17	30.0	27.5	40.3			
18–20	12.9	13.0	21.0			
21–30	14.3	13.0	9.7			
31–40	12.9	17.4	9.7			
40 or over	8.6	11.6	3.2			
				19.40	.150	

Variable	Severity Level (%)			$X2$	p	w
	Exhibition	Fondling	Penetration			
Reason to participate						
Felt good	6.5	4.5	23.0			
Curiosity	43.5	23.9	26.2			
To feel loved	4.8	6.0	3.3			
Told it was "OK"	11.3	13.4	23.0			
Authority used	16.1	6.9	11.5			
Gifts	8.1	10.4	9.8			
Threats	8.1	6.0	1.6			
Force	1.6	9.0	1.6			
				32.42	.004	.41
Initiator						
Other	88.4	90.0	75.8			
Self	1.4	4.3	1.6			
Both initiated	10.1	5.7	22.6			
				10.28	.036	.23
Emotional response: fear						
Not at all scared	42.9	21.7	33.3			
A little scared	17.5	11.6	12.3			
Somewhat scared	17.5	18.8	17.5			
Quite scared	12.7	23.2	15.8			
Very scared	9.5	24.6	21.1			
				12.13	.146	
Emotional response: anger						
Not at all angry	77.4	51.5	66.1			
A little angry	6.5	8.8	12.5			
Somewhat angry	8.1	16.2	8.9			
Quite angry	4.8	7.4	3.6			
Very angry	3.2	16.2	8.9			
				13.42	.098	
Emotional response: guilt						
Not at all guilty	44.3	29.0	42.9			
A little guilty	19.7	20.3	16.1			
Somewhat guilty	18.0	10.1	10.7			
Quite guilty	8.2	14.5	3.6			
Very guilty	9.8	26.1	26.8			
				14.12	.079	
Emotional response: depression						
Not at all depressed	73.8	51.5	58.9			
A little depressed	6.6	17.6	12.5			
Somewhat depressed	14.8	13.2	10.7			
Quite depressed	3.3	8.8	5.4			
Very depressed	1.6	8.8	12.5			
				12.72	.122	
Emotional response: pride						
Not at all proud	75.5	76.1	45.6			
A little proud	8.1	9.0	10.5			
Somewhat proud	9.7	6.0	21.1			
Quite proud	1.6	7.5	7.0			
Very proud	4.8	1.5	15.8			
				24.04	.002	.36

Variable	Severity Level (%)			X^2	p	w
	Exhibition	Fondling	Penetration			
Feelings of victimization						
Not at all victimized	55.6	26.1	29.3			
A little victimized	25.4	20.3	13.8			
Somewhat victimized	12.7	17.4	15.5			
Quite victimized	1.6	13.0	17.2			
Very victimized	4.8	23.2	24.1			
				27.89	.001	.38

Notes: Levels of abuse are mutually exclusive. Percentages of "yes" responses are calculated within level of abuse for each descriptive variable.

1.6%) involved the use of force. The levels of sexual abuse differed in who initiated the behavior $[X^2 (4, N = 201) = 10.28; p < .05]$. Boys who reported fondling or penetration were more likely (10.1% and 22.6% respectively) to have helped initiate the behavior than boys who experienced exhibition (5.7%).

REACTION TO THE INCIDENT   The groups differed in how victimized they felt by the experience $[X^2 (8, N = 190 = 27.89; p < .001]$. Those who reported penetration and fondling (23.2% and 24.1% respectively) were much more likely to feel "very much victimized" than those who reported exhibition (4.8%). The groups also differed in their feelings after the abuse $[X^2 (8, N = 186) = 24.04; p < .01]$. Some boys who reported penetration felt proud after their experience (24.0%), whereas this response was not typical in exhibition and fondling victims (4.8% and 1.5% respectively). The groups did not differ in the degree to which they felt scared, angry, guilty, or depressed.

AGE OF VICTIMS   In order to compare the mean ages of victims at the time of the abuse experience, a one-way analysis of variance (ANOVA) was performed. The results of this analysis revealed that the levels of sexual abuse occurred at different ages $[F (2, N = 198) = 3.29; p < .05]$. Exhibition occurred at a younger age $(M = 8.61)$ than fondling $(M = 9.67)$ or penetration $(M = 9.28)$.

DISCUSSION

In this approximately representative national sample of male students in higher education, 7.3% of the men reported a childhood sexual experience that qualified as abusive according to a set of three criteria: age discrepancy, use of coercion, and/or authority or caregiver role status of the other person. This rate is slightly higher than the 6.4% prevalence reported by Finkelhor (1979) for boys under age 14, a rate based on a definition of abuse related solely to age discrepancy.

Even though the overall rates were similar, however, there was one large distinction between the characteristics of the abusive incidents reported in our study and those recorded by Finkelhor (1979). While Finkelhor reported that 20% of the perpetrators of sexual abuse were female, in this study 42.7% of the other persons were female. To determine whether the difference in proportion of female perpetrators was accounted for by the varying criteria for sexual abuse, the data from our study were rescored according to Finkelhor's (1979) age discrepancy criteria. The use of these criteria in our data set resulted in a prevalence rate for childhood sexual abuse of 5% (compared with Finkelhor's rate of 6.4% in boys younger than 14). However, the proportion of female perpetrators in our data set (34.7%) still was higher than the rate reported by Finkelhor (20%).

Closer inspection of the characteristics of the female others identified in our study revealed that almost one-half of them were babysitters age 14–17. Episodes involving female babysitters comprised a sizable portion of the data base, including 33.9% of penetration experiences, 22.9% of fondling incidents, and 17.1% of exhibition situations. Among the incidents that involved female others, almost one-half the boys participated in the incidents voluntarily, and most did not feel victimized as a result of the experience.

While it was valuable to learn of the existence of this type of sexual experience, these results raise questions about the adequacy of the screening items and the criteria for sexual abuse that were used in the study. The screening questions did not differentiate whether men were reporting being penetrated or were engaging in an act of penetration. When a young girl or boy is voluntarily penetrated by an offender who is a somewhat older babysitter, the episode clearly qualifies as sexual abuse. When a boy voluntarily penetrates an opposite sex, somewhat older teenage babysitter, the situation is a qualitatively different experience.

That such experiences were tapped in the study is supported by the observation that the group that reported penetration was both most likely to feel very victimized and most likely to feel very proud. Perhaps it was inappropriate to include voluntary, heterosexual sexual penetration of female babysitters as sexual abuse. Even though an authority relationship was involved, inspection of the emotional response to such experiences suggests that they are not traumatic and they are a "gray area" between abusive and normative sexual behavior. If the screening items used in future research on sexual abuse were more behaviorally specific, it would be possible to distinguish between acts in which the victim engaged in an act of penetration versus acts in which the victim was penetrated. Then, the differential impact of these different types of penetration experiences could be examined and the appropriateness of classifying them as sexual abuse could be considered.

The results of the study highlight the difficulties of designing a gender-neutral definition of sexual abuse. Future research must address the tendency, revealed in this study, for men to respond to items about childhood sexual intercourse both from the perspective of accomplishing penetration and from the perspective of experiencing penetration. Criteria for sexual abuse of boys may need to acknowledge this dual perspective. However, ad hoc attempts to develop objective, situational, and relationship criteria for sexual abuse often lead to the inclusion of some respondents who participated voluntarily and/or did not feel victimized by the episode. An alternative methodology could involve a cluster analysis of those characteristics that differentiate episodes in which subjects experienced negative emotions and felt victimized, compared with those episodes in which they experienced few negative emotions, felt proud, and did not feel victimized.

At least three explanations could account for differences in the types of sexually abusive episodes identified in this study compared with Finkelhor's work (1979). A primary consideration is the fact that the men in this study were queried about their childhood sexual experiences *after* having responded to items pertaining to attempted and complete heterosexual acts of penetration that they had experienced as adults (i.e., since they were 14 years old). It is possible that this item placement heightened the saliency of experiences that involved penetrating another person. Thus, subjects recalled more incidents as boys in which they attempted or achieved penetration with a female. Second, Finkelhor utilized a small sample that was selected from geographic location, which might not generalize to a national basis. Finally, Finkelhor's data were collected before sexual abuse received recent widespread coverage in the news media. This coverage may have broadened the range of incidents recalled in response to sexual-experience items.

Future research can address these methodological questions regarding differences in the child-abuse prevalence rate depending on the sample, screening questions, and definitional criteria utilized. The cardinal intent of this chapter has been to highlight several methodological problems that may lead to less ambiguous studies in the future. The most important conclusion to be drawn from our study is that, in spite of the inclusion as sexual abuse of some situations that are gray areas, a sizable amount of sexual abuse was identified and the importance of the problem of sexual abuse of boys in our society was supported.

This chapter is based on the master's thesis of the first author. Data collection was supported by grant no. MH 31618 from the National Institute of Mental Health to the second author.

REFERENCES

Bell, A., and M. Weinberg. 1978. *Homosexualities*. New York: Simon and Schuster.

Burgdorf, K. 1980. *Recognition and reporting of child maltreatment: Findings from the National Study of the Incidence and Severity of Child Abuse and Neglect*. Washington, D.C.: National Center on Child Abuse and Neglect.

Cohen, J. 1977. *Statistical power analysis for the behavioral sciences*. New York: Academic Press.

Finkelhor, D. 1979. *Sexually victimized children*. New York: Free Press.

―――. 1984. *Child sexual abuse: New theory and research*. New York: Free Press.

Finkelhor, D., and G.T. Hotaling. 1984. Sexual abuse in the National Incidence Study of Child Abuse and Neglect: An appraisal. *Child Abuse and Neglect* 8: 22–33.

Gold, E.R. 1986. Long-term effects of sexual victimizations in childhood: An attributional approach. *Journal of Consulting and Clinical Psychology* 54: 471–75.

Koss, M.P., C.A. Gidycz, and N. Wisniewski. Forthcoming. The scope of rape: Incidence and prevalence of sexual aggression and victimization in a national sample of students in higher education. *Journal of Consulting and Clinical Psychology*.

Office of Civil Rights. 1980. *Fall enrollment and compliance report of institutions of higher education*. Washington, D.C.: U.S. Department of Education.

Rogers, C. 1979. Findings from a hospital-based sexual abuse treatment program. Paper presented to Children's Hospital Medical Center Conference on Sexual Victimization of Children, Washington, D.C.

Russell, D.E.H. 1983. The incidence and prevalence of intrafamilial and extrafamilial sexual abuse of female children. *Child Abuse and Neglect* 7: 133–46.

U.S. Bureau of Census. 1980. *Current population reports 1980–1981*. Washington, D.C.: U.S. Government Printing Office.

VICTIM RESPONSE STRATEGIES IN SEXUAL ASSAULT

DANIEL L. CARTER
Massachusetts Treatment Center

ROBERT ALAN PRENTKY
Massachusetts Treatment Center

ANN WOLBERT BURGESS
University of Pennsylvania

The past ten years have witnessed a marked increase in empirical research on sexually aggressive behavior. Indeed, Chappell and Fogarty (1978) refer to publicity about rape within the last decade as a "veritable explosion." This publicity and, by inference, an attendant increase in social awareness have led to noteworthy advances in the development and provision of victim services (McCombie 1980; National Center for the Prevention and Control of Rape 1980), the apprehension of suspects (Brodsky 1976), the conviction of suspects (Curtis 1976), rape law reform (e.g., Marsh, Geist, and Caplan, 1982), and research on the sexual victimization of women (e.g., Bart and O'Brien 1984; Brodsky 1976; Burgess and Holmstrom 1974, 1976, 1979; Chapman and Gates 1978; Katz and Mazur 1979; Queens Bench Foundation 1976; Russell 1984).

Over the past decade there has also been a steady increase in the numbers of reported rapes (Federal Bureau of Investigation 1983) as well as a clearer understanding of women's fear of rape (Bart 1981; Burnett, Templer, and Barken 1985; Gordon and Heath 1981; Warr 1985). Warr found that two-thirds of urban women under age 35 ranked fear of rape on the top half of his scale. Warr's data suggest that the majority of women will experience moderate to high levels of fear of rape until their mid-30s.

He contends that fear of rape continues to be a problem of considerable magnitude and consequence. Russell and Howell (1983) conclude from their San Francisco interview survey that sexual violence against women is endemic. Despite the magnitude of the problem and the depth of concern among potential victims, the critical area of victim responses to sexual assault has failed to yield any replicable findings.

Brodsky (1976) showed videotapes of simulated attempted rape scenes to 199 conferees attending a meeting on rape, 18 staff members of a forensic unit in a state mental hospital, and 39 convicted rapists. The subjects were asked to rate, on a five-point scale, the effectiveness of nine behaviors in deterring the rapist. The conferees gave the highest ratings to scenes depicting active resistance (verbal attack) by the victim. The lowest ratings were of scenes in which the victim acquiesced or appealed to the morals of the offender. It is noteworthy that the rapists in this study provided quite different feedback. The highest ratings were given to scenes involving bodily weakness, acquiescence, and moral appeal on the part of the victim.

A study based on reports to the San Francisco police department included interviews with 108 women who had been victims of rape or attempted rape as well as interviews with 73 rapists incarcerated at Atascadero State Hospital (Queen's Bench Foundation 1976). When rape victims were compared with those who had managed to avoid rape (though not necessarily avoid physical assault), it was found that a larger percentage of rape avoiders had screamed, a larger percentage of avoiders had fought physically, a somewhat larger percentage of avoiders had successfully escaped, and a somewhat larger percentage of avoiders resisted by talking to the assailant. A similar study of 50 rapists at Atascadero found that victims who resisted, threatened, or degraded the rapist increased the level of anger in over 66% of attackers. When asked how a woman could make her situation worse, 55% cited resistance (Chappell and James 1976).

There is evidence, however, that fighting back may indeed thwart a sexual assault (e.g., McIntyre, Myint, and Curtis 1979; Sanders 1980). In a recent study by Bart and O'Brien (1984), 51 women who successfully avoided a rape were compared with 43 women who were raped. Bart and O'Brien stress the importance of using multiple assertive strategies, such as using physical force and yelling.

It is interesting to note that rape avoidance may also be a function of specific victim fears and perceptions. Bart (1981) found that victims whose principal fear was being murdered or mutilated were *less likely* to be avoiders (rapes attempted but not completed) than were victims whose principal fear was being raped. Another recent study also found that victim resistance to rape was inversely associated with degree of death anxiety (Burnett, Templer, and Barker 1985). The degree and type of response strategy used in a rape situation are also determined by the victim's perception of how the resistance will affect the outcome—the likelihood that resistance will aid in diverting the assault or avoiding serious physical injury (Abarbanel 1986).

An equivocal picture emerges from these studies, suggesting that offender responses to various victim coping strategies vary widely. Indeed, two studies with what may be construed to be opposing findings were conducted at roughly the same time on rapists incarcerated at the same institution (Chappel and James 1976; Queen's Bench Foundation 1976). Conflicting findings such as these are not atypical and may, in part, be attributable to the manifest heterogeneity among rapists (Knight, Rosenberg, and Schneider 1985). Men who sexually assault adult women are markedly heterogeneous with respect to many facets of their familial, developmental, and criminal histories as well as the motives that drive them to rape. Given this heterogeneity, there can be no single response that is optimally appropriate in all sexual assault situations.

Nevertheless, one victim response in particular—physical combative-ness—has been the subject of considerable scrutiny. In this regard, the statement of Bart and O'Brien (1984) is noteworthy: "But we also know that there is little relationship between women's use of physical resistance and rapists' use of additional physical force over and above the attempted rape" (94). This statement might suggest that most of the rapists in the Bart and O'Brien study used only instrumental force (only that amount of force necessary to gain compliance).

While physical resistance may be effective against such rapists, for rapists whose singular motive is not forcing victim compliance but expressing rage, such resistance may indeed increase the risk of serious or mortal physical injury to the victim. However, physical resistance may also increase the chance that the victim will avoid being raped. In addition, the rapist's response to the victim's physical resistance may provide information that will help the victim in determining the nature of subse-quent resistance strategies. In such instances, the increased risk of physical injury may be acceptable if it serves to increase the probability of escape.

There is clearly a need to refine our understanding of the motives underlying different sexual assaults and how best a victim might respond in such a traumatic and potentially life-threatening situation. In view of such a need, this chapter has two principal goals. The first is to examine empirically the hypothesized interaction of differentiated subgroups of rapists with combative and noncombative victim responses. If such an interaction exists, it is imperative to understand its implications for a potential victim of sexual assault. Thus, the second goal of this chapter is to address that issue by setting forth clinically derived recommendations for alternative resistive responses based upon the presumptive psychological and motivational themes underlying four subgroups of rapists.

METHODS

SUBJECTS

The Massachusetts Treatment Center was established in 1959, under Chapter 123A of the Massachusetts General Laws, for the evaluation and treatment of persons defined by laws as sexually dangerous. This law provides that a person found guilty of a sexual offense can, if he is judged to be sexually dangerous, be committed to the Massachusetts Treatment Center for one day to life under a civil commitment.

Since the establishment of the Massachusetts Treatment Center, over 6,000 sexual offenders have been screened. Of these, approximately 1,500 were judged possibly dangerous and were referred to the center for an intensive 60-day examination. Of the 1,500 men evaluated, approximately 500 have been committed. Of these patients, 270 have been released after varying lengths of treatment, leaving a current population of about 230. Of the present population of 230, 108 are rapists. For the purposes of this report, the term rapist will refer to an adult male whose sexual offenses were committed against adult women (i.e., 16 years of age or older).[1]

This sample of 108 individuals is a select subset of men convicted of sexual assault in Massachusetts and consists primarily of offenders whose offenses were repetitive and/or violent. The average age at commitment for this sample was 27.12 (SD = 8.08), and the average age at present is 32.47 (SD = 9.07). Racially, 81.3% of the sample is Caucasian and 18.7% is nonwhite (black, Hispanic, or native American). The average full-scale IQ for the sample is 100.76, and the average number of years completed in school is 9.39 (SD = 1.89). The average achieved skill level, on a scale of 0 (unskilled) to 6 (professional), is 1.39.

As adolescents, 48% of the men had criminal histories, and 20% had psychiatric histories. As adults, 94% had criminal histories, and 64% had psychiatric histories prior to Massachusetts Treatment Center commitment. The average number of adult serious sexual offenses (i.e., physical contact with victim) for this sample is 2.98, and the average number of juvenile serious sexual offenses is 0.64. A detailed description of this sample may be found in Bard et al. (1985).

TABLE 8.1
VICTIM CHARACTERISTICS (% PRESENT)

Variables	Compensatory (N=173)	Rapist Type Exploitative (N-133)	Displaced-Anger (N=46)	Sadistic (N=37)	X2	df
Relationship to offender						
Stranger	82.1	62.0	70.0	41.9	49.14**	21
Close friend/family	3.2	8.0	2.5	19.4		
Married	19.5	10.4	9.7	28.0	14.09*	9
Race (nonwhite)	3.2	8.0	2.4	2.9	4.38	3
Gender (male)	1.0	0.3	0.3	0.5	3.13	3
Age						
1–10	4.2	7.7	2.5	10.7	15.77	15
41 or older	3.4	5.8	15.0	10.7		
Use of alcohol/drugs at time						
of offense	11.3	36.9	3.8	26.3	18.04**	3

$*p < .10.$ $**p < .001.$

The 389 subjects discussed in this chapter are all surviving victims of the sample of 108 rapists for whom detailed offense-related information was available.[2] (Characteristics of the victim sample are presented in table 8.1.) The primary data source was the offender's clinical file, containing multiple sources of criminal information (e.g., police reports, official versions of each offense, court testimony, parole summaries, and probation records). Access to original reports helped to counteract the retrospective biases inherent in file research that is based largely on archival data (i.e., data that are recorded after events of particular importance have already taken place). Up to 100 variables were coded for each offense, including specific acts committed by the offender on the victim, injuries sustained by the victim, acts performed by the victim on the offender, and victim characteristics.

To maximize the accuracy of the coded information, two trained research assistants, blind to hypothesized relationships among variables under study, encoded data from each file and then met to resolve all discrepancies through a consensus procedure. The consensus codings served as the basis for all analyses. A detailed explanation of the data collection procedure and interrater reliabilities may be found elsewhere (Bard et al. 1985, Knight et al. 1983).

This sample of 108 offenders who were committed to the Massachusetts Treatment Center is a select subset of men convicted of rape in Massachusetts and consists primarily of individuals whose offenses were repetitive (i.e., multiple convictions) and/or violent. Consequently, an important empirical question, as well as a caveat, is the generalizability of this sample to other samples of rapists. Clinical experience, however, derives from a much broader and less selective sample. Over 700 rapists have been evaluated for a period of 60 days; of these only about 230, or one-third, were committed. The remaining two-thirds, deemed not suited for commitment, were returned to the penal system.

Analyses were performed after researchers collapsed data across all victims of rapists representing each of the four subtypes described in this chapter.[3] Thus, the four groups include 173 victims of compensatory rapists, 133 victims of exploitative rapists, 46 victims of displaced-anger rapists, and 37 victims of sadistic rapists.

Victims using combative resistance at any time during the offense (e.g., scratching, kicking, biting, punching, etc.) were compared with victims who did not or could not resist the rapist physically. The two groups were compared with respect to physical injuries sustained by the victim and the use of expressive or gratuitous aggression by the rapist before or during the offense and after the sexual act. The term expressive refers to the aggression stemming from the offender's uncontrollable rage, anger, or need to control the victim.

Expressive aggression is typically evidenced by the use of force far beyond what is necessary to gain victim compliance. While the variable was coded on a scale from 0 (none) to 7 (victim killed or mutilated), it will be reported in tabular form as four points. These four points are: 0 (no expressive aggression), 1 (aggressive verbalizations only), 2–3 (physical, nonbrutal aggression, such as holding, pushing, squeezing, slapping, or pinching), and 4–7 (brutal aggression resulting in long-term or permanent physical injury, ranging from bruises, cuts, and black eyes to mutilation).

CLASSIFICATION PROCEDURE AND RELIABILITY

The subtypes discussed in this chapter derive from a formal taxonomic system developed for the classification of rapists at the Massachusetts Treatment Center (Cohen, Seghorn, and Calmas 1969; Cohen et al. 1971; Prentky, Cohen, and Seghorn 1985; Seghorn and Cohen 1980). Classifications were made in the following manner. The lengthy clinical files were condensed into research files, which included diagnostic and evaluative information, school and employment reports, police reports and court testimony, parole summaries, probation records, social service notes, past institutionalization records, and complete Massachusetts Treatment Center records on familial and developmental history. The research files were read and subtyped independently by two senior clinicians familiar with the subject population. When there was disagreement in primary subtype, the raters met to resolve discrepancies and reach consensus. In the event that discrepancies could not be resolved, a third clinician made an independent rating. If this third judgment failed to promote a consensus of agreement, the case was omitted. This occurred in 8 of 108 cases. In all other cases (95%), consensus was obtained. Interrater reliability on the *initial* pair or ratings prior to consensus is as follows: compensatory (n = 38) = .63; exploitative (n = 31) = .76; displaced anger (n = 25) = .60; and sadistic (n = 14) = .67. A detailed discussion of the reliability of the taxonomy is provided elsewhere by Prentky, Cohen, and Seghorn (1985).

MASSACHUSETTS *
TREATMENT CENTER TAXONOMY

A recent report by Prentky, Cohen, and Seghorn (1985) discusses the latest contribution in an ongoing effort to create a taxonomic system for the classification of rapists. A primary consideration in the development of the Massachusetts Treatment Center classification system concerned the interaction of sexual and aggressive motivations. Although all rape clearly includes both motivations, for some rapists the need to humiliate and injure through aggression is the most salient feature of the offense, while for others the need to achieve sexual dominance is the most prominent feature. It is not possible in the context of this chapter to present, in full, the Massachusetts Treatment Center's taxonomy. Rather, we discuss, in abbreviated fashion, four of the subcategories of rapists. The following descriptions are clinical prototypes and represent the most commonly discussed rape categories in the literature. Specific features of these types will undoubtedly change as they are subjected to ongoing empirical analysis.

For the *compensatory rapist*, the assault is primarily an expression of rape fantasies. There is usually present a history of sexual preoccupation typified by the living out or fantasizing of a variety of perversions, including bizarre masturbatory practices, voyeurism, exhibitionism, obscene telephone calls, cross-dressing, and fetishism. There is often high sexual arousal accompanied by a loss of self-control, causing a distorted perception of the victim/offender relationship (e.g., the rapist may want the victim to respond in a sexual or erotic manner and may try to make a "date" after the assault).

In sum, this is an individual who is "compensating" for acutely felt inadequacies as a male. The core of his fantasy is that the victim will enjoy the experience and perhaps even fall in love with him. The motivation derives from the rapist's belief that he is so inadequate that no woman in her right mind would voluntarily have sex with him. This individual has been described by Guttmacher and Weihofen (1952) as the true sex offender, has subsequently been discussed by other researchers (Kopp 1962, Groth, Burgess, and Holmstrom 1977; Prentky, Cohen, and Seghorn 1985), and is similar to the tentative rapist noted by Brodsky (1976).

For the *exploitative rapist*, sexual behavior is expressed as an impulsive, predatory act. The sexual component is less integrated in fantasy life and has far less psychological meaning for the offender. For this individual,the rape is an impulsive act determined more by situation and context than by conscious fantasy. The assault can best be described and understood as a man "on the prowl," looking for a woman to exploit sexually. The offender's intent is to force the victim to submit sexually, and hence he is not concerned about the victim's welfare.

In some cases, these are poorly socialized, generally antisocial people whose motive to rape tends to surface spontaneously (e.g., while driving down a dimly lit, deserted street and noticing a woman walking toward her car). These assaults often occur within some context (e.g., leaving a party or bar after a number of drinks in the company of a newly acquired female friend with the intention of "going for a walk").

These rapists may also *appear* highly socialized, or at least of high social competence. They tend to be men who cannot believe that a woman could (or should) mean to refuse them sexually. Their sense of sexual entitlement is so high that sexual refusal is an incomprehensible response and is interpreted as a variant of a cat-and-mouse game (e.g., "catch me if you can") or as a necessary response by the victim in order to preserve her image as proper. Most date rape falls into this category.

This offender is the most frequently described subtype of rapist in both the clinical and popular literature. Astor (1975); Brownmiller (1975); Cohen, Seghorn,and Calmas (1969); Gebhard et al. (1965); Groth, Burgess, and Holmstrom (1977); Guttmacher and Weihofen (1952); Kopp (1962); Prentky, Cohen, and Seghorn (1985); Rada (1978); and Scully and Marolla (1985) have all described such an individual.

For the *displaced anger rapist*, sexual behavior is an expression of anger and rage. Sexuality is in the service of a primary, aggressive aim, with the victim representing the hated individual(s). While the offense may reflect a cumulative series of experienced or imagined insults from many people (e.g., family members, wife, or girlfriends), it is important to note that there need not be any historical truth to these perceived injustices. This individual is a misogynist; hence, the aggression may span a range from verbal abuse to brutal murder. Although a sexual impetus (feeling, thought, fantasy, etc.) seems to be a catalyst for the aggression, there does not appear to be a sexual meaning in the assault itself. Sex is used only as a means of humiliating the victim.

In sum, the most distinctive feature of this offender is his persistent and frequently overwhelming anger and negative attitude toward women. This attitude, as well as aggressive and hostile behavior toward women, existed in the life of this offender long before the rape occurred. The rape of women is much more than a predatory act; it is behavior that is activated, sustained, and justified by such an attitude. The displaced-anger rapist is a seldom-identified subtype in the literature, having been described by Cohen, Seghorn, and Calmas (1969); Groth, Burgess, and Holmstrom (1977); and Prentky, Cohen, and Seghorn (1985).

For the *sadistic rapist*, sexual behavior is an expression of sexual-aggressive (sadistic) fantasies. It appears as if there is a fusion or synergism between sexual and aggressive feelings. As sexual arousal increases, aggressive feelings increase and, similarly, increases in aggressive feelings heighten sexual arousal. Anger is not always apparent, particularly at the outset, when the assault may begin as a seduction. The anger may begin to emerge as the offender becomes sexually aroused, often resulting in the most bizarre and intense forms of sexual-aggressive violence. Unlike the displaced anger rapist, the sadist's violence is usually directed at parts of the body having sexual significance (i.e., breasts, anus, buttocks, genitalia, or mouth).

Despite all evidence to the contrary, the offender often experiences the victim as an active participant in the assault. That is, the victim's efforts to defend herself are perceived as part of her own sexual-aggressive fantasy life, hence this offender's belief that the more the victim resists, the more she really wants the rape to occur. Often the feelings of rage are activated or intensified in the offender when the victim, out of abject fear or helpless submission, becomes passive or otherwise unresponsive. Sadomasochistic fantasies consume such men for many years and are lived out in neutralized ways (e.g., bondage, feigned pain, and other ritualistic but noninjurious sadistic acts) with presumably consenting women before the violent, sadistic rapes occur.

Sadism is highest in profile due to its bizarre and sensational nature but is lowest in actual incidence. Sadistically motivated rape has been described by Becker and Abel (1978); Bromberg and Coyle (1974); Cohen, Seghorn, and Calmas (1969); Gebhard et al. (1965); Guttmacher and Weihofen (1952); Groth, Burgess, and Holmstrom (1977); Prentky, Cohen, and Seghorn (1985); Rada (1978); Ressler (1985); and Scully and Marolla (1985).

RESULTS

Overall, the victim sample may be characterized as Caucasian, single, female, and between the ages of 20 and 40. There are, however, some noteworthy subtype differences (see table 8.1). Victims of sadistic rapists were more often married than were victims of displaced-anger and exploitative rapists (28%, 10.4%, and 9.7%, respectively). There is a tendency for victims of sadistic rapists to span a wider age range and for victims of displaced-anger rapists to be somewhat older. This latter finding is consistent with theoretical expectation (Prentky, Cohen, and Seghorn 1985) and is, if anything, smaller in magnitude than predicted. Over one-third (37%) of the victims of exploitative rapists were using alcohol or drugs at the time of the assault, which undoubtedly reflects the situational and contextual nature of those offenses.

These data support the conclusion that most victims are strangers to their attackers. Collapsing data across subtype, we found that 70% of the victims were strangers to the offenders. There were, however, significant subtype differences: 82% of the victims of compensatory rapists were strangers, compared with 42% of the victims of sadistic rapists. Furthermore, 19% of the victims of sadistic rapists were close friends or family members, compared with only 2–3% of the victims of compensatory or displaced-anger rapists.

The amount of expressive aggression before or during the offense was examined in relation to the presence or absence of combative resistance on the part of the victim (see table 8.2).[4] For all rapist types, there was a higher incidence of brutal aggression associated with combative resistance than with noncombative resistance. Only for the exploitative rapists did this difference in the use of brutal aggression not reach significance. Among compensatory rapists, brutal force was associated with 30% of those victims who resisted combatively and 5.4% of those victims who did not. Among displaced-anger rapists, brutal force was associated with 84.7% of those victims who resisted combatively and 18.2% of those victims who did not. Among sadistic rapists, brutal force was associated with 80% of those victims who resisted combatively and 20% of those victims who did not. Finally, among exploitative rapists, brutal force was associated with 62.6% of the victims who resisted combatively and 26.3% of those victims who did not.

Conversely, there is evidence relating nonbrutal physical aggression with noncombative resistance, particularly among the most violent offenders (i.e., displaced-anger and sadistic rapists). Among displaced-anger rapists, nonbrutal force was associated with 15.3% of the victims who resisted combatively and 54.6% of those victims who did not. Among

TABLE 8.2
VICTIM RESPONSE ASSOCIATED WITH EXPRESSIVE AGGRESSION
BEFORE OR DURING OFFENSE (% PRESENT)

Expressive Aggression by Offender	Rapist Type							
	Compensatory		Exploitative		Displaced-Anger		Sadistic	
	C	NC	C	NC	C	NC	C	NC
None	3.3	17.6	0	0	0	18.2	0	20.0
Nonphysical-verbal	6.7	14.9	6.3	15.8	0	9.0	0	0
Physical-nonbrutal	59.9	62.2	31.3	57.9	15.3	54.6	20.0	60.0
Physical-brutal	30.0	5.4	62.6	26.3	84.7	18.2	80.0	20.0
X^2 (df = 3)	29.22***		9.24*		13.46**		15.00**	

Notes: C = Combative resistance by victim.   NC = No combative resistance by victim.
*p < .10.   **p < .005.   ***p < .001.

TABLE 8.3
VICTIM RESPONSE ASSOCIATED WITH EXPRESSIVE AGGRESSION
AFTER SEXUAL ACT (% PRESENT)

Expressive Aggression by Offender	Rapist Type							
	Compensatory		Exploitative		Displaced-Anger		Sadistic	
	C	NC	C	NC	C	NC	C	NC
None	77.5	89.2	68.5	75.0	71.4	90.9	70.0	100
Nonphysical-verbal	9.7	5.4	6.3	7.5	7.2	0	20.0	0
Physical-nonbrutal	6.4	2.7	18.9	15.0	0	9.1	0	0
Physical-brutal	6.4	2.7	6.3	2.5	21.4	0	10.0	0
X^2 (df = 3)	6.57*		6.35*		4.71		2.22	

Notes: C = Combative resistance by victim.   NC = No combative resistance by victim.
*p < .10.

sadistic rapists, nonbrutal force was associated with 20% of the victims who resisted combatively and 60% of those victims who did not.

The amount of expressive aggression after the sexual act was also examined in relation to victim resistance (see table 8.3). There was an inappreciable amount of expressive aggression after the sexual act among compensatory rapists. Among exploitative rapists, between 15% and 19% of the victims were subjected to nonbrutal expressive aggression after the sexual act; however, there was no significant association with victim resistance. Among the more violent offenders, there were nonsignificant associations between expressive aggression and combative resistance. Among displaced-anger rapists, some forms of expressive aggression were associated with 28.6% of those victims who resisted combatively and 9.1% of those victims who did not. Among that same group, brutal aggression was associated with 21.4% of those victims who resisted combatively and none of those victims who did not. A similar pattern was observed among the sadistic rapists, with some form of expressive aggression being associated with 30% of those victims who resisted combatively and none of those victims who did not. It should be pointed out that, overall, there was a very low incidence of expressive aggression after the sexual act (averaging around 20%). Thus, the cell sizes for these comparisons were quite small, rendering the results interpretable at no more than a descriptive level.

The association between victim resistance and physical injury also was examined (see table 8.4).[5, 6] Significantly more combative victims of compensatory rapists had medical problems requiring a physician and suffered cuts, bruises, and abrasions. In addition, significantly more of those same victims were rendered unconscious. There were no significant differences in physical injury between exploitative rapists' victims who did and did not combatively resist. Among victims of displaced-anger rapists, those who combatively resisted were rendered unconscious significantly more often than those who did not so resist. There was also a nonsignificant tendency ($p < .10$) for more of those same victims who combatively resisted to have cuts, bruises, and abrasions. Significantly more combative victims of sadistic rapists had medical problems as well as cuts, bruises, and abrasions. Although the finding is not significant, one-third of the combative victims of sadistic rapists were rendered unconscious as compared with none of the noncombative victims.

TABLE 8.4
Victim Response Associated with Physical Injury (% present)

Expressive Aggression by Offender[a]	Rapist Type											
	Compensatory			Exploitative			Displaced-Anger			Sadistic		
	C	NC	X²	C	NC	X²	C	NC	X²	C	NC	X²
Medical problems requiring a physician	21.7	3.5	6.82***	40.0	25.0	0.81	80.0	40.0	2.39	100	20.0	6.46**
Cuts, bruises, and abrasions	93.8	30.0	18.60****	100	81.8	2.28	100	75.0	3.27*	100	20.0	10.94****
Unconscious	9.7	0	7.66***	6.3	2.4	0.52	30.8	0	4.06**	33.3	0	2.50

Notes: C = Combative resistance by victim.   NC = No combative resistance by victim.
[a]Dichotomous; $df = 1$.   *$p < .10$.   **$p < .05$.   ***$p < .01$.   ****$p < .001$.

DISCUSSION OF FINDINGS

One of the assumptions about rape is the notion that offenders are always strangers to victims (Gelles 1977; Medea and Thompson 1974; Nadelson, Notman, and Hilberman 1980). However, Katz and Mazur (1979) report that the incidence of stranger rape in 18 studies ranged from 27% to 91%, undoubtedly reflecting the wide variation in offenders that were sampled in those studies. Russell's (1984) random sample of 930 women revealed that 44% had been subjected to rape or attempted rape, though only 8% (of the entire sample) had been victimized by a husband. Were it possible to draw any consensus from the literature, it may be tentatively concluded that about two-thirds of adult victims are raped by strangers (Brodyaga et al. 1975; Katz and Mazur 1979).[7]

That statistic is supported by our study, with one important exception. There is evidence that the relationship of offender to victim may, to some extent, be dictated by the type of rapist. In our study, 82% of the victims of compensatory rapists were strangers (and 3% were close friends of the family), while 42% of the victims of sadistic rapists were strangers (and 19% were close friends or family). This finding lends support to hypotheses regarding motives underlying compensatory and sadistic rape. The compensatory rapist is hypothesized to be afraid of familiar women for fear of ridicule and thus is less likely to assault anyone that he knows. The sadistic rapist is more likely to assault a friend or recent acquaintance because he believes, in projective fashion, that the victim derives the same pleasurable experience from the assault that he does.

Another finding in this study is the apparent differential importance of victim alcohol use across rapist types. Over one-third of the victims of exploitative rapists had been drinking at the time of the offense, compared with only 4% of the victims of displaced-anger rapists and 11% of the victims of compensatory rapists. While these figures are unremarkable according to the National Commission on the Causes and Prevention of Violence (Eisenhower 1969), the significantly greater incidence of alcohol use among victims of exploitative rapists does suggest the contextual nature of those offenses (e.g., initial contact being made at a social gathering or in a bar) and supports the hypothesis that such rapes are often impulsive, predatory, and determined more by situational and immediate antecedent factors than by preexisting fantasy.

The reported incidence of physical injury among rape victims varied widely, again underscoring the heterogeneity of sexually assaultive behavior as well as numerous methodologic inconsistencies. The Center for Women Policy Studies found that approximately 63% of rape victims suffered some physical injury (Brodyaga et al. 1975). Schiff (1969) reports that 38% of the victims in his study suffered physical injuries, while Selkin (1975) found that less than 9% of the victims in his study suffered more than cuts and bruises. Burgess and Holmstrom (1974) examined the recorded signs of trauma from the medical records of 146 victims, noting that the symptoms of trauma were considerably higher than the documented evidence of physical injury would suggest. Over half the victims in the Burgess and Holmstrom study had at least one visible bruise or abrasion.

Our study found a much higher incidence of physical injury than generally has been reported in the literature, though these figures represent, of course, the end of a continuum of sexual violence. Most important, serious physical injury (e.g., resulting in unconsciousness) was associated with combative resistance on the part of the victim. As we have emphasized previously, this is *not* a causal relationship. We are reporting preliminary evidence for a correlative relationship. Group differences (combative vs. noncombative resistance) for victims of compensatory, displaced-anger, and sadistic rapists are marked, however, and clearly warrant further scrutiny.

It is noteworthy that there were no significant group differences for the victims of exploitative rapists. Whether or not the victim combatively resisted was unrelated to physical injury. This finding is especially important because it supports the results of earlier studies that found no association between physical injury and combative resistance (Bart and O'Brien 1984; Queen's Bench Foundation 1976; Sanders 1980). It is reasonable to speculate that the group of rapists classified in this study as exploitative represent the largest relatively homogeneous category of adult sexual offenders, perhaps as large as 50%. We hasten to add, however, that the exploitative group reflects the beginning of taxonomic analysis, not the end. There are critical sources of variance within this group that have yet to be accounted for, necessitating a more refined classification system. One step in the evolution of such a system was presented by Prentky, Cohen, and Seghorn (1985), although that system continues to be revised through an ongoing process of empirical and clinical examination (Prentky and Knight 1986, 1987; Rosenberg et al. 1986).

CLINICAL OBSERVATIONS OF VICTIM RESPONSE

While we cannot infer causality from the correlative data presented here (i.e., it cannot be ascertained whether a victim's combative response precipitated or contributed to an increase in violence or was a reaction to violence), the data strongly suggest that it is important to explore strategies that are viable alternatives to physical combativeness, particularly in situations where such resistance proves to be ineffective and may increase the risk of serious injury or even death. Knowledge of alternative strategies may serve to enhance the effectiveness of resistance.

The following discussion is an attempt to provide an overview of possible strategies for resisting rape. The observations and conclusions derive from our joint clinical experience, including extensive contact with victims and offenders as well as the detailed evaluation of more than 300 offender files. This experience allows us to observe a large number of effective and ineffective responses to rape, sometimes with the same offender. While there is a conceptual and clinical foundation for the recommendations that follow, there is, at present, little supportive empirical evidence.

RESPONSE STRATEGIES DEFINED

Studies have examined coping behaviors of victims (e.g., Burgess and Holmstrom 1976, 1979), strategies of rape avoiders and rape victims (e.g., Bart and O'Brien 1984) and victim behavior signaling vulnerability (e.g., Grayson and Stein 1981). Analysis of the various strategies defined in the literature, combined with our clinical experience with both convicted offenders and rape victims, allows us to define a typology of response strategies as follows: escape, verbally confrontative resistance, physically confrontative resistance, nonconfrontative verbal response, nonconfrontative physical resistance, and acquiescence.

ESCAPE We emphasize that escaping the assailant is always the optimum response *when it can be employed successfully.* However deciding whether an escape attempt will be successful is very difficult. If the victim is alone in the woods with nowhere to run or is assaulted by multiple offenders, escape attempts may not only be unsuccessful, but may also be hazardous. If weapons have been brandished, the possible consequences of attempting to escape—and being caught—may make it not worth the risk. If the offender appears to be young and athletic, the probability of a successful escape diminishes.

In general, in a city or urban location, if there are no weapons, if there are other people somewhere in the vicinity, and if there are no encumbrances (i.e., no clothes tied or tangled around the ankles), the probability of successful flight will be increased. Caution must be exercised, however. There is a small percent of individuals (i.e., sadists) for whom unsuccessful flight may only serve to increase arousal and, in so doing, increase the brutality of the attack.

VERBALLY CONFRONTATIVE RESISTANCE   This strategy includes screaming or yelling (e.g., "Leave me alone! Get away.") as a means of attracting attention or asserting oneself against victimization. These verbal responses are strictly confrontative and are intended to convey the message at the outset of the assault that the victim will not acquiesce.

PHYSICALLY CONFRONTATIVE RESISTANCE   Confrontative physical resistance ranges from moderate responses (e.g., fighting, struggling, punching, or kicking) to violent responses (e.g., attacking highly vulnerable areas—face, throat, groin—with lethal intention). These responses are dictated by many critical situational factors such as the location of the assault, the presence of a weapon, the likelihood of help, the size and strength of the offender, and the degree of violence of the assault. When employed successfully, such responses often occur quickly and make use of surprise. The victim can expect that in many cases physical resistance will be met with increased aggression.

NONCONFRONTATIVE VERBAL RESPONSES   These responses are intended to dissuade the attacker (e.g., "I'm a virgin." or "I have my period or cramps."), create empathy (i.e., engaging the offender in conversation and listening and attempting to respond in an understanding way), inject reality (e.g., "I am frightened.") or negotiate (e.g., "Let's talk about this." or "Let's go have a beer.") to stall for time and devise another strategy (e.g., set the stage for an escape). Talking tends to be the safest and most reliable means of reducing the degree of violence (once it is determined that the offender is intending to use violence), though it may not be effective in stopping the assault completely.

In general, nonconfrontative dissuasive techniques do not work (McIntyre, Myint, and Curtis 1979). In the heat of an attack, most rapists will not be concerned about the victim's menstrual cramps or virginity if, in fact, they even believe her. Victims should avoid such references as "I have VD" or "I'm pregnant," as such statements may support the offender's pathological fantasy that the victim is "bad" or promiscuous and thus deserves to be raped. Also threats of reprisal (e.g., "You will be caught and go to jail.") should be avoided.

The safest way to engage the assailant through dialogue is for the victim to appeal to his humanity by making herself a real person and by focusing on the immediate situation (e.g., "I'm a total stranger. Why do you want to hurt me? I've never done anything to hurt you." or "What if I were someone you cared about? How would you feel about that?" and not "This is going to ruin my life."). The attacker can easily dismiss what may happen sometime in the future. He cannot as easily dismiss what the victim is telling him is happening right now. The victim should avoid asking "What if I was your daughter or sister?" because she will not know what meaning such an individual has for the offender.

NONCONFRONTATIVE PHYSICAL RESISTANCE   This technique involves active resistance that does not actually confront the attacker (as in the case of physical confrontation). Nonconfrontative physical responses may be feigned or quite real and uncontrollable. Feigned responses might include fainting, gagging, sickness, or seizure. Uncontrollable or involuntary responses may include crying, gagging, nausea, and loss of sphincter control. In general, these responses may work on occasion, but they are highly idiosyncratic and thus are not reliable. In one important situation (with a displaced-anger rapist), this strategy could be dangerous.

ACQUIESCENCE   Acquiescence implies no counteractive response (offensive or defensive) to thwart the attack. The victim might say something to the effect of "Don't hurt me and I'll do what you want." Acquiescence is often the result of paralyzing fear, abject terror, or a belief that such a response is necessary to save one's life. In most cases, acquiescence need only be a last resort when attempts to stop the attack have failed. Acquiescence may be interpreted by the offender as participation and exacerbate the intensity of the attack.

In general, the decision to submit or acquiesce to an attacker is a difficult one, determined as much by the violence of the assault as by the victim's emotional state and specific fears (e.g., death or rape). Some women will be able to cope much better than others with the knowledge that they submitted. Acquiescence can invoke, in some victims, postassault rage and/or guilt, while other victims may be able to accept and feel comfortable with whatever actions they felt were necessary to survive the assault with a minimum of physical and emotional injury. If, after other strategies have failed, acquiescence is deemed to be the optimum response to protect life and reduce physical injury in a given situation, it is important that the victim be comfortable with such a choice and be aware that postassault guilt feelings will probably arise.

We operate on the assumption that aggression begets aggression. When the amount of rage and aggression obviously exceed what is necessary to force compliance, a violent confrontative response on the part of the victim will generally increase the violence in the assault and place the victim at increased risk for serious physical injury. Gratuitous violence on the part of the rapist places the victim in dangerous, volatile, and unpredictable situations. For that reason, we recommend that the *first* response to violence *not* be violent. If direct dialogue does not begin to neutralize the attacker (i.e., reduce the intensity of the aggression), then the victim will have no recourse but to employ any means available to protect herself and, if necessary, disable the attacker. The foregoing statements are predicated on the assumption that the *most* important outcome of a sexual assault is for the victim to emerge with the fewest emotional and physical scars. Any actions that may increase the violence will tend to undermine that outcome.

RESPONSE STRATEGIES AND RAPIST TYPE

There are four basic responses that we recommend in sexual assault situations and they should generally be used in the following order: verbal confrontation, physical confrontation, nonconfrontative verbal responses, and finally violent confrontation. However, when it seems appropriate to move to nonconfrontative verbal responses, those responses can be tailored to the type of rapist committing the assault (see figure 8.1).[8]

We do *not* expect women to memorize and have immediate access to a complex decision diagram for responding in sexually dangerous situations. Instead, we simply illustrate the adaptation of the victim's response to the offender's behavior. The first response should be one of firm resistance: first verbal, and, if necessary, physical resistance. At that point, however, it is imperative that the victim begin adapting her responses to what she is experiencing

In all cases, if the victim cannot easily escape, firm, confrontative, verbal resistance should be the first response. This verbal resistance alone will be successful in deterring some of the *compensatory rapists*. For these offenders, the victim represents a fantasy object, with the assault fantasized as a fulfilling experience for himself as well as for the victim. Thus, the victim is a potential friend, lover, and mate. The intention is not to hurt the victim. As our data suggest, this rapist type is most likely to be repelled by confrontative resistance and least likely to attempt to injure the victim.

If the attacker remains after verbal confrontation and threatens with a weapon or immediately uses violent force, the victim should respond using verbal dissuasion in an attempt to reduce the attacker's anger and aggression. The objective of this response is to break the confrontation, reduce the tension, and initiate conversation. The victim should try to make herself real rather than a sexualized object. Once the violence ceases, the victim should try to set the stage for escape (e.g., attempt to manipulate the attacker into going to a more populated area).

If the offender does not verbally demean or humiliate the victim and if his behavior or verbalizations are not bizarre or peculiar, it is likely that he is an *exploitative rapist*. For this rapist the victim is viewed as a sexual

FIGURE 8.1
Victim Response Strategies

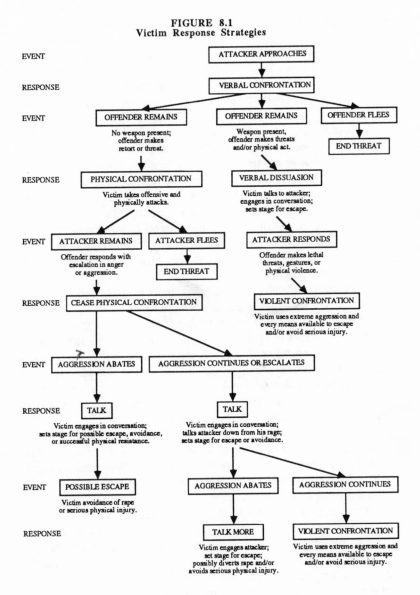

object. The offender believes that he is entitled to sex under any condition, and hence has a callous indifference to the comfort or welfare of the victim. Both verbal resistance and nonconfrontative resistance strategies are appropriate. Once it has been demonstrated that the rapist will likely use whatever force necessary to gain victim compliance, confrontative physical resistance would be unwise unless the victim is confident that it will work. The best strategy, then, is to encourage the rapist to start talking about himself (playing on his narcissism) so that the victim becomes real rather than a sexualized object. Nonconfrontative physical strategies may also work, but they tend to be unreliable and are highly indiosyncratic to the individual rapist. As noted earlier, some of these responses (e.g., crying, nausea, gagging) may be involuntary, in which case the victim may have to overcome the response if it is aggravating the situation.

Many exploitative rapists will certainly be given a moment's pause if the victim appears undaunted and immediately says "You what? Here? Now? Come on, let's sit down here and talk." While admittedly this requires extraordinary presence of mind on the part of the victim, it has the advantage of momentarily catching the rapist off guard. It may not avoid the rape, but it might decrease the amount of physical injury that could result from the assault as well as give the victim time to assess options and set the stage for possible escape.

If the victim is unable to engage the offender in conversation, and the physical attack continues, escalates, or appears to be lethal, the victim should fight with every means available (attack eyes or groin, hit the offender with a rock or stick, etc.) to escape and/or avoid serious injury.

If the assaulter remains after verbal confrontation, has no weapon, and responds with threats or retorts, the victim should immediately resist physically by punching, hitting, kicking, etc. Such physically confrontative resistance is often successful with compensatory rapists and is sometimes successful with exploitative rapists.

If the attacker responds to victim physical confrontation with increased anger and/or violence, the victim should cease physical resistance. If he responds by immediately ceasing his aggressive/violent behavior and is willing to engage the victim in conversation, he is also likely to be an exploitative rapist and the victim should use verbal strategies.

If the attacker continues to escalate aggression/violence, the victim should attempt to begin verbal dissuasive techniques. Again, the object is to break the confrontation, reduce tension, and defuse the violence. If verbal dissuasion is unsuccessful and the violence continues in spite of the victim's attempts, the victim again must do anything to get out of the situation. If verbal dissuasion is successful and the violence seems to diminish, those same responses should be continued, with specific statements tailored to what the rapist is saying.

For the *displaced-anger rapist*, the victim is a substitute for and a symbol of the hated person(s) in his life. The primary motive is to hurt and injure the victim. Aggression may span a wide range from verbal abuse to brutal assault. Continued physical confrontation, unless the victim is reasonably certain that she will be able to incapacitate the attacker, may only justify in the offender's mind the need to "punish" the victim and thus escalate the violence.

In general, nonconfrontative responses are also not recommended. A displaced-anger rapist will not respond empathically to the victim's evident pain or discomfort. Such responses as nausea, gagging, or crying are evidence that the rapist is achieving the desired result. Moreover, acquiescence is not an appropriate response to this type of rapist. Because sexual intercourse is not this offender's primary motive, deterence of the rape will not be accomplished by acquiescing.

The recommended response to such a rapist is verbal, and the words must be carefully chosen. The victim must convince the offender that she is not the hated person (e.g., "It sounds like you're really angry at someone, but it can't be me. We've never even met before."). The victim should avoid statements that may justify the assault in the mind of the rapist. Challenging the fantasy is critical. Statements such as "How do you know that I'm a bitch? You've never met me before. We're strangers. I could be a nice person." may be along the lines of what is appropriate.

For the *sadistic rapist*, the victim is a partner who has been recruited to play out sexual-aggressive or sadistic fantasies. Needless to say, this rapist is an extremely dangerous individual. Because these assaults are brutal and can end with serious physical injury to the victim, it may be a matter of life and death to escape.

If escape is not possible, there are few recommendations we can make. If the victim acquiesces, the sadistic offender may perceive her as an active participant in the assault. This will function to increase his arousal and, hence, his anger. If the victim is physically confrontative, struggles, or otherwise seeks to protect herself, the rapist may also perceive her as an active participant, which also will increase his anger and arousal. Passivity or submission may also serve to intensify feelings of rage in the offender. Once the fused sexual-aggressive feelings are activated, sadists generally will not hear attempts at negotiation, empathy, or dissuasion. Finally, nonconfrontative physical resistance is not effective, as there is a high probability that these behaviors may also be interpreted as participation in the assault.

Because there are no reliably safe and effective responses, the victim must do *anything* necessary to get out of the situation. That may mean feigning participation and, at a critical moment, making maximum use of surprise, attacking the offender's vulnerable areas as viciously as possible. This requires the victim to convert fear into rage and a sense of helplessness into a battle for survival.

DECISION-MAKING PROCESS

We realize that most of our recommendations may be forgotten at the moment of panic when the victim is confronted by a would be rapist. The victim may not have the presence of mind—and perhaps not even the time—to evaluate different responses to rapist types. Believing, however, that knowledge brings an added sense of confidence to an unpredictable and volatile situation, we have tried to reduce much of the foregoing discussion to a systematic decision-making process (see figure 8.1).

The *first* response should always be to attempt to escape. If escape is not possible, the *second* response is firm verbal confrontation. If the attacker persists, there is no weapon present, and no physical violence is occurring, the victim should immediately initiate the *third* response: offensive physical confrontation. If the attacker flees, he probably is compensatory. If he does not flee and responds with physical aggression, the victim should start talking, keeping conversation in the present. The victim should attempt to reduce the aggression, talk the assailant down from his rage, and convey the message that she is a stranger, and that there are other ways to find a sex partner or express anger. The intent is to disrupt the fantasy and, in so doing, challenge the rapist's symbolic conceptualization of the victim.

If the response is positive (i.e., the offender stops, listens, or talks), the same course of action should be continued. If he pays no attention and persists in his attempts to force the victim to submit to sexual activity and if the amount of aggression does not extend beyond that force, the attacker is probably exploitative. The victim should persist in verbal attempts to make herself real by diverting the offender with questions about himself.

If there is a clear escalation in aggression, the victim should try to distinguish between a displaced and a sadistic motive. If the primary intent seems to be to humiliate and demean by word or deed, the offender is more likely to be a displaced-anger rapist. If none of this is present, and the rapist is making demands that are both eroticized and bizarre, then he is probably sadistic. With a displaced-anger rapist, the victim should keep conversation in the here and now and underscore the message that she has not abused him. Because these men have a history of perceived abuse by women, the victim should try to demonstrate some sense of interest, concern, or caring. If the victim determines that the individual is a sadist, she should use extreme violent confrontation and do whatever possible to escape. There is no single response that is likely to deter a sadistic assault, and because these assaults are potentially lethal, the victim must do *whatever* is in her power to survive the attack and attract help.

We have been discussing in the abstract what to do in a highly traumatic situation, and it may seem cavalier or even insensitive to suggest that a victim should perform a quick mental status exam as she is being assaulted. However, all rapes are *not* "blitz" assaults, and victims have often been noted to use multiple strategies over time until one works (Bart and O'Brien 1984). As an overview, as well as an attempt at simplification, the strategies that we have recommended can be briefly summarized as follows:

Step 1. *Firm verbal confrontation.* Firmly tell the attacker to get away and leave you alone.

If step 1 is unsuccessful:

Step 2. *Physical confrontation.* Immediately take the offensive and attack the assaulter with moderate physical aggression (hit, kick, punch, etc.).

If step 2 is unsuccessful:

Step 3: *Nonconfrontative verbal responses.* Attempt to calm the assaulter and talk him down from his rage. Engage him in conversation, and make yourself a real person to him. Challenge his fantasy that you are the person he wants to harm. Set the stage for an escape attempt (e.g., try to talk him into taking you to a more populated area: "Let's go have a drink" etc.).

If step 3 is unsuccessful in neutralizing the violence:

Step 4: *Violent confrontation.* Use extreme aggression, and take any action within your means (kick, punch, bite, strike with rock, etc.) to incapacitate the assaulter and avoid rape or mortal physical injury.

In sum, knowledge may be the only weapon a victim has in a highly dangerous situation. As such, knowledge can provide a sense of power, as well as the confidence necessary to *act* rather than resign out of helplessness.

Preparation of this manuscript was supported by the National Institute of Justice (82-IJ-CX-0058), the office of Juvenile Justice and Delinquency Prevention (84-JW-AX-K010), the National Institute of Mental Health (MH32309), and the Commonwealth of Massachusetts. The authors wish to gratefully acknowledge Murray Cohen, Lita Furby, Raymond Knight, Alison Martino, Peg Salamon, and Theoharis Seghorn for contributions to earlier drafts of this manuscript. They also acknowledge Lucy Berliner and Py Bateman for commentary on an earlier version of this manuscript.

NOTES

1. When this definition could not easily be applied, several additional guidelines were used. First, age discrepancy between offender and victims was examined, as well as the predominant ages of the victims and any victim-age trends that may have existed. Second, an attempt was made to determine from offense profiles whether the psychological meaning of the assault was more characteristic of rape (i.e., vaginal intercourse) or of child molestation (e.g., nongenital sexual acts such as fondling, caressing, and frottage). A serious sexual offense was defined as any sexually motivated assault involving physical contact with the victim and did not require any penetration by the offender. When victim selection appeared to be indiscriminate (i.e., men whose victims were both under and over the age of 16) the subject was excluded from the study. Nine such cases were identified.

2. Nine victims of homicide were excluded from the analyses because it would have been impossible to obtain reliable victim-response information.

3. Subtype assignments were based, in part, on a review of the offender's entire criminal history. Thus, all victims of a given offender, not just the victims associated with the commitment offense, were considered when making a classification. Obviously, there were instances in which a particular offense was not consistent with the subtype assigned (e.g., an offender classified as a displaced-anger rapist may have committed an offense that was predominantly exploitative). Such instances would, however, serve to decrease between-subtype differences, yielding a more conservative estimate.

4. We recognize that a chi-square distribution assumes N independent observations from a normal population, and that this assumption may be violated by collapsing data across multiple victims of the same offender. It was not possible to unconfound the victim offender relationship because many offenders had both combative and noncombative victims. While the chi-squares should be regarded with this caveat in mind, the variability of victims per offender was relatively small, and we do not believe that the stability of the analyses was seriously compromised.

5. It should be noted that we have not examined outcome in terms of completion of sexual assault, only in terms of physical injury. As Bateman (1986) clearly points out, recovery from the trauma of rape may be more difficult than recovery from physical injuries. We fully appreciate this point and intend to examine rape completion in subsequent analyses.

6. It should be noted that the chi-square values presented in table 4 are uncorrected. The Yates (1934) correction for continuity was applied (i.e., .5 was subtracted from the absolute value of each deviation in computing the chi-square in order to correct for bias in determining true probability levels) and significance was confirmed for all previously significant values except for the unconscious victims in the displaced-anger rapist category (corrected chi-square = 2.15, $p <$ .10). For five 2 x 2 contingency tables with a small cell size N (N = 20 or less), the Fisher exact probability test was used (Siegal 1956). Probability levels associated with the Fisher test are the following: for the displaced-anger rapist category, problems requiring a physician (.17), cuts, bruises, and abrasions (.16); for the sadistic rapist category, problems requiring a physician (.01), cuts, bruises, and abrasions (.004), and unconscious (.18).

7. One may reasonably speculate that *nature of relationship* and *degree of violence* are factors importantly related to conviction. That is, when the victim is unknown to the offender and/or when the assault is more physically violent, the probability of conviction increases. Were this speculation valid, the high rates of stranger rape reported in the literature might be spuriously inflated by conviction rates.

8. Our efforts to identify appropriate victim responses to specific subgroups of rapists must necessarily parallel our efforts to validate the classification system. The validity of the sex offender subtypes described here is presently under intensive scrutiny (Prentky, Cohen, and Seghorn 1985; Prentky and Knight, 1986, 1987; Rosenberg and Knight, 1987). As our conceptualization of a valid system for classifying rapists continues to come into focus, it will be necessary to reassess subtype-related victim responses. The recommendations presented here can be no more valid than the offender groups for which they were intended.

REFERENCES

Abarbanel, G. 1986. Rape and resistance. *Journal of Interpersonal Violence* 1: 100–05.

Astor, G. 1975. *The charge is rape*. Chicago: Playboy Press.

Bard, L.A., et al. 1987. A descriptive study of rapists and child molesters: Developmental, clinical and criminal characteristics. *Behavioral Sciences and the Law*. Forthcoming.

Bart, P.B. 1981. A study of women who both were raped and avoided rape. *Journal of Social Issues* 37: 147.

Bart, P.B., and P. O'Brien. 1984. Stopping rape: Effective avoidance strategies. *Signs: Journal of Women in Culture and Society* 10: 83–101.

Bateman, P. 1986. Let's get out from between the rock and the hard place. *Journal of Interpersonal Violence* 1: 105–11.

Becker, J.V., and G.G. Abel. 1978. Men and the victimization of women. In *Victimization of women,* ed. J.R. Chapman and M.R. Gates. Beverly Hills, Calif.: Sage Publications.

Brodsky, S. 1976. Prevention of rape: Deterrence by the potential victim. In *Sexual assault,* ed. M.J. Walker and S.L. Brodsky. Lexington, Mass.: Lexington Books.

Brodyaga, L., et al. 1975. *Rape and its victims: A report for citizens, health facilities, and criminal justice agencies.* Prepared for the National Institute of Law Enforcement and Criminal Justice, Law Enforcement Assistance Administration, Department of Justice. Washington, D.C.: U.S. Government Printing Office.

Bromberg, W., and E. Coyle. 1974. Rape! A compulsion to destroy. *Medical Insight,* April, 21–22, 24–25.

Brownmiller, S. 1975. *Against our will.* New York: Bantam Books.

Burgess, A.W., and L.L. Holmstrom. 1974. Rape trauma syndrome. *American Journal of Psychiatry* 131: 981–86.

———. 1976. Coping behavior of the rape victim. *American Journal of Psychiatry* 133: 413–18.

———. 1979. Adaptive strategies and recovery from rape. *American Journal of Psychiatry* 136: 1278–82.

Burnett, R., D. Templer, and P. Barker. 1985. Personality variables and circumstances of sexual assault predictive of a woman's resistance. *Archives of Sexual Behavior* 14: 183–88.

Chapman, J.R., and M. Gates, eds. 1978. The victimizations of women. In *Volume 3: Sage yearbooks in women's policy studies.* Beverly Hills, Calif.: Sage Publications.

Chappell, D., and F. Fogarty. 1978. *Forcible rape: A literature review and annotated bibliography.* Prepared for the National Institute of Law Enforcement and Criminal Justice, Law Enforcement Assistance Administration, Department of Justice. Washington, D.C.: U.S. Government Printing Office.

Chappell, D., and J. James. 1976. Victim selection and apprehension from the rapist perspective: A preliminary investigation. Paper presented at 2nd International Symposium on Victimology, September, Boston.

Cohen, M.L., T. Seghorn, and W. Calmas. 1969. Sociometric study of sex offenders. *Journal of Abnormal Psychology* 74: 249–55.

Cohen, M.L., et al. 1971. The psychology of rapists. *Seminars in Psychiatry* 3: 307–27.

Curtis, L.A. 1976. Toward a theory of response to rape: Some methodological considerations. In *Victims and society,* ed. E. Viano. Washington, D.C.: Visage Press.

Eisenhower, M.S. 1969. *To establish justice, to insure domestic tranquility*. Final report of the National Commission on Causes and Prevention of Violence. Washington, D.C.: U.S. Government Printing Office.

Federal Bureau of Investigation. 1984. *Crime in the United States. Uniform Crime Reports, 1983*. Washington, D.C.: U.S. Government Printing Office.

Gebhard, P.H., et al. 1965. *Sex offenders: An analysis of types*. New York: Harper and Row.

Gelles, R.J. 1977. Power, sex, and violence: The case of marital rape. *The Family Coordinator* 26: 339–47.

Gordon, M.T., and L. Heath. 1981. The news business, crime and fear. In *Reactions to crime*, ed. D.A. Lewis. Beverly Hills, Calif.: Sage Publications.

Grayson, R., and M.I. Stein. 1981. Attracting assault: Victims' nonverbal cues. *Journal of Communication* 31: 68–75.

Groth, A.N., A.W. Burgess, and L.L. Holmstrom. 1977. Rape: Power, anger, and sexuality. *American Journal of Psychiatry* 134: 1239–43.

Guttmacher, M.S., and H. Weihofen. 1952. *Psychiatry and the law*. New York: W.W. Norton.

Katz, S., and M.A. Mazur. 1979. *Understanding the rape victim: A synthesis of research findings*. New York: John Wiley and Sons.

Knight, R., R. Rosenberg, and B. Schneider. 1985. Classification of sexual offenders: Perspectives, methods and validation. In *Rape and sexual assault: A research handbook*, ed. A. Burgess. New York: Garland Publishing, Inc.

Knight, R., et al. 1983. Linear causal modeling of adaptation and criminal history in sexual offenders. In *Prospective studies of crime and delinquency*, ed. K.T. Van Dusen and S. Mednick. Boston: Kluwer–Nijhoff.

Kopp, S.B. 1962. The character structure of sex offenders. *American Journal of Psychotherapy* 16: 64–70.

Marsh, J.C., A. Geist, and N. Caplan. 1982. *Rape and the limits of law reform*. Boston, Mass.: Auburn House Publishing Co.

McCombie, S.L., ed. 1980. *The rape crisis intervention handbook: A guide for victim care*. New York: Plenum Press.

McIntyre, J.J., T. Myint, and L.A. Curtis. 1979. Sexual Assault: Alternative outcomes. Final report to the National Institute of Mental Health, Grant no. RO1 MH29045.

Medea, A., and K. Thompson. 1974. *Against rape*. New York: Farrar, Straus and Giroux.

Nadelson, C.C., M.T. Notman, and E. Hilberman. 1980. The rape experience. In *Modern legal medicine, psychiatry, and forensic science*, ed. W.J. Curran, A.L. McGarry, and C.S. Petty. Philadelphia: F.A. Davis Co.

National Center for the Prevention and Control of Rape. 1980. *1980 national directory of rape prevention and treatment resouces.* Rockville, Md.: National Institute of Mental Health.

Prentky, R.A., and R.A. Knight. 1986. Impulsivity in the lifestyle and criminal behavior of sexual offenders. *Criminal Justice and Behavior* 13: 141–64.

Prentky, R.A., and R.A. Knight. 1987. *Motivational components in a taxonomy for rapists: A validational analysis.* Typescript.

Prentky, R.A., M.L. Cohen, and T.K. Seghorn. 1985. Development of a rational taxonomy for the classification of sexual offenders: Rapists. *Bulletin of the American Academy of Psychiatry and the Law* 13: 39–70.

Queen's Bench Foundation. 1976. *Rape victimization study: Final report.* San Francisco: Queen's Bench Foundation.

Rada, R.T. 1978. *Clinical aspects of the rapist.* New York: Grune and Stratton.

Ressler, R.K. 1985. Violent crime. *FBI Law Enforcement Bulletin* 54(8): 10.

Rosenberg, R., and R.A. Knight. 1987. Determining male sexual offender subtypes using cluster analysis. Typescript.

Rosenberg, R., et al. 1986. *Validating the components of a taxonomic system for rapists: A path analytic approach.* Typescript.

Russell, D.E.H. 1984. *Sexual exploitation.* Beverly Hills: Sage Publications.

Russell, D.E.H., and N. Howell. 1983. The prevalence of rape in the United States revisited. *Signs: Journal of Women in Culture and Society* 8: 4.

Sanders, W.B. 1980. *Rape and women's identity.* Beverly Hills, Calif.: Sage Publications.

Schiff, A.F. 1969. Statistical features of rape. *Journal of Forensic Sciences* 14: 102–11.

Scully, D., and J. Marolla. 1985. "Riding the bull at Gilley's": Convicted rapists describe the rewards of rape. *Social Problems* 32: 251–63.

Seghorn, T., and M. Cohen. 1980. The psychology of the rape assailant. In *Modern legal medicine, psychiatry, and forensic science,* ed. W. Curran, A.L. McGarry, and C. Petty. Philadelphia: F.A. Davis Co.

Selkin, J. 1975. Rape: When to fight back. *Psychology Today,* January, 71–76.

Siegal, S. 1956. *Nonparametric statistics for the behavioral sciences.* New York: McGraw-Hill Book Co.

Warr, M. 1985. Fear of rape among urban women. *Social Problems* 32: 238–50.

Yates, F. 1934. Contingency tables involving small numbers and the chi-square test. Supplement to *Journal of Royal Statistical Society* 1: 217–35.

9

SEXUALIZED THERAPY
Causes and Consequences

ROBERTA APFEL
Harvard Medical School

BENNETT SIMON
Harvard Medical School

Overt sexual contact between patient and therapist is a disturbing strain of pathology in the psychotherapeutic process. In this chapter, we mean to examine this "disease" in its own right, but even more importantly, to learn about this abnormal manifestation of the normal. Our approach involves the use of two complementary pairs of conceptual terms. The first pair is Freud's concept of genitality and Erikson's concept of generativity. One can analyze overt sex between patient and therapist as a failure of genitality and/or as a failure of generativity. The second complementary pair involves the language of individual conflict and the language of social psychiatry. That is, one can analyze patient-therapist sexual contact as a problem within the individuals involved and/or as a problem within a social network, specifically the community of therapists.

In this review, we have drawn upon data from several sources and have utilized our own experiences in consultation, supervision, and therapy. We have also talked with other psychoanalysts about their experiences in analyzing and/or supervising cases involving previous sexual contact. We have no first- or second-hand information on the personal therapy of therapists who seduced patients; we suspect there are few cases in which these therapists seek treatment.

Sections adapted from "Sexualized Therapy: Causes and Consequences" by Roberta Apfel and Bennett Simon, in *Sexual Exploitation of Patients by Health Professionals*, ed. A.W. Burgess (New York: Praeger Publishers, 1986), reprinted with permission of Praeger Publishers, and from *Psychotherapy and Psychosomatics* 43: 57–68, 1985.

Although our analysis aims at objectivity and scientific examination, this is not a value-free or morally neutral discussion. The two stances we take are not compatible: (1) the clinical stance of what is most effective and objective in psychotherapy for patients, and (2) the personal stance of moral indignation toward therapists who are sexually involved with patients. Rehabilitation and prevention for therapists and patients are potentially frustrating ventures.

CAUSES OF THERAPIST-PATIENT SEXUAL CONTACT

FAILURE OF GENITALITY

All that involves the genitals is not "genital." The so-called genital phase of development begins in puberty with the biological capacity for orgasm, but the term "genital" also refers to "attitudes and feelings which connote non-narcissistic *object love*, the capacity for true intimacy and the security for flexible ego regression" (Moore and Fine 1968, 48). Implied in Freud's usage, this definition today is part of common usage.   Sexual involvement between therapist and patient may not even involve the genitals, although the range of activities is as broad as sexual behavior in other relationships. The genital phase integrates phallic, anal, and oral components. One predominant group of male therapists who initiate sex with patients are people who have achieved some measure of genital integration in their lives. However, they are perhaps unknowingly experiencing deintegration or regression from the genital phase because of stresses in their lives (e.g., the issues of aging of self and spouse, death and sickness of parents, incestuous and competitive feelings toward adolescent children, professional disappointments in career aspirations, and failures to analyze successfully the impact of these expectable life events). Actual genital inadequacy—impotence or inept sexual technique—characterizes the midlife therapist in contacts with patients. The patient often is seduced into sexual activities that may be flattering, tender, and exciting, but scarcely give the patient much genital pleasure.

Thus, the nature of the sex play in these instances is also a caricature of the flexible ego regression that is part of our working definition of genitality. The easy playfulness of mature sexuality, which ideally allows freedom for imaginative expression of individual sexual preferences, is conspicuously missing.

One goal of psychotherapy and psychoanalysis is for the patient to develop a broadened view of imaginative possibilities and problem-solving techniques and solutions to conflicts. When in the course of therapy a conflictual instinctual wish is directly gratified, there is concrete ego regression, rather than the more desirable, flexible, and abstract ego exploration that ultimately leads to a deeper satisfaction and maturation.

For example, a female patient, in the course of intensive psychotherapy came in touch with a previously warded-off yearning for maternal intimacy. When the male therapist invited her to sit on his lap and suck on his breast he foreclosed the possibility for creative transformation of the woman's yearning. Instead, he repeated the trauma of inappropriate and ill-timed parental intervention that fixates on a specific form of expression, and he precluded the possibility for imaginative discovery of alternative expressions.

We believe it is nourishing to the patient's ego to expand on fantasies and associations in the safety of a therapeutic relationship, with actual physical distance existing between therapist and patient. However, some therapists directly gratify a patient's wish.

Another way of looking at the impact of the seduction in the example cited is to note that the patient is forced to wonder and worry about the therapist's sanity and reliability. This undoubtedly recreates a childhood situation of insecurity about parents and reinforces trauma, instead of providing a setting in which the trauma can be disentangled and understood by the adult mind and in which a new model for a relationship can evolve. Just as appropriate regression in thought and feeling is foreclosed by sexual contact between patient and therapist, so are the possibilities for developing the intimacy appropriate to the therapeutic relationship.

Real-life intimacies between adults may involve an interplay of narcissistic and nonnarcissistic features, but mature intimacy allows for separateness and separation. Reports of patient-therapist sexual intimacies, even in literature touting favorable therapeutic outcome (Shepard 1971), indicate three outcomes for the therapist-patient relationship: (1) bondage by therapist of patient, (2) jilting of patient by therapist according to therapist's timetable, and (3) bondage by patient of therapist. Some form of bondage, whether subtle or obvious occurs inevitably in all patient-therapist sexual relationships. Bonding, which occurs in all therapies, at times can feel like bondage to the patient or therapist. However, actual physical contact implies promises for a type of concrete intimacy and bodily linkage that gives the feelings of bondage considerable reality and permanence.

The intimacy of therapy grows slowly in an atmosphere in which the patient trusts that no exploitation will occur. We emphasize that this trust is not to be taken for granted and evolves through many interchanges, including ones in which the patient may temporarily feel a breach of trust or be convinced that the therapist is exploiting him/her in some way. The latter is inevitable, but the magnitude of the feelings of exploitation must be such that the patient and the therapist can negotiate difficulties. In other words, development of the trust necessary for intimacy must involve the experience of mistrust and its subsequent resolution. Some of the difficulties in resolving are usefully considered as transference, some as transference/countertransference issues, and some as based on misunderstandings or even mischief.

The sexual situation presents not only possibilities for deep intimacy, but the likelihood of situations of mistrust and exploitation that are not negotiable. Consider the typical situation of therapist-patient sexual contact: the therapist charges the patient a fee while having sexual relations with him or her. In therapy, the fee situation elicits feelings of mistrust and fears of exploitation. The resolution of feelings about fee becomes even more difficult when the patient is having sex with the therapist.

In one case example of this a 35-year-old woman came for consultation for anxiety during her therapist's vacation. In a tearful, agitated state, she revealed that she had seen her therapist three times a week for almost ten years. The consultant suspected a need to review this long-lived therapy but was startled to hear more details of the "treatment." The patient said that she had started with twice-weekly therapy and soon began to have sex regularly with the male therapist during one of these sessions; she continued to pay for both weekly visits. In addition, for the last year the patient was seeing the therapist a third time each week. During that time, she was typing for the therapist and was being paid by him. When the consultant suggested that this therapy sounded exploitive and not in the patient's best interest the patient became furious and defended her therapist vehemently. She said her only problem with the therapist was his having taken a vacation with his family and thus being temporarily separated from her. The patient stated that she had no need for further consultation.

Undoubtedly, there are several dynamic constellations underlying the therapist's behavior, and we do not propose that any single one accounts for the sexual encounter. However, one discernable configuration is the operation of a rescue fantasy, in particular the type alluded to by Freud (1910, 1915). Freud argues that rescue fantasies typically are part of the parental complex. We surmise that several male therapists who seduce female patients desire to "rescue" sexually the woman from a terrible fate or problem. Thus, the therapist is likely to be acting out (and reenacting) his own childhood Oedipal fantasy, with the female patient being the suffering mother whom he rescues (or seduces away from) the wicked father.

From the side of the female patient, there is a mirroring rescue fantasy. She is playing out her fantasy of exclusively possessing the father or of saving the father from a woman (the mother) who does not make him happy. Similarities to situations of father/daughter incest reported by Herman (1981) are striking.

When the therapist is depressed and sexually inadequate, he or she may be "propped up" by the sexual activity with the patient. In at least one instance, it was clear that the therapist's sexual inadequacy was a painful secret that the female patient had to keep to protect her internal fantasy picture of the male therapist.

Genitality as we have used it, is therefore equated with maturity, with adulthood. Erikson was one of the authors who contributed to this usage. Yet in his studies of adult life, Erikson (1963) also uses the term in a more specialized sense to refer to the stage of young adulthood. Genitality is paired with the term *intimacy*: and its failure leads to isolation.

FAILURE OF GENERATIVITY

Generativity (including procreativity) is the term Erikson applies to the developmental tasks of adulthood. The failure to develop or to sustain generativity leads to stagnation and self-absorption. The virtue specific to generativity is care. Similar views of adulthood are presented by other writers such as Jaques (1965), who introduced the term *midlife crisis*, a crisis that can lead to either spiritual regeneration or spiritual death.

According to Erikson, generativity encompasses procreativity, productivity, and creativity and implies as well the capacity for self-generation or regeneration with further identity development. The associated virtue is care, care of persons, of products, and of the ideas one has learned to care about (Erikson 1964). To understand why sex between patient and therapist constitutes a problem in the therapist's generativity, consider Erikson's description of the larger consequences of foiled generativity: "Where such enrichment fails altogether, regressions to an obsessive need for pseudo-intimacy takes place, often with a pervading *sense of stagnation*, boredom, and "interpersonal impoverishment" (Erikson 1968).

One common type of sexual contact between patient and therapist that has come to our attention clinically involves the middle-aged male therapist caught in a nexus of personal and professional dissatisfactions, often unacknowledged. He is covertly and sometimes overtly depressed. His marriage is in difficulty, he is likely to be experiencing sexual problems and dissatisfaction, and he does not feel particularly successful in the rearing of his children. He is also beset by doubts either about his own professional competence or about the efficacy of his practice of psychotherapy and psychoanalysis. His basic commitments and relationships are largely ambivalent. His aspirations for generativity have been disappointed and frustrated by external reality and inner ambivalence.

The scenario frequently involves a neurotic male therapist who is a basically humane person striving for generativity. He is not a psychopathic or perverted opportunist; if he were, it would be easier to dismiss the problem. He was motivated to become a psychotherapist at least in part out of a desire to be generative. He may often rationalize sexual relations with patients as a sign of caring.

Both patients and therapists may attribute benefit to the patient from the sexual relationship. However, the same benefit may well have accrued from therapeutic strategies without the physical contact. For example, a few women patients in subsequent therapies credit the sexual therapist with having helped to foster self-esteem, especially via support of intellectual/academic achievements. They feel grateful and say they could not have been successful without the special care of that therapist's approach.

However, there are some fallacies in this reasoning. The specialness of the patient has the effect of attributing more to the therapist, making him seem more special and stroking his narcissism. It detracts from the patient's sense of self-worth in that the patient senses that his or her achievements are totally dependent on the therapist. We believe that the relative good that results in such cases may be more a tribute to the capacities of the patients to make the best out of bad situations than to the clinical shrewdness of the therapists.

In our estimation, patient-therapist sex never has a favorable outcome for the patients' development. Positive features reported to us by patients and in the literature could, we believe, have been achieved in therapy by other means, thus averting the largely negative consequences of the sexual relationship. In addition, we see three ways in which sex with one's therapist thwarts the generativity of the patient: (1) it creates difficulties in subsequent therapies and life, (2) it introduces inhibitions into relationships, and (3) it causes repetition of a pathological pattern and the fixation on this repetition.

Case examples illustrate this failed generativity. In one case, a middle-aged woman entered therapy for concerns about a new career after having raised four children. She was able to work through her competitive issues with her husband, her ambivalence toward her mother and her identification with her academic but withdrawn and sadistic father and become generative in her own scientific work. Her history of sex with a previous therapist emerged as most significant in the termination phase of therapy; this history had been addressed during the therapy, but its full significance became clear only at the end. Ordinary fees and vacations were experienced by the patient as major exploitations and became occasions for tumultuous upheaval in the therapy. The patient maintained a fantasy wish that following termination her current therapist would sexually seduce her as had the previous therapist. However, such a seduction would reinforce the patient's inner conviction of being a helpless victim, thus undoing and disproving all the gains of therapy. In addition, the patient needed to assume control over the termination pace and date and was unable to terminate in a definitive, mutually agreed-upon manner. Although the woman's conflict over her own independence probably antedated her sexual relationship with the therapist, it had been reinforced by that relationship.

This case illustrates one patient's difficulty in terminating therapy. Another frequent negative outcome for therapy subsequent to a patient-therapist sexual relationship is premature termination or inability to reenter therapy for fear of betraying the original offending therapist or of parting with the fantasized relationship. The following case illustrates a tragic outcome.

A talented woman writer at age 22 was involved sexually with a psychoanalyst who offered—in treating her depression—to undo an earlier trauma with a seductive father but who, in fact, repeated and reinforced this traumatic experience. Despairing, the woman ended the analysis and forswore entering any form of psychotherapy again. Professionally successful by age 35 she remained conflicted about marriage and children and wanting to have a family. She sought help from a so-called avant-garde therapy group that shared her rejection of the psychiatric establishment and became involved in a "therapeutic" community in which everyone shared everything—feelings, sex, food, and living quarters. In this setting, the woman's isolation and depression worsened, and she attempted suicide. She was treated medically and in conventional individual and group psychotherapy. The patient failed to develop any trusting relationship and eventually killed herself.

The repetition of a patient's traumas through sexual exploitation by the therapist is not always fatal, but it can be apparent even to the patient who feels helpless to alter it. One 30-year-old woman, married to a physician and in the midst of her first pregnancy, sought help because of anxiety about her adequacy to be a mother. During the initial consultation, she revealed that she was the oldest child of a tumultuous marriage and had experienced a frightening, mutually seductive relationship with her father that precipitated her flight from home at age 17. Soon thereafter, she entered into a therapeutic relationship with a male psychologist; within a few months, he began to have intercourse with her. The relationship continued for about one year, when the psychologist announced that he was moving away and starting a new life. The woman took a near-lethal overdose of barbituates (that the psychologist had helped her to obtain) and a few days later awoke from coma in the hospital intensive care unit. After recovery, the patient made several unsuccessful attempts at therapy and in her early 20s was hospitalized for severe depression. In the psychiatric unit, she met a medical student who helped her in a seemingly miraculous short-term therapy and with whom she fell in love. After her discharge, she and the student began an affair, and eventually they married.

After the consultation, the patient did not return for another visit. She communicated to the psychiatrist that she felt he had not believed her story and that she had decided that conventional therapy was not for her. She later consulted with "Dr. Jones," a notorious charlatan with a reputation for sexual liaisons with patients.

In summary, it seems that sex between the patient and the therapist replicated the pathogenic relationship between the woman and her father and made it difficult for her to relate to a reputable therapist. The patient's decision not to return to the consultant may have been influenced unconsciously by the consulting therapist's excessive zeal to rescue the woman from her terrible therapeutic history. A major countertransference problem in subsequent therapy is that although the content of the new therapist's rescue fantasy may differ from that of the previous seducing therapist, the desire to rescue persists and remains pathogenic.

The fixating power of the sexual relationship with the therapist is reflected in the observation of Masters and Johnson (1970) that in cases where the sexual liaison with the therapist accomplishes orgasmic return, "there is no assurance of ability to transfer this facility in due course to the rejected husband. Any woman's inherent demand for exchange of vulnerabilities is markedly enhanced by this presumed therapeutic procedure" (390).

A 25-year-old, depressed man sought therapy for difficulty in fulfilling his vocation as a teacher. He entered treatment with a male therapist who was completing his own training. The patient's conflict centered around the issue of how to accept love, help, and mentoring from the same man with whom he was involved in an intense competition. Given the grim details of his childhood, he could easily have been confusing competition with moral combat.

In his late teenage years, the patient had briefly been in therapy with an older, much admired college teacher. The therapy culminated in a homosexual relationship lasting almost one year. The young man felt some sexual attraction toward his new therapist, typically when he could not accept the intensity of his competitive feelings toward the man he admired. He was recurrently in danger of botching opportunities for significant professional advancement and personal fulfillment. Vigorous and repeated interpretation of the fixating significance of the sexual relationship with the first therapist allowed the patient to avoid further self-destructive behavior and proceed on the path toward expressing his own generative capacities. Sexual collusion with this man would have foreclosed the possibility of creating a resolution.

In simplest terms, the failure of generativity as expressed in patient-therapist sex is the failure to create the capacity for a different and better life. There are two kinds of problems in subsequent clinical work with patients who do seek consultation: (1) how best to help them separate from their current enmeshment, and ((2) how to develop principles of treatment in the new therapy.

INDIVIDUAL CONFLICT AND THE SOCIAL NETWORK OF THERAPISTS

The interaction between the individual offending therapist and the community of practitioners who constitute his or her peer reference group does not provide any simple means for effective preventive action. Further, recent literature documents the difficulty and unreliability of self-policing within the profession. In 1976, Stone reviewed self-regulation and indicated that there are "four possible avenues for punishing, disciplining or deterring sexual activity between patient and therapist (criminal law, civil law, professional associations, and state licensing boards). None of these avenues seems to provide an effective system of control. In the end, in this, as in most other things, patients must depend on the decent moral character of those entrusted to treat them." Another article in the same journal issue documents how little disciplinary action medical associations and licensing boards took against 98 alcoholic physicians— a group with an impressive record of public sanction in terms of numerous arrests, jailings, and loss of driver's licenses (Bissell and Jones 1976). A more recent study by Grunebaum, Nadelson, and Macht (1973) further documented the difficulties of the Massachusetts branch of the American Psychiatric Association in effectively prosecuting and disciplining offending psychiatrists.

Compounding the legal problems is the dense network of denial, minimization, and rationalization on the part of many members of the profession. A psychoanalyst colleague has asserted that the offenders in question must be ill-trained and marginally licensed; the colleague is oblivious to the fact that one psychoanalytic society confronted four of its members within five years with documented patient-analyst sex. A recent case in California led to a $5.8 million malpractice settlement against a prominent psychoanalyst, a former president of his psychoanalytic society.

Has sex between patient and therapist become acclaimed as acceptable and desirable therapy? Freud commented on the matter in his famous 1931 letter to Ferenczi on the latter's technical innovation of touching, hugging, and kissing patients:

> Now picture what will be the result of publishing your technique. There is no revolutionary who is not driven out of the field by a still more radical one. A number of independent thinkers in matters of technique will say to themselves: Why stop at a kiss? . . . and then bolder ones will come along who will go further, to peeping and showing—and soon we shall have accepted in the technique of analysis the whole repertoire of demiviergerie and petting parties, resulting in an enormous increase of interest in psychoanalysis among both analysts and patients (Jones 1957, 164).

Certain features of the Freud-Ferenczi relationship as narrated by Jones (1957) can tell us something universal about patient-therapist sexual relationship. For many years, the relationship between Freud and Ferenczi was marked by a total devotion and even submission of Ferenczi to Freud and Freud was bothered by a certain cloying docility in Ferenczi. Later, Ferenczi rebelled against Freud through the introduction of a technique that often included direct physical, affectionate contact between analyst and patient. These ideas became the topic of serious public debate within the psychoanalytic movement. The Freud-Ferenczi dispute highlights how in conflicts over authority within the psychoanalytic movement, sexual contact becomes the battle cry of freedom of the young against the old. This kind of rebellion is different from debate, an art that is not especially well practiced by analysts. Rebellion and setting up a new school seem to come easier than extended debate over therapeutic issues.

The Freud-Ferenczi exchange opens up three issues. First, institutions, professional organizations, and other groups must strike a balance between the preservation of the group itself, its history, and its traditions and the continued renewal of ideals and mutual goals. In the maturation process of institutions, there is always a shift from the original purpose toward the preservation of the institutions per se; the danger is unquestioning acceptance of old ideas–a certain path to eventual extinction. From the beginning, the psychoanalytic movement was revolutionary and innovative. It was quickly beset by the task of how to encourage honest debate and accumulate new ideas.

One reason why debates are difficult within the field of psychotherapy is that for therapists, the technique and theory they espouse are closely wedded to their temperament and unconscious needs. But a relationship between one's personality and one's mode of practicing psychotherapy is not to be decried, but rather to be the topic for continuous self-scrutiny, both by individuals and by communities of psychotherapists. By having sex with patients, therapists declare that there is no need for them to sublimate and channel personal needs and motives, no need to examine and to integrate their personalities with the accumulated practice and experience of other therapists.

What is needed, both in spirit and in practical institutional arrangements, are ways in which individual therapists can express dissent, air new discoveries, offer and devise new techniques, and express their individuality. Simultaneously, there must be ways for these dissenting ideas to be argued, to be tested, and to receive consensual understanding.

Second, professional institutions must provide nurturance and a sound milieu in which to practice the craft of psychotherapy. Nurturance includes a tolerance for dissent, a willingness to set limits, and a provision for teaching, support, and comfort.

When the necessary nourishment is not available from peers and colleagues, therapists practice in isolation and feel abandoned and ignored. Then, outlandish behavior can be a way for therapists to demand that the community take notice; even if the recognition is disapproval, it may feel better than apathy. Sexual intimacy with patients has the aspect of such outlandish behavior, a cry for help often followed by a defiant or passive refusal to accept therapy or supervision. Part of nurturing is policing, a function that has been inadequately performed by professional organizations. It is far easier to provide a scientific or social forum than to apprehend and punish offenders. Yet corrupt activities become quickly known within the general community, and the concomitant loss of pride discredits the entire professional organization.

Third, we have all witnessed the way in which the so-called sexual revolution has been accompanied by sexual therapies. Ironically, the defenders of sex with patients are looking for greater freedom from narcissistic bondage and justify the practice as a way to help share and permit growth. In our experience, exactly the opposite occurs; the trade-off is failed generativity—there is truly an inhibition of growth for both participants and a degeneration for the human community.

CONSEQUENCES OF THERAPIST-PATIENT SEXUAL CONTACT

In our experience, as well as in studies reported in the literature, the effects on the patient of therapist-patient sex range from instances where the patient seems more or less to have buffered the ill-effects of the relationship to instances of psychosis and suicide. Within this range of outcomes, recurrent psychodynamic themes emerge.

AMBIVALENCE TOWARD THERAPISTS AND THERAPY   Ambivalent feelings may be expressed in the patient's trouble finding a therapist, frequent changes of therapist and therapeutic modality, and major delays or avoidance in seeking needed therapy. It is not uncommon to hear that a patient has seen several therapists within one two-month period following a sexual relationship with a therapist. Normally, any one of the therapists would have been acceptable, but at this vulnerable time, each therapist was seen as having committed an error serious enough to invite mistrust. Exaggerated and continuing allegiance to the former therapist often compounds the difficulty in finding a new therapist.

QUESTIONING OF REALITY AND SANITY   Patients who are not ordinarily psychotic may experience a split between their view of the actual sexual relationship and their view of the rationalization and deception involved. The patient's sense of reality is particularly unstable if the offending therapist has provided elaborate therapeutic justifications for the relationship, rather than honestly admitting to more ordinary motives for sex.

REPLAY OF PATHOGENIC CHILDHOOD SITUATIONS   Childhood experiences may be repeated, reinforced, and even escalated by a therapy that should have been aimed at correcting these traumas. If the patient as a child was sexually abused by a family member, the therapist may repeat the role of abuser. The secrecy demanded by the offending therapist often causes the guilty sense of complicity with parental seductiveness to resurface.

BONDAGE TO ONE THERAPIST   Bondage may result from the actual physical contact and surrender of independent judgment that accompany a sexual relationship. Bondage is often a two-way situation; the therapist may be as much a slave of the patient as the patient of the therapist. The only possible termination is abrupt withdrawal of one party, leaving the other feeling wounded and betrayed.

PERSISTENCE OR WORSENING OF ORIGINAL SYMPTOMS   The symptoms that brought the patient to therapy, such as sexual dysfunction, may continue. There may be illusory gains; the patient may enjoy sex, but only with the therapist. Discussion of other symptoms (e.g., inadequate work performance, chaotic relationships, or inappropriate partner choices) may be circumvented. As mentioned earlier, some women feel that the male therapist with whom they had a sexual relationship actually helped them in academic or vocational achievement. Close scrutiny both of some published accounts (McCartney 1966; Shepard 1971) and of patients we know suggests that these women continue to belittle their own achievements by ascribing their successes to the therapist.

CONSTRICTED INTIMACY WITH MEN   Already troubled marriages become more so, and we have seen instances of reactive sexual difficulties in spouses or worsening of existing difficulties. Even more than other extramarital affairs, the patient-therapist liaison can make the spouse or potential partner seem inadequate and beyond redemption. Masters and Johnson (1970) made a similar observation that in cases in which a sexual liaison with a therapist accomplished orgasmic return, this ability did not necessarily transfer to the spouse or partner. The offending therapist rarely acknowledges that the patient's acting out of hostility may be fostered, a hostility that had been interfering with intimacy.

RAGE AND DESIRE FOR REVENGE   Feelings of rage may be crystallized, particularly at the time of the breakup in the sexual relationship, and may be directed toward all people of the therapist's gender. The patient's angrily ending the relationship is typically precipitated by the realization either that the therapist has other sexual partners or that the therapist has no intention of making a lifelong commitment to the patient. In some instances, the intensity of murderous rage may evoke primitive, psychotic defenses on the part of the patient in order to spare the therapist.

EXCESSES OF GUILT AND SHAME   Patients sexually involved with their therapists universally feel guilt and shame. One important aspect of these feelings is the patient's conviction that they failed to satisfy the needs of the therapist, who at times may have accused the patient of being insensitive to the therapist's needs. This sense of failure, combined with guilt and shame over complicity, further impairs the shaky self-esteem that originally brought the patient to therapy. Masochistic character traits and the tendency toward self-blame are thereby reinforced, rather than modified.

Somewhat to our surprise, we came to realize that a particular aspect of the patient's shame had to do with various infantile sexual activities engaged in and initiated by the therapist. In our case material, coitus was the exception; nursing, fondling, and oral sex was the rule—often performed in a manner more humiliating than gratifying. The patients went to great lengths to protect the original therapist by not revealing details of these activities to subsequent therapists.

STIFLED IMAGINATION   Because the sexual contact is rarely playful and diverse and is instead ritualized and repetitive, there is a concreteness and immediacy to the nature of the activities. The sexual activity seems literally to limit the range of topics that patient and therapist can discuss.

CREATION OF A CRISIS SITUATION   The ending of the sexual contact is often without a therapeutic termination and referral, leaving the patient stranded in crisis and severely disorganized. The reverberations of such traumatic endings will be felt for many years, particularly at the time of termination of subsequent therapy. The time of abrupt termination, however, is critical to revelation of the sexual relationship and presents an opportunity for consultative intervention.

CONSULTATION AND EVALUATION

If the therapy has been terminated abruptly, the patient comes seeking consultation in a state of mistrust, confusion, and great need. The consultant may be skeptical of the patient's story or horrified by the revelation of misconduct by a colleague. Faced with a patient in turmoil who is unwilling or unable to reveal the relationship, the consultant may be unsure of how to uncover the shameful secret. Generally, the combination of the patient's state and the array of details presented leaves little room for doubt about the truthfulness of the account. In our experience, stories of bizarre sexual practices with the previous therapist confirm the tale, rather than weaken its credibility. We doubt there exists a condition of an isolated delusion about patient-therapist sex without other evidence of psychotic thinking or behavior being present.

The consultant must listen with interest and objectivity. Frank questioning and honest curiosity about details of the account encourage the patient to speak. The consultant's role is to help the patient believe and integrate the reality of the experience, rather than to question the account or to establish its veracity.

Although contacting the previous therapist generally is valuable professional practice, in this situation the patient may have strenuous objections to or painfully ambivalent feelings about such contact. The consultant also may feel ambivalent and must acknowledge these feelings and defer a decision on contact with the previous therapist until the patient's feelings have been explored and a working relationship developed.

In choosing a mode of treatment, the consultant should not automatically reject the previous mode of therapy (e.g., individual psychotherapy) if that mode is warranted. The value of a support group of patients with similar experiences has been demonstrated as one validating experience (Schoener, Milgrom, and Gonsiorek 1981). Long-term group therapy, with its diffused transference relationship, also may be beneficial. In addition, the possible value of an interruption or postponement of therapy should be considered. This is not the same as dismissal or abandonment, which are antitherapeutic and which can deepen the patient's despair.

A similar open-mindedness should accompany the selection of a new therapist by the consultant, and the consultant should continue some supervising interest in the subsequent therapy. The gender of the new therapist may be important to the patient. In our experience, women patients who had participated in a sexual relationship with a male therapist generally sought a new female therapist. The discussion of the new therapist's gender may be an important first step in clarifying some issues that were acted out but not analyzed in the previous therapy. Subsequent therapies are workable with therapists of either gender (Mogul 1982).

The consultant indicates trustworthiness to the patient by straightforward discussion of fees, hours, and availability. These will be recurrent issues in long-term therapy, and patients will be forever sensitive to real or imagined lapses on the part of the therapist. Occasionally, a patient may need hospitalization; this too must be discussed honestly.

There are patients who, having been treated once in a "special" way, continuously both wish for and dread any other form of special treatment. The main form of special treatment that therapists and patients are at risk of colluding about is the exemption of the patient (and the therapist) from confronting long-term painful feelings. As subsequent therapists, we have become angry and frustrated with patients, and we are particularly aware of the dangers of unanalyzed countertransference hate. Some patients are impressively skilled and experienced at inducing in the therapist all the conflicting feelings that they as patients wish to disclaim.

For example, in one case it became clear how the patient's persistent self-denigration and masochistic behavior was employed as a transference weapon to devalue and torture the therapist. In the previous treatment, the therapist exploited the patient's helplessness, thus averting the need for either of them to experience the extent of the patient's conflicts about her own competitiveness and aggression toward men. In order to persist in analyzing these conflicts, the next therapist must resist the temptation either to rescue or to withdraw. Unfortunately, the sexual relationship with the previous therapist makes the subsequent analysis more difficult.

Termination of therapy is almost certain to be difficult and prolonged. Consultation and supervision are especially useful at this time. Dread of abandonment, fears of not being able to function independently, fears for the well-being of the therapist, rage at the therapist, and many other individual feelings may emerge. For some patients, the second termination highlights the degree to which they may have preserved the illusion of a continuing relationship with the first therapist.

A serious question is whether or not and under what circumstances it can be therapeutically beneficial for the patient to press charges against the offending therapist. The question is a complex one, and the therapist can err by colluding with the patient to avoid even discussing the possibility or by urging such action in a coercive manner. The potential benefits for the patient include the opportunity to turn passivity into activity in a socially constructive manner. Patients frequently are concerned, and often with good reason, about the previous therapist's repeating sexual offenses with other patients (Kardener 1974; *Roy v. Hartogs*). Reporting may thus be an expression of genuine altruistic motive and hence of considerable value in enhancing the patient's self-esteem. To pose the question and examine it with the patient is to keep alive and in focus major issues dealing with the real world. The one stance that is clearly unacceptable and antitherapeutic is ignoring the question altogether.

We cannot offer any formula for how therapists should deal with the issue of reporting, except to suggest that they address it in the manner that will best facilitate thorough analysis of how the patients cope with painful realities. The obligation to analyze patients' behaviors in this area may run counter to therapists' professional obligations, namely, to report unethical behavior (American Psychiatric Association 1973; American Psychological Association 1977). We concur with Stone's (1983) recommendation that a consultant other than the treating therapist handle issues of reporting and of possible litigation. If the consultation concluded with referral to long-term therapy, the original consultant might be the best individual to deal with the patient in professional and legal matters. For the therapist to be involved beyond the usual therapy situation risks the repetition of an aspect of the earlier sexual relationship, that is, the engaging in an activity allegedly for the patient's benefit but beyond the usual degree of professional involvement. It may, however, be necessary at times for the therapist to testify in a hearing or to submit a letter of opinion to an examining board. Decisions about the therapist's role should be discussed over the course of therapy, as both feelings and circumstances may change.

Pressing charges carries its own risks. It can be painful, arduous, humiliating, expensive, and inconclusive. Furthermore, litigation is slow and may keep alive, with full intensity, the ambivalent relationship with the previous therapist. In addition, neither therapist nor patient should minimize the importance of the amount of money that the patient spent on the previous therapy and might spend on litigation. In some cases, the patient is left without resources to continue needed therapy. Pressuring the former therapist (either through legal action or through professional societies) to reimburse the patient may be not only a moral issue, but an absolute necessity.

Finally, we offer a suggestion to all new therapists. Probably the best mix of attitudes includes a large measure of respect for the power of good psychotherapy, a fair bit of curiosity about how patients and therapists become involved in sexual situations, a sprinkling (no more) of competitive wishes to demonstrate one's professional superiority, a concern and balanced respect for the patient, and a measure of regard for the basic dignity of the profession.

REFERENCES

American Psychiatric Association. 1973, The principals of medical ethics with annotations especially applicable to psychiatry. *American Journal of Psychiatry* 139: 1048–64.

American Psychological Association. 1977. Ethical standards of psychologists. *APA Monitor*, March, 22–23.

Erikson, E. 1963. *Childhood and society.* 2d ed. New York: W.W. Norton and Co.

———. 1964. *Insight and responsibility.* New York: W.W.Norton and Co.

———. 1968. *Identity, youth, and crisis.* New York: W.W. Norton and Co.

Freud, S. 1910. A special type of choice of object made by men. *Standard Edition* 11: 163–75.

———. 1915. Observations on transference love, *Standard Edition* 12: 157–71.

Grunebaum, H., C. Nadelson, and C.B. Macht. 1973. Sexual activity with a psychiatrist: A district branch dilemma. Paper presented at 129th annual meeting, American Psychiatric Association.

Herman, J. 1981. *Father-daughter incest.* Cambridge Mass.: Harvard University Press.

Jaques, E. 1965. Death and the mid-life crisis. *International Journal of Psychoanalysis* 46: 502–14.

Jones, E. 1957. *The life and work of Sigmund Freud, vol. 3.* New York: Basic Books.

Kardener, H. 1974. Sex and the physician-patient relationship. *American Journal of Psychiatry* 131: 1134–36.

Masters, W.H., and V.E. Johnson. 1970. *Human sexual inadequacy.* Boston: Little, Brown and Co.

McCartney, J.L. 1966. Overt transference. *Journal of Sexual Research* 2: 277–37.

Mogul, K.M. 1982. Overview: The sex of the therapist. *American Journal of Psychiatry* 139: 1–11.

Moore B.E., and B. Fine. 1968. *Glossary: American Psychoanalytic Association.* 2d ed. New York: American Psychoanalytic Association.

Roy v. Hartogs, 366 N.Y.S 2d. 297, 81 misc. and 2d 350 (1975).

Schoener, G., J. Milgrom, and J. Gonsiorek. 1981. *Responding therapeutically to clients who have been sexually involved with their psychotherapists.* Minneapolis: Walk-in Counseling Center, Inc.

Shepard, M. 1971. *The love treatment: Sexual interest between patients and psychotherapists.* New York: Syden.

Stone, A.A. 1976. The legal implications of sexual activity between psychiatrist and patient. *American Journal of Psychiatry* 133: 1138–44.

————. 1983. Sexual misconduct by psychiatrists: The ethical and clinical dilemma of confidentiality (commentary). *American Journal of Psychiatry* 140: 159–97.

SELF-BLAME IN RECOVERY FROM RAPE

Help or Hindrance?

BONNIE L. KATZ
The Urban Institute

MARTHA R. BURT
The Urban Institute

When the antirape movement first began in the early 1970s, the multitude of ways that women victims found to blame themselves for the assault emerged as one of the most striking experiences of many rape hotline counselors. Helping women deal with feelings of self-blame became a major goal for rape crisis centers, and understanding why women engaged in self-blame became a major task of the antirape movement. Faced with so many instances of self-blame by so many different women in such different rape situations, feminist analysts of rape quickly recognized that societal rather than individual forces must be at work. Women began exposing the cultural supports for victim-blaming, the ways in which women are held responsible for anything sexual that happens to them, and the ways that the culture excuses rapists and denies the disastrous impact of rape. Throughout this period and to the present in most rape crisis centers, freeing women from the crippling effects of self-blame has been a central premise of the antirape movement.

However, more recently a thesis that self-blame is an adaptive response to a crisis (Janoff-Bulman 1979, 1982) has caught the interest of academic social psychologists and of some therapists who counsel rape victims. This chapter presents the first published data on self-blame from rape victims themselves. It addresses the adequacy of the hypothesis that self-blame is adaptive (i.e., good for you) and asks, What is the role of self-blame in recovery from rape?

PREVIOUS RESEARCH

Studies of the aftermath of rape have yielded extensive descriptions of cognitive, affective, behavioral, and physiological effects—most frequently referred to as rape trauma syndrome. There are several commonly reported and accepted features of this syndrome (for a review of this literature, see Burt and Katz 1985). Generally, a rape is followed immediately by a period of intense disruption in all areas of functioning, lasting from a few hours to a few weeks. Then, the rape victim experiences a gradual reorganization of internal and external functions which usually develops into a successful readjustment to life. Most current researchers report that after six months to one year following a rape, the majority of women have recovered. However, some recent reports in the research literature show that a sizable minority of women do not consider themselves to be recovered, even after several years have passed since the rape (Burgess and Holmstrom 1979; Nadelson et al. 1982).

Research has found that throughout the stages of recovery, certain emotions are consistent. The most prominent emotion reported has been fear of being raped again and in association with rape-related cues (Calhoun, Atkeson, and Resick 1982). Anxiety and depression have also been the focus of much discussion and research (e.g., Kilpatrick, Veronen and Best 1986; Frank and Stewart 1984). Issues of the rape victim's feelings of guilt and responsibility for having caused the attack and subsequent self-blame, have also been addressed (e.g., Janoff-Bulman 1979).

The phenomenon of rape victims, expressing the view that they themselves must be at fault for having been raped has been at the center of much debate over the theoretical significance of rape, both psychologically and sociopolitically. It has been cited as evidence for female masochism as well as a clear result of the socialized feminine role and identity. However, research has not documented the role of self-blame in the recovery process of women who have actually experienced a rape (as opposed to college student responses to hypothetical vignettes).

Janoff-Bulman (1979, 1982) and her colleagues have suggested that one type of self-blame (behavioral) is an important aid in recovering from rape, while another type (characterological) is detrimental. Despite some experimental support for this assertion from college-student samples (most of whom presumably have not been raped), no compelling evidence suggests that women who have actually experienced a rape recover more successfully when they blame themselves more. We believe that the concern with self-blame in the current literature, coming from an attribution theory standpoint, has contributed little to the understanding of recovery from rape and has instead been focused on elaborating abstract tenets of attribution theory. The use of the self-blame construct in the attribution-theory framework is, furthermore, contrary to our understanding of the recovery process for rape victims and requires further examination.

The focus on self-blame has been primarily the province of social psychologists interested in attribution theory, and Janoff-Bulman's (1979, 1982) constructs of behavioral and characterological self-blame generally have been adopted. *Behavioral self-blame* is defined as seeing one's own behavior as contributing to causing the event. *Characterological self-blame* is defined as seeing one's character as contributing to causing the event. In this formulation, victims either blame themselves for engaging in (or failing to engage in) a specific activity, thus attributing blame to their own behaviors, or else blame themselves for some enduring trait or character flaw. Janoff-Bulman has posited that behavioral self-blame represents a victim's attempt to reestablish control following a victimization and that characterological blame, in contrast, is a result of low self-evaluation and self-derogation.

Current theories of self-blame as a response to victimization are primarily functional; that is, they posit that the attribution of blame to oneself serves a particular psychological purpose (Miller and Porter 1983). Theorists propose three particular functions of self-blame: (1) it allows the woman to perceive herself as being more in control and therefore more able to avoid future victimization (Wortman 1976), (2) it allows the victim to maintain a view of the world as a just and orderly place in which bad things happen only to people who deserve them (Lerner 1980), (3) it enables the victim to explain why the incident happened as it did and to find meaning in it (Frankl 1963).

These three functions are consistent with the theory of coping developed by social psychologists researching cognitive processes following victimization (Bulman and Wortman 1977; Janoff-Bulman and Frieze 1983; Taylor 1983; Wortman 1983). Janoff-Bulman (1985) has summarized this theoretical framework and suggests that the major impact of any victimization lies in its destruction of basic cognitive assumptions about how the world operates and that coping with the traumatic event requires the individual to rebuild those cognitive assumptions.

Janoff-Bulman asserts that three beliefs are especially affected because their upheaval destroys a person's ordinary functional stability. These are the belief in personal invulnerability, the perception of the world as meaningful, and the view of oneself in a positive light. The stronger an individual holds these beliefs prior to the victimization, the more adjustment problems the victim is predicted to experience following the event.

Janoff-Bulman views behavioral self-blame as one adaptive strategy that women use following rape to reconstruct their conceptual worlds in a way that lets them not only readopt their prior cognitive assumptions, but also acknowledge and accept their own victimization experiences.

Applying these ideas about blame, victimization impact, and adaptive coping strategies to the process of recovery following rape has proved to be quite appealing, especially to other social psychologists. The ideas provide a conceptual framework with which to approach this difficult area and suggest explanations for frequently reported phenomena. However, Janoff-Bulman and her colleagues have promoted these concepts as being pertinent to rape without actually studying them directly in women rape victims. Although victims of various traumatic experiences clearly have many reactions in common (Figley 1986), there are compelling reasons to believe that rape victims differ from victims of most other stressful events in the way society views and treats them. It has been well documented that society often sees rape victims as responsible for their assaults, perhaps more than other victim groups. Accordingly, women who are raped begin with a self-incriminating social ideology, and it seems likely that for them, self-blame would have a different value than for victims whom society does not see as culpable.

Janoff-Bulman's research methods also contribute to doubts about her interpretation that behavioral self-blame is a helpful response while characterological self-blame is a detrimental one. In her 1979 study, Janoff-Bulman collected questionnaire data from rape crisis center counselors, asking them to indicate their impressions of the extent to which their clients made statements reflecting behavioral vs. characterological self-blame. Counselors' judgments and interpretations of what their clients had told them over time provided the data. The results reported are based on replies from 38 crisis centers. Janoff-Bulman's demonstration of the link between characterological self-blame and depression was based on a study of college student subjects who completed personality inventories and then indicated the extent to which they thought they would blame themselves if they found themselves in several different hypothetical scenarios.

In her 1982 study, Janoff-Bulman conducted another analogue experiment using female college students as subjects. She asked them to assume the role of either victim or observer and to indicate how much they blamed the victim (which was, for half the subjects, themselves) for the rape. The attributions of blame by these subjects were interpreted as if they were made by victims, and the generalizability of results to actual victims was argued on the basis of differences in blame attributions by observers vs. victims. Janoff-Bulman considered her hypothesis to be confirmed by her finding that women who had high self-esteem tended to blame themselves more than low self-esteem women in response to assuming the victim role in imagined rape scenarios. Although the questions asked in this study were interesting and important ones for understanding the cognitive processes of observers, victim counseling experience will attest that many rape victims come to understand that their real reactions differ substantially from any prerape ideas they may have had about how they would react to a rape.

Despite Janoff-Bulman's findings and their use by other researchers, our theoretical approach to the study of rape would predict an entirely different role for self-blame in recovery. We believe the rape recovery process involves psychodynamic and sociocultural as well as cognitive elements (for an elaboration of this view, see Burt and Katz 1987). We also see recovery as a process of rebuilding, but believe this process involves re-evaluating one's own identity as well as one's relationships to the social and cultural world. In keeping with our theoretical perspective, we expect that self-blame would not be helpful to recovery, but that it would instead compound the victim's struggle against society's (and her own internalized) view of rape victims as culpable and somehow damaged.

It may be that reasserting control over oneself and one's environment is, in fact, a task of recovery, but the concept of self-blame is broader than the simple idea of control and has less sanguine aspects. In addition to being an indicator of the wish to feel in control, self-blame, even behavioral blame, may be motivated by a woman's conscious or unconscious endorsement of the societal attitude that she is responsible for the rape. Blaming herself may also be an expression of a woman's feelings of guilt or shame about having participated in the attack, even if she does not feel that she was responsible for causing it.

This distinction between feeling responsible for causing a rape vs. feeling shame for having accepted the necessity of minimal participation in order to survive may prove to be useful in understanding both the sources and the role of self-blame in recovery. Even if a woman blames only her own behavior, she is nonetheless directing her anger and despair at herself. It seems rather impossible to separate the characterological and behavioral components (for a discussion of this problem in research, see Miller and Porter 1983).

METHODS

In our study, elements of the questionnaire and interview were designed to let us explore the role of self-blame more directly than others have done and to elaborate on its relationship with other variables. We were especially interested in variables that were either theoretically related to the self-blame construct or that have been discussed by other researchers. Specifically, we have used our data to look at the association of self-blame with the prior relationship with the rapist, with the victim's self-esteem, with indicators of prerape psychopathology, with indicators of psychological distress, and with the length of time it takes for the victim to feel recovered.

Data presented here were collected as part of a larger research project designed to develop measures of growth outcomes following rape, to explore the effects of counseling interventions, and to delineate patterns of recovery from rape. The data set contains a rich array of information regarding rape and its impact, including items relevant to the understanding of self-blame.

SAMPLE

Participants in this study were referred to the Urban Institute by five Washington-Baltimore rape crisis centers located in socioeconomically and racially diverse communities; in addition, some were recruited through newspaper announcements. Of women completing both questionnaires and interviews ($N = 80$), 74 came from rape crisis centers and 6 came from responses to newspaper announcements. Of the 33 women completing questionnaires only, 4 came from rape crisis center referrals and 29 from the newspaper announcements. Data reported in this chapter came from the 80 women who completed interviews and the 7 women who completed only questionnaires but for whom we also have self-blame data.

The sample was designed to include about 35% individual and 35% group counseling clients, plus 30% women who had received hospital treatment only, with little or no follow-up. In addition, the sample was designed to include at least 30 women who had been raped by nonstrangers. Therefore, this sample is not representative of all rape victims or of all rape victims using rape crisis center services. Instead, it is a sample stratified by type of counseling use and representative within these strata. The 80 women interviewed represent 42% of the 190 women contacted by centers and 52% of the 155 women who authorized the centers to release their names to us (18% of the women contacted by centers refused to participate).

Women were included in the study if they had been raped, if they were 18 or older at the time of the rape for which they came to the crisis center (the index rape), if they had no known history of father-daughter or repeated incest, if the rape occurred at least six months prior to the interview, if counseling (for those who received it) occurred at least three months prior to the interview, and if they had no physical handicap that would prevent them from being interviewed with the standard protocol. Marital rapes were excluded. Women who had been assaulted prior to the index rape (including as children) were not excluded.

Selected demographic features of the sample are as follows. The sample was 81% white, 17% black, and 1% each Asian and Hispanic. Of the study participants, 15% of the sample rated themselves as lower or working class, 24% as lower middle class, 43% as middle class, 18% as upper middle class, and 1% as upper class. At the time of the rape, 21% of the women were ages 18–20, 39% were 21–25, 21% were 26–35, and 19% were 36 or older. For 15% of the women, six months to one year had passed since the rape. Another 15% were one to one and one-half years postrape, 20% had been raped one and one-half to three years earlier, 26% were three to five years postrape, 11% were five to eight years out, and 13% had been raped more than eight years before participating in the study. In the sample, 88% of the women were attacked by a lone assailant, while 12% were attacked by two or more persons.

Prior relationships with the rapist varied widely among participants: 62% were total strangers, 9% were raped by men they had just met in the interaction that ended with the rape, and 9% knew of the rapist (but did not know him well). Solid acquaintances attacked 11% of the women, 4% were attacked by close friends, 5% by former boyfriends or husbands, and 1% by a current boyfriend. This distribution underrepresents women raped by nonstrangers. Women sustained various degrees of injury: 34% had none; 41% had minor bruises and scratches; 14% had bruises that took two weeks or longer to heal. Serious injuries that did not require hospitalization were suffered by 6% of the women, while another 6% were injured seriously enough to require hospitalization, operations, and rehabilitation.

PROCEDURE

Questionnaires were sent to participants as soon as they set up interview appointments, with instructions to complete the questionnaire and bring it to the interview. Questionnaires took the average respondent two to three hours to complete. Most respondents completed the questionnaire without difficulty. Several women needed help with one or two sections, and three women completed the questionnaire by having the interviewer read them the entire questionnaire and record their answers. Respondents who were not going to be interviewed also received a supplemental questionnaire concerning their history, demographics, and description of the assault.

Interviews were scheduled at times and places convenient for the respondents. The most frequent meeting place was the respondent's home, but only if that could be arranged to take place when no one else was present. Other meeting places were the researchers' offices, the researchers' homes, and public places such as quiet restaurants. The interviewers made extensive notations during the interviews and also tape-recorded all but one interview (the woman refused taping). Interviews took an average of three to four hours (with a few as long as six hours) and included a ten- to fifteen-minute break in the middle. A few interviews had to be completed in two sessions. The authors themselves conducted all the interviews.

All women were paid $20 upon completion of the interview. The end of the actual interview was always followed by an opportunity for the participant to ask the interviewer questions and generally to decompress. A follow-up letter was sent after the interview, thanking the participant and providing her with a referral list of local rape crisis centers. In addition, follow-up calls were made to many participants to see how they were feeling and to determine their view of the study and their participation in it.

MEASURES

The questionnaire used 17 instruments, including some previously standardized and some developed by the authors for this study. Most items were Likert scales with from four to seven points for endorsement. We included measures to ascertain selected personality characteristics, various aspects of self-concept, psychiatric symptomatology, beliefs and attitudes about rape and about sex roles, experiences in counseling, approaches to coping with the rape, and views of the impact of the rape and the recovery process. The questionnaire is described in more detail elsewhere (Burt and Katz 1987).

The interview used a semistructured format. It included sections on the respondent's use of rape crisis and other counseling services, her history and demographics, her social-relationship history and current romantic relationship, a timeline of significant events in her life extending from a year before the rape until the present, a description of the assault and her thoughts and feelings during it, persistent or permanent physical problems resulting from the rape, her relationship to the rapist(s), disclosure patterns and others' reactions, the recovery process (including the presence of other stressors, turning points or stages, ways the victim or her life changed, thoughts about causes of rape, feelings about rapist, self-blame, sexual functioning, coping strategies, the victim's definitions of recovery, and her perception of her own progress toward recovery), and advice to other women who have been raped.

The specific variables we discuss in this chapter are drawn from both interview and questionnaire data as follows. The issue of self-blame was measured in several ways; for material discussed here we used two measures. The first was part of a broader interview question regarding attribution of blame: "Many women think a lot about blame after a rape experience. I'd like you to take 100% of the blame for your rape and divide it up. Tell me how much you would give to the rapist, to society, to yourself, or elsewhere, then (right after the rape) and now." Women were subsequently prompted to give their immediate postrape responses and their current feelings. The self-blame attribution made for immediately postrape was used in our analysis to measure the women's feelings of self-blame that are specific to the rape.

The second measure of self-blame was a factor score derived from a questionnaire instrument titled "How I See Myself Now" (Burt and Katz 1987). The factor was labeled guilt/blame based on its highest-loading items and consisted of responses to seven-point scales describing the following dimensions: not guilty/guilty; not fearful/fearful; not anxious/ anxious; not clear about my needs/ clear about my needs (R); not nervous/ nervous; not trusting of myself/trusting of myself (R); not deserving blame/deserving blame. Items marked (R) load negatively on the factor. This measure of self-blame tapped current feelings (as opposed to those immediately following the rape). Furthermore, it probed for generalized feelings of guilt and blame, rather than those feelings focused exclusively on the rape.

We used the Rosenberg self-esteem scale (Rosenberg 1965) to measure self-esteem. We asked women to indicate on a timeline the point at which they felt they had recovered from the rape or when in the future they felt they would recover. We then calculated the number of months between the rape and the self-reported recovery and used this as one recovery index. To provide a gross indicator of preexisting psychopathology, we included a question asking each woman whether she had ever been psychiatrically hospitalized and whether she had ever seriously considered or attempted suicide. We measured the amount of counseling women had received by asking them about the duration and frequency of all counseling contacts; we calculated the number of hours spent in counseling since the rape and created a variable with five categories, from 0 hours to 40 or more hours.

Respondents reported their prior relationship with the rapist in response to the question: "Did you know the rapist? If so, what was the relationship, and how long had you known him?" We coded the relationship on a seven-point continuum, from total stranger to current boyfriend. Specific aspects of the relationship were rated by women who knew the rapists on a seven-point scale: "Before the rape, how well would you have said that you knew him?. . . Please rate this from one to seven, where one is not at all well and seven is extremely well"; "Before the rape, how close would you have said you were with him?. . . Please rate from one to seven, not at all close to extremely close"; "Before the rape, did you feel this was a man you could trust?" We also coded the respondents' open-ended descriptions of their assaults and their relationships for the extent of the interaction they had with the rapist(s) prior to the rape and for whether the rape occurred as part of an interaction that began with the victim voluntarily accompanying the rapist.

Negative symptomatology was measured using the brief symptom inventory (Derogatis and Spencer 1982), the profile of mood states (McNair, Lorr, and Droppelman 1971), the modified fear survey (Resick et al. 1984), and the impact of events scale (Horowitz, Wilmer, and Alvarez 1979). These instruments collectively measured fear, anxiety, depression, other psychiatric symptoms, avoidance, intrusion of thoughts about the rape, and mood states. Victims' responses were summarized by 28 separate scales and subscale scores. To reduce the data and derive a single indicator of symptomatology, we entered the scores for each of the 28 scales and subscales into a factor analysis. Using a principal components factor analysis, we found that the first principal component of the unrotated factor matrix accounted for 49.9% of the variance among the 28 scale scores; every score loaded on this unrotated factor, with loadings from .422 to .957. This yields an Armor's *theta* value of .963 (Armor 1974), indicating an extremely high level of internal consistency. Accordingly, we used each respondent's factor score on this factor as our indicator of the presence of negative symptomatology.

RESULTS

We first explored the nature of self-blame immediately following the rape by determining its frequency and extent. Women's self-blame immediately following the rape ranged from 0% to 100%. On average, respondents indicated that they ascribed 28% of the blame for the rape to themselves immediately following the rape. At the time of the interview, the proportion of blame attributed to self had dropped to a mean of 8.6%. The difference between these means was highly significant [$t(86)=-5.644$, $p < .0001$]. This drastic reduction in felt responsibility for having caused the rape yielded quite distinct frequency distributions for self-blame now vs. then, as depicted in figure 10.1.

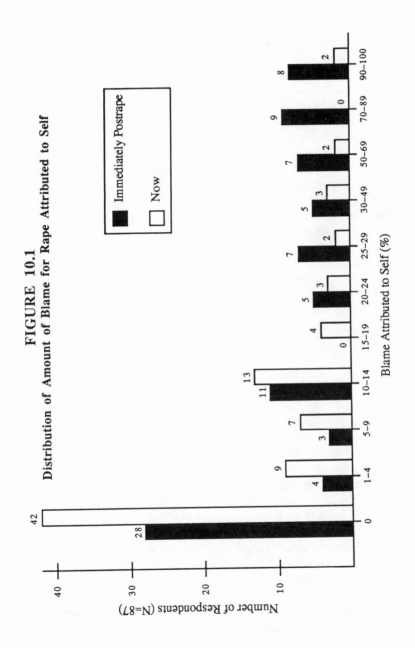

FIGURE 10.1

Distribution of Amount of Blame for Rape Attributed to Self

Of the women, 32% (28) felt immediately that they deserved no blame for the rape; this increased to 48% of the sample (42 women) who felt that they were not to blame by the time the interview took place. At the time of the interview, 90% of the women felt that they deserved less than 20% of the blame for the rape; two women felt that they were wholly responsible for the rape. In contrast, only 53% of the women had felt little self-blame (less than 20%) immediately following the rape.

This reduction in variance in the current self-blame variable makes it less useful than the earlier self-blame variable for exploring relationships with other variables. Preliminary analysis yielded no significant correlations between current self-blame specifically for the rape and any of the variables of interest. Accordingly, the remainder of our self-blame analyses were performed using the "then" levels of blame specifically for the rape and the more generalized blame measure contained in the guilt/ blame factor score for the measure of current self-blame. These two measures correlate with each other at a marginally significant level [r (74) = .206, $p < .08$].

Examination of the correlations between the variables of interest and our measure of self-blame reveals that most of our expectations were confirmed (see table 10.1). Our respondents' level of self-blame right after the rape was significantly and positively correlated with one prerape psychopathology indicator prerape psychiatric hospitalization history [r (87) = .197, $p < .05$] but not the other (prerape suicidality).

All of the variables indexing the prerape relationship with the rapist were highly correlated with self-blame. More familiarity [r (87) = .276, $p < .01$], more closeness [r (87) = .336, $p < .002$], and more trust [r (87) = .331, $p < .002$] were all significantly associated with higher levels of self-blame for the assault.

We explored this association further using a one-way analysis of variance; relationships were dichotomized into total strangers vs. all other relationships. We found that women raped by nonstrangers felt significantly more self-blame than did women who were raped by strangers [F (1,81) = 14.885; $p < .0009$]. Women who reported voluntarily accompanying the rapist in the interaction that ended in the assault also reported especially high levels of self-blame, whereas women who felt forced to go with the assailant tended to blame themselves less [r (87) = .416, $p < .001$]. (See Katz and Burt [1986] for further discussion of the importance of the stranger/nonstranger dimension.)

Self-blame immediately following the rape was also correlated with variables that reflected postrape events and the recovery process. The more women felt they had blamed themselves for the rape, the higher their current levels of psychological distress as measured by negative symptomatology [r (87) = .194, p < .05]. Higher levels of self-blame were also associated with more hours of counseling since the rape [r (87) = .285, p < .01], and with the length of time women felt it took (or would take) them to be "recovered" [r (73) = .297, p < .01]. Similarly, the more women had blamed themselves for the rape, the lower their current levels of self-esteem [r (76) = -.241, p < .05].

The factor-score measure of current generalized guilt/blame also yielded interesting results. First, despite this measure's more generalized, nonrape-specific nature, the rape victims in our sample reported significantly more guilt and self-blame on this measure than a comparison sample of non-raped women [N = 164, t (113; 164) = 5.734; p < .0001]. Second, the items comprising the measure, selected as they were by factor analysis from among 43 self-descriptors (many of which had positive connotations), strongly suggest that guilt and blame were associated with negative rather than positive or "taking control" feelings. The other items on this scale—fearful, anxious, unclear about needs, nervous, not trusting self—paint a rather unhappy picture of a rape victim troubled by guilt and blame.

TABLE 10.1.
CORRELATIONS OF SELF-BLAME WITH OTHER VARIABLES

Variable	Immediately Postrape Blame to Self (%)	Current Guilt/ Blame Factor Score (%)
Prerape suicidality	N.S.	N.S.
Prerape psychiatric hospitalization	.197**	N.S.
Relationship with rapist prerape	.276***	N.S.
Prerape trust in rapist	.331***	N.S.
Prerape closeness with rapist	.336****	N.S.
Voluntarily going with rapist	.416****	N.S.
Negative symptomatology	.194**	.295ᵃ***
Postrape suicidality	.315ᵇ***	N.S.
Postrape psychiatric hospitalization	.225ᵇ*	N.S.
Hours of counseling since rape	.285***	.196*
Time to recovery by self-report	.297ᶜ***	N.S.
Self-esteem	-.241ᵇ	-.310ᵃ***
Romantic self-image	N.S.	-.231ᵃ**
Self-rating of recovery	N.S.	-.209*
Satisfaction with self now	-.245**	-.385ᵃ****

Notes: N = 87 unless otherwise specified. N.S. = not significant.
ᵃN = 113   ᵇN = 76   ᶜN = 73
*p < .06.   **p < .05.   ***p < .01.   ****p < .001

Table 10.1 presents zero-order correlations of guilt/blame factor scores (current generalized self-blame) with selected variables. By the time this measure was taken, the effect of the prerape relationship to the rapist had dissipated considerably; none of these variables correlated significantly with current guilt/blame. However, current generalized guilt/blame did correlate significantly with our global measure of negative symptomatology $[r (113) = .295, p < .01]$, general self-esteem $[r (113) = -.310, p < .01]$, romantic self image—a measure of self-esteem in the context of romantic relationships $[r (113) = -.231, p < .05]$, and satisfaction with oneself now $[r (113) = -.385, p < .001]$. It also had marginally significant relationships with hours of rape-related counseling $[r (87) = .196, p < .06]$ and with self-rating of recovery $[r (87) = -.209, p < .06]$.

In addition to the correlations presented in table 10.1, current generalized guilt/blame was highly correlated with several factors measuring coping styles. Guilt/blame was positively correlated with avoidance behaviors $[r (113) = .234, p < .02]$; nervous/anxious behaviors $[r (113) = .207, p < .03]$; cognitive behaviors $[r (113) = .189, p < .05]$; and self-destructive behaviors $[r (113) = .342, p < .0003]$. Construction of these coping measures is described in Burt and Katz (1987). The only coping measure not associated with the guilt/blame factor was expressive behaviors—a measure reflecting the healthiest approach to recovery of accepting one's feelings and working them through. As described by Burt and Katz (1987), high scores on coping measures were associated with high negative symptomatology (fear, anxiety, and depression) and low self-esteem.

DISCUSSION

In every instance, the reported correlations confirm our expectation that high degrees of self-blame indicate distress rather than an adaptive recovery mechanism. Although it is clear from our results and previous research that self-blame is indeed a common response to rape, it is noteworthy that most women assign more of the blame to other sources. The shift over time of blame for the assault away from oneself and onto other causes of rape appears to be one element of the process of recovery.

Our finding that 68% of the respondents blamed themselves at least in part for the rape is consistent with Janoff-Bulman's (1979) results. She reported that counselors indicated that 74% of their clients blamed themselves somewhat for the rape. Of these, 69% were seen as behavioral self-blamers while 19% were classified as characterological self-blamers. The similarity of our findings provides some validation of our use of a retrospective self-report measure and also of Janoff-Bulman's reliance on counselor estimates. Janoff-Bulman's findings are probably based primarily on women's feelings soon after their assaults, since the majority of crisis center contacts are likely to be made early in the recovery process. It is important to consider that by the time of our interviews with the respondents, an average of 45 months had passed since the rape and significantly fewer women blamed themselves at all.

Another issue that our data address is Janoff-Bulman's contention that self-blame may aid in recovery because it enables women to feel that they are more in control and thus more able to avoid future victimization. We expected that regaining control would be a key focus of recovery, although we did not accept the notion that such control is achieved through blaming oneself. In asking women to describe what they felt it meant to be recovered, only 8% mentioned control in their responses. Similarly, only 5% of our respondents mentioned gaining control as a task of recovery, and only 4% listed feeling in control as one of the things they had left to work through. Thus, it appears that even if self-blame does enhance feelings of being in control, there is no evidence that it promotes better recovery in the large percentage of women for whom control is not a prominent issue.

For those women who do focus on regaining control following rape, there are paths besides self-blame for doing so. Rape crisis center counselors, for instance, often help women cognitively reframe the event: "You did a good job taking care of yourself, making choices in the situation that kept you safe (alive). If you had responded differently, you might have been hurt more severely—you were there, you evaluated the situation as well as you could, and you acted, trusting your own intuition and thinking." Interventions such as these impart to the victim a sense of competence and control in much the same way Janoff-Bulman argues that self-blame attributions have been proposed to do. However, these interventions help the victim feel successful and give her credit, rather than support her belief that it is the responsibility of individual women like herself to prevent rapes. The fact that the level of self-blame attributions depends so closely on the prerape victim-rapist relationship is consistent with the popular notion that if a woman is raped by someone she knows, then she is suspect for having failed to prevent it.

Our data also counter other assertions regarding self-blame. In our study, we asked rape victim respondents who had received counseling to tell us, in an open-ended format, what were the most helpful things their counselors said to them. Among comments this interview question elicited, the most frequently mentioned as helpful (endorsed by 65% of the women interviewed) were statements by counselors to victims that "you are not to blame." This is clearly at odds with Janoff-Bulman's experience of such statements causing victim distress. It may be that this difference can be explained by the different populations; recovery from rape is indeed a different task than is adjustment to a terminal or debilitating illness or injury, despite their commonalities.

Self-blame per se is an endorsement of a negative view of oneself, both as a woman and as a rape victim. We found that higher levels of initial self-blame were significantly associated with the presence of more negative symptomatology such as fear, anxiety, and depression. This relationship between self-blame and psychological distress is further demonstrated by the positive correlations between self-blame and several indicators of postrape difficulties. The more women blamed themselves for the rape, the more suicidal they had been since the rape, the greater the likelihood that they had been psychiatrically hospitalized, and the lower their self-esteem. This negative correlation between self-blame and self-esteem directly contradicts Janoff-Bulman's supposition that behavioral self-blame is likely to be associated with high self-esteem. Her argument for the adaptive function of self-blame is based on this premise; the clear relationship in our sample between self-blame and low self-esteem indicates that her argument has little basis in reality as experienced by actual rape victims.

The extent to which women blamed themselves also was associated with the amount of counseling they received; more blame accompanied more hours of counseling. It appears, then, that women who felt more at fault for their rapes experienced greater psychological distress, felt worse about themselves, and, therefore, sought counseling in order to get help. They may have stayed in counseling longer because they had to deal not only with the rape, but also with their eroded self-image.

The fact that more self-blame was also correlated with a longer recovery period adds further support to our assertion that self-blame is experienced by most rape victims as negative and distressing, rather than as comforting or helpful to recovery. It may be that, like other uncomfortable symptoms (such as intrusive memories or phobic fears), self-blame functions as a motivator for women to seek help and to change their situations. In this regard, self-blame might appear to be associated with growth through the recovery process or with successful adjustment to the rape. This currently popular notion that self-blame enhances recovery is unlikely to be true, given the understanding of self-blame and its correlates that this study has provided. Self-blame should, instead, be added to the list of negative symptoms that occur frequently following rape, and its effects should be considered along with those of other distressing thoughts and emotions.

This chapter is based on data collected with support from a grant from the National Institute of Mental Health, no. 1 RO1 MH38337. The views expressed are solely those of the authors and do not reflect those of the sponsor, the Urban Institute, or its trustees or supporters.

REFERENCES

Armor, D. 1974. Theta reliability and factor scaling. In *Sociological Methodology*, 1973–1974, ed. H.L. Costner. San Francisco: Jossey-Bass.

Bulman, R.J., and C.B. Wortman. 1977. Attributions of blame and coping in the "real world": Severe accident victims react to their lot. *Journal of Personality and Social Psychology* 35: 351–63.

Burgess, A.W., and L.L. Holmstrom. 1979. Adaptive strategies and recovery from rape. *American Journal of Psychiatry* 146: 1278–82.

Burt, M.R., and B. Katz. 1985. Rape, Robbery, and Burglary: Responses to actual and feared criminal victimization, with special focus on women and the elderly. *Victimology* 10: 1–3.

———. 1978. Dimensions of recovery from rape: Focus on growth outcomes. *Journal of Interpersonal Violence*. Forthcoming.

Calhoun, K., B. Atkeson, and P. Resick. 1982. A longitudinal examination of fear reactions in victims of rape. *Journal of Counseling Psychology* 29: 655–61.

Derogatis, L.R., and P.M. Spenser. 1982. *The brief symptom inventory administration, scoring, and procedures manual—I*. Baltimore: Clinical Psychometric Research.

Figley, C.R., ed. 1985. *Trauma and its wake*. New York: Brunner/Mazel.

Frank E., and B.D. Stewart. 1984. Depressive symptoms in rape victims: A revisit. *Journal of Affective Disorders*. 7: 77–85.

Frankl, V. 1963. *Man's search for meaning*. New York: International Universities Press.

Horowitz, M., N. Wilmer, and W. Alvarez. 1979. Impact of event scale: A measure of subjective stress. *Psychosomatic Medicine* 41: 209–18.

Janoff-Bulman, R. 1979. Characterological versus behavioral self-blame: Inquiries into depression and blame. *Journal of Personality and Social Psychology* 37: 1798–1809.

———. 1982. Esteem and control bases of blame: "Adaptive" strategies for victims versus observers. *Journal of Personality* 50: 118–92.

———. 1985. The aftermath of victimization: Rebuilding shattered assumptions. In *Trauma and its wake*, ed., C.R. Figley. New York: Brunner/Mazel.

Janoff-Bulman, R., and I.H. Frieze. 1983. A theoretical perspective for understanding reactions to victimizations. *Journal of Social Issues* 39: 1–17.

Katz, B.L., and M.R. Burt. 1986. Effects of familiarity with the rapist on post-rape
recovery. Paper presented at annual meeting, American Psychological Association, Washington, D.C.

Kilpatrick, D.G., L.J. Veronen, and C.L. Best. 1985. Factors predicting psychological distress among rape victims. In *Trauma and its wake,* ed. C.R. Figley.
New York: Brunner/Mazel.

Lerner, M.J. 1980. *The belief in a just world: A fundamental delusion.* New York:
Plenum.

McNair, D., M. Lorr, and L. Droppelman. 1971. *Profile of mood states scale
manual.* San Diego: Educational and Industrial Testing Service.

Miller, D.I., and C.A. Porter. 1983. Self-blame in victims of violence. *Journal
of Social Issues* 39: 139–52.

Nadelson, C.C., et al. 1982. A follow-up study of rape victims. *American Journal
of Psychiatry* 139: 1266–70.

Resnick, P.A., et al. 1984. Assessment of fear reactions in sexual assault victims:
A factor analytic study of the Veronen-Kilpatrick modified fear survey. Univer-
isty of Missouri-St. Louis. Typescript.

Rosenberg, M. 1965. *Society and the adolescent self-image.* Princeton, N.J.:
Princeton University Press.

Taylor, S. 1983. Adjustments to threatening events: A theory of cognitive
adaptation. *American Psychologist* 38: 1161–73.

Wortman, C.B. 1976. Causal attributions and personal control.. In *New directions
in attribution research, vol. I,* ed. J. Harvey, W. Ickes, and R.F. Kidd. Hillsdale,
N.J.: Erlbaum Associates.

———. 1983. Coping with victimization: Conclusions and implications for
future research. *Journal of Social Issues* 39: 195–221.

CHAPTER

11

RESPONDING TO THE NEEDS OF RAPE VICTIMS

Research Findings

LINDA E. LEDRAY

Hennepin County Medical Center

In the past ten years, significant advances have been made in research dealing with sexual assault and the treatment of its survivors. This chapter presents the results of a research study evaluating the relative efficacy of two methods of treating victims of sexual assault. The study attempted to overcome many of the methodological problems inherent to this area of research.

The early descriptive studies of the responses of sexual assault survivors looked for a pattern in these responses in an attempt to better understand the victim (Sutherland and Scherl 1970; Burgess and Holmstrom 1974; Notman and Nadelson 1976). Later studies have employed the use of standardized tests to evaluate the change over time of specific symptoms identified in the earlier studies. The symptoms that have attracted the most research attention are depression, anxiety, phobic fear, self-esteem, self-blame, anger, and sexual dysfunction.

The availability of standardized measures of these symptom patterns, such as the Beck depression inventory (BDI), the Hamilton depression rating scale (HDRS), the symptom checklist (SCL-9OR), the multiple affect adjective checklist (MAACL), and many others with demonstrated reliability and validity have made the researcher's job much easier. A limited number of unique symptoms are now often the primary dependent variables evaluated over time in rape research. Depression, anxiety, and fear are the primary variables of interest in this study.

PREVIOUS RESEARCH

DEPRESSION

Atkeson and colleagues (1982) used both the Beck depression inventory (Beck et al. 1961) and the Hamilton depression rating scale (Hamilton 1960) to evaluate the incidence, severity, and duration of depressive symptoms in 43 female rape victims over a one-year period. They compared their population to 21 nonrape matched controls at two weeks, one month, two months, four months, eight months, and one year after rape. Both measures showed a significant difference across assessment periods between the victim and nonvictim groups.

The level of depression was also evaluated by Ellis, Atkeson, and Calhoun (1981), who used the BDI to study 27 adult female rape victims one year following a rape. They found the one-year BDI score for the victim group, which had not been involved in periodic assessment with the opportunity to discuss the assault, well within the subclinical range of depression.

Another research group (Frank, Turner, and Duffy 1979) used the BDI to assess 34 rape victims within one month after the assault. Consistent with the earlier reports was their finding that considerable depression was present in their group during the first month. One problem in evaluating this and other studies is that the amount of support or psychological treatment received by the victims was not addressed.

In a study looking at fear and anxiety, Kilpatrick, Veronen, and Resick (1979) included the SCL-9OR (Derogatis 1977) and found that the 46 recent rape victims scored significantly higher than the 35 nonvictims on eight of the nine symptom scales at the six- to ten-day and the one-month assessment points. A subsample involving 20 victims and 20 controls was tested later at one year (Kilpatrick, Resnick, and Veronen 1981). The assessment battery included the SCL-9OR, the modified fear survey (MFS) (Veronen and Kilpatrick 1980), the profile of mood states (POMS) (McNair, Lorr, and Droppleman 1971), and the state-trait anxiety inventory (STAI) (Spielberger, Gorsuch, and Lushene 1970). The between-group difference was only significant at the one-month assessment point, as a result of the moderately high level of depression in the victim group.

There are still relatively few systematic research studies available that specifically evaluate depression in rape victims. However, all of the available data indicate that depression is a major problem through the first one or two months after rape. There appears to be a rapid initial decline in the level of depression during the first few weeks, with the level of depression returning to near normal levels by three to four months in those patients seen and assessed periodically. It also appears from the research by Ellis, Atkeson, and Calhoun (1981) that another group of rape victims may continue to experience persistent problems with depression long after the assault.

ANXIETY AND FEAR

The primary initial reaction to rape is often anxiety and fear, not only of injury, but also of death. This fear does not end when the rape is over, but may continue for many weeks, months, and even years. Veronen and Best (1983) evaluated rape victims and nonvictim controls using the Wolpe-Lang fear survey (Wolpe and Lang 1964), plus additional items of fear reported by rape victims, and the SCL-9OR along with a state-trait anxiety inventory. Although they found generalized distress was extremely disruptive during the first month, only fear and anxiety continued at a high level in the victim group throughout the first year. The most problematic fears included rape cues, fear of vulnerability to future attack, and rape-precipitated concerns (such as the necessity of testifying in court). The fear of being alone, and thus more vulnerable, was the most frequent fear and was reported by 80% of the sample.

In an earlier interim report on this study, Kilpatrick, Veronen, and Resnick (1979) indicated that the rape victim sample included only those victims receiving counseling. (It is important to note that as few as 3% of rape victims request counseling directly after the assault, and reporters appear to have more frequent postassault problems [Kilpatrick, Best, and Veronen 1983]. Since it is likely that only distressed victims seek treatment, existing studies using samples of reporters, especially reporters who also request treatment, may greatly overestimate the extent of the impact to the victim.) This early report indicated 46 rape victims and 35 nonvictim controls were evaluated at six to ten days, one month, three months, and six months after the rape.

Neither the interim report nor the 1983 report stated whether treatment was initiated during the evaluation period, though one might expect it had been since the victims came to the center specifically for counseling. The researchers reported that victims scored significantly higher than nonvictims on 25 of their 28 indicators of fear or anxiety through the first month. While the victims' general distress had subsided, at three and six months they still scored significantly higher than the nonvictim group on trait-anxiety and phobic-anxiety measures. Their fear and anxiety had stabilized after the first month, but at a significantly higher level than found in a nonvictim group.

In another study with a smaller sample of 15 rape victims (Veronen and Kilpatrick 1982), the increase in most symptoms occurred at the three-month follow-up point, which was two months after the victims' stress inoculation training subsided. It is possible that treatment continued through the three-month assessment point in the earlier study and that there may have been a posttreatment increase in fear and anxiety in both studies.

Calhoun, Atkeson, and Resnick (1982) reported the results of additional measures used with the same sample reported by Atkeson et al. (1982) on depression. Victims were initially significantly more fearful than nonvictims on measures of overall fear as well as on most of the six subscales, and although there was an initial decline, they remained significantly more fearful through the 12-month assessment point. It is interesting to note the initial rapid decline during the first two months, which is very much like the initial decline in BDI scores discussed earlier. Calhoun, Atkeson, and Resnick also indicated that victims reported frequent nightmares, generalized anxiety, and fear of a wide range of stimuli associated with the rape. Though no systematic assessment was completed, Burgess and Holmstrom (1974) and Notman and Nadelson (1976) reported the same clinical impression from victim interviews.

Generally, it appears that the most distressing period with the most problematic symptoms for rape victims occurs during the first one to two months after rape. It is during this period that the victims report the highest levels of depression, fear, and anxiety. While there appears to be a dramatic decline in reported symptoms for most victims by the three-month assessment period, some victims do report less significant but continued distress for one to six years later. However, few studies have assessed long-term impact.

STUDY GOALS

To be most effective, treatment must recognize the importance to the patient of depression, anxiety, and fear. The symptoms represent potentially difficult issues that must be understood and resolved. This study sought to develop and evaluate a treatment model designed to address the unique needs of rape victims, especially during the first few months when the symptoms are the most distressing.

The study evaluated the impact of rape and the relative efficacy of two methods of treating rape victims: supportive crisis counseling and guide to goals. *Supportive crisis counseling* was selected because it is widely used by rape crisis centers throughout the country as the treatment method of choice with rape victims. This method also appeared to fit the needs of rape victims because of its emphasis on early intervention in a period of significant distress. In addition, crisis theory assumes that the individual in crisis is a normal individual dealing with an overwhelming crisis; psychopathology is not implied.

Guide to goals was selected for evaluation because it appeared to meet treatment needs. It places the locus of control in the hands of the patient, not the counselor. The process of goal development facilitates the patient's learning to regain control. Guide to goals has been shown to be an efficacious treatment technique in short-term counseling with other populations (Smith 1976; Goldstein 1962). In particular, the use of guide to goals with other patient populations has resulted in significant gains on measures of depression, anxiety, and self-esteem. Guide to goals also allows for goals that address specific as well as general problems.

In addition, the study emphasized developing, implementing, and systematically evaluating a treatment model for rape victims that would be cost effective and that could be easily replicable in the clinical setting. The clinical relevance of treatment methods and procedures were always of central concern.

Two primary hypotheses were tested: (1) that psychological treatment would reduce the negative impact of the rape and facilitate behavioral changes in the desired direction faster than medical care only, and (2) that guide to goals would reduce the negative impact of the rape and facilitate behavioral changes in the desired direction faster than supportive counseling. Additional hypotheses included the expectation that rape would indeed have a negative impact on the victim, which would result in feelings of depression, anxiety, hostility, fear, and generalized distress. It was also expected that there would be a general decline in these symptoms over time, even in the control population.

METHODS

STUDY SAMPLE

All females 16 years of age and older who came to the Hennepin County Medical Center's (HCMC) emergency department, who stated that they had been raped, and who agreed to participate were included in the study. Victims were not asked to participate if they were unconscious on admission to the emergency department, unable to speak English, or had either physical or psychological trauma necessitating admission to an inpatient facility. Individuals were also excluded if they were severely mentally retarded and thus unable to understand the necessary consent issues and forms.

Only 15% of the rape victims initially asked to participate in this study refused to do so. Another 5% who initially agreed to participate dropped out during the following year. There were no significant differences in the dropout rate across treatment conditions. Ninety-eight rape victims remained active participants throughout the year and formed the basis for the study.

Of the 98 active cases, only 6.7% were married, although an additional 7.7% were living with a male. The highest percentage, 68.9%, were single and living alone or living with a female roommate; 2.6% were widowed; 11.9% were divorced. While the majority (82.5%) were white, 10.3% were black, which is more than twice the percentage of black females in the general population of Hennepin County. Ages ranged up to 78 years; the majority of victims (81.9%) were less than 30 years old. Only 37% had completed high school. Of the victims, 42% were either students, homemakers, or working at unskilled jobs; 11% were professionals; 24% were technical employees; and 4% were identified prostitutes. As might be expected with a young, often unemployed population, 36.1% earned less than $5,000 per year.

RESEARCH DESIGN

A 2 x 2 randomized factorial block design was employed. Each victim was randomly assigned to one of four treatment conditions. In order to maintain some consistency in group size, researchers completed randomization blocks of 40, with 10 subjects allocated to each treatment condition for every 40 consecutive subjects. Because important treatment differences began during the first contact in the emergency room, researchers were unable to wait to make the random assignment after the initial dropout occurred between the emergency room and the 24- to 48-hour visit. As a result, differences resulted in the four treatment group sizes.

GROUP 1: CONTROL ($N = 15$) Group 1 was treated in the same manner and received the same care that was in place prior to the implementation of the research program. The victims were given a medical evidentiary exam and provided with care of medical injuries sustained during the assault. Because the literature indicated rape victims improve over time even without treatment, the progress of this group on the dependent measures was utilized to evaluate the effectiveness of treatment in relation to the improvement seen over time without treatment.

GROUP 2: GUIDE TO GOALS ($N = 24$) Group 2 received an evidentiary exam and was provided with care of injuries. In addition, the nurse counselors negotiated treatment goals using the guide-to-goals format.

GROUP 3: SUPPORTIVE COUNSELING ($N = 31$)   In addition to receiving a medical evidentiary exam and care of injuries, the third group was provided with supportive counseling.

GROUP 4: SUPPORTIVE COUNSELING AND GUIDE TO GOALS ($N = 27$) Group 4 received an evidentiary exam, care of injuries, and a combination of supportive counseling and the use of treatment goals in the guide to goals format.

TREATMENT PROCEDURES

MEDICAL TREATMENT.   Medical treatment was provided for all the victims by the hospital staff and included an evidentiary exam and care of injuries. Sexually transmitted disease and pregnancy testing, preventive care, and disease treatment were also available.

GUIDE TO GOALS FORMAT III   Guide to goals is an adaptation of goal-attainment scaling (GAS), an evaluation device developed by Kiresuk and Sherman (1968). As the name implies, guide to goals developed from the general tradition of goal-focused counseling. At its simplest, guide to goals involves setting a goal, implementing counseling, determining subsequent goal attainment, and using this information to modify future activities.   Goal-oriented counseling and feedback are interrelated operations of the overall treatment approach.

Goals were negotiated between the rape victim and counselor by means of a five-point scale referred to as a goal attainment guide, of observable outcomes. The use of this guide involved: (1) selecting the goal areas, (2) weighting these areas according to their comparative importance, (3) selecting a follow-up time interval, (4) filling in a scale of potential outcomes for each interval, (5) determining and listing realistic strategies to facilitate reaching the desired goal, and (6) aggregating the scores on the individual scales through the calculation of a summary goal attainment score. Patients reviewed and revised goals and strategies at each follow-up contact point.

Follow-up checks by the project director indicated that all of the patients completed at least three goals, many completed five, and in some cases old goals were discarded and new goals were developed. The goals were not used in data analysis, as several patients indicated such use of this very personal information would make them feel uncomfortable.

SUPPORTIVE COUNSELING   The supportive counseling component was based on crisis intervention theory. During the six-month pilot phase, the following seven components of supportive counseling were established:

1. Being an empathetic, accepting, and respectful listener to whom the victim can express her feelings

2. Responding to the victim as a normal, healthy individual who is currently in a state of emotional disequilibrium as a result of a serious life crisis

3. Being nonjudgmental by recognizing that it is the subjective experience of rape that is important and that it is not the counselor's job to determine if the victim was "really" raped

4. Assisting the victim in regaining or maintaining control of herself and her situation, ensuring that she knows she has the ability to make choices, and providing her with the necessary information to make informed choices

5. Treating the victim as separate from the rape

6. Assisting the victim in identifying and dealing with the response of her social support network

7. Addressing issues of personal safety

MEASUREMENT INSTRUMENTS

Follow-up measures were completed at each contact point. These measures included the Beck depression inventory (Beck et al. 1961), the SCL-9OR (Derogatis 1977), goal attainment scaling (Kiresuk and Sherman 1968), an assault data base, consumer satisfaction measures, and structured interviews developed specifically for the study.

PROCEDURE

One of four nurse researchers/counselors were on call 24 hours per day, seven days per week, and came into the emergency department whenever a rape victim was admitted. The counselor who first met with the victim followed the same victim for a one-year period, with a minimum number of contacts being those that occurred at two days, three weeks, six weeks, three months, six months, and one year after the assault. An independent follow-up worker also saw the victim at these times in order to complete the goal attainment follow-up guides used to measure observable behavioral changes.

The study was introduced to the victim and informed consent obtained at the 24–48 hour visit. The same nurse counselor who had met with the victim in the emergency room contacted her to explain the study, obtain consent, and offer additional supportive services to those in the treatment groups.

RESULTS

The focus of the main analysis was based on the study hypotheses. This focus was: (1) to determine if there was a treatment effect, (2) to determine if there was a goal-setting effect, (3) to determine if there was a counseling effect, (4) to determine the relative efficacy of goal setting and supportive counseling, and (5) to determine if there was an interactional effect between goal setting and counseling. The primary dependent variables used to evaluate treatment outcome were depression, anxiety, generalized distress, and behavior changes in the desired direction.

IMPACT ON DEPRESSION

Two measures of depression and its severity were used, the BDI and the SCL-90R depression scale. There were no pretreatment measures of depression. The first testing point was two days after treatment had begun, in two counseling sessions. These sessions included the emergency-room visit and a one-hour counseling session. In some cases, additional telephone contacts offered support or answered patient questions.

The two-day assessment indicated that there were already differences among the groups. Ordinarily, an analysis of covariance (ANCOVA) would be performed to remove any pretreatment differences that may have resulted even after randomization of victims to treatments. However, because the initial assessment of depression occurred after treatment had already begun, statistically removing any initial differences in the treatment groups would be, in effect, removing the initial treatment effect we were attempting to measure. Therefore, we did not attempt any covariance analyses.

The BDI scores at the two-day testing point indicated a higher level of depression in the control group than in the three treatment groups (see figure 11.1). This trend continued through the one-year testing point. Three of the four groups showed the steepest decline in self-reported depression during the first three weeks, with the group means reaching normal limits of less than 10 in both goal-setting groups (groups 2 and 4) at that time. This same "normal" level was reached in the counseling group (group 3) at the three-month point. Only the no-treatment control group remained slightly above normal throughout the year.

Though less than 10 is usually used to indicate a normal level of depression, a group mean of 10 indicates many scores were above "normal." Because of this, an additional analysis was completed to determine by treatment group the frequency of scores that were less than 10 (normal), 10–19 (mildly depressed), 20–29 (moderately depressed),

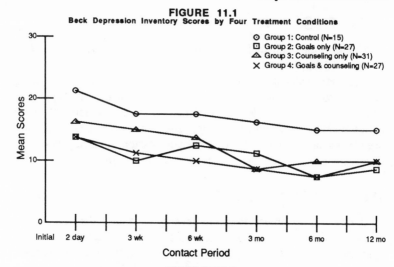

FIGURE 11.1
Beck Depression Inventory Scores by Four Treatment Conditions

○ Group 1: Control (N=15)
□ Group 2: Goals only (N=27)
△ Group 3: Counseling only (N=31)
✕ Group 4: Goals & counseling (N=27)

Contact Period

TABLE 11.1

FREQUENCY DISTRIBUTION OF BECK DEPRESSION INVENTORY
SCORES BY TREATMENT GROUP AT THREE WEEKS

		Treatment Group		
Score	Control	Goals	Supportive Counseling	Goals and Counseling
0–9	8	11	14	16
10–19	1	4	6	3
20–29	2	1	4	6
30 or above	2	0	3	0
Totals	13	16	27	25

and 30 or greater (severely depressed). A chi-square analysis indicated that the categoric distribution of depression scores was not different across treatment groups. A second chi-square analysis comparing a binary partition of BDI scores (0–9 and 10 or greater) in the four treatment groups was also not significant. Frequencies of BDI scores by treatment group at the three-week testing point are presented in table 11.1

A two-way analysis of variance (ANOVA) was completed on the BDI scores at each point in time to determine whether there were any interactions between the goal-setting and counseling treatment groups (see table 11.2). No significant differences were found in the main effects or between the counseling (groups 3 and 4) and no counseling (groups 1 and 2) groups. The two-way interaction between counseling and goals was also nonsignificant. This was true at all points in time.

TABLE 11.2

BECK DEPRESSION INVENTORY SAMPLE BY TREATMENT GROUP

Treatment Group	Size through 6 months	Size through 12 months
Control (group 1)	6	3
Goals (group 2)	10	7
Counseling (group 3)	15	10
Goals and counseling (group 4)	9	6
Total	40	26

The repeated measures of analysis of variance on the BDI data through six months indicated a significant treatment effect [F (4, 144) = 5.08, $p <$ .001]. Two of the three treatment contrasts were clearly significant: (1) the control group vs. the three treatment groups ($p < .001$) and (2) the goals groups vs. no goals ($p < .001$).

Next the treatment-by-time interaction of the BDI scores was tested by means of the Wilkes multivariate test of significance. No time-by-treatment interaction was found [F (12, 87) = .657, $p = .787$]. Each treatment group thus followed the same general pattern, or slope, over time. A time or trend effect was also tested with the Wilkes multivariate test of significance. The results indicated a significant, but weak, overall trend [F (4, 33) = 2.69, $p < .05$]. The type of trend was found to be only linear [F (1, 36) = 10.25, $p < .01$] and is toward a lower level of depression over time, based on the BDI scores (see figures 11.1 and 11.2).

FIGURE 11.2
Beck Depression Inventory Scores by Two Treatment Conditions

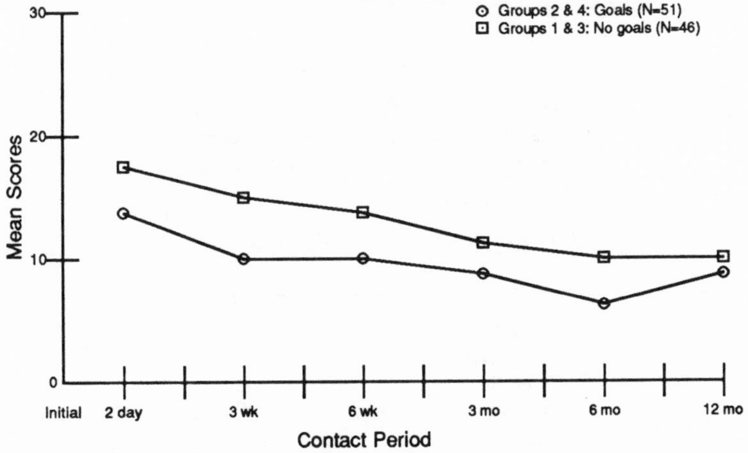

A repeated-measures analysis was also completed on the SCL-9OR depression scale. The homogeneity-of-variance assumption was satisfied through six months. The initial results indicated there was an overall treatment effect [$F (3, 33) = 4.80, p < .01$], so three treatment contrasts were tested. All three contrasts were significant: control vs. the three treatment groups ($p < .01$), counseling vs. no counseling ($p < .05$), and goals vs. no goals ($p < .001$). Additional analysis using Wilkes multivariate tests of significance indicated no time x treatment interaction. There was a very significant trend effect [$F (4, 30) = 21.42, p < .001$. The trend was both linear [$F (1, 33) = 40.38, p < .00001$] and quadratic [$F (1, 33) = 11.51, p < .001$].

FIGURE 11.3
Symptom Checklist Depression-Scale Scores by Four Treatment Conditions

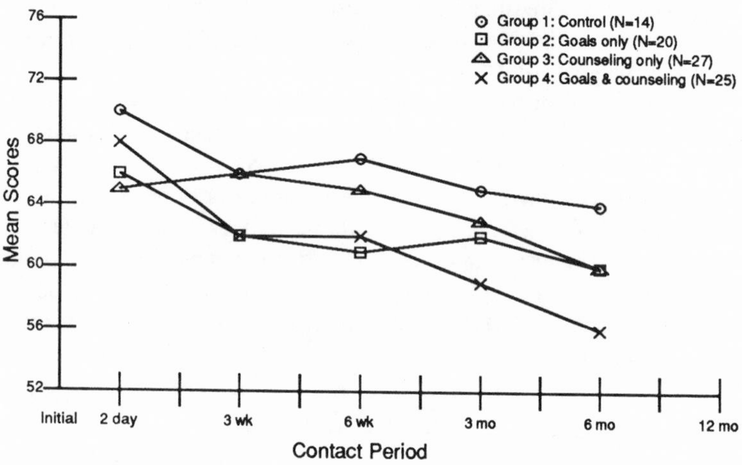

⊙ Group 1: Control (N=14)
□ Group 2: Goals only (N=20)
△ Group 3: Counseling only (N=27)
✕ Group 4: Goals & counseling (N=25)

TABLE 11.3

CORRELATION OF BECK DEPRESSION INVENTORY SCORES
AND SYMPTOM CHECKLIST DEPRESSION SCORES AT
CONTACT POINTS FOR TREATMENT GROUPS

Contact Point	Median r[a]
2 days	.74*
3 weeks	.74*
6 weeks	.81*
3 months	.81*
6 months	.81*

[a] Median r calculated across treatment groups.   *$p < .01$.

When the SCL-9OR depression scale mean group scores were plotted (see figure 11.3), the slope of the curve was found to be similar to the BDI scores (see figures 11.1 and 11.2). So that this similarity could be evaluated, a correlation between the BDI and SCL-9OR depression scale scores was completed for each group; the median correlation across groups at each point in time indicated the scores were highly related (see table 11.3).

An ANOVA based on the SCL-9OR depression scale indicated a significant difference between the control group and the three treatment groups at the two-day testing point ($p < .01$) and a difference approaching significance at the three-week point ($p = .06$) and at the six-month point ($p=.07$).

In general, it appeared that all treatment groups reported less depression over time, with a generally linear decline. The three treatment groups recovered faster than the control groups, and the goal-setting groups recovered faster than the counseling groups. However, the mean scores of all victim groups remained at a high normal level of depression, even at the one-year assessment point.

IMPACT ON ANXIETY

Two SCL-9OR anxiety scales were used as dependent measures of differential impact based on treatment group assignment. The repeated-measures analysis of the first of these, the phobic-anxiety scale, indicated the multivariate assumption of equal pattern of variance was violated at six months; thus the analysis was completed through three months only. After finding a significant overall treatment effect ($p < .05$), researchers analyzed additional treatment contrasts.

Three nonorthogonal contrasts were completed. All three were significant. The most highly significant was the control group vs. the three treatment groups ($p < .01$). The goals vs. no goals group and the counseling vs. no counseling contrasts were also both significant ($p < .05$).

The analysis showed there was no time-by-treatment effect, indicating that the treatment groups had the same slope over time. There was, however, a significant overall time effect [$F (3, 40) = 38.98, p < .00001$], indicating an overall improvement (decrease) in level of phobic anxiety over time. The univariate test of components or direction of the trend indicated the trend was linear ($p < .00001$) and quadratic ($p < .00001$). This indicated a slight change in the slope of the curves in more than one direction over time.

The SCL-9OR phobic-anxiety group mean scores were also plotted over time (see figure 11.4). The control group consistently reported more

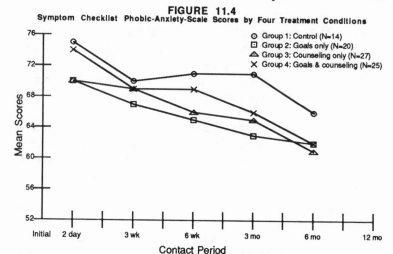

FIGURE 11.4
Symptom Checklist Phobic-Anxiety-Scale Scores by Four Treatment Conditions

phobic anxiety. An analysis of variance indicated the difference between the control group and treatment groups was statistically significant at the three-month point ($p < .05$). There was also a statistically significant counseling effect at this point, with group 1 and group 2 (no counseling) reporting a combined score significantly above group 3 and group 4 (counseling) ($p < .01$). This significance is an artifact of the excessively high phobic anxiety reported by the control group (group 1). The phobic anxiety level in group 2 is actually below group 3 and group 4 at the three-month reporting point. There was also a significant difference between the three treatment groups and the control group at the six-week point ($p < .05$).

The anxiety scale of the SCL-9OR was also analyzed in the same manner as the phobic-anxiety scale. There was a significant overall treatment effect found on the repeated measures analysis [$F (3, 33) = 3.76$, $p < .01$], so additional contrasts were completed. The three treatment contrasts were once again all significant: control vs. three treatment groups ($p < .01$), counseling vs. no counseling ($p < .01$), and goals vs. no goals ($p < .01$). There was a significant treatment-by-time interaction with this scale [$F (12, 79) = 2.46, p < .01$], indicating differences in change over time between the treatment groups. The trend effect was significant [$F (4, 30) = 23.12, p < .00001$]. The trend was linear ($p < .00001$), quadratic ($p < .00001$), and cubic ($p < .01$).

When the group means of the SCL-9OR anxiety scale were plotted over time, the results were very similar to the phobic-anxiety scale. (see figure 11.5). Once again, the control group consistently reported more anxiety than the treatment groups. An analysis of variance indicated the difference was significant at the three-month point in time ($p < .01$).

FIGURE 11.5
Symptom Checklist Anxiety-Scale Scores by Four Treatment Conditions

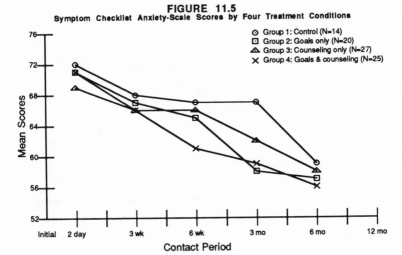

Overall, the two anxiety measures evidenced a steady decline in level over time. The decline was most rapid during the first three weeks and most pronounced in the three treatment groups.

IMPACT ON BEHAVIOR

The goal-attainment follow-up guides developed by independent researchers blind to treatment group assignment were used as the measure of successful behavioral change. The changes indicated on the guide to goals format were evaluated using the formula developed by Kiresuk and Sherman (1968). According to these computations, a maximum score of 100 would indicate more than the expected change in the desired direction on all goals. A score of 0 would indicate less than the expected changes on all goals, and a score of 50 would indicate that, on an average, the expected changes were made on all goals. Goals were written with the expectation that they would be achieved by the end of six months.

All four groups began at essentially the same point and there was a steady upward trend in the scores for all groups, indicating successful behavioral change (see figure 11.6). The primary change occurred in the two goal-setting groups, 2 and 4 (see figure 11.7). An analysis of variance indicated the difference between the goal-setting vs. no goal-setting groups was significant at the three-week point ($p < .01$) and at the six-month point ($p < .05$) and approached significance at six weeks ($p < .10$). The difference between the supportive-counseling and no-counseling groups was not statistically significant at any point in time (at three weeks p was .870, and at six months it was .643).

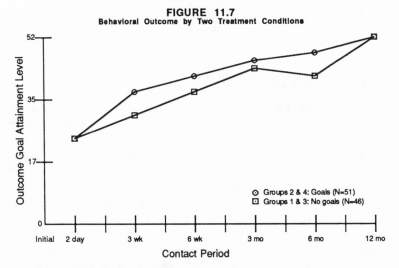

FIGURE 11.6
Behavioral Outcome by Four Treatment Conditions

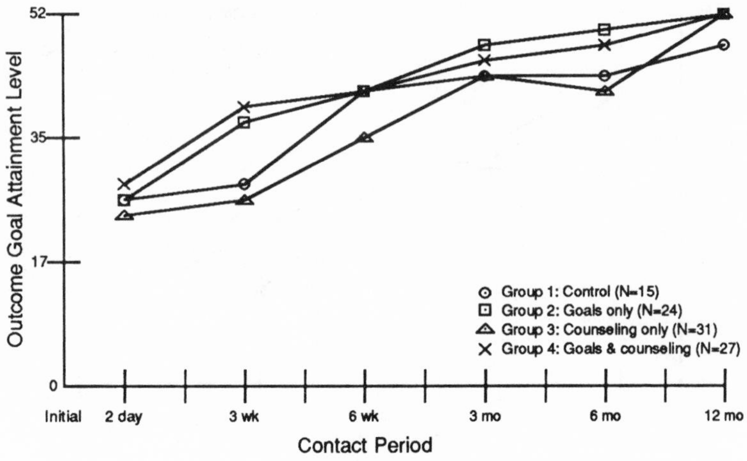

FIGURE 11.7
Behavioral Outcome by Two Treatment Conditions

SUMMARY OF FINDINGS

The data indicated that rape had a significant negative impact on the victims studied. Initially this impact was severe, and the SCL-9OR profiles of the victims even appeared similar on analysis to an inpatient psychiatric population. Abnormally high levels of anxiety, phobic anxiety, and depression were used as the primary dependent measures of treatment outcome in this study. Consistent with the findings of other researchers (Atkeson et al. 1982; Frank, Turner, and Duffy 1979; and Kilpatrick, Resick, and Veronen 1981), considerable depression, anxiety, and phobic anxiety were found on initial assessment. It is, however, important to note that this response was not ongoing. Rather, it appeared to be time limited in most cases, especially with treatment. A more rapid decline in symptomatology was noted in the first three weeks to three months, though the residual levels remained at high normal levels throughout one year. This too is consistent with the earlier research findings.

TABLE 11.4
SUMMARY OF FINDINGS: ANALYSIS OF VARIANCE

			Treatment Point			
Measure	2 Days	3 Weeks	6 Weeks	3 Months	6 Months	1 Year
Beck depression inventory	N.S.	Goals vs. no goals; $p < .06$	N.S.	N.S.	N.S.	N.S.
Symptom checklist depression	Control vs. 3 treatments; $p < .01$	Control vs. 3 treatments; $p < .10$	N.S.	N.S.	Control vs. 3 treatments; $p < .10$	N.S.
Symptom checklist phobic anxiety	N.S.	N.S.	Control vs. 3 treatments; $p < .05$	Control vs. 3 treatments; $p < .05$	N.S.	N.S.
Symptom checklist anxiety	N.S.	N.S.	N.S.	Control vs. 3 treatments; $p < .01$	N.S.	N.S.
Symptom checklist GSI	N.S.	N.S.	N.S.	N.S.	N.S.	N.S.
Goal attainment scaling	N.S.	Goals vs. no goals; $p < .01$	Goals vs. no goals; $p < .10$	N.S.	Goals vs. no goals; $p < .05$	N.S.

Note: N.S. = Not significant.

TABLE 11.5
SUMMARY OF FINDINGS: REPEATED-MEASURES CONTRASTS

Measure	Three Treatments vs. Control	Goals vs. No Goals	Counseling vs. No Counseling
Beck depression inventory	$p < .001$	$p < .001$	N.S.
Symptom checklist depression	$p < .01$	$p < .001$	$p < .05$
Symptom checklist phobic anxiety	$p < .01$	$p < .05$	$p < .05$
Symptom checklist anxiety	$p < .01$	$p < .01$	$p < .01$
Symptom checklist GSI	$p < .05$	$p < .05$	N.S.

Note: N.S. = Not significant.

A difference between the three treatment groups and the control group was identified at the first posttreatment assessment point two days after the emergency department visit. This difference reached significance on the SCL-9OR depression scale ($p < .01$) (see tables 11.4 and 11.5). This is consistent with crisis counseling theory, which stresses the importance of early intervention during the crisis period, when the individual is in the midst of turmoil and thus the most amenable to change (Aguilera and Messick 1982).

The analysis of variance completed on the BDI depression scale did not find any statistically significant differences between the four groups at any point in time, nor were any significant treatment-interacting effects found. The SCL-9OR depression scale ANOVA did, however, show a significant difference between the control group and three treatment groups at the two-day point, and differences that approached significance were evident at three weeks and six months. Both measures indicated a trend in which the control group reported a consistently higher level of depression than any treatment group. In addition, the difference between the two groups using guide to goals vs. the two non-goal-setting groups approached significance on the BDI at the three-week point. Repeated measures analysis completed on a more select group confirmed this trend.

The repeated-measures analysis indicated there was significant improvement over time in the three treatment groups when compared with the control group ($p < .001$) and in the goal-setting groups when they were compared to the nongoal-setting groups ($p < .001$). The difference between the supportive counseling groups and the no-counseling groups was not significant in this analysis.

The BDI repeated-measures analysis, due to the nature of the procedure, included only treatment completers who were evaluated at each and every point in time. It is possible that the group differences were significant in this analysis and only indicated a trend in the ANOVA due to the additional benefits of the full treatment protocol received by treatment completers. It is unlikely that the differences were the result of chance because they were so highly significant and because they confirmed the trend identified in the ANOVAs.

Multivariate analysis of the SCL-9OR phobic anxiety scales also found a significant treatment effect ($p < .05$), and all three treatment contrasts were significant as well. The ANOVA indicated a significant difference between the control group and the three treatment groups at three months on both the phobic-anxiety scale ($p < .05$) and the anxiety scale ($p < .01$).

Overall, it appeared that both treatments were effective in reducing symptomatology in rape victims. The repeated-measures contrasts consistently found highly significant differences between the control group and the three treatment groups. In addition, consistently high differences were found between the goals vs. no goals groups. While significant differences were also found between the counseling and no-counseling groups, the differences were not as highly significant nor as consistently found. Guide to goals thus appears somewhat more effective than supportive counseling, though both have been shown to have significant benefits to rape victims.

DISCUSSION

A major limitation of this study was the lack of pretreatment assessment. The study was not introduced to the subjects, nor was consent obtained, until the two-day postrape visit. However, because subjects were randomly assigned to treatment conditions and because no other significant differences were found among the groups, it is likely that the differences on the dependent measures were indeed the result of the treatment received in the emergency department and during the two days prior to assessment. As the ethical issue of introducing a study of this nature to individuals in intense emotional turmoil is a consideration, one possible compromise for future research might be to collect observational data. This would provide some basic information on the victim's pretreatment level of functioning, which could then be used in determining significant pretreatment group differences.

The generalizability of the results is also somewhat limited, as the sample was composed primarily of young, poor, white, marginally educated, and marginally employed women. These differences may reflect the population served by the facility where the study was completed, the target group for rape, or those victims willing to report rape. Since there were few significant demographic differences between those victims who agreed to participate and those who did not, the sample does not reflect self-selection of that nature. It is interesting to note that this sample is similar to the samples reported by other rape researchers.

For the most part, the measurement instruments used to evaluate the dependent measures were adequate. However, it is unfortunate that there were no counselor-completed measures of depression and anxiety that could have been compared to the self-report measures. While the two measures of depression correlated more highly with each other than with the measure of anxiety, there was nonetheless a moderately high correlation between the measures of depression and anxiety. It would be helpful in future research to differentiate more closely between components of depression and anxiety to ensure that separate parameters are indeed being measured.

The primary significance of this study is that it represents the first randomly controlled, systematically evaluated outcome study of rape victims to demonstrate the efficacy of a treatment model. Other studies either have had no control group or have not been able to demonstrate a significant difference between treatment and spontaneous remission of symptoms. While withholding treatment from victims of such an overwhelming crisis is an important concern, the use of a control group is crucial because of the spontaneous remission of symptoms documented in women not receiving treatment (Kilpatrick, Resick, and Veronen 1981). Future research might be able to maintain the treatment comparison cells without the control condition. One treatment would, of course, need to be especially effective in this type of study to demonstrate a significant improvement over an alternative treatment condition. In this study, guide to goals was able to demonstrate this level of effectiveness.

Another strength of this study is its clinical relevance, cost effectiveness, and duplicability in a wide range of clinical settings and with staff from various disciplines and professional backgrounds. This is especially important with rape victims because they are treated in hospitals, rape crisis centers, mental health clinics, and by private clinicians. Both treatment methods evaluated can be utilized by individuals with minimal psychotheraputic training. They are easy for both the counselor and the patient to understand and employ.

Rape is a serious life crisis, and its impact is immediate. Many researchers do not make contact and begin treatment and assessment until weeks or months after the assault. This study made contact within 72 hours of the rape and began systematic assessment within two days after contact. The cooperation of the hospital emergency department staff and the coordination of services that allowed for the establishment of a protocol of this nature were essential to the success of this project.

The study's importance is that, as a result of its demonstration that a clinically useful and cost-effective treatment model could be incorporated into a hospital setting, Hennepin County Medical Center now has a sexual assault resource service. Based on the initial results of this research, the county commissioners voted to fund the clinical component of the research project as an integral part of the county's service delivery system.

REFERENCES

Aguilera, D.C., and J.M. Messick. 1982. *Crisis intervention: Therapy for psychological emergencies.* New York: Mosby.

Atkeson, B.D., et al. 1982. Victims of rape: Repeated assessment of depressive symptoms. *Journal of Consulting and Clinical Psychology* 50: 96–102.

Beck, A.T., et al. 1961. An inventory for measuring depression. *Archives of General Psychiatry* 4: 56–171.

Burgess, A.W., and L.L. Holmstrom. 1974. Rape trauma syndrome. *American Journal of Psychiatry* 131: 981–86.

————. 1976. Coping behavior of the rape victim. *American Journal of Psychiatry* 133: 413–17.

Calhoun, K.S., B.M. Atkeson, and P.A. Resick. 1982. A longitudinal examination of fear reactions in victims of rape. *Journal of Counseling Psychology* 29: 655–61.

Derogatis, L. 1977. *SCL-9OR manual I.* Baltimore: Johns Hopkins University Press.

Ellis, E.M., B.M. Atkeson, and K.S. Calhoun. 1981. Short report: An assessment of long-term reaction to rape. *Journal of Abnormal Psychology* 90: 263–66.

Frank, E., S.M. Turner, and B. Duffy. 1979. Depressive symptoms in rape victims. *Journal of Affective Disorders* 1: 269–77.

Goldstein, A.P. 1962. *Therapist-patient expectancies in psychotherapy.* New York: Macmillan Publishing Co.

Hamilton, M. 1960. A rating scale for depression. *Journal of Neurology, Neurosurgery, and Psychiatry.* 23: 56–62.

Kilpatrick, D.G., C.L. Best, and L.J. Veronen. 1983. Rape victims: Have we studied the tip of the iceberg? Paper presented at the meeting of the American Psychological Association, August, Anaheim, Calif.

Kilpatrick, D.G., P.A. Resick, and L.J. Veronen. 1981. Effects of a rape experience: A longitudinal study. *Journal of Social Issues* 37: 105–22.

Kilpatrick, D.G., L.J. Veronen, P.A. Resick. 1979. The aftermath of rape: Recent empirical findings. *American Journal of Orthopsychiatry* 49: 658–69.

Kiresuk, T., and R. Sherman. 1968. Goal attainment scaling: A general method for evaluating community mental health programs. *Community Mental Health Journal* 4: 443–53.

McNair, D., M. Lorr, and L. Droppleman. 1971. *Profile of mood states (manual)*. San Diego, Calif.: Educational and Industrial Testing Service.

Notman, M.T., and C.C. Nadelson. 1976. The rape victim: Psychodynamic considerations. *American Journal of Psychiatry* 133: 408–12.

Smith, D. 1976. Goal attainment scaling as an adjunct to counseling. *Journal of Counseling Psychology* 23: 22–27.

Spielberger, C.D., R.L. Gorsuch, and R.E. Lushene. 1970. *The state-trait anxiety inventory*. Palo Alto, Calif.: Consulting Psychologists Press.

Sutherland, S., and D.J. Scherl. 1970. Patterns of response among victims of rape. *American Journal of Orthopsychiatry* 40: 503–11.

Veronen, L.J., and D. Kilpatrick. 1980. Self-reported fears of rape victims: A preliminary investigation. *Behavior Modification* 4: 383–96.

Veronen, L.J., and C.L. Best. 1983. Assessment and treatment of rape-induced fear and anxiety. *The Clinical Psychologist* (Summer): 99–101.

Veronen, L.J., and D.G. Kilpatrick. 1982. Stress inoculation training for victims of rape: Efficacy and differential findings. Paper presented at meeting of Association for Advancement of Behavioral Therapy, Los Angeles, Calif.

Wolpe, J., and P.J. Lang. 1964. A fear survey schedule for use in behavior therapy. *Behavior Research and Therapy* 2: 27–30.

PART 2

The Social Context of Rape and Sexual Assault

CHAPTER
12

SEXUAL SOCIALIZATION AND ATTITUDES TOWARD RAPE

ILSA L. LOTTES
University of Pennsylvania

Traditionally, explanations and theories about rape and rapists' motivations have been dominated by the psychiatric perspective. However, social scientists recently have stressed that sociocultural factors should be investigated for their influence on men's sexually assaultive behavior. Scully and Marolla (1985a) are among the researchers who have argued that an "alternative perspective" that emphasizes sociocultural factors can provide insights into the causes of sexual aggression. The premise of this perspective is that "deviant behavior is learned in the same way as conforming behavior, that is, socially, through interaction with others. Learning includes not only the techniques of committing the crime, but also motives, drives, rationalizations, and attitudes that are compatible with the behavior" (Scully and Marolla 1985a, 306).

In the first part of this chapter three common etiologies of rape are defined: psychopathological, sociocultural, and physiological. Studies and arguments that support primarily the sociocultural perspective are presented. In the second part of this chapter, callous attitudes toward rape victims are discussed. Social scientists have claimed that such attitudes (1) facilitate sexual aggression by helping rapists justify and deny the negative effects of their crimes and (2) severely hinder both the reporting of rape and the recovery of rape victims.

ETIOLOGY OF RAPE

The psychopathological explanation of rape assumes that men who rape are psychologically maladjusted and different from other men. Marolla and Scully (1982) point out that clinical studies conducted by research psychologists have been unable to demonstrate that rapists are more pathological as a group than other groups of sex offenders or criminals. Koss and Leonard (1984) reviewed psychological studies of sexually aggressive men and concluded that the empirical evidence to support the existence of psychopathology among groups of incarcerated rapists or self-identified sexually aggressive men was inconclusive and weak. For example, Perdue and Lester (1972) found no significant differences in the Rorschach protocols of rapists and those who had committed nonsexual aggressive crimes. Abel, Becker, and Skinner (1980) state that research suggests that fewer than 5% of rapists were psychotic at the time of their rape. Schwendinger and Schwendinger (1983) emphasize that although a small number of rapists are psychotic and their crimes can be especially terrifying and dangerous, the majority of rapists are not psychotic.

However, on the basis of the results of a study comparing the Minnesota multiphasic personality inventory (MMPI) profiles of exposers, rapists, and assaulters, Rader (1977) concludes that individuals who had committed offenses involving both violence and sex had profiles indicating significantly more psychological disturbance than individuals committing offenses involving either only sex or only violence. Even though Koss and Leonard (1984) found low incidences of neurotic and psychotic diagnoses for sexually aggressive men in the studies they reviewed, they emphasize that researchers (Armentrout and Hauer 1978; Cohen et al. 1971; Langevin 1983; McCaldon 1967) did attribute to rapists antisocial traits such as hostility, resentment, and a low capacity for warmth, trust, compassion, and empathy.

In contrast with the psychopathological explanation for rape, recent studies and feminist literature (Clark and Lewis 1977; Griffin 1971; Medea and Thompson 1974; Russell 1975) have provided evidence and arguments for a sociocultural explanation of rape. Supporters of this view argue that rape occurs in cultures characterized by other forms of violence, that rape is largely an act of male domination, and that rape results from social inequities between the genders.

From this perspective, rape is not primarily the result of an idiosyncratic or intrapsychic problem but, like most behavior, is learned through interaction with others. Rape is regarded as a logical and psychological extension of a dominant ideology that degrades women and justifies coercive sexuality. Adherents of the sociocultural etiology do not consider most rapists as sick and psychologically distinct from other groups of men. They hypothesize that rapists' belief systems about what constitutes acceptable and desirable sexual and gender role behavior are not extremely different from those of other men. In this view, rape is a sociocultural phenomenon and is supported by attitudes that emphasize differential power roles for men and women.

A third approach to the etiology of rape emphasizes purely physiological motives. Rape is regarded as the expression of a male's uncontrollable desire for sex. In this view, male sexuality is to be feared because of its powerful, explosive, and demanding nature. This perspective assumes that sexual repression or a lack of sexual outlets will contribute to sexually aggressive male acts.

Some support for this explanation of rape is provided by LeVine (1959) from his study of the Gusii in southwestern Kenya. The Gusii culture was characterized by a high incidence of rape and by attitudes that greatly inhibited both female sexual expression and nonmarital sexual relations. However, LeVine's work also could be interpreted as supporting a sociocultural explanation of rape, since the Gusii culture was also characterized by male dominance, low female status and power, high rates of crime and violence, and adversarial sexual relations. LeVine reported that rape could be viewed as an extension of the legitimate aggressive pattern of male/female sexual interactions to illegitimate contexts.

Symons (1979) argues that sexual desire is involved in rape motivation. He writes that men's sexual impulses are part of "human nature" and that men tend to desire "no-cost, impersonal copulations" (284–85). Consequently, men will rape when they feel that (1) force is the only means to sexual access to a woman and/or (2) the probability of negative consequences resulting from a rape is low. Even if one accepts Symons's premise that men are prone to acts of sexual aggression, the two foregoing conditions he cites imply that men's sexual urges are affected by rational and controllable factors, factors that can be influenced by society. Symons's arguments suggest that rape would be lower in societies that (1) made sexual access to women easier and (2) made rape a high-risk act with severe consequences. Thus, Symons's view that rape has a sexual motivation does not imply that sociocultural factors have no influence on men's decisions to rape.

The complex phenomenon of rape has no easy or simple explanations. Groth, Burgess, and Holmstrom (1977) emphasize the variability of both sexually aggressive behavior and the motivations for such behavior. Interactions and combinations of psychological and physiological charac-

teristics with sociocultural factors must be investigated for their association with sexual aggression. Malamuth (1986) writes that: "to understand
the causes of sexual aggression it is essential to consider the role of
multiple factors, such as those creating the motivation to commit the act,
those removing or reducing internal and external inhibitions that might
prevent it from being carried out, and those providing the opportunity to
act" (953).

Malamuth's (1984, 1986) recent evidence suggests that combinations
of variables produce far better predictions of sexual aggression than any
single variable. Other researchers (Albin 1977; Mahoney, Shively, and
Traw 1986; Scully and Marolla 1984, 1985a, 1985b) have argued that the
focus on a single explanatory model, the psychopathological one, has
hindered an understanding of rape and has led to misconceptions about
both the prevalence and characteristics of sexually assaultive males. They
urge that more consideration be given to sociocultural factors that might
contribute to rape.

CULTURAL VARIATION OF RAPE

Sanday's (1981) cross-cultural study of rape in 95 tribal societies supports
the sociocultural explanation of rape. Of the 95 societies, 47% were
classified as rape free, 35% were placed in an intermediate category, and
18% were classified as rape prone. Sanday found that in rape-prone
societies, compared with the rape-free societies, female power and authority were lower, males expressed contempt for women as decision makers,
the genders were separated, interpersonal violence rates were high, and
toughness and aggression were highly valued male characteristics. In the
rape-free societies, women were highly valued and respected. Variables
measuring sexual repression did not discriminate rape-prone from rape-
free societies. Sanday concludes that "violence is socially, not biologi-
cally programmed. Rape is not an integral part of male nature, but the
means by which men programmed for violence express their sexual
selves" (Sanday 1981, 25–26).

Using the standard cross-cultural sample (Murdock and White 1969), a
sample of 186 nonindustrialized cultures representative of the six major
culture regions of the world, Reiss (1986) found that significant predictors
of rape-prone societies were endorsement of the macho personality and a
belief in the inferiority of females. Macho attitudes included acceptance
of physical aggression, high risk-taking, and a casual attitude toward
sexuality. Reiss rejects Brownmiller's (1975) theses that (1) rape is a
crucial weapon used by all men to intimidate and exploit women, and (2)

all men are innately aggressive, bestial, and animalistic. Citing cross-cultural evidence, Reiss states that "males have always had strong kinship reasons to protect their daughters and wives from sexual violence by other men" (Reiss 1986, 191). Reiss notes also that the cross-cultural coding of rape proneness by both Broude and Greene (1976) and Sanday (1981) showed that about half of their societies had either low rape rates or no evidence of rape and that for many of the other societies there was no evidence that rape was supported as a threat to intimidate women.

A study by Lottes (1984) supports Reiss's arguments about the cultural variation of rape. She found that in cultures with high rape rates, women had lower status, fathers had less contact with infants and children, and torturing and killing of enemies were common in comparison with cultures with low rape rates.

Schwendinger and Schwendinger (1983) include anthropological evidence to support their claim that social conditions, rather than the idiosyncrasies of rapists should be examined as causes of sexual violence. In denying the universality of rape, they argue that rape, gender inequality, and socioeconomic relations are interrelated. They write that "rape is no longer considered apart from other forms of violence against women or isolated from the general level of violence in a society . . . rape does not exist in a social vacuum because it is an individual crime. It is dynamically related to constellations of harmful practices that vary from one society to another" (Schwendinger and Schwendinger 1983, 13).

The United States has a substantially higher incidence of rape than other countries. Citing statistics from the FBI's 1977 *Uniform Crime Reports*, Abramson and Hayashi (1984) note that the reported rapes per 100,000 were 34.5 in the United States, 10.7 in West Germany, 10.1 in England, 3.2 in France, and 2.4 in Japan. Researchers have argued that the high incidence of rape in the United States suggests that it has cultural supports. Russell (1982) interprets her findings of the high prevalence of rape (24%) and attempted rape (31%) in a random sample of San Francisco female residents as supporting a sociocultural view of rape. Burkhart and Stanton (forthcoming) also state that the numerous studies (Cate et al. 1982; Kanin and Parcell 1977; Korman and Leslie 1982; Koss 1981, 1985; Lane and Gwartney-Gibbs 1985; Makepeace 1981; Meyer 1984; Muehlenhard et al. 1985; Mynatt and Allgeier 1985; Parrot 1985; Parrot and Lynk 1983; Rapaport and Burkhart 1984; Schultz and DeSavage 1975; Sweet 1985) documenting high rates of sexual aggression by college students support the thesis that rape is a culturally sanctioned phenomenon in the United States.

CHARACTERISTICS OF SEXUALLY AGGRESSIVE COLLEGE MALES

Recent studies by several researchers support the sociocultural perspective. In a sample of 175 college males, Mosher and Anderson (1984) found that a measure of macho personality with three components—calloused sex attitudes toward women, a conception of violence as manly, and a view of danger as exciting—was significantly correlated with a history of self-reported sexual aggression against women. Using the same measure of macho personality, Mahoney, Shively, and Traw (1986) found that for college males with coital experience, the macho personality variable was the best predictor of self-reported sexually coercive/assaultive behavior.

Rapaport and Burkhart (1984) found that (1) scores on the two Burt (1980) scales measuring adversarial sexual beliefs and acceptance of interpersonal violence and (2) the score on a scale measuring acceptance of males using force to engage in sexual acts with women were significantly positively correlated with self-reported coercive sexual behavior with females. This same study did not show significant correlations between the Burt measures of sexual conservatism and sex-role stereotyping and reports of sexually coercive behavior.

In a sample of 392 college males, Tieger (1981) found that "normal" men who rated themselves as more likely to rape if they could be certain they would not get caught scored lower on the femininity scale of the Bem sex role inventory and indicated beliefs that minimized the violent and negative impact of rape on a victim, blamed the victim, sympathized with the rapist, and considered sexual aggression an appropriate and well-received action. As Bandura (1973, 1978) and Bandura, Underwood, and Fromson (1975) point out in elaborating social learning theories of aggression, such a belief pattern suggests the existence of cognitive structures that assist men in disinhibiting sexual aggression. Malamuth, Feshbach, and Jaffe (1977) also theorize that sexual arousal and aggression are linked more by learned inhibitory and disinhibitory cues than by biological instinct.

Briere and Malamuth (1983) conducted a study, the results of which they interpret as supporting a sociocultural theory of rape. Their study compared the ability of attitudinal and sexual variables to predict males' self-reported likelihood of sexually aggressive behavior. Variables measuring sexual frustration or sexual malajustment were not predictive of either likelihood to rape or likelihood to use sexual force. The one sexual variable that was significantly related to sexual aggression was sexual experience: males with more sexual experience were more sexually aggressive. This finding appears to be inconsistent with a view that rape is related to sexual repression. In contrast to most of the sexual variables, a variety of rape-supportive attitudes, such as blaming the victim for rape and regarding sexual violence as sexually stimulating to women, were significant predictors of self-reports of both likelihood to rape and likelihood to use sexual force. Briere and Malamuth conclude that their finding of a "linear relationship between degree of force-rape inclinations and rape-supportive beliefs suggests an 'aggression toward women' continuum with respect to attitudinal correlates, rather than a view of rape as a discrete phenomenon with its own unique antecedents" (Briere and Malamuth 1983, 321–22).

In another recent study, Malamuth, Check, and Briere (1986) found that men who said they would find being sexually forceful with women sexually arousing also accepted rape-supportive attitudes, approved of aggression in nonsexual situations, and reported a high likelihood of themselves being sexually coercive. Variables assessing sexual attitudes, inhibitions, experience, and knowledge did not differentiate those men who indicated they would be aroused by using force. These researchers interpreted their findings as supporting the sociocultural etiology of rape advocated by feminist ideology.

Kanin's (1984) study of date rape on a college campus gives additional support to a sociocultural explanation of rape. He found that date rapists were products of a highly sexually oriented peer-group socialization, which started in the early years of high school. The peer groups of these men accepted the view that the sexual conquest of women enhanced their self-worth. Compared to sexually nonaggressive men, the rapists had had more sexual partners and were "dramatically more" sexually active (Kanin 1984, 99). Yet the rapists were significantly more likely to rate their sex life as unsatisfactory. Kanin concludes that differential socialization, resulting in the rapists placing a higher value on both a large number of sex partners and frequent sexual activity, contributes to the behavior of rapists.

Using the self-reports of a sample of college men, Koss (1981) found that compared with sexually nonaggressive men, sexually aggressive men (1) viewed sexual aggression as normal, (2) had conservative attitudes toward female sexuality, (3) reported greater rape-myth acceptance, (4) regarded heterosexual relationships as game playing, (5) held women more responsible for rape prevention, and (6) reported traditional beliefs about women's roles. For males, the foregoing six attitude measures were significantly intercorrelated. In a discriminant analysis, Koss et al. (1985) found that the rape-supportive attitudes, rather than the psycho-pathological variables, differentiated between sexually aggressive and sexually nonaggressive men.

The Koss results support Burt's (1980) thesis that attitudes about rape are part of a belief system that includes attitudes about sexuality and gender roles. As Koss writes, her "results offer indirect support for the social control model of rape in that they suggest that the more a man accepts culturally transmitted sexual stereotypes, the more likely he is to hold rape-supportive beliefs" (Koss 1981, 35).

DIFFERENTIAL SEX-ROLE SOCIALIZATION AND HETEROSEXUAL INTERACTIONS

Farrell (1978), Makepeace (1981), and Weis and Borges (1975) argue that popular conceptions of dating and courtship contribute to male sexual aggression. Women have been socialized not to make sexual advances to men, not to acknowledge an enjoyment of their sexuality, not to respond to a man's sexual advances without offering at least some initial resistance, and not to have sexual relations unless they are involved in a love relationship. In contrast, men have been encouraged to enjoy their sexuality and pursue sexual encounters with numerous partners.

Johnson and Goodchilds (1973), Russell (1975), and Stock (1983) all emphasized that for men sexual conquest is one measure of status, self-esteem, and masculinity. Person (1980) writes that "there is a wealth of clinical evidence to suggest that in this culture, genital sexual activity is a prominent feature in the maintenance of masculine gender while it is a variable feature in feminine gender. . . . In men, there is such a rigid link between sexual expression and gender that their sexuality often appears driven rather than liberated" (619–20).

To achieve their sexual goals, men have been taught that they must initiate sexual activity and often overcome a woman's resistance. According to Farrell (1978), the pressure and expectation for men always to be the initiator leads many men to develop strong feelings of insecurity and anger about being rejected. Since women have been socialized to be the limit setters in sexual interactions, men's perception that women, not themselves, control and manipulate sexual involvement further increases their anger and insecurity. This anger and fear of rejection contributes to men's developing adversarial views of heterosexual relationships and callous, contemptuous attitudes toward women, characteristics that have been associated with sexually aggressive men.

Perper (1985) argues that rape arises from the reactions that some men have to women's rejection strategies. Men find their sexuality devalued by actual or feared rejections of women they like. According to Perper, these rejected men feel that women always have power, and they see themselves as begging for the women's sexual favors. In rape, socially and sexually powerless men "can possess what they do not have in reality: the power to possess a woman and to punish her for her resistance" (Perper 1985, 195). Fremont's (1975) description of one of the convicted rapists he interviewed supports the rejection motivation: "Rape was his way of striking back at society and women for actual or potential rejection" (249).

In his interviews with men about rape, Beneke (1982) found that men acknowledged societal pressures to have "a lot of sex with a lot of different women" (44) and that some men viewed sex as an achievement through which they gained status and power and expressed dominance and hostility. Beneke claims that if sex is regarded as an achievement, then for some men the mere presence of an attractive woman would make them feel like a failure. Beneke quotes one man:

> A lot of times a woman knows she's looking really good and she'll use that and flaunt it, and it makes me feel like she's laughing at me and I feel degraded. I also feel dehumanized, because when I'm being teased, I just turn off, I cease to be human.... If I were actually desperate enough to rape somebody, it would be from wanting the person, but also it would be a very spiteful thing just being able to say, "I have power over you and I can do anything I want with you," because really I feel they have power over me just by their presence. (Beneke 1982, 20–21)

In describing one pattern of rape, the power rape, Groth (1979) states that the goal of the rapist is to achieve sexual intercourse with his victim as evidence of conquest. Groth says that this sexual conquest serves to assert the rapist's competence, validate his masculinity, and compensate for underlying feelings of inadequacy and lack of control.

Russell (1975) also identifies our culture's differential sex role socialization and the American dating system as contributors to rape. Russell claims that traditional sex roles have encouraged submissiveness, passivity, weakness, kindness, compassion, patience, acceptance, and dependence in women while promoting aggression, strength, force, dominance, superiority, competitiveness, and toughness in men. She points out that women have not been socialized to develop skills that allow them to communicate their feelings assertively to men and that men have been encouraged to pursue sexual relationships that exclude caring, respecting, and loving. In addition, men have not been socialized to be emotional, affectionate, warm, or tender. Russell argues that this differential gender socialization of both opposite qualities and opposing roles and goals in sexual and dating situations contributes to male sexual aggression against women. She concludes that "rape is the logical consequence of the lack of symmetry in the way males and females are socialized in this society"

(Russell 1975, 275). Similarly, Burt (1980) writes that, "rape is the logical and psychological extension of a dominant-submissive, competitive, sex role stereotyped culture" (229).

Giarrusso and colleagues (1979) found that male and female adolescent respondents had divergent expectations and perceptions about important aspects of heterosexual interactions. The adolescents accepted traditional, stereotyped attitudes about male and female roles in dating relationships. However, female respondents held a less sexualized view of the world than did males. Whereas females often did not acknowledge that dressing or acting certain ways or going particular places on dates indicated their desire for sexual intimacy, males frequently regarded such behaviors as a signal for them to make a sexual advance. Abbey (1982) found that college males also were more likely than college females to perceive the world in sexual terms and to interpret friendly behavior by a woman as a signal for a man to make a sexual advance. Giarrusso et al. point out that their study refutes the assumption that sexual attitudes and behaviors have become more egalitarian.

Carroll, Volk, and Hyde (1985) found that male and female college students differed significantly in their sexual attitudes, sexual behavior, and motives for engaging in sexual intercourse. For example, 24% of the males reported more than 16 sex partners (as compared with 2% of the females), and 84% of the males (as compared with 42% of the females) reported that they had engaged in sexual relations without emotional involvement. Compared with 50% of the males, only 9% of the females indicated they would not feel guilty or anxious about having a "one-night stand." Males' motives for sexual intercourse more often included pleasure, fun, and physical reasons, whereas females' motives emphasized love, commitment, and emotion. The authors concluded that their data do not support the view that male and female gender roles are converging.

Laplante, McCormick, and Brannigan (1980) and McCormick (1979) found that college men and women still accept the traditional sexual script that dictates that men should use any strategy to influence women to have sex and that women should either submit passively to a sexual advance or use any strategy to convince a man not to pursue sexual intercourse. Abel, Becker, and Skinner (1980) and Kanin and Parcell (1977) also emphasize that, although America has become more sexually permissive, this has not led to major changes in sex roles. Men are still regarded as conquerors and women as passive receptors.

Giarrusso et al. (1979) conclude that the fact that males and females have different expectations and goals for dates and attribute different meanings to each other's behaviors contributes to a situation where date rape is likely. Similarly, Weis and Borges (1975) write that: The stereotyped notions of male and female roles and their relationship to conceptions of masculine and feminine sexuality, coupled with a situation that is fraught with ambiguous expectations, provide the ingredients for systematically socialized actors who can participate in the drama of rape" (110).

ATTITUDES TOWARD RAPE

IMPACT OF RAPE ATTITUDES

Burt, Brownmiller, and Weis and Borges have argued that widely accepted myths about rape support and promote rape. Burt (1980) defines these myths as "prejudicial, stereotyped, or false beliefs about rape, rape victims, and rapists" (217). Brownmiller (1975) writes that our culture promotes attitudes providing men with an "ideology and psychologic encouragement to commit their acts of aggression without awareness, for the most part, that they have committed a punishable crime, let alone a moral wrong" (439). Weis and Borges (1975) claim that the mythology of rape "allows the man both to engage in the otherwise forbidden behavior and to rationalize and justify it after the event" (111).

The widespread acceptance of rape myths has been demontrated by Barnett and Feild (1977), Burt (1980, 1983), Feild (1978), Russell (1975), and Williams and Holmes (1981). For example, in a study comparing 36 rapists with a general-public sample of 598 adults on their justifications and definitions of violence, Burt (1983) found that, although the rapists' attitudes were more extreme, rapists and the general public held many of the same beliefs about violence and its justification. Burt claims that these rape myths and attitudes about violence are used as psychological releasers or neutralizers, allowing potential rapists to turn off social prohibitions against injuring or using others.

Consistent with Burt, Marolla and Scully (1982) note that "the critical importance of rape mythology is that it provides men with a structural position from which to justify sexually aggressive behavior" (5). Scully and Marolla (1984, 1985a, 1985b) found that the myths that women both enjoy and are responsible for their rape were used by convicted rapists to excuse and justify their crimes and to deny the negative effects of their actions on their victims. They report that the vast majority of rapists in their study never thought of the possibility of prison because they did not define what they had done as wrong.

Alford and Brown (1985), who assesses sexuality variables for a sample of incarcerated rapists and college students, conclude that their research supports the view that rape myths both contribute to rape and help an assailant deny his offense. In his study of college date rape, Kanin (1985) found that a majority of rapists accepted attitudes justifying forceful and surreptitious techniques to induce a woman to have sex.

Koss and Leonard (1984) define the following beliefs as rape supportive: (1) rape is not a serious crime, (2) women are responsible for rape prevention, (3) women provoke and want men to use force in sexual interactions, (4) relationships between men and women are adversarial and manipulative, (5) a man's role is to convince a reluctant woman to have sex, (6) some amount of force is a legitimate strategy to get sex , and (7) women do not find offensive the forceful strategies men use to obtain sex. These researchers stress that the results of studies investigating "the relationship between sexual aggression and rape-supportive attitudes are remarkably consistent" (Koss and Leonard 1984, 223).

Convicted rapists (Burt 1983; Groth 1979; Marolla and Scully 1982; Feild 1978), self-reported sexually aggressive college men (Kanin 1985; Koss et al. 1985; Malamuth, 1986; Rapaport and Burkhart 1984), and men who indicate a likelihood to rape if they could be assured of no punishment (Briere and Malamuth 1983; Check and Malamuth 1983; Greendlinger and Byrne, 1987; Malamuth 1981; Malamuth and Check 1980; Malamuth, Haber, and Feshbach 1980; Muehlenhard et al. 1985; Tieger 1981) all have been reported as accepting rape supportive beliefs or accepting them more than other groups of men who indicate no sexually aggressive tendencies. Malamuth, Check, and Briere (1986) found that men who indicated they would be highly sexually aroused by using force with women in sexual situations also reported greater acceptance of rape-supportive attitudes than men who indicated no sexual arousal concerning using force with women. In addition, Malamuth (1983) found that rape-supportive attitudes were a significant predictor of laboratory aggression against women.

Although some researchers have emphasized that rape-supportive attitudes facilitate sexual aggression by helping rapists to justify and deny their crimes, social scientists have attributed other harmful effects to these attitudes. Russell (1982) has stated that the low reporting rate of rape is due to the widespread acceptance of rape-supportive attitudes. Ehrhart and Sandler (1985) claim that widely accepted myths about rape contribute to a blaming-the-victim attitude, which makes it more difficult for rape victims to seek help and recover from their assaults. Deming and Eppy (1981) state that "attribution of responsibility to the victim distinguishes rape from other violent crimes and adds to the particular trauma of the rape experience for the victim" (366). Scully and Marolla (1985a) note that rape myths produce damaging effects on the victim by shifting the responsibility for the act from the offender to the victim and by denying or reducing the perceived injury to the victim.

Cann, Calhoun, and Selby (1979) point out that a victim's recovery depends heavily on how the people she encounters after the rape assign responsibility to the crime. Burt and Estep (1981) emphasize that the victim is subjected to callous attitudes in intrapersonal, interpersonal, and institutional areas. Weis and Borges (1975) stress that, in reporting their experience to police or in court, rape victims often complain that they are made to feel that they, rather than their attackers, are to blame.

Williams (1984) has described the harsh treatment of rape victims as a secondary victimization caused by negative, judgmental attitudes toward a victim and resulting in lack of support, condemnation, and/or alienation of the victim. She writes, "Responses to victims are capricious products of public attitudes. Consequently, such attitudes have the potential for becoming an integral part of victimization, or conversely, a part of the recuperative process which must follow a crisis such as rape" (Williams 1984, 68–69). Williams found that victims from communities with greater acceptance of rape-supportive attitudes tended to blame themselves more, feel unjustifiably responsible for their rape, experience more trauma, and find recovery more difficult and painful than victims from communities with less acceptance of such attitudes.

Groth (1979) stresses that persistent misconceptions and fallacies about rape have led institutions to adopt ineffective treatment programs for offenders and ineffective protective strategies for potential victims. Burkhart and Stanton (forthcoming) and Burt and Albin (1981) emphasize that acceptance of rape myths leads to (1) denial that interactions that legally should be classified as rape actually are labeled rape and (2) not-guilty verdicts in experiments involving mock jury trials. For example, many people believe that a woman can only be raped by a stranger, that the assailant always has a weapon, or that women will always suffer obvious physical injuries from the rape. Rose (1977) contends that rape myths have contributed to rape legislation that is callous toward rape victims. Thus, social scientists have argued that rape myths not only facilitate acts of sexual aggression and influence the recovery of rape victims, but also enter into decisions to arrest, prosecute, convict, sentence, and treat offenders.

EXAMPLES OF CALLOUS ATTITUDES TOWARD RAPE VICTIMS

WOMEN ENJOY SEXUAL VIOLENCE   One rape myth or rape-supportive attitude cited by social scientists is that women enjoy sexual violence. Albin (1977) emphasizes that the psychoanalytic perspective, promoted by Freud and his followers, presents a masochistic view of female sexuality. According to this perspective, (1) a woman derives pleasure from suffering for a lover, (2) rape is the natural outcome of a woman's pain-inflicting psyche, and (3) rape, in either fantasy or fact, satisfies a woman's self-destructive needs.

Burt and Estep (1981) report that about one-fifth of an adult sample believed the myth that women enjoy sexual violence. Malamuth, Haber, and Feshbach (1980) found that a significant portion of college students thought that some women would enjoy being raped. Although men reported this belief more often than women, women generally indicated that, although they personally would not derive pleasure from being raped under any circumstances, they thought about one-fourth of the female population would derive some pleasure from a rape.

In contrast, Dean and deBruyn-Kops (1982), Ehrhart and Sandler (1985), and Griffin (1971) state that women do not secretly want to be raped. They pointed out that virtually all rape victims report feelings of terror, humiliation, and degradation after their rape. Russell (1975) notes that her interviews with 90 rape victims "emphatically contradict the prevalent view" that "women enjoy being raped" (13).

Hariton and Singer (1974) and Masters and Johnson (1979) report that fantasies of being raped, overpowered, or forced to submit by a man are common sexual fantasy themes of females. However, Greendlinger and Byrne (1987) argue that fantasies of forced sexual encounters have been falsely labeled as rape fantasies (i.e., they are not fantasies of real rapes). Johnson and Goodchilds (1973) and Weis and Borges (1975) point out that women's fantasies of being sexually overpowered usually include a congenial, attractive, desired assailant and do not involve excessive force, physical hurt, or pain.

Stock (1983) found that when women were exposed to realistic depictions of rape, they were not aroused and had negative feelings toward such depictions. In contrast, when women were exposed to the eroticized "rape myth" version of forced sex commonly found in pornographic literature, they reported higher levels of positive feelings and sexual arousal. Consistent with Stock's results, Bond and Mosher (1986) found that guided imagery of an erotic fantasy of "rape," in comparison with realistic imagery of rape, elicited distinctly different affective and subjective responses. They write, "Not only do women not enjoy the experience of being raped, they do not even enjoy the experience of imagining being raped" (Bond and Mosher 1986, 177). They found that women who imagined a realistic rape reported feelings of shame, depression, pain, disgust, and anger and not feelings of sexual pleasure, arousal, or enjoyment. In contrast, women who imagined an erotic fantasy of "rape" did report some feelings of sexual pleasure, arousal, and enjoyment.

For a sample of over 200 college women, Kanin (1982) found that females who engaged in realistic rape fantasies regarded these as negative fantasy experiences. He concludes that "the conscious fantasizing of rape as a sexually rewarding event appears to be something of a rare phenomenon" (Kamin 1982, 119). Russell (1975) and Weis and Borges (1975) emphasize that voluntary fantasizing about rape and actually wanting to be raped are two different things. Many people enjoy fantasizing about events they don't want to actualize, and unlike a real rape situation where women are not in control and are usually afraid or terrified, a woman is in control of her fantasies.

SEX IS THE PRIMARY MOTIVATION FOR RAPE   A second rape attitude cited by researchers as a myth is that sex rather than power is the primary motivation for rape (Burt and Estep 1981; Beneke 1982; Cherry 1983; Dean and deBruyn-Kops 1982; Deming and Eppy 1981; Griffin 1971; Russell 1975; Weis and Borges 1975). From their analysis of the motivations of over 500 rapists, Groth, Burgess, and Holmstrom (1977) found that rape was more an expression of power or anger than sexual desire. They state, "Rape, then, is a pseudo-sexual act, a pattern of sexual behavior that is concerned much more with status, aggression, control, and dominance than with sensual pleasure or sexual satisfaction. It is sexual behavior in the service of nonsexual needs" (Groth, Burgess, and Holmstrom 1977, 1240). Amir's (1971) finding that 71% of the rapes he studied were premeditated also refutes the general acceptance of the irresistible, uncontrollable sexual impulse theory of rape motivation.

In reviewing theories of sexual aggression, Deming and Eppy (1981) discount the view that a need for sexual outlets is related to rape. They note that studies show that convicted rapists (1) were involved in a consenting relationship at the time of their offense, (2) indicated high levels of sexual dysfunction and low levels of pleasure during the rape, and (3) used more excessive force, brutality, or humiliation than necessary for sexual release.

Ehrhart and Sandler (1985) emphasize that rape is primarily an act of violence and aggression and not a result of a man's uncontrollable sexual urges. Scully and Marolla (1985a) write, "Certainly from the victim's perspective rape is not a sexual act. . . . It is the ultimate violation by one human being of another's right to physical and bodily autonomy" (307). Similarly, Brownmiller (1975) argues that "rape is not a crime of irrational, impulsive, uncontrollable lust, but is a deliberate, hostile, violent act of degradation and possession on the part of a would-be conqueror designed to intimidate and inspire fear" (439).

Schwendinger and Schwendinger (1983) also claim that rape is not primarily an act of frustrated sexual passion. If rape were simply a result of sexual repression, then legalization of prostitution should result in a decline of sexual crimes. But, as they point out, Las Vegas, Nevada, which has legalized prostitution, also has one of the highest rape rates in the United States; in three cities (Gary and Terre Haute, Indiana, and Honolulu, Hawaii), rape rates declined after prostitution was prohibited. Although the accuracy of statistics involving rape is always questionable, there appears to be no evidence that availability of prostitutes decreases the incidence of rape. The Schwendingers state that the power and dominance factors in the rape of women seem also to apply to homosexual rape of men in prisons. They cite the work of Davis (1968), who studied homosexual prison assaults. According to Davis, the primary goal of a sexual aggressor is the conquest and degradation of his victim, rather than sexual release.

WOMEN ARE RESPONSIBLE FOR RAPE PREVENTION   Another commonly accepted rape attitude is that women are responsible for rape prevention. Schultz and DeSavage (1975) report that college students, courts, prosecutors, policemen, and jurors often hold a victim at least partially responsible for her rape. The victim is viewed as a seductress or as a pushover. Weis and Borges (1975) also note that "victims are thought to have asked for it, and deserved whatever they got" (98). They also write that a "woman is consistently taught that she is both defenseless and responsible for the prevention of her victimization" (Weis and Burgess 1975, 119–120).

Cherry (1983) and Williams (1984) claim that society (including the victim) attributes responsibility for rape to the victim, which is not true for other crimes. In their cross-ethnic, nonstudent sample, Williams and Holmes (1981) found a strong tendency for respondents to assign responsibility for both cause and prevention of rape to women. In a study of black, white, and Hispanic teenagers, Goodchilds and Zellman (1984) found that although the teenage respondents assigned most of the responsibility for a rape to the man, nearly one-third of the responsibility was assigned to the woman in response to 27 acquaintance-rape vignettes.

Ehrhart and Sandler (1985) note that "rape is the responsibility of the rapist, not the victim" (17). They argue that a person carrying money does not expect to be robbed; likewise, a woman who dresses or acts in certain ways does not expect or ask to be raped. Quoting statistics compiled by the National Commission on the Causes and Prevention of Violence comparing the crimes of homicide, assault, robbery, and rape, Brownmiller (1975) reports that rape victims were assigned the least responsibility for precipitating the crime, 4% compared with between 6% and 22% for the victims of other crimes.

ONLY CERTAIN WOMEN ARE RAPED   Dean and deBruyn-Kops (1982), Deming and Eppy (1981), Ehrhart and Sandler (1985), and Weis and Borges (1975) have noted among myths about rape the attitude that rape happens only to certain kinds of women. Burt and Albin (1981) report that almost 70% of an adult sample agreed with the following statement: "In the majority of rapes, the victim was promiscuous or had a bad reputation." The research of L'Armand and Pepitone (1982) supports the view that "nice women" are considered less likely to become rape victims or to have caused or precipitated their rape. They found that in making judgments about rape, college students blamed the victim more for her rape when she was thought to have had some sexual experience, either limited or extensive, than when no information about the victim's sexual history was given. Pugh (1983) found that, unlike the verdicts given by women, men gave significantly more guilty verdicts when the victim was thought to have "high moral character" than a "low moral character." Pugh concludes that his study supports the view that men consider certain women legitimate targets for sexual exploitation and that these women do not make credible rape charges.

However, Griffin (1971) states that the belief that mainly "bad girls" get raped has no basis in fact. She reports that in a study of rape victims from the District of Columbia, 82% were found to have a "good reputation" (Griffin 1971, 32).

WOMEN FALSELY REPORT RAPE   Beneke (1982), Dean and deBruyn-Kops (1982), Deming and Eppy (1981), and Rose (1977) have emphasized the widespread acceptance of another rape attitude: that women falsely report many rape claims. Burt (1980) found that more than half of a sample of adults agreed that at least 50% of reported rapes are only reported because "the woman was trying to get back at a man she was angry with or was trying to cover up an illegitimate pregnancy" (229). Burt and Estep (1981) point out that rape victims report challenges to their credibility and honest intent from police officers, prosecutors, and medical personnel. These authors also state that rape victims often have to defend themselves against charges that they (1) are covering up or excusing an illegitimate pregnancy, (2) are out to get revenge against their assailant, (3) acted negligently, precipitating or provoking the attack, or (4) offered insufficient resistance.

Nevertheless, Ehrhart and Sandler (1985) report that most women do not falsely report a rape. According to these authors, only about 2% of all rapes and related sex charges have been determined to be false.

WOMEN ARE LESS DESIRABLE AFTER RAPE   Several social scientists have argued that the belief that a woman is less desirable after she has been raped prevents many rape victims from reporting their attack and makes recovery from the experience more difficult. Burt and Estep (1981), Rose (1977), and Russell (1975) emphasize that rape victims report feeling impure, devalued, guilty, and stigmatized. Weis and Borges (1975) write that "public exposure of rape will subject the victim to the risk of stigmatization on three levels: negative status is conferred because she is known as a victim and loser, because an actual act of intercourse with an illegal partner has become common knowledge, and because a most intimate experience can be discussed openly" (132).

Using a divergent sample of over 1000 subjects, Williams (1979) found that 45% of Mexican Americans, 31% of blacks, and 13% of whites agreed with the statement, "Once a girl is raped, her reputation is ruined." Williams reports that compared to black or white women, the Mexican-American rape victims had the most difficulty recovering from a rape. Feild (1978) also found that his sample of over 1000 adults attached a negative stigma to rape victims. Feild cites victimization research indicating that people are quite willing to attribute fault or to assign responsibility to a victim of a crime or accident.

Ryan (1972) also describes the common tendency to blame a victim despite the obvious contradiction in that expression. In this view, the negative status attached to rape victims contributes to the lack of credibility of victims' claims and interferes with their right to be acknowledged as legitimate victims.

Griffin (1971) and Weis and Borges (1975) argued that many men consider rape victims as "damaged goods." According to Weis and Borges, men are reluctant to pursue long-term relationships with a raped woman "for fear of contagion of social stigma and loss of self-esteem resulting from settling for an inferior woman" (106). These authors claim also that the inferior, negative view of raped women makes them a more justifiable target for further exploitation.

RAPE MAY BE JUSTIFIED   Recent research (Goodchilds and Zellman 1984; Wheeler and Utigard 1984) indicates that a significant number of both high school and college students believe that rape is justified in some situations. Burt and Estep (1981) and Weis and Borges (1975) argue that many adults consider certain types of women to be legitimate targets of sexual victimization and also describe situations in which rape is regarded as justified. For example, rape or forced sex was considered justified by the respondents when some degree of acquaintance between the victim and her attacker was implied.

Dean and deBruyn-Kops (1982) and Parrot and Allen (1984) state that people commonly accept the idea that one can be raped only by a stranger. Forced sex between acquaintances is regarded differently and usually is not defined as rape. Shotland and Goodstein (1983) found that when they presented descriptions of date situations involving forced sex that could legally be defined as rape, respondents generally said the male's behavior was wrong but was not rape.

Mahoney (1983) notes that a significant percentage of males have what he refers to as "male sexual access rights" (431–32). According to Mahoney, these rights specify certain conditions under which the males have the right of sexual access to a female, regardless of her unwillingness. For example, he found in a sample of college males that 45% thought it was acceptable for a male to hold a female down and physically force her to engage in intercourse if she got him sexually excited and that 36% said this behavior was acceptable if she let him touch her breasts.

Giarrusso, Johnson, Goodchilds, and Zellman (1979) found that over 50% of the male high school students they interviewed thought that it was acceptable for a male to hold a female down and force her to have sexual intercourse when she gets him sexually excited, when she has led him on, or when she says she's going to have sex with him and then changes her mind. More than a third of these men considered forced sex acceptable if the male had spent a lot of money on the female, if they had been dating for a long time, if the male was so aroused he could not stop, if she let him touch her above the waist, or if she was stoned or drunk. These same authors (Zellman et al. 1981) report that high school students of both genders, in responding to a variety of acquaintance-rape vignettes, considered forced sex as legitimate and acceptable.

Fischer (1985) found that 19% of a sample of college men rated nine acquaintance rape situations (the same situations used by Giarrusso et al.) as "not definitely unacceptable" and that only 14% of the men rated the male's forced-sex behavior as "definitely unacceptable" in all nine situations. In his study of 71 date rapists, Kanin (1984) found that these men interpreted their victim's responsiveness to consensual "foreplay" as a signal that both invited and justified a sexual attack, despite the victim's verbal or physical protests. Kanin (1985) also reports that 86% of the rapists and 19% of a control group justified rape if the woman was viewed as a teaser, an economic exploiter, or "loose." In addition, 80% of the rapists and 40% of the controls indicated that their reputations would be enhanced among their friends if they were thought to have tried to force a teaser, exploiter, or loose woman to have sex. Goodman (1982) reports the results of a study indicating that college men rated nonconsensual intercourse on dates as more acceptable if the woman initiated the date, when the couple went to the man's apartment, and when the man paid for the date. Thus, empirical studies have indicated that people do justify force in various sexual situations.

CORRELATES OF RAPE ATTITUDES

Burt (1980) investigated correlates of rape myth acceptance for a sample of nearly 600 Minnesota adults. She found that rape myth acceptance was part of a larger, related attitude structure, which included beliefs about gender roles, sexuality, and violence. In a regression analysis, Burt found that the attitudinal variables of sex role stereotyping, acceptance of violence against women, and adversarial sexual beliefs had the strongest associations with rape myth acceptance. In addition, she found that younger, better-educated, and less sexually conservative adults reported less rape-myth acceptance. Using Burt's scales and an additional scale measuring general acceptance of violence, Check and Malamuth (1983) found in a sample of Canadian college students high intercorrelations among sex role stereotyping, rape myth acceptance, acceptance of violence against women, and acceptance of general violence.

Consistent with these findings, the cross-cultural study by McConahay and McConahay (1977) shows that sex role stereotyping is associated with an acceptance of violence in general and violence specifically against women. These researchers did not find significant correlations between violence and sexual permissiveness measures. The McConahays interpret their results as supporting a theory of violence based more on social learning than on physiological or instinctual factors.

Other studies show that attitudes about rape are related to beliefs about women's roles. Krulewitz and Payne (1978) report that in a college student sample feminist views about women's roles were related to attitudes toward rape. Profeminist males gave less support than nonfeminist males to the belief that a victim wanted to be raped. Profeminist females were more likely to classify a forced-sex situation as rape than were females with nonfeminist views. The more traditional females required proof of a greater degree of assailant force before they would believe a victim's account of rape.

Shotland and Goodstein (1983) found that college students with more egalitarian views about women blamed a rape victim less often for her rape. Acock and Ireland (1983) found that college students who expressed more traditional attitudes about appropriate sex roles viewed a rape victim as less respectable and blamed her more for the rape. Wheeler and Utigard (1984) found that sex-role stereotyping and acceptance of interpersonal violence correlated significantly with beliefs justifying forced sex.

In a study of college students, Fischer (1985) found that more traditional attitudes toward women, more acceptance of a double standard of sexual behavior (i.e., they had more approving attitudes toward premarital and extramarital sex for themselves but not for a steady sex partner or spouse), more sexual partners, and less acceptance of homosexuality were associated with a greater acceptance of date rape. In another sample of college students, Lottes (1986) found that adversarial sexual beliefs, nonegalitarian gender-role beliefs, traditional attitudes toward female sexuality, and macho personality were significant predictors of callous attitudes toward rape victims. In a sample including both students and nonstudents, Costin (1985) found that respondents who reported a greater acceptance of rape myths had beliefs restricting the roles and rights of women.

In a British nonstudent sample, Howells and associates (1984) report that, compared with males with egalitarian attitudes toward women, males with more traditional attitudes perceived a rape victim as suffering less psychological disturbance as a result of the rape and attributed more blame and causation for the rape to the victim and less to the assailant.

In another nonstudent sample, Feild (1978) found that people with more traditional views of women's roles were more likely to attribute blame to the rape victim, regard sex as the motivator for rape, and view a victim as less attractive after a rape. In a sample including whites, blacks, and Mexican Americans, Williams (1979) reported that more traditional attitudes about gender roles and women's liberation were linked with attributing more fault to a rape victim and defining fewer forced sexual encounters as rape.

The results of the foregoing studies consistently show that respondents with male-dominant, restrictive beliefs about women's roles tend to have callous attitudes toward rape victims. Studies whose results support the sociocultural etiology of rape show that compared to sexually nonaggressive men, men with a history of sexual aggression and men who indicate a tendency to commit sexually aggressive acts report greater acceptance of callous rape attitudes. Future researchers need to investigate and identify societal factors that contribute to the development of male-dominant/callous attitudes and egalitarian/victim-supportive attitudes. A knowledge of such factors is an important step toward developing and enacting policies that promote a less rape-prone society.

REFERENCES

Abbey, A. 1982. Sex differences in attributions for friendly behavior: Do males misperceive females' friendliness? *Journal of Personality and Social Psychology* 42: 830–38.

Abel, G., J.V. Becker, and L.J. Skinner. 1980. Aggressive behavior and sex. *Psychiatric Clinics of North America* 3: 133–51.

Abramson, P., and H. Hayashi. 1984. Pornography in Japan. In *Pornography and Sexual Aggression*, ed. N. Malamuth and E. Donnerstein, 173–83. New York: Academic Press.

Acock, A.C., and N.K. Ireland. 1983. Attribution of blame in rape cases: The impact of norm violation, gender, and sex role attitude. *Sex Roles* 9: 179–93.

Albin, R.S. 1977. Psychological studies of rape. *Signs: Journal of Women in Culture and Society* 3: 423–35.

Alford, A.C., and G.E. Brown. 1985. Virgins, whores, and bitches: Attitudes of rapists toward women and sex. *Corrective and Social Psychiatry* 31: 58–61.

Amir, M. 1971. *Patterns in forcible rape*. Chicago: University of Chicago Press.

Armentrout, J.A., and A.L. Hauer. 1978. MMPIs of rapists of adults, rapists of children, and non-rapist sex offenders. *Journal of Clinical Psychology* 34: 330–32.

Bandura, A. 1973. *Aggression: A social learning analysis*. Englewood Cliffs, N.J.: Prentice-Hall.

———. 1978. Social learning theory of aggression. *Journal of Communication* 3: 12–29.

Bandura, A., B. Underwood, and M.E. Fromson. 1975. Disinhibition of aggression through diffusion of responsibility and dehumanization of victims. *Journal of Research in Personality* 9: 253–69.

Barnett, N.J., and H.S. Feild. 1977. Sex differences in university students' attitudes toward rape. *Journal of College Student Personnel* 18: 93–96.

Beneke, T. 1982. *Men on rape*. New York: St. Martin's Press.

Bond, S.B., and D.L. Mosher. 1986. Guided imagery of rape: Fantasy, reality, and the willing victim myth. *The Journal of Sex Research* 22: 162–83.

Briere, J., and N.M. Malamuth. 1983. Self-reported likelihood of sexually aggressive behavior: Attitudinal versus sexual explanations. *Journal of Research in Personality* 17: 315–23.

Broude, G.J., and S.J. Greene. 1976. Cross–cultural codes on twenty sexual attitudes and practices. *Ethnology* 15: 409–29.

Brownmiller, S. 1975. *Against our will: Men, women and rape*. New York: Simon and Schuster.

Burkhart, B., and A.L. Stanton. Forthcoming. Sexual aggression in acquaintance relationships. In *Violence in intimate relationships*, ed. G. Russell. Elmsford, N.Y.: Pergamon.

Burt, M.R. 1980. Cultural myths and supports for rape. *Journal of Personality and Social Psychology* 38: 217–30.

————. 1983. Justifying personal violence: A comparison of rapists and the general public. *Victimology* 8: 131–50.

Burt, M.R., and R.S. Albin. 1981. Rape myths, rape definitions, and probability of conviction. *Journal of Applied Social Psychology* 11: 212–30.

Burt, M.R., and R.E. Estep. 1981. Who is a victim? Definitional problems in sexual victimization. *Victimology* 6: 15–28.

Cann, A., L. Calhoun, and J. Selby. 1979. Attributing responsibility to the victim of rape: Influence of information regarding past sexual experience. *Human Relations* 32: 57–67.

Carroll, J.L., K.D. Volk, and S.H. Hyde. 1985. Differences between males and females in motives for engaging in sexual intercourse. *Archives of Sexual Behavior* 14: 131–40.

Cate, R., J. Henton, F. Christopher, and S. Lloyd. 1982. Premarital abuse: A social psychological perspective. *Journal of Family Issues* 3: 79–90.

Check, J.V.P., and N.M. Malamuth. 1983. Sex role stereotyping and reactions to depictions of stranger versus acquaintance rape. *Journal of Personality and Social Psychology* 45: 344–56.

Cherry, F. 1983. Gender roles and sexual violence. In *Changing boundaries: Gender roles and sexual behavior*, ed. E. Allgeier and N. McCormick, 245–60. Palo Alto, Calif.: Mayfield Publishing.

Clark, L., and D. Lewis. 1977. *Rape: The price of coercive sexuality*. Toronto: The Women's Press.

Cohen, M.L., et al. 1971. The psychology of rapists. *Seminars in Psychiatry* 3: 307–27.

Costin, F. 1985. Beliefs about rape and women's roles. *Archives of Sexual Behavior* 14: 319–26.

Davis, A.J. 1968. Sexual assaults in the Philadelphia prison system and sheriffs' vans. *Transaction* 8 (December): 15.

Dean, C.W., and M. deBruyn-Kops. 1982. *The crime and the consequences of rape*. Springfield, Ill.: Charles C. Thomas.

Deming, M., and A. Eppy. 1981. The sociology of rape. *Sociology and Social Research* 65: 357–80.

Ehrhart, J.K., and B.R. Sandler, B.R. 1985. *Myths and realities about rape*. Washington, D.C.: Project on the Status and Education of Women.

Farrell, W. 1978. How we teach our men to be "rapists." *Forum* 7: 10–13.

Feild, H.S. 1978. Attitudes toward rape: A comparative analysis of police, rapists, crisis counselors, and citizens. *Journal of Personality and Social Psychology* 36: 156–79.

Fischer, G.J. 1985. *College student attitude toward date rape: Cognitive predictors*. Paper presented at annual meeting, Society for the Scientific Study of Sex, San Diego, Calif.

Fremont, J. 1975. Rapists speak for themselves. In *The politics of rape*, ed. D. Russell et al., 243–56. New York: Stein and Day.

Giarrusso, R., et al. 1979. *Adolescents' cues and signals: Sex and assault*. Paper presented at annual meeting, Western Psychological Association, April, San Diego, Calif.

Goodchilds, J., and G. Zellman. 1984. Adolescent sexual signaling and sexual aggression. In *Pornography and sexual aggression*, ed. N. Malamuth and E. Donnerstein, 233–43. New York: Academic Press.

Goodman, H. 1982. Assertiveness breeds attempt. *Psychology Today*, December: 75.

Greendlinger, V., and D. Byrne. 1987. Coercive sexual fantasies of college males as predictors of self-reported likelihood to rape and overt sexual aggression. *The Journal of Sex Research* 23: 1–11. Forthcoming.

Griffin, S. 1971. Rape: The all-American crime. *Ramparts* 10: 26–35.

Groth, N. 1979. *Men who rape*. New York: Plenum Press.

Groth, A.N., A.W. Burgess, and L.L. Holmstrom. 1977. Rape: Power, anger, and sexuality. *American Journal of Psychiatry* 134: 1239–43.

Hariton, E., and J. Singer. 1974. Women's fantasies during sexual intercourse. *Journal of Consulting and Clinical Psychology* 42: 313–22.

Howells, K., et al. 1984. Perceptions of rape in a British sample: Effects of relationship, victim status, sex, and attitudes to women. *British Journal of Social Psychology* 23: 35–40.

Johnson, P., and J. Goodchilds. 1973. Comment: Pornography, sexuality, and social psychology. *Journal of Social Issues* 29: 231–38.

Kanin, E.J. 1982. Female rape fantasies: A victimization study. *Victimology* 7: 114–21.

———. 1984. Date rape: Unofficial criminals and victims. *Victimology* 9: 95–108.

———. 1985. Date rapists: Differential sexual socialization and relative deprivation. *Archives of Sexual Behavior* 14: 219–31.

Kanin, E.J., and S.R. Parcell. 1977. Sexual aggression: A second look at the offended female. *Archives of Sexual Behavior* 6: 67–76.

Korman, S.K., and G.R. Leslie. 1982. The relationship of feminist ideology and date expense sharing to perceptions of sexual aggression in dating. *The Journal of Sex Research* 18: 114–29.

Koss, M.P. 1981. *Hidden rape on a university campus.* Rockville, Md.: National Institute of Mental Health.

———. 1985. The hidden rape victim: Personality, attitudinal, and situational characteristics. *Psychology of Women Quarterly* 9: 193–212.

Koss, M.P., and K.E. Leonard. 1984. Sexually aggressive men: empirical findings and theoretical implications. In *Pornography and sexual aggression,* ed. N. Malamuth and E. Donnerstein, 213–32. New York: Academic Press.

Koss, M.P., et al. 1985. Nonstranger sexual aggression: A discriminant analysis of the psychological characteristics of undetected offenders. *Sex Roles* 12: 981–992.

Krulewitz, J.E., and E.J. Payne. 1978. Attributions about rape: Effects of rapist force, observer sex and sex role attitudes. *Journal of Applied Social Psychology* 8: 291–305.

Lane, K.E., and P.A. Gwartney-Gibbs. 1985. Violence in the context of dating and sex. *Journal of Family Issues* 6: 45–59.

Langevin, R. 1983. *Sexual strands, understanding and treating sexual anomalies in men.* Hillside, N.J.: Lawrence Erlbaum Associates.

LaPlante, M., N. McCormick, and G. Brannigan. 1980. Living the sexual script: College students' views of influence in sexual encounters. *The Journal of Sex Research* 16: 338–55.

L'Armand, K., and A. Pepitone. 1982. Judgements of rape: A study of victim-rapist relationship and sexual history. *Personality and Social Psychology Bulletin* 8: 134–39.

LeVine, R.A. 1959. Gusii sex offenses: A study in social control. *American Anthropologist* 61: 965–90.

Lottes, I.L. 1984. An investigation into the validity of two model societies proposed to aid analysis, comparison, and understanding of cultural patterns and differences. Typescript.

———. 1986. Predictors of attitudes toward rape in a college population. Ph.D. diss., University of Pennsylvania.

Mahoney, E.R. 1983. *Human sexuality.* New York: McGraw-Hill.

Mahoney, E.R., M.D. Shively, and M. Traw. 1986. Sexual coercion and assault: Male socialization and female risk. *Sexual Coercion and Assault* 1: 2–8.

Makepeace, J.M. 1981. Courtship violence among college students. *Family Relations* 30: 97–102.

Malamuth, N. 1981. Rape proclivity among males. *Journal of Social Issues* 37: 138–57.

————. 1983. Factors associated with rape as predictors of laboratory aggression against women. *Journal of Personality and Social Psychology* 45: 432–42.

————. 1984. Violence against women: cultural, individual, and inhibitory causes. Paper presented at annual meeting, American Psychological Association, Toronto, Canada.

————. 1986. Predictors of naturalistic sexual aggression. *Journal of Personality and Social Psychology*. 50: 953–62.

Malamuth, N., and J. Check. 1980 Penile tumescense and perceptual responses to rape as a function of victim's perceived reactions. *Journal of Applied Social Psychology* 10: 528–47.

Malamuth, N., J. Check, and J. Briere. 1986. Sexual arousal in response to aggression: Ideological, aggressive, and sexual correlates. *Journal of Personality and Social Psychology* 50: 330–40.

Malamuth, N., S. Feshbach, and Y. Jaffe. 1977. Sexual arousal and aggression: Recent experiments and theoretical issues. *Journal of Social Issues* 33: 110–33.

Malamuth, N., S. Haber, and Seymour Feshbach. 1980. Testing hypotheses regarding rape: Exposure to sexual violence, sex differences, and the "normality" of rapists. *Journal of Research in Personality* 14: 121–37.

Marolla, J., and D. Scully. 1982. *Attitudes toward women, violence, and rape: A comparison of convicted rapists and other felons.* Rockville, Md.: National Institute of Mental Health.

Masters, W., and V. Johnson. 1979. *Homosexuality in perspective.* Boston: Little, Brown.

McCaldron, R.J. 1967. Rape. *Canadian Journal of Corrections* 9: 37–43.

McConahay, S.A., and J.B. McConahay. 1977. Sexual permissiveness, sex-role rigidity, and violence across cultures. *Journal of Social Issues* 33: 134–43.

McCormick, N. 1979. Come-ons and put-offs: Unmarried students' strategies for having and avoiding sexual intercourse. *Psychology of Women Quarterly* 4: 194–211.

Medea, A., and K. Thompson. 1974. *Against rape.* New York: Farrar, Straus, and Giroux.

Meyer, T.J. 1984. "Date rape": A serious campus problem that few talk about. *The Chronicle of Higher Education,* 5 December, 1: 12.

Mosher, D.L., and R.A. Anderson. 1984. Macho personality, sexual aggression, and reactions to realistic guided imagery of rape. Typescript.

Muehlenhard, C.L., et al. 1985. Men's attitudes toward the justifiability of date rape: Intervening variables and possible solutions. Paper presented at meeting of Society for the Scientific Study of Sex, Midcontinent region, June, Chicago, Ill.

Murdock, G.P., and D.R. White. 1969. Standard cross cultural sample. *Ethnology* 8: 329–69.

Mynatt, C.R., and E.R. Allgeier. 1985. Sexual coercion: Victim reported effects of acquaintance and social contact. Paper presented at meeting of Society for the Scientific Study of Sex, Midcontinent Region, June, Chicago, Ill.

Parrot, A. 1985. Comparison of acquaintance rape patterns among college students in a large coed university and a small women's college. Paper presented at annual meeting of Society for the Scientific Study of Sex, San Diego, Calif.

Parrot, A., and S. Allen. 1984. Acquaintance rape: Seduction or crime? Paper presented at meeting of the Society for Scientific Study of Sex, Eastern Meeting, April, Philadelphia, Pa.

Parrot, A., and R. Lynk. 1983. Acquaintance rape in a college population. Paper presented at annual meeting of the Society for Scientific Study of Sex, November, Chicago, Ill.

Perdue, W.C., and D. Lester. 1972. Personality characteristics of rapists. *Perceptual and Motor Skills* 35: 514.

Perper, T. 1985. *Sex signals, the biology of love.* Philadelphia: ISI Press.

Person, E.S. 1980. Sexuality as the mainstay of identity: Psychoanalytic perspectives. *Signs* 5: 605–30.

Pugh, M.D. 1983. Contributory fault and rape convictions: Loglinear models for blaming the victim. *Social Psychological Quarterly* 46: 233–42.

Rader, C.M. 1977. MMPI profile types of exposers, rapists, and assaulters in a court services population. *Journal of Consulting and Clinical Psychology* 45: 61–69.

Rapaport, K., and B.R. Burkhart. 1984. Personality and attitudinal characteristics of sexually coercive college males. *Journal of Abnormal Psychology* 93: 216–21.

Reiss, I.L. 1986. *Journey into sexuality: An exploratory voyage.* Englewood Cliffs, N.J.: Prentice-Hall.

Rose, V.M. 1977. Rape as a social problem: A byproduct of the feminist movement. *Social Problems* 25: 75–89.

Russell, D. 1975. The politics of rape. New York: Stein and Day.

———. 1982. The prevalence and incidence of forcible rape and attempted rape of females. *Victimology* 7: 81–93.

Ryan, W. 1972. *Blaming the victim.* New York: Vintage.

Sanday, P.R. 1981. The socio-cultural context of rape: A cross-cultural study. *The Journal of Social Issues* 37: 5–27.

Schultz, L.G., and J. DeSavage. 1975. Rape and rape attitudes on a college campus. In *Rape Victimology*, ed. L.G. Schultz, 77–90. Springfield, Ill.: Charles C. Thomas.

Schwendinger, J.R., and H. Schwendinger. 1983. *Rape and inequality.* Beverly Hills: Sage Publications.

Scully, D., and J. Marolla. 1984. Convicted rapists' vocabulary of motive: Excuses and justifications. *Social Problems* 31: 530–44.

Scully, D., and J. Marolla. 1985a. Rape and vocabularies of motive: Alternative perspectives. In *Rape and sexual assault: A research handbook,* ed. A.W. Burgess, 294–312. New York: Garland Publishing.

————. 1985b. "Riding the bull at Gilleys": Convicted rapists describe the rewards of rape. *Social Problems* 32: 251–63.

Shotland, R.L., and L. Goodstein. 1983. Just because she doesn't want to doesn't mean it's rape: An experimentally based causal model of the perception of rape in a dating situation. *Social Psychological Quarterly* 46: 220–32.

Stock, W. 1983. Women's affective responses and subjective reactions to exposure to violent pornography. Paper presented at annual meeting of Society for the Scientific Study of Sex, November, Chicago, Ill.

Sweet, E. 1985. Date rape, the story of an epidemic and those who deny it. *MS./ Campus Times,* October, 56–59.

Symons, D. 1979. *The evolution of human sexuality.* New York: Oxford University Press.

Tieger, T. 1981. Self-rated likelihood of raping and social perception of rape. *Journal of Research in Personality* 15: 147–58.

Weis, K., and Borges, S. 1975. Victimology and rape: The case of the legitimate victim. In *Rape victimology,* ed. by L.G. Schultz, 91–141. Springfield, Ill.: Charles C. Thomas.

Wheeler, J.R., and C.N. Utigard. 1984. Gender stereotyping, rape attitudes, and acceptance of interpersonal violence. Paper presented at combined annual meeting of the Society for the Scientific Study of Sex and the American Association of Sex Educators, Counselors, and Therapists, June, Boston, Mass.

Williams, J.E. 1979. Sex role stereotypes, women's liberation, and rape: A cross-cultural analysis of attitudes. *Sociological Symposium* 25: 61–97.

Williams, J.E. 1984. Secondary victimization: Confronting public attitudes about rape. *Victimology* 9: 66–81.

Williams, J.E., and K.A. Holmes. 1981. *The second assault, rape and public attitudes.* Westport, Conn.: Greenwood Press.

Zellman, G., et al. 1981. Teenagers' application of the label "rape" to nonconsensual sex between acquaintances. Symposium presentation at meeting of American Psychological Association, August, Los Angeles, Calif.

CHAPTER
13

VULNERABILITY TO SEXUAL ASSAULT

SUZANNE S. AGETON
University of Colorado

Of all the issues related to sexual assault, perhaps none generates more intense interest than that of vulnerability. It touches every woman, and there are few who have not thought about their own vulnerability to this crime. Beyond the individual level, however, only in the last two to three decades have sociologists and social psychologists begun to develop theories to account for the distribution of rape and sexual assault observed in different groups and populations. These explanations range from global, social-structural arguments to more limited ecological or subcultural perspectives.

At the broadest level, it has been argued that all women are vulnerable to sexual assault because of the sharp sexual stratification in most societies and because of the female socialization process, which trains women to be submissive and acquiescent. Rape and sexual assault are viewed as the natural outgrowth of power relationships that emerge when sexual stratification is marked within a society (or within major subgroups within a society). It is acknowledged that cultures or societies (as well as subgroups within) may vary in the degree to which they are sexually stratified, and hence vulnerability to sexual assault should vary as well. Although these arguments from feminist and conflict theory have not received much empirical testing, recent research by Sanday (1981) and Williams and Holmes (1981) has begun to fill this gap.

Less global theories of vulnerability to sexual assault have focused on ecological and subcultural themes. These approaches argue for differential risk on the basis of such factors as low socioeconomic status, minority-group membership, residence in a high-crime area, and the existence of subcultures of violence (Amir 1971; Curtis 1976). To a large extent, these explanations are based on victim data generated from criminal justice, hospital emergency room, and rape crisis center files. The disproportionate number of lower-class, minority women found in these samples, for example, has led to theorizing that these groups face a higher risk of sexual assault.

All of these theories have some currency and support, but they generally have not been verified on representative samples of women. Knowledge about vulnerability to sexual assault is still tied to known or officially reported cases, which are unlikely to be typical of all sexual assault cases. Comparisons of victims and nonvictims derived from a general population survey are needed to determine whether the images we have of victims, created partly from feminist ideology and partly from official records, are accurate.

To address this issue, one objective of the Sexual Assault Project, which is discussed in this chapter, was to use a national probability sample of adolescents to test some generally stated ideas about vulnerability to sexual assault. The availability of a representative sample of adolescents, which contained a reasonable sample of sexual-assault victims, offered a unique opportunity. Through comparison of the victims with a control group on several factors believed to be related to vulnerability to sexual assault (race, social class, sex-role attitudes, and a deviant lifestyle), some understanding of the concept of differential risk could be achieved.

This effort was viewed as exploratory, and consequently no single theoretical framework was imposed. Two theoretical perspectives pervaded this effort, however, one by happenstance and one by choice. The National Youth Survey, the larger study out of which the Sexual Assault Project (SAP) grew, had as a primary objective a test of an integrated theory of delinquent behavior. This theory incorporates a number of sociopsychological concepts, including strain, commitment, and conventional and delinquent bonding. Although these variables are not generally part of the theorizing about risk of sexual assault, it seemed reasonable to take advantage of their presence. Consequently, included in the victim-control comparisons are several of these factors.

By choice, we decided to analyze the risk of sexual assault from a sex-role perspective. Within the sexual-assault literature, two of the basic themes regarding risk of sexual assault are tied to this perspective and yet are inherently contradictory. On the one hand, it is argued that females who conform to the traditional female role model are more vulnerable to sexual aggression because of their passivity and general acquiescence to male demands (Brownmiller 1975; Gager and Schurr 1976; Weis and

Borges 1973). On the other hand, it is asserted that liberated women face a higher risk of sexual aggression because of their nonconformity and violation of traditional norms for female behavior (Adler 1975; Hayman 1972; Lee 1972). This circular reasoning leads to two alternative conclusions: (1) all women are equally at risk of sexual assault, regardless of their sex-role attitudes and behavior, or (2) traditional and nontraditional sex-role attitudes are related. While both of these positions seem untenable (certainly neither is supported by the available data), it is less than clear what role, if any, sex-role attitudes and behavior play in affecting vulnerability to sexual assault.

In an effort to address the inconsistencies in the literature and to assess empirically the impact of sex-role attitudes and behavior on sexual assault, we chose to conceptualize vulnerability in sex role terms and to test this scheme with sexual-assault data drawn from a national probability sample of adolescents.

CONCEPTUALIZATION OF VULNERABILITY

Sexual-assault literature, especially that influenced by feminist analyses (Brownmiller 1975; Gager and Schurr 1976; Griffin 1971), has stated that the role of the traditional female, resulting from conventional female socialization, is structurally conducive to assuming the role of rape victim. From childhood, females learn to be submissive and subordinate, to direct their attention toward being attractive and appealing, rather than assertive and competitive (Weitzman 1975). This identification process is operative in all major social institutions (home, school, and the peer group), as well as being supported by image reinforcement in the mass media. The result of this comprehensive socialization process, according to some researchers, is that women become vulnerable to sexual aggression because of their propensity, ingrained by conventional sex-role training, to acquiesce to such behavior. Weis and Borges (1973) define the socialization process of the female as one that molds her into a victim and provides the procedure for legitimizing her in the role. Similarly, Russell (1975) argues that acceptance of the feminine mystique increases a woman's risk of rape.

Other researchers provide empirical evidence that women are often ambivalent and passive in the face of sexual aggression. In a study of male sexual aggression on a university campus (Kirkpatrick and Kanin 1957), it was noted that an ambivalent resistance was often offered by college women who encountered sexual aggression. While a large number

expressed anger, their responses were more often characterized by inde-
cision, guilt, and embarrassment. In another study assessing potential
responses to a sexual assault, female respondents were much less likely
than male respondents to select a physically aggressive response to a
hypothetical assault (Tolor 1977).

Despite the pervasiveness of this argument, we are not convinced that
traditional sex-role socialization is related to vulnerability to sexual
assault. First, if the female socialization process is as universal as the
perspective implies, there would be no variability on this factor, and thus
it could not help to explain differential vulnerability to sexual assault.
However, the assumption that all or most females in our society experience the same type of sexual socialization is unjustified. The socialization
process is not necessarily traditional, complete, or identical for all women.
Race and class status, among other factors, influence and differentiate sex-
role socialization, as has been described most recently by Williams and
Holmes (1981). Thus it is possible, in line with the sex-role perspective,
that those women most traditionally socialized are more at risk of a sexual
assault; however, we think it as likely that vulnerability to sexual aggression and assault is tied to unconventional sex-role attitudes as to traditional
ones. Women whose attitudes flaunt or denigrate traditional sex-role
patterns and norms may be equally at risk. In sum, we are inclined to
believe that sex-role attitudes are not strongly related to risk of a sexual
assault. This is not to say that sex-role attitudes may not contribute to a
sexual assault or interact with other factors to increase vulnerability, but
we do not expect that their contribution will be primary.

The second major theme focuses on the impact of sex-role behavior,
particularly inappropriate role behavior, on vulnerability to sexual assault.
Women whose behavior is inconsistent with that typically expected of
them by society have often been considered open to sexual aggression. It
is argued that women who go out alone at night, frequent bars, and display
other unusual female-role behavior are more likely to be sexually assaulted than those who behave in accordance with traditional expectations
(Lee 1972; Hayman 1972). Women who overplay their sexuality (according to some undefined set of social norms) or who use it for economic gain
are believed legitimate victims (they are said to have precipitated their
own victimization).

The belief that certain women have created their own vulnerability by
their unconventional and deviant behavior is widespread and has been
reinforced by the findings from several studies. Results from a survey of
Michigan policemen indicate that most of these men charged with enforc-
ing the sexual-assault laws believe that some women deserve to be raped
(Pope 1974). Additionally, a study assessing judicial attitudes toward

rape victims (Bohmer 1974) indicates that judges feel there are types of women who are raped because they are "asking for it." Furthermore, there are innumerable studies involving rape cases indicating that such factors as the victim's previous sexual experiences, marital status (divorced women are less likely to be believed than married ones), and relationship with the offender often influence juries to acquit (Cann, Calhoun, and Shelby 1977; L'Armand and Pepitone 1977; Kalben and Zeisel 1966; Jones and Aronson 1973). Finally, there are suggestions throughout the literature that adolescent women who engage in such deviant activities as running away from home, hitchhiking, drug use, and frequent sexual intercourse are, by the nature of these activities and the environments they occur in, setting themselves up for a sexual assault (Nelson and Amir 1975; Konopka 1976; Russell 1975; Robert 1966).

Besides involvement in delinquent or deviant activities, assuming a liberated sexual lifestyle may also increase a female's vulnerability to sexual assault. The more open sexual attitudes associated with changes in conventional female roles may make men expect sexual intercourse and be less likely to accept refusals (Adler 1975). Williams and Holmes (1981) argue that the occurrence of date rapes may increase as a result of liberated behavior on the part of women:

> The liberated woman is often sexually active and will not rely on moral or virginal protestations to reject a sexual advance. As a result, situations in which unsuccessful seductions become rapes—"date rapes"—are likely to increase. If a woman says "no," it is likely a matter of personal choice and as Weis and Borges note, "since both participants 'lose face' when the refusal is blunt and without the usual justifications, the rejected suitor may take it as a personal attack" (1973: 97) and respond with physical force. (Williams and Holmes 1981, 10; reprinted with permission)

While there appears to be rather widespread support both in the literature and among the public for this argument, no sound data indicate that women who behave in unconventional ways are, in fact, more vulnerable to sexual victimization. Data on the frequency of antisocial behavior among groups of known rape or sexual-assault victims are incomplete or nonexistent. More important, no controlled data are available to ascertain whether victim rates of such behavior are comparable to those of nonvictims from the same race and class groups. Without such data, the evidence that atypical female role behavior raises the risk of sexual assault is inferential at best. We assumed that there would be no significant relationship between these two factors.

To address the issues concerning vulnerability to sexual assault, we used data from the Sexual Assault Project (SAP) to explore the relationship between sex-role attitudes and behavior and risk of sexual assault. We anticipated that these factors would not significantly influence vulnerability to sexual assault. The data also permitted an assessment of the influence of race and social class on the risk of sexual assault, and several other general attitudinal and behavioral variables tied to an integrated delinquency theory were assessed as well. Comparisons were made on these variables between victim and nonvictim groups.

RESEARCH DESIGN

The SAP grew out of a larger study on delinquent behavior, the National Youth Survey (NYS). The NYS used a longitudinal, sequential design with multiple birth cohorts. The sample, selected in 1976, was a national probability sample of youth aged 11 through 17 and included seven birth cohorts (1959–65). The total youth sample was interviewed initially between January and March 1977 concerning the respondents' victimization and involvement in delinquent behavior during calendar year 1976. The second, third, fourth, and fifth surveys were conducted during these same months in successive years. By the fifth survey (1981), the panel was 15 through 21 years of age. The cumulated data across the five years of the study cover the entire adolescent period.

Because the original NYS interview contained self-reports of sexual assaults from both victims and offenders, the basic data were available from which to develop a more comprehensive study of sexual assault among adolescents. Funding for the SAP began in 1978, and for the last three years of the NYS (1978 through 1980), specific information about any reported sexual assaults was obtained from all of the self-identified victims and offenders. These data, plus the general attitudinal and behavioral data gathered in the NYS, provided the basis for the findings reported in this chapter.

STUDY SAMPLE

NYS SAMPLE

The NYS employed a probability sample of households in the continental United States in 1976 based on a multistage, cluster-sampling design. At each stage, the probabilities of selection were established to provide a self-weighting sample. Seventy-six sampling units were selected, with probability of selection being proportional to size. Approximately 8,000 households were chosen for inclusion in the sample, and all youth living in these households who were 11 through 17 years of age on December 31, 1976, and who were physically and mentally capable of being interviewed were eligible respondents for the study. Out of a total of 2,360 eligible youth, 635 (27%) did not participate in the study due to parental refusal, youth refusal, or inability to establish contact with the respondent. The remaining 1,725 agreed to participate in the study, signed informed consents, and completed interviews in the initial survey (1977).

An age, sex, and race comparison of nonparticipating eligible youth and participating youth indicated that the initial loss rate from any particular age, sex, or racial group appeared proportional to that group's representation in the population. Further, with respect to these characteristics, participating youth appeared to be representative of the total 11 through 17-year-old youth population in the United States as established by the U.S. Census Bureau.

Across the five years of the study, the total sample loss was 231 youth, or 13.4% of the original first year participants. Tests for selective loss on basic demographic characteristics suggested that although there was some selective loss over time with respect to race, class, and place of residence, the cumulative loss rates were very small. Overall there was no evidence that the participating samples for years 2 through 5 lost their representativeness by sex, age, race, social class, or place of residence.

SEXUAL ASSAULT SAMPLE

For purposes of this research, *sexual assault* was defined to include all forced sexual behavior involving contact with the sexual parts of the body. Thus, the definition could encompass forcible rape, incest, sodomy, and fondling but not exhibitionism or other sexual acts where no contact was established. Attempted sexual assaults were counted. In addition, we allowed the force component to be as mild as verbal pressure or as severe as a physical beating or injury from a weapon.

This relatively broad definition was chosen because of our interest in the range of forced sexual experiences among adolescents, specifically the so-called date rape. We suspected that many adolescents experience forced contact, with the sexual parts of their bodies, that does not conclude with forceful sexual intercourse. Nonetheless, many of these acts qualify as sexual assaults and may have significant implications for adolescents whose sexuality is just emerging. Limiting queries to forcible rapes would have excluded a priori all forced sexual acts that fell short of rape. Although this definition may have included behaviors that were not sexual assaults, we believed a broad definition was necessary to capture the range of sexual assaults that adolescents experience.

Out of the NYS sample, those respondents who self-identified as sexual assault victims became the sexual-assault victim sample. This self-identification process had two stages. Initially, each repondent was asked several questions to determine whether he or she had experienced a possible sexual assault. These questions were embedded in a larger set of delinquency and victimization items. They were designed to cover the continuum of sexual-assault behavior from the stereotypic violent stranger assault to the date-rape situation. A response of one or more to either of the following questions tentatively placed the respondent in the sexual assault victim sample: How many times in the last year have you (1) been sexually attacked or raped or an attempt made to do so, and/or (2) been pressured or pushed by someone such as a date or friend to do more sexually than you wanted to do?

In addition to the specific sexual-assault questions, reports of physical assaults were followed up to ascertain whether a sexual assault had occurred as well. If it had, these cases were added to the pool of potential victims.

The original NYS interview only contained the first question. The second question was added to the 1978 interview in an attempt to broaden and specify the types of forced sexual behavior we wanted to study. Specifically, we wanted to capture those forced sexual behaviors that occur in the context of a date but may not be defined as rape or even as sexual assault.

One drawback to this expansion was that we created overlap in the items and thus the possibility of multiple reports of the same incident. Therefore, respondents were asked to tell us the total number of sexual assaults that had occurred during the year whenever both of the sexual-assault questions was answered. This procedure enabled us to provide a nonredundant count despite the overlapping questions.

The second stage in the self-identification process involved reading to all potential victims a general description of the sexual situations we were defining as sexual assaults. This second-level filter of potential sexual-assault cases was deemed necessary for two reasons. First, since the SAP was essentially a secondary research effort tied to an ongoing study of delinquent behavior, the goals of the primary study had to be given priority. This meant that a detailed description of sexual assault and the gathering of precise information on what sexual behavior occurred during the assault were precluded for fear of jeopardizing respondent participation in the larger study. Consequently, the presentation of a general description of sexual assault to all potential respondents was judged critical to ensure that only legitimate cases were pursued. In addition, it was felt that the age of the respondents might work against a clear understanding of the initial questions and that it would be wise to give all potential victims a consistent description of the behavior of interest. The reading of a general description would also permit respondents to deselect themselves before the questioning began if the behavior they had reported did not fit the description read to them.

The broad description of sexual assault was read to all potential victims as part of the general introduction to the specific sexual-assault questions. The description stated the following:

> The following set of questions is related to the event you reported earlier in the interview of having been pressured by someone to do more sexually than you wanted to do. For purposes of this interview, we are interested in the sexual situation in which someone pressured you into contact with the private parts of your body or theirs. Please remember that all your answers are confidential and that your name will not appear anywhere on the interview.

Respondents who passed through both stages of the self-identification process were considered legitimate victims and were asked the special sexual-assault questions at the end of the regular interview. This process was followed for each of the three years (i.e., 1978, 1979, and 1980).

For the period 1978–80, this process generated 172 completed interviews with female adolescent victims.[1] Approximately 20 cases were lost due to refusal, deselection, or interviewer error, with the majority lost by deselection. Respondent comments and interviewer observations suggest that the preponderance of the deselections were legitimate.[2]

ANALYSIS PROCEDURES

To reduce the disparity in sample size between the female victim group and all nonvictimized females in each year, we developed procedures to select a control group from the sample of females who had not reported any sexual assaults in each year. In each year, all females who reported no sexual assaults as either a victim or offender were eligible for the control group. The victim and control samples were matched only on sex, because to match on any other variables could have obscured potential differences between victims and nonvictims. For each year, systematic samples of approximately the same size as the female victim group were drawn from the nonvictim, nonoffender female sample. For each year (1978, 1979, 1980), statistical comparisons were conducted between these control groups and the samples from which they were drawn on a number of relevant variables: age, social class, race, and self-reported delinquency.

No significant differences were observed. Although these tests cannot ensure that no biases are present in the control groups, they do indicate that the control groups were representative of the larger samples from which they were drawn, at least on the variables examined.

In order to determine whether female adolescent sexual-assault victims may be distinguished from the nonvictimized female youth population, a series of *t*-tests (and chi-square tests where appropriate) was conducted. These analyses were undertaken with several variables. The two key variables, *attitudes toward sex roles* and *deviant lifestyle*, were measured in the following ways. First, the sex-role scale was designed to assess the extent to which adolescents adhere to traditional expectations regarding appropriate role behavior for men and women. The intent of the scale was to focus on both behavior and characteristics of men and women, as well as role responsibilities of each gender within their relationships with each other. The second variable was measured by general reports of involvement in all types of delinquent behavior, as well as by a specially constructed *deviant lifestyle* measure. This measure was composed of five deviant behaviors often cited in the literature as related to adolescent sexual assault: running away from home, hitchhiking, prostitution, sexual intercourse, and being drunk in a public place. In addition to the two specific variables, all of the basic sociodemographic variables were examined (race, age, social class, and place of residence). Comparisons were made as well on a large number of environmental, attitudinal, and behavioral measures.

VICTIM AND CONTROL-GROUP COMPARISONS

1978 COMPARISONS

None of the sociodemographic comparisons produced any statistically significant differences. Also most of the attitudinal and behavioral measures did not show substantial differences between the victim and control groups. In particular, the two groups were not differentiated on the sex-role attitudes scale. Some significant differences were observed, however, on measures related to peer group. The victims had a significantly more delinquent peer group than the controls ($t = 3.99$, $p < .00$). Regarding involvement in delinquent behavior, the victims received significantly less disapproval from their peers than the controls received from their peers ($t = 2.57$, $p < .01$). Although there was no significant difference between the victims and the controls on the attitudes-toward-deviance scale, the peer group findings suggest that the victims are more exposed to delinquency from their peers, both attitudinally and behaviorally.

While no significant difference appeared on the general delinquency scales or on the deviant-lifestyle measure, the victim and control group were differentiated on several of the offense-specific scales. Of the delinquency scales analyzed, the four presented in table 13.1 show significant differences. In all cases, the sexual-assault victims were substantially more delinquent than the control group. It is obvious from the size of the standard deviations, however, that there was considerable overlap in the distributions. While the mean values of the two groups were statistically distinct on these scales, it is unlikely that there can be much predictive power in these differences.

TABLE 13.1
SIGNIFICANT MEAN ($\bar{X}$) DIFFERENCES BETWEEN
VICTIMS AND CONTROLS ON SELF-REPORT DELIQUENCY
AND VICTIMIZATION SCALES, 1978

Scale Name	Victim $\bar{X}$	SD	Control $\bar{X}$	SD	t-Value	p
Minor assault	1.48	3.78	0.23	0.64	2.59	.01
Minor theft	0.70	1.92	0.10	0.43	2.42	.05
Crimes against persons	1.78	4.14	0.32	0.92	2.72	.01
School-related delinquency	9.90	13.77	4.48	8.77	2.63	.01
Nonsexual victimization	5.24	9.93	0.89	1.29	3.45	.00

A final measure on which we compared the groups was the total amount of nonsexual victimization experienced. The data in table 13.1 clearly indicate that the controls experienced substantially less victimization of all kinds than did the victims.

In summary, the data indicate that female adolescent sexual-assault victims in 1978 were not distinct from nonvictims demographically or on either the sex-role attitudes scale or the deviant-lifestyle scale; however, the victims engaged in delinquency and were supported in their behavior by their peers to a significantly greater extent than the control group members. They also had experienced significantly more nonsexual victimization than the controls.

On the basis of these data alone, one would conclude that attitudinally and demographically, female sexual assault victims are not particularly distinguishable from their nonvictimized peers. Their involvement in delinquent behavior and the character of their peer groups, however, do differentiate them from the nonvictims. It may be that these features affect vulnerability to sexual assault or are simply idiosyncratic to the 1978 victims.

1979 COMPARISONS

The 1979 victim and control group comparisons on sociodemographic variables evidenced no significant differences by age, race, social class, or place of residence. None of these tests even approached statistical significance. The victim group did experience more disruptive events in the family, such as divorce or extended unemployment, than did the control group ($t = 3.16$, $p < .01$); nonetheless, these data, like those from 1978, suggest that there are not strong, consistent sociodemographic differences between female adolescent sexual-assault victims and nonvictims.

Unlike the 1978 findings, the attitudinal measures showed several significant differences between the two groups, which are summarized, along with the self-report delinquency data, in table 13.2. The control

TABLE 13.2
SIGNIFICANT MEAN ($\overline{X}$) DIFFERENCES BETWEEN VICTIMS AND CONTROLS ON ATTITUDINAL AND BEHAVIORAL SCALES, 1979

Scale Name	Victim $\overline{X}$	SD	Control $\overline{X}$	SD	t-Value	p
Family variables						
Family normlessness	9.38	3.15	8.13	2.64	−2.42	.05
School variables						
Involvement in school academics	6.88	3.45	8.13	2.98	2.05	.05
School normlessness	10.59	3.17	9.50	2.43	−2.03	.05
Peer variables						
Importance of peer aspirations	15.46	3.54	13.46	3.45	−3.30	.00
Exposure to delinquent peers	28.42	7.67	21.69	5.85	5.52	.00
Commitment to delinquent peers	4.43	1.28	3.98	1.06	−2.13	.05
Perceived peer disapproval of delinquent behavior	41.98	6.13	44.93	5.55	2.82	.01
Peer pressure for drinking and drug use*	11.08	3.70	8.51	2.49	−4.58	.00
General variables						
Attitudes toward deviance	36.78	6.37	40.32	5.15	3.43	.00
Trouble from drinking*	7.12	3.23	5.47	1.26	−3.63	.00
Trouble from drug use*	6.77	2.89	5.44	1.40	−2.59	.01
Delinquent behavior and victimization						
Felony assault	0.70	2.34	0.02	0.13	−2.31	.05
Crimes against persons	4.10	13.15	0.15	0.81	−2.38	.05
Index offenses	0.86	2.76	0.02	0.13	−2.42	.05
General delinquency	95.51	140.24	36.32	79.97	−2.90	.01
School related delinquency	30.35	55.43	6.83	17.44	−3.21	.01
Nonsexual victimization	3.79	6.54	0.76	1.28	−3.58	.00

*These measures were available for all subjects only in 1979 and 1980.

group was substantially more involved in school academics than were the victims and less likely to believe that rules had to be broken in order to achieve conventional goals at school (school normlessness). The controls also evidenced substantially less normlessness in the family context than did the victims. Furthermore, there was a significant difference between the groups on their attitudes toward deviance, with the victims less likely than the controls to judge deviant acts as wrong.

The peer group findings are similar to, if not stronger than, those from the 1978 data. The sexual-assault victims seemed to view their peer relations as significantly more important than the controls did. Furthermore, their peers were substantially more delinquent than those of the controls, and the victims asserted a greater commitment to these peers, even though they were delinquent. The peers of the victims also seemed to provide an atmosphere supportive of delinquency to a substantially greater extent than the peers of the control group members. Finally, on a new scale available in 1979 and 1980, which measured peer pressure for drinking and drug use, the controls reported substantially less pressure of this type than did the victims.

When self-reported delinquency scores were compared, the victims had higher mean scores than the controls on all of the scales examined. Several of these differences achieved statistical significance (see table 13.2). Unlike 1978, the victims and controls were distinguished on a general measure of delinquency as well as on a measure of all serious offenses, the index-offense scale. The mean differences on these two scales between the two groups were substantial and suggest real differences in the levels of involvement in these offenses by the victims and the controls. Again, however, the magnitude of the standard deviations indicates that although the two groups were statistically different on these measures, there was considerable overlap in the scores.

The amount of nonsexual victimization reported by the 1979 victims was significantly higher than that reported by the controls, as may be seen in table13. 2. The victim mean was approximately five times that of the control mean.

In summary, although there were few demographic distinctions between the 1979 victims and controls, there were numerous attitudinal and behavioral ones. The most consistent of these include the following: the victims' tendencies to be involved with and supportive of delinquent peers, substantially greater involvement in delinquent behavior on the part of the victims, and a significant difference in the amount of nonsexual victimization experienced by the two groups, with the victims reporting more of this victimization. Because these three differences were also evidenced in the 1978 comparisons, some patterns began to emerge that may alter our conceptualization regarding vulnerability to sexual assault. It is beginning to appear that deviant behavior, albeit not the specific types included in the deviant-lifestyle scale, is related to sexual assault. Sex-role attitudes again did not distinguish the groups, reinforcing our belief that this set of attitudes is peripheral to the risk of a sexual assault.

1980 COMPARISONS

As in the previous two years, no significant differences between the victim and control groups were observed on any of the sociodemographic variables; however, the family life of the victims was disrupted by significantly more traumatic events, such as divorce and death, than that of the controls ($t = 2.04, p < .05$). Thus, although the two groups were not demographically distinct, it does appear that the home environment of the victim group was substantially less stable than that of the control group.

Significant findings from the comparisons between the victims and controls on several attitudinal, behavioral, and self-report delinquency measures are presented in table 13.3. One pattern in these results indicates that the victims generally had less involvement with their families and poorer family relationships than did the control group. Specifically, they felt less successful at maintaining a good relationship with their families, were less involved in family activities, and felt more estranged from their families than did the controls.

The data in table 13.3 also confirm the association between victims and delinquent peers that was observed in the 1978 and 1979 findings. The 1980 victims had peers who were less likely to disapprove of delinquent acts, more involved in delinquent behavior, and more likely to approve of drinking and drug use than the peers of the control group members.

Two final comments about the results reported in table 13.3 seem appropriate. First, the significant difference between the two groups on the attitudes-toward-deviance scale suggests that the victims judged more deviant behaviors as acceptable than did the controls. This finding in conjunction with the peer-group results indicates that the victims were behaviorally and attitudinally more tolerant of delinquent behavior than were the controls. Second, for the first time we see a significant difference between the victims and controls on the sex-roles attitudes scale. The direction of the scores indicates that the controls held significantly more traditional values than did the victims. This finding would suggest that the risk of sexual assault is higher among females who hold nontraditional sex-role values; however, no differences between the victims and controls were observed on this scale in either of the other years.

The differences in frequency of self-reported delinquency between the victim and control groups were similar to those reported previously. The victims reported higher mean scores than the controls on all of the delinquency scales, and these differences were significant for the scales listed in table 13.3. This table also reflects the significant differences between the two groups on the trouble-from-drinking scale and on the drug-use-and-nonsexual-victimization scale. For these measures, the victims again reported the higher scores, indicating more problems from drinking and drug use and more victimization in general.

TABLE 13.3
SIGNIFICANT MEAN ($\overline{X}$) DIFFERENCES BETWEEN VICTIMS AND CONTROLS ON ATTITUDINAL AND BEHAVIORAL SCALES, 1980

Scale Name	Victim $\overline{X}$	SD	Control $\overline{X}$	SD	t-Value	p
Family variables						
Family aspirations—						
current success	16.85	5.12	19.11	4.15	2.37	.05
Involvement in family activities	7.26	4.25	9.63	3.42	2.62	.01
Social isolation from family	11.19	4.29	9.31	3.14	−2.44	.05
Perceived negative labeling						
by family	25.67	7.13	22.69	4.94	−2.38	.05
School variables						
Social isolation from school	11.12	2.77	9.95	2.31	−2.05	.05
Peer variables						
Perceived peer disapproval of						
delinquent behavior	40.90	6.86	44.71	5.17	3.07	.01
Exposure to delinquent peers	28.72	9.21	20.36	5.89	−5.28	.00
Peer pressure for drinking						
and drug use*	11.71	4.16	8.15	2.23	−5.22	.00
General variables						
Attitudes toward deviance	36.65	5.98	39.83	5.22	2.78	.01
Attitudes toward sex roles	19.73	5.09	22.13	4.81	2.37	.05
Attendance at religious services	2.31	1.32	2.96	1.38	2.34	.05
Trouble from drinking*	7.32	3.18	5.28	0.57	−4.32	.00
Trouble from drug use*	7.11	3.22	5.13	0.35	−3.68	.00
Delinquent behavior and victimization						
Minor assault	1.71	4.83	0.08	0.40	−2.32	.05
Public disorder	30.50	81.14	1.13	2.29	−2.51	.05
Status offenses	54.19	70.32	13.85	32.12	−3.61	.00
Crimes against persons	2.29	5.76	0.10	0.52	−2.62	.01
General delinquency A	103.46	138.67	18.50	36.93	−4.10	.00
General delinquency B	49.00	73.41	10.63	25.56	−3.42	.00
School-related delinquency	21.21	36.20	4.08	14.89	−3.03	.00
Deviant lifestyle	48.83	88.46	10.65	25.77	−2.87	.01
Nonsexual victimization	3.90	5.77	0.77	2.00	−3.55	.00

*These measures were available for all subjects only in 1979 and 1980.

The 1980 comparisons produced results generally similar to those reported for 1978 and 1979. One slight change is that the 1980 findings indicate that the victims felt isolated from their families, and that the family environment was not stable. This finding was noted in the 1979 results as well, but the estrangement and separation from the family was not reported so strongly then.

GENERAL SUMMARY

In summarizing the findings from 1978 through 1980, we have operated under the assumption that significant differences that appear in two or more years are likely to reflect real, substantive distinctions between sexual-assault victims and controls. Hence, we confine our comments generally to variables that meet this criterion.

Despite some popular beliefs that sexual-assault victims are disproportionately lower-class, minority, urban women, the SAP data show no significant differences between victims and nonvictims on these characteristics. The only two demographic variables that differentiated the victims and controls for two or more years was the family-crisis scale. In two of the three years, the victims reported significantly more disruptive events in their homes, such as divorce and extended unemployment, than did the controls. Although we have no data that supports a direct connection between this factor and the risk of sexual assault, it may be that this experience interacts with other factors to influence vulnerability. An unstable home environment may leave an adolescent female without the basic emotional and physical support she needs during a period of rapid sexual, biological, and psychological development. If she turns to male friends or dates for this support, her needs may be taken advantage of or misinterpreted. Although this line of reasoning is conjecture, the findings do imply that a family environment punctuated by disruptive events may contribute to the risk of sexual assault.

Some of the strongest findings from these analyses are associated with the peer group and involvement in delinquent behavior. For all three years, sexual-assault victims had a significantly higher exposure to delinquent peers and received support from these friends for unconventional, delinquent acts. In addition, the victims themselves were significantly more involved in a wide variety of delinquent behavior, including serious offenses. They also reported significantly more trouble from drinking and drug use than did the controls. Not surprisingly, in two of the three years the victims reported receiving significantly more peer pressure for drinking and drug use than did the controls. In line with their behavior, the victims displayed far more tolerant attitudes toward deviance than did the controls.

Although the findings are somewhat inconsistent, it does not appear that sex-role attitudes play a major role in differentiating victims from controls. In two of the three years examined, no significant differences were noted between the two groups on this scale. When a difference did emerge, it was consistent with the behavioral findings in that the victims were more nontraditional in both attitudes and behavior. We conclude from these results that sex-role attitudes are unrelated to the risk of a sexual assault, but that deviant or inappropriate role behavior is related.

Taken in concert, all of these findings indicate that engaging in delinquent behavior and being part of a delinquent network influence the risk of being sexually assaulted (and victimized in other ways as well). Although the specific delinquencies previously associated with sexual assault (hitchhiking, prostitution, running away from home, etc.) did not significantly differentiate victims from controls, the two groups were distinctly different in terms of the character of their peer networks and their involvement in general and serious delinquency. It appears that teenage females who were generally delinquent were advertising their unconventionality in ways that jeopardized their control of sexual situations. If one is behaviorally and attitudinally delinquent, conventional protestations with regard to requests for sexual intercourse may fall on deaf ears. Confining a delinquent image to nonsexual behavior may not be possible.

PREVICTIMIZATION COMPARISONS

If victims and controls can be distinguished after the assault has occurred, one obvious question is whether those differences existed prior to the assault and might in some way account for the different experience of the two groups.[3] Most sexual-assault research projects cannot address this question adequately because they have no prospective data (those gathered prior to or simultaneous with the report of an assault). In this case, we were fortunate that the SAP grew out of a larger study that had collected two years of data on all subjects before the research on sexual assault was formally begun. Consequently, we were able to compare victims and controls two years before victimization on a number of variables, particularly some of those on which they differed significantly in the year of the assault.[4]

The comparison groups consisted of all victims in 1978 who had not reported a sexual assault in 1976 or 1977 and a group of controls who reported no sexual assaults across the entire study period.[5] The data in table 13.4 reflect significant mean differences between these two groups for the years 1976 and 1977 on several attitudinal variables.

TABLE 13.4

MEAN DIFFERENCES BETWEEN FUTURE SEXUAL-ASSAULT VICTIMS (V)
AND CONTROLS (C) ON SELECTED ATTITUDINAL SCALES

Scale Name	1976						1977					
	V	SD	C	SD	t	p	V	SD	C	SD	t	p
Family and school variables												
Family normlessness												
	9.19	2.82	8.06	2.42	–2.16	.05	8.46	2.95	7.75	2.23	1.39	N.S
School normlessness												
	11.05	2.97	10.50	2.80	–0.96	N.S	10.77	2.81	9.70	2.61	–1.98	.05
Peer variables												
Perceived peer disapproval of delinquent behavior												
	35.04	6.33	37.98	5.39	2.52	.01	36.12	5.10	38.09	4.91	1.98	.05
Exposure to delinquent peers												
	17.01	6.26	14.71	5.14	–1.92	N.S	17.40	5.54	14.11	3.95	–3.31	.00
General variables												
Attitudes toward deviance												
	31.18	4.20	33.10	3.13	2.64	.01	30.98	4.08	32.44	3.31	1.99	.05

Notes: Victim group is composed of all victims who reported a sexual assault for the first time in the study in 1978 ($N = 55$). To ensure that the controls had no reported sexual assaults across the entire study period, the control group from wave 5 was used ($N = 48$).
t = t-Value.   N.S = Not significant.

The data show that several of the variables that separated the groups after the sexual assaults also did so as much as one to two years prior to the assaults. The victims appeared to be less well bonded than the controls, both at home and at school, though the differences between the two groups were not consistently significant. Regarding their peer networks, the victims consistently reported greater exposure to delinquent peers and approval from these peers for illegal behavior. In addition, the victims reported substantially more tolerant attitudes toward deviance in both 1976 and 1977. While these peer and attitudinal differences did not translate into any significant differences in delinquent behavior in 1976 and 1977, the victims did consistently report higher mean frequency scores on all of the delinquency scales in these years.

The peer differences between the groups persisted into 1978, when the first sexual assaults were reported. Furthermore, in that year we observed several significant differences between all of the 1978 victims and the controls on some of the delinquency scales (see table 13.1). In all instances, the victims reported significantly higher levels of involvement in delinquent behavior than did the controls.

These findings suggest that the cumulative effect of associating with delinquent peers and engaging in a fair amount of delinquency may be to raise substantially the risk of sexual assault. We speculate that there are two primary reasons why this may be so. First, the settings and circumstances in which delinquency occurs are likely to be conducive to many forms of deviance. For example, even though a female victim may have intended only to steal some drugs and get high with her friends, the situation could easily evolve into one that ends with a forced sexual experience. Second, a female involved in delinquent behavior may project a generally deviant image, which carries with it expectations about sexual behavior. Consequently, she may not be successful in restricting her deviant behavior to nonsexual acts.

Overall the data in table 13.4 indicate that victims and controls were substantially different in terms of peer networks and attitudes toward deviance at least two years prior to the first reported assaults. The victims also appeared to be less well integrated into home and school environments than the controls. Although there were not any significant differences in delinquency between the victims and controls prior to any reported assaults (in 1976 and 1977), the victims always reported higher delinquency involvement. By 1978 when the first assaults were reported, the two groups were statistically separated on several delinquency scores, as well as on many of the peer variables.

These results imply that certain factors, such as exposure to delinquent peers, may be predictive of sexual assault. Thus, we completed a discriminant analysis to see how well the variables would do in discriminating the victims from the controls. Seven variables were used in the analysis: (1) *exposure to delinquent peers,* (2) *attitudes toward deviance,* (3) *perceived peer disapproval of delinquent behavior,* (4) *family normlessness, and the self-reported delinquency scales,* (5) *crimes against persons,* (6) *public disorder,* and (76) *school-related delinquency* (see appendix A for a complete description of each of these measures).

The discriminant analysis was conducted on the 1978 victims with no prior assaults ($N = 55$) and a control group with no reported assaults throughout the entire study period ($N = 48$). Data for 1977 were used in the analysis so that the ability of the variables to separate the two groups prior to the occurrence of any sexual assaults could be assessed.

Only four of the variables evidenced any statistical ability to distinguish between the two groups: exposure to delinquent peers, attitudes toward deviance, crimes against persons, and public disorder. Among these, exposure to delinquent peers was by far the most powerful; its contribution to the discriminant function was four times that of the other variables. However, these four variables were not very successful in assigning the individual cases to the correct groups; only 57% of the victims and 67% of the controls were correctly classified using these variables. Furthermore, as the total variance existing in the variables was less than 10%

(eigenvalue = 0.075), these factors cannot be considered very useful for discriminating between victims and controls.

In conclusion, while victims and controls may be distinguished prior to an assault by such factors as peer networks and deviance attitudes, these variables do not accurately predict who will be victimized and who will not. Being delinquent and operating in a delinquent environment is clearly related to sexual victimization, but it is not sufficient, in and of itself, to predict this outcome accurately. It seems likely that the ability to account for the occurrence of sexual assault rests on the integration of a number of variables, only some of which have been measured and analyzed here. A much more detailed and comprehensive research effort is needed before we can identify the full constellation of factors leading to sexual assault.

UNIQUENESS OF SEXUAL-ASSAULT VICTIMS

It has generally been assumed that sexual assault is in a special category among violent crimes because of its sexual component. Similarly, victims of sexual assault often have been viewed and treated differently from female victims of other physical assaults. Yet to our knowledge, no empirical data support this premise. In fact, researchers in the rape and sexual-assault area have commented on the need to compare sexual assault with other assault victims in order to understand better the risk of experiencing either kind of assault (Katz and Mazur 1979). Knowledge of differences or similarities between these victim groups may indicate whether vulnerability to sexual assault is any different from vulnerability to assault in general.

To address this issue, we compared the sexual-assault victims with victims of other physical assaults. We used the first report of an assault, either sexual or not, from the years 1978 through 1980. The -assault group was identified by a response of one or more to any of the following questions: How many times in the last year (1) has something been taken directly from you, (2) have you been beaten or threatened with a beating, and/or (3) have you been attacked with a weapon? To avoid the potentially confounding influence of prior assaults on later attitudes and behavior, we excluded from this analysis anyone who reported an assault, sexual or otherwise, in the first two years of the NYS (in 1976 or 1977).

We compared three groups: sexual-assault victims only (N = 39), nonsexual-assault victims only (N = 80), and victims of both types of assault within the same year (N = 13). These three groups were compared on a number of demographic and attitudinal variables as well as on their self-reported delinquency. In all analyses, the data came from the year of the reported assault(s).

Demographically, the three groups were not distinguishable. We found no significant differences by race, social class, age at the time of assault, place of residence, or number of family crises. Comparisons on three attitudinal scales (attitudes toward deviance, attitudes toward sex roles, and attitudes toward interpersonal violence) produced no significant differences among the groups. The only differences were noted on the behavioral measures. On two of the self-reported delinquency scales, damaged property and home-related delinquency, the victims who had experienced both types of assault reported significantly higher involvement than either of the other assault groups ($p < .05$). No significant differences were observed between the groups on the other behavioral variable examined, exposure to delinquent peers.

While variables other than those examined may differentiate the victim groups, there is nothing in these findings to suggest that they were distinct from one another. In fact, the only significant findings placed the two single assault groups together and differentiated them from the victims of both kinds of assault, as might have been expected. Overall, these results imply that sexual-assault victims are not substantially different from other physical assault victims demographically or on a variety of attitudinal and behavioral measures. There was nothing in the factors analyzed to differentiate the risk of sexual assault from that of other kinds of physical assault.

The study on which this chapter is based was supported by two grants from the Center for the Prevention and Control of Rape, National Institute (MH 31751), for the period July 1978 through 1983.

NOTES

1. Although a few male victims did appear in the sample, they are not included in the analyses presented. To include them could result in misleading conclusions regarding the majority of adolescent sexual-assault victims.

2. For a detailed description of the sexual assault victim sample, plus a description of the validity of the data, refer to chapter 2 in Ageton 1983.

3. Some of the variables that differentiated the groups after the sexual assaults were measured concurrently with the report of a sexual assault. Thus, for example, differences on the self-report delinquency scales reflect differences between the victims and controls that occurred simultaneously with the report of a sexual assault. However, most of the distinguishing variables reflect differences between the two groups after the sexual assault had occurred.

4. We were unable to compare the two groups on the attitude-toward-sex-roles scale since it was not added to the interview until 1978.

5. When the SAP began in 1978, we expanded the set of questions that could identify victims. In 1976 and 1977, there was only one question about being sexually assaulted. Therefore it is possible that some of the victims who reported in 1978 would have reported earlier if the broader set of questions had been in use.

REFERENCES

Ageton, S. 1983. *Sexual assault among adolescents.* Lexington, Mass.: D.C. Heath and Company.

Adler, F. 1975. *Sisters in crime.* New York: McGraw-Hill.

Amir, M. 1971. *Patterns in forcible rape.* Chicago: University of Chicago Press.

Bohmer, C. 1971. Judicial attitudes toward rape victims. *Judicature* 58: 303–7.

Brownmiller, S. 1975. *Against our will: Men, women and rape.* New York: Simon and Shuster.

Cann, A., L.G. Calhoun, and J.W. Shelby. 1977. Sexual experience as a factor in reactions to rape victims. Paper presented at meeting of American Psychological Association, August, San Francisco.

Curtis, L.A. 1976. Rape, race and culture: Some speculation in search of a theory. In *Sexual assault: The victim and the rapist*, ed. M.J. Walker and S.C. Brodsky, 117–34. Lexington, Mass.: Lexington Books.

Gager, N., and C. Schurr, 1976. *Sexual assault: Confronting rape in America.* New York: Grosset and Dunlap.

Griffin, S. 1971. Rape: The all-American crime. *Ramparts* 10: 26–35.

Hayman, C. 1972. Roundtable: Rape and its consequences. *Medical Aspects of Human Sexuality* 10: 152–61.

Jones, C., and E. Aronson. 1973. Attribution of fault to a rape victim as a function of respectability of the victim. *Journal of Personality and Social Psychology* 26: 415–19.

Kalven, H., and H. Zeisel. 1966. *The American jury.* Boston: Little, Brown and Co.

Katz, S., and M.A. Mazur. 1979. *Understanding the rape victim: A synthesis of research findings.* New York: John Wiley and Sons.

Konopka, G. 1976. *Young girls: A portrait of adolescence.* Englewood Cliffs, N.J.: Prentice-Hall.

L'Armond, K., and A. Pepitone. 1977. On attribution of responsibility and punishment for rape. Paper presented at meeting of American Psychological Association, August, San Francisico, Calif.

Lee, B. 1972. Precautions against rape. *Sexual Behavior* 2: 28–30.

Nelson, S., and M . Amir. 1975. The hitchhike victim of rape: A research report." In *Victimology: A New Focus*, ed. I. Drapkin and E. Viano. Lexington, Mass.: Lexington Books, D.C. Heath and Company.

Pope, D. 1974. Rape survey of Michigan police. Paper presented at the Seminar for the International Association of Women Police, October Kalamazoo, Mich.

Robert, P. 1966. *Les bandes d'adolescents*. Paris: Ed. Ouvrières.

Russell, D.E.H. 1975. *The politics of rape*. New York: Stein and Day.

Sanday, P.R. 1981. The socio-cultural context of rape: A cross-cultural study. *Journal of Social Issues* 37: 5–27.

Tolor, A. 1977. Women's attitudes toward rape. Fairfield University, Fairfield, Conn: Mimeo.

Weis, K., and S.S. Borges. 1973. Victimology and rape: The case of the legitimate victim. *Issues in Criminology* 8: 71–115.

Weitzman, L.J. 1975. Sex role socialization. In *A Feminist Perspective*, ed. J. Freeman. Palo Alto, Calif.: Mayfield.

Williams, J.E., and K.A. Holmes. 1981. *The second assault: Rape and public attitudes*. Westport, Conn.: Greenwood Press.

CHAPTER 14

ADOLESCENTS AND THEIR PERCEPTIONS OF SEXUAL INTERACTIONS

JACQUELINE D. GOODCHILDS
University of California, Los Angeles

GAIL L. ZELLMAN
The Rand Corporation

PAULA B. JOHNSON
California School of Professional Psychology, Los Angeles

ROSEANN GIARRUSSO
University of California, Los Angeles

This chapter discusses four subsections of a larger study examining the sexual socialization of adolescents, defined as the set of attitudes and expectations about sexually intimate relationships that evolve and coalesce as an individual becomes sexually mature and sexually active. These four subsections address: (1) adolescent perceptions of responsibility for dating outcomes, (2) adolescents' cues and signals concerning sexuality, (3) adolescents' expectations for dating relationships, and (4) teenagers' application of the label "rape" to nonconsensual sex between acquaintances.

We recruited the subjects in 1978 through a youth employment branch office of the California state employment office. Each respondent was paid $5 for the approximately one-hour session. Written consent was obtained from the participants and from their parents. Our interviewers were clinical psychology or social work graduate students in their 20s, matched to the subject in sex and ethnicity.

The study sample was made up of 432 Los Angeles adolescents, one-half of each sex and one-third each of the three major ethnic groups in the area (white, black, and Hispanic). Concerning background demographics, our sample was fairly characteristic of the local adolescent population, even in ethnic compositions. The youths represented a broad range of education and occupation of parents, and most of the participants were still in school. Of the respondents, 37% were age 14 or 15, 39% were age 16, and 33% were age 17 or 18. (While the females were significantly older than the males, we took this into account in our analyses.) In addition, 33% of the subjects expected not to attend or complete college, and 49% came from father-absent homes.

In terms of reported sexual behavior, our sample was active. Overall, 61% reported having had sexual intercourse. The figure for males was 71%; the figure for females was 51%. While these percentages are considerably higher than those of Vener and Stewart (1974) and Miller and Simon (1974), they closely approximate those of Sorenson (1972). Our figures are also close to those of Zelnick and Kantner (1977), who reported a rate of 54% when their sample of 1,232 white and 654 black females ages 15 through 16 was equally weighted. Virtually all adolescents in our sample reported at least some dating experience (89%), and 69% reported that they knew what the opposite sex "was like." Comparative data are not available on these figures.

The study sample is unique in focusing on younger people than are generally surveyed in university-based research on sexual behavior. Additionally, because they were precollege age, the respondents represent a broader cross-section of their own age group than the self-selected college samples that form the subject pool for much of the psychological research in this area.

PERCEPTIONS OF RESPONSIBILITY FOR "DATING" OUTCOMES

The construct of power as employed in social psychological theory and research is unclear. Value-laden both positively and negatively, it is variously conceptualized as a personal-quality trait, as a social-structural fact, and as a situational-specific product of some particular interpersonal interaction, Despite the confusion, power remains a fascinating rubric.

In this study, it is power as responsibility with which we are concerned, and we acknowledge that the label takes on several shades of meaning in this context—most notably, responsibility implying control and responsibility implying blame. In respect to dating, there is even the odd paradox of a person's being regarded as "responsible" for outcomes as a direct consequence of having behaved "irresponsibly." Contradictory concepts notwithstanding, to our adolescent subjects assigning responsibility was an intuitively meaningful task.

MEASUREMENT AND ANALYSIS

The interviewers read each subject a series of short stories (vignettes), each involving a boy/girl brief encounter, and then asked two main questions about each vignette: (1) How much was the boy responsible for what happened? (2) How much was the girl responsible for what happened? It is the "responsible for what happened" data that are relevant to considerations of power in close relationships.

The vignettes read to our subjects each involved a "guy" and a "girl" who were at least minimally attracted to one another and who found themselves alone together—they had the time and the place to have sex. Outcome was whether they did, or did not have sex; a couple could agree not to have sex; they could agree to have sex; or they could disagree (for a total of six situations).[1] In cases of conflict, the girl could be in favor of having sex and the boy opposed, or the boy could be the one in favor and the girl opposed, and each of the two types of disagreement could be resolved either way. It should be noted that we make no assumptions about the relative frequency of the six outcomes in the real world.

Following are two vignettes to illustrate first the agreement not to have sex and then disagreement with sex as the outcome:

A girl and a guy who live in the same neighborhhod know each other fairly well but have not dated. One evening the guy comes over to watch TV. The girl's parents are not at home. They sit on the couch and hold hands and begin to kiss. After while, he starts to unbutton her blouse, but then they both pull away. They agree that they like each other, but only as friends, They decided they do not want to have sexual intercourse, and they do not.

One evening a guy and a girl who know each other from school but have not dated are listening to records in a back room of the girl's house. They start dancing, and after a while, they begin to kiss. Later on the girl slips her hand inside the guy's shirt. He says that he doesn't want her to do that, but she continues to touch and kiss him, and then says that she wants to have sex with him, The guy says that he doesn't want her to, but the girl says that she will tell lies about him if he doesn't. Though the guy does not want to, they have sexual intercourse.

TABLE 14.1
RESPONSIBILITY FOR OUTCOME: ALL VIGNETTES

| | Conflict | | | | Consensus | |
| | Boy | Girl | Boy | Girl | | |
Outcome	Yes	No	No	Yes	Boy	Girl
Have sex	84	27	35	79	66	65
Do not have sex	54	45	44	58	49	47

Note: Entries are average estimated percentage.

TABLE 14.2
RESPONSIBILITY FOR OUTCOME: "RAPE" VIGNETTES

| | Relationship | | | | | |
Boy's Action	Just Met		Casual Aquaintance		Dating	
Threatens verbal harm	78	34	80	33	78	35
Threatens physical harm	84	25	83	28	84	28
Uses physical force	91	17	90	18	86	23

Notes: Rape vignette situation is boy wants sex, girl says no, couple has sex. Within each cell, the number on the left is responsibility assigned to the boy; number on the right is responsibility assigned to girl. Entries are average estimated percentage.

The first two entries in table 14.1 (boy says yes, girl says no, they have sex) represent the prototype for acquaintance or date rape. Because that particular sequence of acts was our main concern, we used 27 different versions of that scenario. We varied three things at three levels. One variable was setting: the incidents took place (1) at work, (2) at the girl's home, or (3) at a party. Interestingly, setting did not affect responses. However, the other two variables did affect responses—see table 14.2. For the second variable, force, the boy was described as (1) threatening to spread rumors or tell lies about the girl, (2) threatening to hurt her, or (3) actually using physical force—pushing her down, or slapping and hitting her. The third variable, relationship, defined the couple as (1) just met and previously unacquainted, (2) known to each other and friendly but never having dated, or (3) in a dating relationshp. All 27 "rape" vignettes ended with the line, "Though the girl does not want to, they have sexual intercourse."

In the following examples of these stories, readers should note that the word *rape* is not used, that the situations do not involve strangers, and that the sexual attack is not completely out of context:

A guy and a girl who are dating are at a friend's party one evening, and decide to sit out in the yard. It is very dark and after a while, they start to kiss and hug. The guy slips his hand under his girlfriend's blouse, but she pulls away and tells him to cut it out. Her boyfriend says that he wants to have sex with her and when she refuses, he threatens to hurt her. Though the girl does not want to, they have sexual intercourse.

As part of her after-school job a girl is working alone in a basement checking supplies. A guy she has not met but who works in the same place comes into the room where she is and they start talking. They find they have many interests in common and after a while they hold hands and kiss. Then the guy grabs the girl and tries to slip his hand under her blouse. She struggles, but he holds her and tells her he wants to have sex with her. The girl refuses, but the guy hits her several times and forces her to the floor. Though the girl does not want to, they have sexual intercourse.

In all, 32 separate vignettes were used.. Each subject responded to the 5 standard (or control) stories, plus a subset of 9 of the 27 rape scenarios, presented in randomized order. The design for the rape vignettes was a balanced, incomplete block arrangement that provided full information to test all main effects and two-way interactions and provided three-fourths of the information to test the one three-way interactions (thus making it possible to estimate that effect as well.)

Two analyses of variances (ANOVA) were required for each dependent measure: an analysis of the rape stories and a separate, simpler, two-way analysis of the basic six situations, employing subjects' average responses across the rape stories as the values for the first two entries in table 14.1. Superimposed upon each of the two ANOVAs is a between-subject 2 x 3 factorial incorporating the variables of subject sex and subject ethnicity (see table 14.3).

From the two responsibility questions we derived four dependent measures: (1) response to question 1, or how much was the boy responsible, expressed as a percentage; (2) response to question 2, or how much was the girl responsible; (3) the boy's relative responsibility, or question 1 minus question 2; and (4) total responsibility assigned within the dyad, or question 1 plus question 2. Although the results for the summation variable are given in the ANOVA tables, they are difficult to interpret satisfactorily. Our original notion—and the reason for asking two separate responsibility questions—was that subjects might consistently in some situations assign less total responsibility to the dyad, placing more on fate or circumstances; however, the results are unclear, with some evidence that subjects did feel constrained to make their responses add up. Thus, we considered only the results indexed by the first three dependent measures.

TABLE 14.3
RESPONSIBILITIES FOR OUTCOME: ANOVA *F* VALUES

| Source | | | Measure | |
	Boy	Girl	Difference	Sum
All vignettes				
Outcome (O)	175.44	51.39	34.44	137.87
Conflict (C)	317.22	391.02	540.67	19.46
O x C	189.21	214.46	343.64	43.54
"Rape" vignettes				
Force (F)	196.97	222.03	299.38	17.59
Relationship (R)	7.99	10.26	12.82	1.72
F x R	5.68	2.82	5.40	0.40

Note: $p < .001$ for all tabled effects except F x R for girl's responsibility ($p < .05$) and R and F x R for sum (both not significant).

RESULTS

Only the means across sex and ethnicity are presented in tables 14.1 and 14.2 because differences associated with those subject characteristics were slight and largely insignificant. Hispanic adolescents tended on the rape stories not to differentiate between the two kinds of threat; any other ethnic differences were of response levels, not patterns, and thus are of no interest in this context. As for sex of subjects, there were no differences in the way teenage boys and teenage girls viewed the apportioning of responsibility in either the rape or the control vignettes. This agrees with the bulk of current sex-role research, which finds perception differences for target sex but not by subject sex; nevertheless, we expected that in this particular content area (cross-sexual encounters) there would be differing viewpoints.

For the standard six-situation stories, the two main effects and their interaction term were significant. Apparently interpreting the no-sex outcome as a situation in which nothing much happened, subjects generally assigned more responsibility to both parties when the outcome was to have sex. For the four standard stories in which there was conflict, the initiator was seen as more responsible (on average 69% vs. 37%) regardless of outcome. The person who says "let's do it" was seen as powerful;

the naysayer received little recognition. However, there is also a strong sex-linked asymmetry in the data for the conflict stories with sex as an outcome; a boy was seen as more responsible for winning than was a girl (84% vs. 79%) and more responsible for losing when losing means having sex (35% vs. 27%). In a sense, the male wins by more and loses by less in this kind of situation.

Table 14.2 presents the means for the second set of analyses, that of the rape stories. In this set also the two main effects and their interaction are significant for the three dependent variables of interest. Clearly, the level of force is critical; responsibility for the outcome was increasingly assigned to the male actor as he was described as threatening verbal harm (79% to him vs. 34% to her), threatening physical harm (84% vs. 27%), or actually using physical force (89% vs. 20%). Although the relationship factor is independently important it is evident that relationship made a difference only at the highest level of force. Unlike the just met and the casual acquaintance pairs for which responsibility became dramatically more one-sided when the boy was described as physically abusing the girl, the ratio shifted hardly at all for a dating couple. It seems that to these adolescents, a girl cannot escape a considerable share of responsibility for her boyfriend's behavior, even if he physically assaults her.

CONCLUSION

Indications are that a new generation is entering into the adult world of relationships, especially that of sexual intimacy between a man and a woman, with traditional views. The expectations that the responses of both male and female teenagers revealed—expectations for non-egalitarian sex roles and that the man is the sexual aggressor—are unrealistic in terms of what the last ten years of research have taught us about interpersonally satisfying relationships and human sexuality. We are led to question how it can be that these young people seemed not to have heard anything about the so-called revolution in sex roles and in sexual behaviors.

When presented with a consensus situation, our subjects did assign responsibility equally to the two participants, and they liked those people. (For each story they were asked whether they thought they would like the boy and the girl and whether they thought the couple would see each other again.) The consensus stories scored highest on all three measures. That is not to say that these adolescents expected to encounter such behavior or even aimed to act that way themselves, but at least they appreciated an agreeable dyad.

CUES AND SIGNALS
CONCERNING SEXUALITY

A second subsection of questions attempted to illuminate the high incidence of acquaintance (or nonstranger) rape in this population (Zellman 1976; Amir 1971). Nonstranger rape, as contrasted with stranger rape, is that which occurs within the context of normal social interaction between persons who are acquainted with one another. To understand the dynamics of this type of rape, we examined the dynamics of the larger dating context, particularly the expectations that young men and women bring to a dating situation as a result of differing socialization experiences.

Specifically, we hypothesized that some proportion of nonstranger rapes result from differential socialization concerning the meaning of certain cues (e.g., a male interprets a female's behavior as consensual while a female interprets a male's behavior as coercive). In the following sections we discuss situations and behaviors that adolescents perceived as signals for sex and some circumstances that they reported as legitimizing the use of force for sex.

SITUATIONAL CUES

Participants were asked to respond to a list of five things that "a guy and a girl" might do together. For each question stem, respondents were asked to indicate on two five-point scales (from "definitely" = 1 to "definitely not" = 5) whether the situation provided a signal or cue that the male or female target person wanted to have sex. For example, one question stem asked, "If a guy and a girl go to the guy's house alone when there is nobody home, does that mean: The guy wants to have sex? The girl wants to have sex?" The other situations included going to a park or beach at night, going to a party where there were drugs or a party where the couple took drugs, and going somewhere together after meeting for the first time in a public place.

The results are presented in table 14.4. A three-factor mixed ANOVA was performed on these data, with sex of subject the between-subjects factor and sex of target person and question stem the two repeated measures. There was a main effect for sex of subject [F (1, 142) = 17.36, $p < .001$], indicating that male respondents saw both male and female target persons as wanting sex more than did female respondents. Males tended to perceive the situations as "sexier" than did females ($\overline{X}$ for males = 2.95; $\overline{X}$ for females = 3.32). A main effect for sex of target person was also found [F (1, 142) = 64.23, $p < .001$], indicating that both males and females saw male targets as wanting sex more than female targets ($\overline{X}$ for

TABLE 14.4
SITUATIONAL CUES

| | Subject | | | | |
| | Female | | Male | | |
Situation	F	M	F	M	Total
Guy's house alone	2.86	2.49	2.63	2.26	2.56
Park/beach at night	3.07	2.86	2.69	2.57	2.80
Take drugs together	3.68	3.58	3.18	3.13	3.39
Party with drugs/alcohol	3.81	3.71	3.10	3.01	3.41
Meet for first time					
in public place	3.83	3.53	3.56	3.36	3.60
Total	3.41	3.23	3.03	2.87	

Notes: Means are for 5-point scale. Low score indicates more interest in sex.
F = female target. M = male target.

male target = 3.05; $\bar{X}$ for female targets = 3.22). Not surprisingly, the various situations were seen quite differently, [F (4, 568) = 44.38, $p <$ .001]. The means in table 14.4 have been ordered according to reported sexiness of the situation, ranging from "going to a guy's house alone" (the highest cue value for sex) to "meeting for the first time in a public place." Statistically significant interactions with the question source point to more subtle variations in appropriateness of specific situations.

BEHAVIORAL CUES

Eight questions were asked about how a guy and a girl might behave when they were alone together. For each question, respondents were asked to indicate on a five-point scale (again from "definitely" = 1 to "definitely not" = 5) whether the situation provided a signal or cue that either the male or female target person wanted to have sex. These behaviors were clustered into three types. Three behaviors—talking a lot about sex, telling someone that he or she is sexy, and telling someone that he or she is good-looking—were grouped together as verbal behaviors. Grouped as physical behaviors were playing with the other person's hair, tickling/ wrestling with the other person, and continually looking at him or her or into his or her eyes. Finally, telling someone that you love him or her or that he or she is understanding were combined as romantic verbal behaviors.

The results are presented in table 14.5. A three-factor mixed ANOVA revealed much the same pattern of results as was obtained for the situational cues. Male respondents saw all three types of behavior as more indicative of sex ($\bar{X}$ for males = 2.40; $\bar{X}$ for females = 2.47), and all respondents perceived male targets as more interested in sex than female targets ($\overline{X}$ for male target = 2.27; $\overline{X}$ for female target = 2.59). The main effect for question type [F (2, 284) = 50.34, p < .001] establishes a strong difference between the three types of behaviors in their cue value for sex. Verbal cues were seen as most potent, followed by physical behaviors and romantic verbal behaviors.

TABLE 14.5
BEHAVIORAL CUES

| Behavior | Subject | | | | |
| | Female | | Male | | |
	F	M	F	M	Total
Verbal	2.38	2.29	2.06	2.01	2.18
Physical	2.63	2.68	2.19	2.20	2.42
Romantic verbal	2.94	2.63	2.60	2.58	2.69
Total	2.65	2.53	2.28	2.26	

Notes: Means are for 5-point scale. Low score indicates cue for sex.
F = female target. M = male target.

The meaning of these effects is tempered by the finding of a three-way interaction between sex of subject, sex of target, and question type [F (2, 284) = 4.69, p < .01]. It appears that male respondents did not differentiate between male and female use of the three types of behaviors, whereas female respondents did. An inspection of the cell means reveals that the only behavior that females perceive as being equally "sexy" for both targets is physical behavior, while both verbal and romantic verbal behaviors were seen as more suggestive of sex when used by male than by female targets. Moreover, when female respondents were talking about female targets they saw love (romantic verbal behaviors) and sex (physical behaviors) as different from each other, a distinction they did not make about males.

CIRCUMSTANCES LEGITIMIZING FORCE QUESTIONS

To explore which cues are perceived as a signal that the female has forfeited her right to say no to sexual intercourse, we asked respondents "Under what circumstances is it okay for a guy to hold a girl down and force her to have sexual intercourse?" Seventy-two percent of the samples responded that there were never any circumstances under which the use of force was okay.

TABLE 14.6
CIRCUMSTANCES LEGITIMIZING FORCE

Circumstance	Females	Males
He spends a lot of money on her	88	61
He's so turned on he can't stop	79	64
She's had sexual intercourse with other guys	82	61
She is stoned or drunk	82	61
She lets him touch her above the waist	72	61
She says she's going to have sex with him then changes her mind	69	46
They have dated a long time	68	57
She's led him on	73	46
She gets him sexually excited	58	49

Note: Entries are percentage responding that it is not acceptable to force sex.

However, when respondents were given a series of specific circumstances to respond to, many of them changed their opinions. Nine circumstances were presented (e.g., "the girl has led the guy on" or "the couple have dated a long time") and are listed in table 14.6. For each circumstance, the respondent indicated on a five-point scale how acceptable was the use of force. Those who responded that force was definitely not acceptable in any of these circumstances were compared with those who responded with any degree of uncertainty. The percentage responding "never" to all the force items decreased to an alarming 34%. A significantly larger percentage of females (44%) as compared with males (24%) rejected the use of force across all nine circumstances [$X^2 (1 \ df) = 5.58, p < .02$].

When the circumstances were ranked according to their overall mean acceptance scores, force was seen as most acceptable "when a girl gets a guy sexually excited," and least acceptable "when a guy spends a lot of money on a girl." A rank order correlation of +.93 reveals that males and females ranked these circumstances in very similar ways.

A principal-components factor analysis confirmed that the force items were measuring the same concept, so subject responses were summed across items to provide an index of overall acceptance of force. The correlation between this force acceptance score and chronological age, measured in months, was essentially zero, suggesting that within this relatively restricted age range, more than biological age is required to pick up developmental changes in attitude on this question.

CONCLUSIONS

Our findings indicate that male and female adolescents did have divergent expectations about some aspects of heterosexual interaction, expectations that influenced their perceptions and opinions. Despite research that shows a decline in the "double standard" (Reiss 1967) and an increase in the rates of premarital intercourse for females (Childman 1979), it appears that things have not changed all that much for this new generation of teenagers. The males in our sample still saw the world as "sexier" than did the females. Moreover, both males and females still felt that males were more interested than females in having sex. Both verbal and nonverbal (physical) behaviors, as well as situational cues, appear to be interpreted in accordance with stereotypic notions about sex roles. These findings are consistent with the work of LaPlante, McCormick, and Brannigan (1979), work which shows that young people still adhere to a "sexual script" in which the male is expected to be the aggressor and the female is expected to be the pace setter. Thus, although we do see sex differences in levels, there seems to be overall acceptance of the same old stereotyped relationships.

The fact that males and females attributed different meanings to the same behaviors and contexts is particularly disturbing in light of our finding that adolescents seemed relatively accepting of forced sex in certain circumstances. A likely scenario involved a young man's interpreting a young woman's behavior as indicative of sexual intent or perhaps even a tacit agreement to sexual intercourse, whereas, the young woman was unaware of this indication and acted accordingly. Our findings suggest that in such a conflict, there may well be a resolution through the use of force, setting the stage for nonstranger rape.

EXPECTATIONS
FOR DATING RELATIONSHIPS

Dating and sexual behavior are an area of major concern to adolescents (Chilman 1978; Hopkins 1977; Sorenson 1972). The attitudes and perceptions they bring into social relationships affect how happily and smoothly these interactions go. Because dating and sexual behavior are quintessentially interpersonal behaviors, the fit between the actors' attitudes and perceptions is of prime importance. When couples have convergent perceptions concerning the meanings of cues and behaviors in dating situations, they are more likely to have satisfying interactions and are less likely to experience conflict that could lead to rape.

One focus of this subsection was the adolescents' understanding of the meaning of behavioral and situational cues in these relationships. In interviewing male and female adolescents and asking them what hypothetical males and females similar to themselves would think and do in a range of situations, we had an opportunity to assess cross-sex attitudinal convergence in both respondents and hypothetical actors.

A number of different patterns of results might be possible. For example, male and female respondents might agree that male and female actors would agree about the meaning of cues—a situation of total harmony. Respondents might agree that actors would disagree. A third pattern would involve disagreement between the respondents and projected disagreement between the actors. Male respondents might predict the male sees a sexual meaning in a given cue while the female actor does not; female respondents would expect male actors to see the cue as neutral while the female imbues it with sexual meaning. A fourth pattern would find both respondents expecting actor agreement but disagreeing about its content.

A major purpose of this subsection is to examine these patterns of convergence and divergence in the meaning of cues. A second purpose is to assess the importance of developmental factors in these perceptions. Are older adolescents more likely than younger ones to perceive harmony or discord between actors? If there are age effects, are they largely a function of reported social experience?

MEASUREMENT AND ANALYSIS

To assess the effect of reported social experience we constructed an index composed of four concepts:

1. Whether or not a respondent reported any prior dating experience

2. How much sexual experience he or she reported

3. Whether or not she or he had ever been in a (self-described) "committed relationship"

4. Whether or not the respondent felt he or she knew what the members of the opposite sex were like

Dating experience was measured by two questions, one asking if the respondent had ever dated and another asking how many people he or she generally dated. If the answer to either of these was positive, or if the respondent was married or in a committed relationship, he or she scored as having dated. By these criteria, 93% of our sample had dated.

Sexual experience was initially measured by six items ranging from holding hands to having had sexual intercourse. Of the sample, 24% had experiences that were limited to holding hands, kissing, holding, necking, hugging, or petting above the waist only. Another 15% of the sample had also experienced petting below the waist, but not intercourse. The majority of the sample (61%) had experienced sexual intercourse. Finally, we measured whether or not the adolescent felt that she or he knew pretty well what the opposite sex was like. A "yes" response was scored as positive. Any other response was scored as zero.

Correlations among experience items were moderate and generally positive. Although ethnic groups varied as to levels of experience, the relationships among the items were remarkably similar. The four derivative items were added to form an experience index, which was then trichotomized. High scores were those who met the criteria as having dated, who reported that they knew what the opposite sex was like, and who responded positively to all four of the sexual experience items; they represented 34% of the sample; low scorers represented 26%. Correlation between chronological age and score on the self-reported sexual experience for the sample as a whole was .07. Therefore, age and self-reported experience were treated separately in the analyses.

Using a 2 x 3 x 3 (sex, ethnicity, age) unweighted means analysis (to control for age differences), we examined how our respondents viewed a range of cues relevant to the dating situation. A second set of 2 x 2 x 3 weighted means analyses substituted the self-reported social-experiences index for chronological age. Blacks tended to score consistently high on this index, probably because of norms about reporting sexual behavior and because of behavioral norms. The limited variance in their scores caused us to exclude black respondents from this second set of analyses.

The findings are stunning in their consistency. Across a range of situations and concepts, we found strong and consistent sex differences and few effects of chronological age or reported sexual experience. As a result, we do not include the age and experience variables in our discussion of the findings. While there were some main effects of ethnicity, they did not interact with sex effects. Since people date mainly within ethnic groups, these ethnic effects were not central to the purpose of this substudy.

DATE CHARACTERISTICS

Using an open-ended format, respondents described attributes of a desirable date. Attributes mentioned were intelligence, social background, religious preference, values, shared interests, and physical appearance.

Females were significantly more likely to mention personality and sensitivity, while males mentioned physical appearance. Respondents with more sexual experience mentioned physical appearance more than those with less experience.

A second set of questions concerned a more unstable, controllable set of characteristics of a date. These questions asked respondents to indicate whether wearing a particular article of clothing indicated the wearer wanted sex. Clothes for girls included items such as a low-cut top, shorts, tight jeans, and transparent clothes. For boys we asked about wearing an open shirt, tight pants, jewelry, and tight swim trunks.

Generally, respondents indicated that clothes do not serve as a signal function for sex. Means for both sexes on all items but the see-through clothes were greater than 3.0, the neutral point of the five-point scale (with 1 = "definitely" and 5 = "definitely not"). In general, the means for both male and female respondents were higher—that is to say, less sexual—for male clothing. Overall, a pattern of sex differences emerged, as shown in table 14.7.

TABLE 14.7
PERCEPTIONS OF ATTIRE AS A SIGNAL FOR SEX

		Respondents	
Attire	*Females*	*Males*	$N^\cdot$
Female			
Low-cut top	3.4	3.2*	427
Shorts	3.9	3.5***	428
Tight jeans	3.5	3.1***	428
See-through blouse	2.1	1.9*	430
No bra	3.3	2.9**	425
Male			
Open shirt	3.6	3.4**	430
Tight pants	3.4	3.3	429
Jewelry	4.2	3.8***	430
Tight swim trunks	3.3	3.2	430

Note: Entries represent mean response indicated on a 5-point scale with 1 = "definitely" and 5 = "definitely not."
$\cdot N$ less than 432 reflects missing scores on some items.
*$p < .05$ for sex difference.   **$p < .01$ for sex difference.   ***$p < .001$ for sex difference.

Female respondents were signficantly less likely to see clothing of any type worn by either sex as a signal for sex than were male respondents. Sex differences were larger for female clothes due to a tendency on the part of the male respondents to rate these items as more likely to indicate that the wearer wants sex, whereas they agreed more closely with female respondents that male apparel did not signal sexual interest.

These findings point to a problem in that young girls, following fashion, may be viewed by boys as inviting sexual advances. While some might argue that the primary purpose of being "in style" is to attract male attention, a young girl may be acting more from a need for (female) peer approval than from a desire to attract male attention.

A third set of date characteristics questions concerned the date's prior reputation. We told respondents, "Suppose a girl dates a guy that she's heard has had sex with a lot of girls." Then we asked, "Do you think she would expect him to come on to her?" Interviewers provided categories— definitely, probably, maybe/don't know, probably not, definitely not. When the respondent had provided an assessment, the interviewer then said, "Would she feel that she had agreed to have sex because she had accepted a date with a guy with that kind of reputation?" Male and female respondents generally agreed that a female accepting a date from a male with a reputation would expect a sexual advance. The mean for both male and female respondents was 1.7, or between "definitely" and "probably." However, females were significantly less likely than males to feel that a female who had accepted a date with a male with a reputation had agreed to sex. The mean for females was 2.9; for males, 2.5.

This pattern of respondent agreement changed abruptly when it was the female actor who had a reputation. Interviewers told respondents, "If a guy dates a girl that he's heard has had sex with a lot of guys, do you think he will come on to her?" Respondents of both sexes agreed that a sexual advance was likely, but females were more likely to think so (female mean = 1.5, male mean = 1.8). Female respondents were also significantly more likely to feel that the male had a right to expect sex from his date when she had a "tarnished reputation" (female mean = 1.8; male mean = 2.2). This finding is particularly interesting because there was a strong tendency throughout our study for female respondents to view the world in a less sexualized way than males, to be less likely to expect a sexual advance, and to be less likely to feel that a sexual advance was justified. Concerning these reputation items, female respondents were consistent in being more likely than male respondents to protect an innocent female against an experienced male date, but when the female had been a "bad girl" the female respondents judged her more harshly than did males. However, both males and females held attitudes that "she deserved it."

LOCATION

In defining and understanding a dating situation, place may be as important as the actors themselves. We asked respondents a series of questions about the meaning of place in dating situations; specifically, interviewers told respondents, "I'm going to read you a list of things that a guy or the girl might do together. Some of these things might be signals that the guy or the girl wants to have sex. For each one, I'd like your opinion about whether it is or isn't a signal for sex. Assume that you don't know anything else about these people besides what I tell you." We then asked respondents to comment on the meaning of a variety of places in terms of whether the guy wanted to have sex, and then separately whether the girl wanted to have sex. We asked about meeting for the first time in a public place and going somewhere together, going to the boy's house alone when there was nobody home, going to a park or beach alone together at night, going to a party where there were drugs or alcohol, and finally the signal value for sex of smoking marijuana, taking drugs, or drinking together.

TABLE 14.8

PERCEPTIONS OF LOCATION AS A SIGNAL FOR SEX

Location	Actor	Respondent Females	Respondent Males	N^a
If a guy and a girl:		Does that mean the guy/girl wants to have sex?		
Meet for the first time				
in a public place and	Male	3.7	3.3*	430
go somewhere together	Female	3.8	3.4*	429
Go to the boy's house				
alone when there is	Male	2.5	2.0*	430
nobody home	Female	2.9	2.4*	430
Go to the park				
or the beach alone	Male	3.0	2.5*	430
together at night	Female	3.3	2.6*	430
Go to a party where				
they know there will	Male	3.6	3.0*	430
be drugs or alcohol	Female	3.7	3.0*	430
Smoke marijuana,				
take drugs, or	Male	3.3	2.7*	430
drink alcohol together	Female	3.5	2.8*	430

Note: Entries represent mean response indicated on a 5-point scale with 1 = "definitely" and 5 = "definitely not."
$^a N$ less than 432 reflects missing scores on some items.
*$p < .001$ for sex difference.

Overall, the rating patterns of male and female respondents were similar, as shown in table 14.8. Respondents generally agreed that any given situation was less likely to indicate the female wanted sex, though the differences were small. Male and female respondents also rated places in the same order, with meeting in a public place and going somewhere together being lowest ranked as a signal for sex and going to the guy's house alone when there was nobody home being ranked highest.

However, we still found large and consistent sex differences on every location item. Overall, we found that female respondents were consistently less likely to view any location or activity as a signal for sex for male or female actors. Respondent age and level of reported social experience also made a difference—the youngest respondents were less likely to see place as a signal for sex. Those with more reported social experience were more likely to see place in this way. These results suggest additional problems between the sexes in social situations. Specifically, males may attach a sexual meaning to a female's being in a given place, a meaning that she does not intend.

DATE BEHAVIOR

The most immediate stimulus in a dating situation is the behavior of the persons involved. In order to assess the meaning that a range of date behaviors had for our respondents, we told them, "When a guy and girl are alone together they might do or say things that could mean that they are interested in having sex. I'm going to read you a list of things and I'd like you to tell me if any of these things mean a guy is interested in having sex." The list included the following: if a guy talks a lot about sex; if he plays with a girl's hair; if he tells her he loves her; if he starts tickling or wrestling with her; if he tells her how sexy she is; if he tells her how understanding she is; if he tells her how good looking she is; if he is always looking at her or in her eyes. After each behavior, we asked, "Is he interested in having sex?" When these questions were completed, we asked the same questions with the female portrayed as the actor.

As shown in table 14.9, we found a consistent tendency for female respondents to view the behaviors of both male and female actors as less expressive of an interest in sex than males did. Female respondents were also more likely than males to make a distinction between males and females. When a female actor told her partner he was good looking or that she loved him, female respondents saw this as indicating less interest in sex than these same pronouncements made by males.

ETHNIC DIFFERENCES

Black males reported the most sexual experience and were more likely than other males to view date characteristics and behavior as indicating a desire for sex. Hispanic girls were the most different from males. They reported the least sexual experience of all girls and were the least likely of all sex and ethnic groups to attribute sexual meaning to date characteristics or behavior. These ethnic differences probably represent cultural differences in socialization and social behavior as well in norms for reporting sexual experiences.

TABLE 14.9
Perceptions of Behavior as a Signal for Sex

Behavior	Actor	Females	Respondent Males	N^a
If a person does this, is he/she interested in having sex?				
Talks a lot about sex				
	Male	2.0	1.7**	429
	Female	2.0	1.8**	430
Plays with partner's hair				
	Male	2.9	2.4***	430
	Female	2.9	2.4***	429
Tells partner he/she loves him/her				
	Male	2.4	2.1*	430
	Female	2.7	2.1***	429
Tickles or wrestles with partner				
	Male	2.3	1.8***	430
	Female	2.3	1.8***	430
Tells partner how sexy he/she is				
	Male	2.0	1.7**	429
	Female	2.1	1.8***	429
Tells partner how understanding he/she is				
	Male	3.0	2.7*	430
	Female	3.2	2.8**	430
Tells partner how good looking he/she is				
	Male	2.5	2.2**	430
	Female	2.9	2.3***	430
Is always looking at partner or in partner's eyes				
	Male	2.6	2.1***	430
	Female	2.7	2.2***	428

Note: Entries represent mean response indicated on a 5-point scale with 1 = "definitely" and 5 = "definitely not."
$^a N$ less than 432 reflects missing scores on some items.
*$p < .05$ for sex difference.   **$p < .01$ for sex difference.   ***$p < .001$ for sex difference.

Within ethnic groups, sex differences were generally smallest among whites. This may be a function of their greater exposure to the cultural mainstream, including feminist ideology, or it may simply reflect socioeconomic status differences in our sample—whites tended to come disproportionately from better-educated families with professional backgrounds.

However, it is cross-ethnic group similarities, rather than differences, that are noteworthy. There were virtually no sex-by-ethnic-group interactions in the data presented above. The noted "main effect" gender differences held for all three sampled ethnic groups.

CONCLUSIONS

The findings show significant and consistent sex differences in how adolescent respondents viewed the characteristics of dates and in the meaning they attached to behavioral and situational cues in dating situations. Female respondents saw things in a less sexualized way—how people dress, act, or where they go were less likely to be taken as cues by female respondents that the actor desires sexual relations. In contrast, male adolescents tended to see the motivations of both male and female actors as sexual.

Female respondents made consistent distinctions between the motivations of male and female actors. Invariably, they attributed greater sexual meaning to the behaviors of male than to female actors. Male respondents were not oblivious to sex differences. They also tended to attribute less sexual meaning to the behaviors of female actors, but the differences were smaller and somewhat less consistent.

Though far less significant and consistent, findings for chronological age and reported social experience suggest that the divergence in views that we found between male and female respondents tends to increase, rather than decrease, with increasing age and experience. Our data do little, however, to illuminate the process by which dating and sexual attitudes are socialized. The lack of strong and consistent age or reported experience differences suggests that attitudes about dating and sex are already in place by age 14, a finding that is consistent with other data on socialization.

Overall, these findings are not encouraging, suggesting as they do significant differences in the way male and female adolescents view the social world. The fact that they tend to agree that actors will disagree about the meaning of cues lends a further discouraging note.

APPLICATION OF THE LABEL *RAPE* TO NONCONSENSUAL SEX BETWEEN ACQUAINTANCES

Nonstranger or acquaintance rape, defined as nonconsensual sex that occurs within the context of an ongoing interpersonal relationship, is a difficult concept for individuals, law-enforcement officials, and poli-cymakers. While legal definitions of rape in all states are broad, with most states defining rape as sexual penetration of a woman by a man not her husband without the woman's consent, working definitions are far more narrow.[2] Weis and Borges (1973) suggest that nonconsensual sex is considered rape only if the assailant is a violent stranger, if the incident is reported immediately, and if the victim can provide evidence of her active resistance.

Acquaintance rape generally lacks these elements of "real" rape. The victim and perpetrator know each other and may even be dating or married. Often, they have had consensual sex prior to the incident in question. Force may be lacking. In all cases, the victim was in voluntary association with the alleged perpetrator. Consequently, the meaning and legal status of nonconsensual sex between acquaintances are unclear.

Police and prosecutor decisions generally work to exclude nonconsen-sual sex between acquaintances from the category of rape. District attorneys often decide not to prosecute cases of nonstranger rape because they believe jurors will not label nonconsensual sex between acquain-tances as rape, and therefore will not find the defendant guilty even if they are convinced that nonconsensual sex occurred. The police "unfound" about one in five reported rapes, which means they do not treat them as crimes and therefore do not recommend prosecution. Unfounding occurs for a variety of reasons, among them a prior relationship between victim and offender (Gager and Schurr 1976).

In the course of our study of adolescent sexual socialization, we addressed the issues of how nonconsensual sex between acquaintances is perceived. We wanted to examine how teenagers view nonconsensual sex between acquaintances and under what circumstances adolescents will label nonconsensual sex between acquaintances as rape. We asked our sample of 432 Los Angeles teenagers to respond to a series of vignettes about nonstranger rape. Each vignette involved a guy and a girl who were at least minimally attracted to one another and who found themselves alone together. For the purposes of this subsection, we were most interested in the question: "Do you think this was rape?" (For a description of the rape vignettes, see the discussion earlier in this chapter.)

The rape vignettes were subjected to ANOVA; analysis of the basic six possible outcomes was limited to an analysis of means. Superimposed on the rape ANOVA was a between-subject factorial ANOVA that included the subject's sex.

RESULTS

As shown in table 14.10, respondents clearly differentiated between the situations. When consensus prevailed, respondents were quite convinced that the activity was not rape, whether or not the actors had sex. Similarly, when sex did not occur, subjects were quite certain the activity (or lack thereof) was not rape, though there were slight indications that lack of consensus was bothersome to some subjects.

TABLE 14.10
OVERALL APPLICATION OF RAPE LABEL

Outcome	Conflict		Consensus
	Boy Wants Sex Girl Doesn't	*Boy Doesn't Girl Wants Sex*	
Have sex	2.45	3.60	4.84
Don't have sex	4.66	4.70	4.85

Note: Entries represent mean response to situation noted across levels of force, relationship, and setting on a 5-point scale, with 1 = "definitely yes," and 5 = "definitely no."

Most significant for understanding labeling are the two situations in which sex occurs in the face of conflict between the partners about whether it is desired. The first of these is the classic case in which the male desire for sex overcomes the female's wish to avoid it. In the second of these, it is the girl who successfully presses for sex against the wishes of the guy. Means for both these situations were much lower than for any of the other situations, indicating that conflict resulting in sex was the situation most likely to be labeled as rape by teenagers. Yet a comparison between the means shows a substantial difference between the two situations—subjects were less likely to apply the rape label to the situation in which the girl is the one who wants sex. This differentiation reflects stereotypes our subjects held about male/female relationships (e.g., that guys always want sex, and that guys ultimately control sexual outcomes.) The classic situation produced the most rape labeling and represents the situation most problematic to society.

Table 14.11 represents the main effects for that cell. Two of the three variables, level of force and degree of relationship, had strong, statistically significant effects on rape labeling; the third variable, the setting in which the incident occurred, had no discernable effect. At the lowest level of force, threat of rumors, the average respondents did not think the nonconsensual sex portrayed in the vignette was rape. When the level of force increased to threat of hurt, more subjects thought the activity was rape. When the scenario involved use of physical force, most subjects did apply the rape label. The effects of relationship were less dramatic but equally clear. As the reported relationship progressed from "just met" to "dating," subjects were less apt to apply the rape label; in fact, they were quite unsure about whether rape occurred between dating partners.

TABLE 14.11
APPLICATION OF RAPE LABEL BY LEVEL OF FORCE,
RELATIONSHIP, AND SETTING

Level	Force	Relationship	Setting
1	3.10	2.30	2.41
2	2.42	2.40	2.47
3	1.82	2.64	2.46

Notes: Entries represent mean response to cell 1 vignettes by level of force, relationship, and setting. For force, level 1 = "threat of rumors," level 2 = "threat of hurt," level 3 = "use of physical force." For relationship, level 1 = "just met," level 2 = "known but never dated," level 3 = "dating." For setting, level 1 = "at work," level 2 = "at her house," level 3 = "at a party."

TABLE 14.12
APPLICATION OF RAPE LABEL BY LEVELS OF FORCE AND RELATIONSHIP

	Relationship		
Force	*Just Met*	*Known But Never Dated*	*Dating*
Threat of rumors	3.06	3.04	3.19
Threat of physical force	2.21	2.47	2.59
Physical force	1.63	1.69	2.14

Note: Entries represent mean response to cell 1 vignettes by level of force and relationship specified.

Table 14.12 presents the means for the interaction of force and relationship. This interaction is significant at $p < .001$. Here we see that when the couple was portrayed as having just met or being known to each other but never having dated, subjects consistently were more apt to apply the rape label to incidents involving physical force. However, the effects of force were much reduced when the couple was presented as dating. Adolescents appeared reluctant to label nonconsensual sex within a dating relationship as rape, even when physical force was involved.

CONCLUSIONS

Our teenage subjects clearly understood the difference between consensual and nonconsensual sex. When consensus reigned between partners, the outcome—whether sex or abstention—was not labeled as rape. But respondents did not label all nonconsensual sex as rape. When consensus was lacking and sex occurred, judgments of whether the activity was rape depended heavily on who was pushing for sex, how hard they pushed, and the nature of the relationship. For example, sex that occurred when the girl wanted it and the boy did not was much less likely to be labeled as rape than when sex occurred over the girl's objections. Our subjects were most likely to apply the rape label to situations in which the boy used physical force and the couple had just met. They were least likely to use the rape label when consensual sex occurred between dating partners and when a minimum of force was used.

Interestingly, there were no main effects by sex of subject in our analyses of rape labeling. Male and female subjects showed no consistent difference in labeling instances of nonconsensual sex as rape. These data demonstrate that young people of both genders expected that forced sex may be legitimate and acceptable across a range of circumstances.

Responses to an additional question amplify these findings. Subjects were asked, as a final question following each vignette, "Do you think that this girl would want to see this boy again?" The results indicate that subjects assumed she would not. Levels of force and relationship each significantly influenced these assessments. As level of force increased, subjects were more likely to assume the girl would want to avoid the boy in the future. As level of relationship progressed from "just met" to "dating," subjects assumed more willingness on the part of the girl to see the boy again.

These data show a perfect fit between rape labeling and presumed willingness on the part of the girl to see the boy again. Those situations least likely to be described as rape were those in which future contact was seen as most desired by the girl. Girls in dating relationships were judged most likely to want future contact.

In our sample, nonconsensual sex and rape were far from synonymous. The closer an instance of nonconsensual sex between acquaintances came to the "classic rape"—in which the assailant was a stranger and violence was used—the more likely it was to be labeled as such. The farther it diverged—as when the actors were dating and only threats of verbal abuse were used—the less likely was the situation to be labeled rape. In other words, our subjects' views of what constitutes rape were inconsistent with the legal definition, but were consistent with the narrower working definition of rape used by police and prosecutors. Thus, police, prosecutors, and policymakers unfortunately may be correct when they assume that the general public, jurors, and judges are reluctant to label nonconsensual sex between acquaintances as rape. Victims of nonstranger rape are likely to receive little sympathy from individuals or institutions unless the situation mimics the classic rape.

It is this situation that has led groups like the American Civil Liberties Union (ACLU) to support legislation that would eliminate use of the word *rape*, substituting instead terms such as *sexual assault* or *sexual battery*. They argue that these latter terms are less emotion-charged and less subject to distortion on the basis of sex-role stereotypes. Our data suggest these efforts may be well placed. Our teenage sample applied the rape label to nonconsensual sex between acquaintances with apparent reluctance and considerable selectivity. Nonstranger rape, for many, is not rape at all.

NOTES

1. An illogical (to an adult) configuration in which neither partner wants sex and sex occurs is missing. We know from talking to the adolescents in our sample that this configuration seems plausible and even likely to some. We regret the omission.
2. A few states have altered rape legislation in recent years to include marital rape.

REFERENCES

Amir, M. 1971. *Patterns in forcible rape*. Chicago: University of Chicago Press.

Chilman, C. 1978. *Adolescent sexuality in a changing American society*. Washington, D.C.: National Institutes of Health.

————. 1979. *Adolescent sexuality in a changing American society: Social and psychological perspectives*. (DHEW Publication no. NIH 79–1426) Washington, D.C.: U.S. Government Printing Office.

Gager, N., and C. Schurr. 1976. *Sexual assault: Confronting rape in America*. New York: Grosset and Dunlap.

Hopkins, J.R. 1977. Sexual behavior in adolescence. *Journal of Social Issues* 33: 67–85.

LaPlante, M., N. McCormick, G. Brannigan. 1979. Living the sexual script: College student's views on influencing sexual encounters. Typescript.

Miller, P.Y., and W. Simon. 1974. Adolescent sexual behavior: Context and change. *Social Problems* 22: 58–76.

Reiss, I. 1967. *The social context of premarital sexual permissiveness*. New York: Holt, Rinehart, and Winston.

Sorenson, R. 1972. *Adolescent sexuality in contemporary America: Personal values and sexual behavior, ages 13–19.* New York: World.

Vener, A.M., and C.S. Stewart. 1974. Adolescent sexual behavior in middle America revisited; 1970–73. *Journal of Marriage and the Family* 36: 728–35.

Weis, K., and S. Borges. 1973. Victimology and rape: The case of the legitimate victim. *Issues in Criminology* 8: 71–115.

Zellman, G.L. 1976. Identifying a set of studies on problems of the victim: Rape victims. In *Criminal justice research and development,* National Advisory Committee on Criminal Justice Standards and Goals. Washington, D.C.: U.S. Government Printing Office.

Zelnick, M., and J.F. Kantner. 1977. Sexual and contraceptive experience of young unmarried women in the United States, 1976 and 1971. *Family Planning Perspectives* 9: 55–71.

CHAPTER
15

RAPE-LAW REFORM
An Analysis

MARY ANN LARGEN
Wellesley College

RAPE: THE COMMON-LAW TRADITION

Criminal laws of the United States regarding the crime of rape were
derived from British common law that had been carried over into the laws
of the colonies. According to common law, the crime consisted of carnal
knowledge of a woman by force and against her will. Under the common-
law concept of *carnal knowledge* both rape (forcible carnal knowledge)
and fornication or adultery (consensual carnal knowledge) were criminal.
Rape was distinguished from the other forms of illicit sex by the nonconsent of the victim.

As the states began codification of their common laws, sexual relations
with minor females was prohibited under *statutory rape* laws. These laws
were originally intended less to protect immature minors than to preserve
public morals. Nonetheless, both offenses were treated as heinous
offenses, often carrying a maximum penalty of life imprisonment or, in
some instances, death.

Both the fine distinction between carnal knowledge offenses and the
severity of punishment for rape gave rise to a legal tradition permeated
with fear of false accusations of rape. No theorists were more influential
in this regard than the 17th-century jurist, Lord Chief Justice Matthew
Hale, and the Edwardian-era scholar, John Henry Wigmore. Hale's belief
that rape is "an accusation easily made, and hard to be proved, and harder
to be defended by the party accused, though ever so innocent" was
reflected in both American jury instructions and standards of proof (Hale
1847, 634). Similarly, Wigmore's worry about sexually precocious
minors and unchaste women who fantasize about rape gave rise to the
corroboration doctrine, and influenced such practices as the routine
polygraph examination of victims (Wigmore 1970).

Though neither man's assertions were supported by empirical data, they received widespread endorsement by such august legal bodies as the American Bar Association. (Wigmore's legal text, *Evidence*, remains a basic authoritative legal source in the law schools of today.) As a result, criminal law in the United States would reflect a concept of rape as a sexual, rather than violent, offense and would impose a vast array of safeguards against false accusations by the turn of the 20th century.

Among those safeguards were the "Lord Hale jury instruction" and a prompt reporting requirement. The latter requirement was instituted as a test of complainant credibility and was similar in intent to the corroboration doctrine. That doctrine held that a conviction for rape could not rest on the unsupported testimony of the complainant alone, and corroborating evidence provided an objective standard by which to measure complainant credibility. Similarly, overt acts of resistance by the victims were determined to be an objective standard by which to test nonconsent by the victim.

The imposition of a resistance standard reflected the difficulty of the courts in determining how *force* should be established. According to common law, force was perceived as a means of showing nonconsent, rather than a separate element of the offense. The use of force was criminal only if the victim's state of mind (nonconsenting) met the statutory requirement. Therefore, in applying the consent standard, the courts settled upon resistance as the outward manifestation of nonconsent. By the early 1970s, resistance standards varied by state. In some states, only such resistance as was reasonable under the circumstance was expected. In others, nothing short of resistance "to the utmost" (i.e., resistance to the point of death or serious injury) would satisfy the requirement.

In addition to these safeguards, the nonconsent element of the offense gave rise to the presumptive admissibility of evidence concerning the victim's past sexual conduct and reputation. Such evidence was admissible only concerning the issue of consent and was intended to show the likelihood that the complainant had consented. In this regard, complainant credibility could be impeached and/or complainant character or reputation impugned at trial. To those outside the legal system, admissibility of such evidence reflected the view that rape victims were responsible for the conduct of the perpetrator due to some participatory misconduct of their own or that victimization was deserved due to the immorality or irresponsibility of the victim. It was this issue, perhaps more than any other, that finally led to a call for major overhaul of the nation's rape laws.

RAPE-LAW REFORM:
ORIGINS AND GOALS

The need for rape-law reform was evident long before the decade of the 1970s. Carnal-knowledge statutes were vague and presented a confusing overlap with other statutes. Certain assaultive acts were not identified as offenses and did not fall under the purview of criminal law. Violations of male victims, even young children, were generally treated as less serious offenses and rape of a spouse was no rape at all. Further, introduction of prior sexual-conduct evidence had become a common defense technique for confusing juries with irrelevancies. Judicial interpretation of the law had obviously been difficult and had resulted in great conflicting opinion and guidelines for administrators.

Some attempts to correct problems with standards of proof had occurred in many states during the 1950–60 codification of statutes. But in the view of some later legal scholars, these efforts had frequently exacerbated, rather than solved, the problems. Nonetheless, it was not until several factors converged at the beginning of the 1970s that a serious effort would be made to change the law.

Those factors included a growing public alarm over an increase in sexual assault that was outstripping all other major categories of crime, a growing body of empirical research disproving long-held myths and misconceptions about the crime, the reemergence of the women's rights movement, and an influx of women into law and lawmaking professions..

Public concern over the spiraling rape rate was based on crime statistics showing an unabated increase in rape for over a decade and on data showing rape to have the highest report-unfounding (i.e., no basis for pursuing an investigation) rate and the lowest arrest and conviction rate of any major crime. This data contributed to a public perception of the criminal-justice system as being unable, or unwilling, to halt the trends. The women's rights movement further fueled public discontent by its encouragement of former victims to speak publicly about insensitive and indifferent treatment they had experienced in the criminal-justice system. These disclosures fostered a recognition of the need for systemic change, change that women activists felt must begin with the law itself.

To this end, movement activists organized to develop a rape-law reform agenda, solicit public support for reform, and present their case to state legislatures. The public and political climate was favorable to these citizen-initiated efforts to change substantive criminal law, but, it was the growing presence of women and sympathetic men within the legal and lawmaking professions that reduced most of the resistance to change.

Although women legislators were frequently at the forefront of reform efforts, nowhere was the presence of women more keenly felt than within the defense bar.

Then, as now, defense attorneys were disproportionately represented in state legislatures. Therefore, strong opposition from the defense bar could have defeated rape-law reform efforts. However, the dissension among states' bar members and members of such organizations as the American Civil Liberties Union (ACLU) effectively undermined the strength of the opposition. Therefore, without significant opposition but with significant public support, reformers would succeed in some measure to change the criminal statutes of all 50 states by the beginning of the next decade.

Although rape-law reform eventually became a process that brought together a great variety of individuals and organizations with varying interests and objectives, both the basic rape-law reform goals and the rape-law reform process were established by the women activists who had initiated the reform drive. The strategies and objectives of many later reform leaders would be more conservative, but the legislative, rather than common-law, process for achieving reform remained the same. That process offered access to (and influence with) lawmakers, an access that the case-law process did not permit private citizens. It also permitted immediate, rather than long-term change, and, more certainty of success.

Nonetheless, even the lawmaking process was not without its critics. Along with defense attorneys, there were legal scholars who shared the fear that legislative reform might undermine the rights of criminal defendants. Some of these scholars warned of the dangers of haste and political compromise. Authors of one law reform analysis, funded by the U.S. Department of Justice, predicted disarray of criminal laws, confusion among criminal justice administrators, and a backlash from the legal community against victims (Chappell, Duncan, and Reich 1976). The reason for such alarm was clear: many of the proposed law reforms unquestionably represented a major, if not radical, departure from the legal theory and tradition of over two centuries.

Although the substance of reforms sought were complex and controversial, the basic goals of reformers were simple enough. Among them were an end to perceived abuses of rape complainants, a recognition of the crime as one of violence, more effective administration of criminal justice, and increased capability of the law to act as a deterrent. To achieve these goals, advocates sought changes in standards of proof to prevent complainant abuse, to encourage victim reporting and cooperation with the criminal justice system, and to enhance the successful prosecution of cases. These changes would also include abolishment of cautionary jury instructions and an end to the presumptive admissibility of complainant conduct and reputation evidence.

Efforts to redirect the attention of the law from the victim's behavior (resisting) and state of mind (nonconsenting) to the defendant's behavior (force) were reflected in proposals for elimination of the term *rape*, with all its traditional carnal knowledge connotations, and substitution of some term emphasizing offender conduct (i.e., *sexual assault, sexual battery, criminal sexual conduct,* etc.). The change in terminology was usually sought in conjunction with a legal concept of rape broadened from a singular act of forcible penetration of a nonconsenting female to a broad range of forcible and coercive acts against persons of either sex and irrespective of spousal relationship. This range of conduct was to be graded under a degree scheme that tailored charges and penalties to the actual acts and circumstances of an offense as well as to offense serious-ness. The new legal concept was intended to emphasize the violent or abusive nature of the offense. The grading scheme was intended to enhance the ability of the criminal-justice system to deal more appropri-ately and successfully with the crime. However, not all states would find these changes acceptable.

The potential of law reform to achieve significant change in the criminal-justice treatment of the offense would ultimately be shaped more by the substantive nature of the legislatively enacted reforms than by the simple success of legislative enactment itself. In this regard, predictions that the legislative process would produce disarray in nationwide criminal law would prove correct.

LEGISLATIVE SUCCESS: SIGNIFICANT CHANGE, PASTICHE OF NEW LAWS

The goals of the early reformers called for comprehensive, not selective, change, and for real, rather than symbolic, reform. However, the politics of compromise among the various interest groups both within and without the legislative system did not always produce comprehensive or real change. In addition, the relative uniformity of nationwide rape law would be replaced by a complex array of state laws with differing consequences for victims.

Certain features of reform were numerically more successful than others. Rape shield laws restricting the scope of cross-examination about the complainant's prior sexual conduct were the most vigorously opposed. Yet despite opposition on the grounds that such laws might abridge the defendant's Sixth Amendment rights, shield laws were eventually adopted by every state. The concept of curbing courtroom abuse of complainants was a popular one, and there was little agreement with the opposition's position. Nonetheless, the degree to which evidence remained admissible would ultimately depend to a large extent on whether or not the new law still made it necessary to prove nonconsent.

Other greatly successful reform features included repeal of prompt reporting requirements and the corroboration doctrine in states that had them prior to the reform drive. Somewhat less successful initially were efforts to abolish cautionary jury instructions. But in later years, the majority of states applying such instructions would eliminate them either through law or through practice.

Efforts to abolish resistance standards were far less successful, due to the fact that the majority of states retained nonconsent as a constituent element of the crime. Approximately 38 states still impose a resistance standard, but statutory or case law redefinition of *force* to include coercion and intimidation has brought a general lowering of that standard. Nonetheless, the stringent "resistance to the utmost" standard still exists in a number of states.

Also less successful during the peak years of the rape-law reform drive were efforts to repeal spousal immunity from prosecution. In more recent years, however, the spousal exemption has been totally or partially abolished through the actions of either the courts or the legislatures of 29 states.

Proposals for repeal of common-law statutes met with mixed results. Numerically, approximately 24 states repealed their common-law statutes, but the crime of *rape* with its traditional formulation is still to be found in 25 states and the District of Columbia. While a few states retain their common-law statutes virtually unchanged, the majority have made some attempt to broaden the offense concept in terms of the force and acts involved in the crime. A number of these states added new offenses (e.g., *carnal abuse, sexual misconduct*, etc.) to their carnal-knowledge statutes. These new offenses generally involve criminal acts against minors or nonconsensual sexual contact. Other states simply gender-neutralized certain offenses, such as sodomy, relabeling it "deviant criminal conduct" or some similar appellation. Still other states have unified former common-law offenses under a degree structure that simply carries over the penalties provided under previous law and makes little or no change in the requisite elements of each offense.

Theoretically, the creation of new but separate offenses meets the reform goal of broadening the range of prohibited criminal acts, as does the consolidation of unchanged, but formerly separate, offenses. Gender neutralization, in either case, is seen as more equitable treatment of the sexes. But the retention of lesser penalties for some assaultive acts, regardless of the degree of force or injury involved, signifies the inability of some lawmakers to accept the premise of sexual assault as a crime of violence rather than as a sexual crime.

Of those states attempting a real, rather than symbolic, statutory restructuring, most adopted an assault and battery model. Rape is defined by such terms as *sexual assault, sexual battery,* etc., and statutes are gender neutralized. Force requirements are generally lessened, and the proscribed acts are broadened to include criminal sexual contact and object penetration. Degrees of the offense are determined by such factors as acts committed, type of force applied, age of victim, and, sometimes, relationship between victim and offender.

Theoretically, this broadened concept of the offense acknowledges the crime as much broader in scope and consequence than the offense under common law. However, these statutes carry forward the carnal-knowledge concept of rape in requiring proof of nonconsent and, frequently, resistance. This implies that the sexual rather than assaultive nature of the offense remains preeminent in the eyes of the law. Certainly, proof of the offense still rests on the behavior and state of mind of the victim, regardless of any theoretical argument to the contrary.

Very few states departed radically from common law in redefining the rape offense. Of those who did, the most commonly emulated law-reform model was that of the Michigan criminal-circumstance model, enacted in 1974. The Michigan criminal sexual conduct statute defines criminal conduct as penetration or contact occurring under certain circumstances that presume criminal intent and lack of consent. Under this statutory scheme, nonconsent is presumed, making victim resistance and corroborating evidence irrelevant under law. Evidence concerning the complainant's prior sexual conduct with others than the accused is also generally irrelevant and is admissible only under severely limited circumstances. Force is presumed and is treated as an aggravating factor for determining charges and penalties.

The criminal-circumstance model, more than any other rape-law reform model, encompasses fully the reform goal of significant change in criminal law. However, most states were simply unwilling to make such a great departure from the carnal-knowledge concept of rape. For some lawmakers, the mental leap from illicit sex to violent crime was more than they could achieve. For them, meeting the public demand to do "something" about rape was enough.

The current disarray in nationwide sexual-assault laws resulted in part from this reticence, in part from the politics of legislative negotiation and compromise, and in part from a lack of tested law-reform models. The complexity of many reform bills made the impact of the proposed law difficult to predict. The departure from common law reflected in many reform proposals also made impact difficult to predict. This encouraged many states to adopt a piecemeal or selective approach to law reform or to adhere cautiously to traditional statutory structures.

A POSTREFORM ANALYSIS

The intent of the study discussed in this chapter was to provide some insight into the impact of rape-law reforms in selected states. The study examined the accomplishments of rape-law reform in light of the original intent. Impact in areas central to the concerns of reformers was measured by perceptions of changes related to the original reform goals. Those changes included the victims' experiences within the criminal-justice system, the scope and type of cases coming into the criminal-justice system, and the impact of selected reform features on criminal-justice decision making and processing of cases.

The data base for assessing rape-law reform impact was derived from structured interviews with principals in both the criminal-justice and victim-advocacy communities who work with sexual assault cases on a daily basis. The surveys identified the most significant features of rape-law reform, and provided insight into the individual and collective impact of reform features.

Interviews were conducted with a total of 151 persons in three states. These states were selected on the basis of their longevity in implementing reformed laws and their variations in statutory structures. Specifically, each state's law represented a different rape-law reform model (i.e., Georgia law represented the common law model; Florida law, the sexual-battery model; and Michigan law, the criminal-circumstance model). This mix permitted some assessment of law-reform impact under diverse legal concepts of the crime. Surveys were distributed fairly evenly among the critical actors in the justice system: the sample included 21% prosecutors, judges, and victim counselors; 20% defense attorneys; and 17% police.

PERCEPTIONS OF REPORTING TRENDS

Reforms designed to make standards of proof more realistic and to provide some privacy protection during trials were partly intended to encourage victims to report and to remain cooperative with the criminal-justice system. Critics of the proposal for lowered standards of proof believed the reforms would result in a deluge of fabricated complaints to police. The findings from this study indicate increasing numbers of reports of sexual assault, but there was no evidence of an increase in fabricated complaints by adult victims. To the contrary, the repeal of legal safeguards was not seen as having generated an increase in false reporting. Fabricated reports were generally described as "few and far between" and as not outweighing the advantages of the reforms. The majority of police described fabricated reports as so infrequent that they pose no significant problems for the system. However, the increasing report rate itself was described as posing problems for understaffed police, prosecutor, and public-defender offices.

Across all sites in this study, major increases in the reporting of sexual-assault crimes were indicated, although there was no consensus regarding reasons for the increase. Some respondents saw it as related to an increase in the incidence of the crime or to the increasingly violent nature of the crime. Others saw social factors, such as changing public attitudes, more victim-support services, and less willingness of women to tolerate sexual abuse, as responsible for the increase. Certain features of law reform, when known to the victim, were credited with encouraging reporting. However, the finding of an increase in the reporting of cases formerly less likely to have been reported suggests that the reporting of nonstereotypical or difficult cases may have been a major factor in the increase.

PERCEPTIONS OF CHANGES
IN CASE CHARACTERISTICS

Across all sites, reports of crimes involving acquaintances, incest, and to a lesser degree, spouse or male victims were seen as increasing. Similarly, complaints with little or no corroborating evidence were seen as increasing; as were reports by victims whose lifestyles may not conform to jurors' expectations. The reporting of crimes with these characteristics were deliberately encouraged by states that had broadened, or changed, the legal concept of the crime. This trend, however, appears to have occurred regardless of any change in legal concept.

This finding is significant. It suggests that states that have abandoned the carnal-knowledge concept of rape have actually ratified a value shift in social norms already occurring prior to rape-law reform efforts. In addition, it has implications for states whose laws are still designed primarily for the prosecution of carnal-knowledge offenses.

PERCEPTIONS OF CASE CHARACTERISTICS' IMPACT ON INVESTIGATION AND PROSECUTION

Evidentiary features of cases were generally seen by respondents as less problematic for the criminal-justice system than features involving certain victim and/or offender characteristics. Evidentiary characteristics such as delayed reports, lack of eyewitnesses, incomplete penetration, or absence of physical injury were seen as particularly less difficult for police in the post-reform era. Prior to law reform, delayed complaints or lack of corroborating evidence would have hindered investigation or led to an unfounding of the complaint. According to respondents, repeal of corroboration requirements had facilitated police investigation and lessened the likelihood that a noncorroborated case would be routinely unfounded. Therefore, at this level of case processing, one feature of rape-law reform would appear to have accomplished the goal of enabling police to get more cases into the system.

However, when reports involved nonstereotypical victim/offender characteristics, perceptions of police decision making were less uniform. On a descending scale, police were reported to investigate and/or make an arrest in slightly more than one-half of the cases involving casual or nonintimate acquaintances (Ga., 64%; Fla., 61%; Mich., 52%); but in slightly less than half the cases involving victims and assailants of the same sex (Ga., 42%; Fla., 44%; Mich., 52%). As the level of intimacy increased, police action was perceived as decreasing. When cases involved past or current sexual intimates, police were reported to investigate and/or make arrests even less frequently (Ga., 33%; Fla., 34%; Mich., 34%). Finally, when cases involved spouses, action was still less frequent (Ga., 8%; Fla., 26%; Mich., 33%). Because of the similarity of responses across sites with varying legal concepts of the crime, this finding suggests that police discretion may remain as much a determining factor as the law in cases with nonstereotypical victim/offender characteristics.

At the prosecution stage of case processing, evidentiary features of cases were seen as slightly more significant in decision making. Lack of corroborating evidence, in particular, was seen as making prosecution somewhat more difficult. In the words of one prosecutor, "Juries are not always willing to accept the word of the victim alone." However, lack of corroboration was not seen as quite as significant to prosecution decision-making as it was in the pre-reform era.

When the difficulty of prosecuting cases with nonstereotypical victims and offenders was rated, responses varied by site. Respondents in Georgia, where statutory language is not gender neutralized, found cases involving victims and assailants of the same sex as "very difficult" more frequently than did respondents in Florida and Michigan (Ga., 66%, Fla., 43%; Mich., 32%). Fewer respondents in Michigan, where nonconsent is presumed, found cases involving casual or nonintimate acquaintances as very difficult than did respondents in the other states (Ga., 31%; Fla., 45%; Mich., 20%). Similarly, a significant number of Michigan respondents found cases involving past or present intimates as very difficult but less so than the other states (Ga., 74%; Fla., 86%; Mich., 63%). Marital rape cases were seen by the states as equally difficult (Ga., 85%; Fla., 85%; Mich., 62%); but again, somewhat less so in Michigan.

These findings suggest the more closely related the parties in a case, the more difficult that case is for the prosecution under any law-reform model. They also suggest that when nonconsent is a necessary element of the prosecution's proofs, the difficulty is enhanced. With many recent studies showing an almost 50% incidence of rape in dating situations alone, it is likely that this trend in the reporting of cases viewed as difficult for the prosecution will continue, if not increase. Therefore, these findings may have implications for states where the law retains a carnal-knowledge formulation.

PERCEPTIONS OF CHANGES IN VICTIMS' EXPERIENCES IN THE CRIMINAL-JUSTICE SYSTEM

REPORTING   As indicated earlier, social factors were seen as more responsible for increased reporting trends than were legal factors. However, a number of respondents in this study noted that when a victim knows or becomes aware of changes in the law, either through the experience of others, exposure to press accounts, or calls to a rape crisis center, law reform may serve to encourage reporting. At this stage of decision making, a belief that police can act on a complaint regardless of evidentiary or other problems is important.

PROSECUTION   Respondents were more likely to credit rape-law reform with influencing victims' decisions regarding remaining in and cooperating with, the criminal-justice system. Those reform features cited as having this influence were the lowered standards of proof, lesser or no emphasis on victim resistance, and rape shield laws. Degree schemes that facilitate appropriate charging and/or plea bargaining were also credited with speeding the conclusion of a case while avoiding the unwanted publicity of a trial. Similarly, shield laws that narrow proofs early in the trial process also were credited with expediting the conclusion of a trial.

CRIMINAL JUSTICE ATTITUDES   There was no consensus that private attitudes among those in the criminal-justice system had greatly changed. But there was some agreement that behaviors had changed, resulting in an improved experience for victims within the system. The most frequently cited change occurring in the view of victim advocates was a greater sensitivity on the part of police in dealing with complainants. Police themselves frequently cited law reforms on evidentiary matters as facilitating their investigations and enhancing their credibility with victims.

The change most noted by researchers doing this study was a change in attitudes among many defense attorneys. While a number of attorneys in this study expressed the traditional antagonism toward or disbelief in rape complainants, a surprising number expressed more enlightened views toward complainants and toward their own roles. Specifically, a significant number expressed the view that badgering victims was counterproductive to their clients' interests. In other words, they found that it is not necessary to defend one's client by destroying the complaining witness. These findings suggest that if the experience of victims within the criminal-justice system has not yet met the high standards desired by reformers, it has nonetheless improved during the postreform era.

PERCEPTIONS OF CHANGES IN JURY BEHAVIORS

Among the many reasons given for the low conviction rates during the prereform period was jury distrust of rape complainants. In this study, no consensus was found as to whether juror attitudes had significantly changed in the postreform period. Perceptions of jury attitudes and behaviors varied across sites and jurisdictions within each site. Many of those who expressed the view that today's juries are more enlightened regarding rape credited that change more to social than to legal factors. The women's movement in particular was seen as legitimizing the concerns of rape victims, while the public-education programs of rape crisis centers were seen as increasing public awareness. However, some who shared the view of a better educated public were quick to say the largely superficial change disappeared at the outset of actual jury duty. Nonetheless, across sites there was some agreement among prosecutors and defense attorneys that trials involving injurious assaults against strangers were now more likely to result in convictions. Convictions in less injurious assaults or cases involving acquaintances remained a problem in most jurisdictions.

Most respondents, particularly those in the southern states, were not gracious in their assessments of juries. At best, juries were described as "having their own standards" for judging a case. At worst, they were perceived as still focusing on the sexual, rather than violent, aspects of the crime and as applying their conservative attitudes toward women and sexuality to their judgments. As one judge put it, "Juries still think good women don't get raped and bad women deserve it."

These perceptions suggest that rape-law reform has not had the desired effect on jury attitudes and behaviors intended by reformers. They indicate that social factors may have influenced jury attitudes in certain jurisdictions or in cases conforming to social stereotypes. However, they also indicate less or no effect in cases not conforming to jury expectations. While the significance of law reform cannot be fully determined on the basis of this informal data, it cannot be fully disregarded as a factor in jury decision making. The fact that jury bias was seen as having more influence on prosecutor decision making in states where legal standards of proof more closely reflect the private standards of jurors is significant.

PERCEPTIONS OF INDIVIDUAL REFORM FEATURES

In assessing the rape shield provision and elimination of the corroboration requirement, the only statutory changes common to all states, a majority of respondents agreed that these reform features were fair, needed, and advantageous to the prosecution.

RAPE SHIELD PROVISION   Across all sites, there was general agreement that the rape shield provision was intended to protect victims/witnesses from courtroom abuse and to preserve the integrity of the trial system by dictating relevancy of evidence to the courts. There was also agreement that the shield provision resulted from the excesses of defense attorneys and the failure of the judiciary to exercise proper discretion. The majority of all respondents saw the shield provision as encouraging victims to remain in the system (94%), increasing the likelihood cases would be accepted for prosecution (86%), improving victim treatment at trial (93%), and increasing the likelihood of conviction (90%).

In addition to the curbing of trial badgering of complainants, the most commonly cited advantage of the shield provision was a greater trial focus on relevant issues. Some defense attorneys found the shield disadvantageous in that it "prevents the introduction of *all* relevant evidence"; but, 53% of defense attorneys believed irrelevant evidence still found its way into trial. Defense strategies for countering the loss of a former advantage were reported to be the introducing of more innuendo at trial and making full use of exceptions to the shield. Only defense attorneys in the southern states saw appeal on constitutional grounds as a viable option. The Michigan shield has been upheld by the state supreme court as constitutional.

CORROBORATION REQUIREMENTS Across all sites, there was general agreement that the statutory elimination of the corroboration requirement was intended to remove an unnecessary evidentiary obstacle to prosecution and to allow for prosecution of more cases. The majority of all respondents saw this feature of rape-law reform as increasing the likelihood cases would be accepted for prosecution (83%) and increasing the likelihood of conviction (83%). It was seen as benefiting victims and facilitating cases because convictions could now be obtained on the basis of the complainant's testimony alone.

Perceptions of impact on the criminal-justice system did vary across respondent roles. Over half the defense attorneys interviewed (55%) and some police (30%) expressed the view that this feature of law reform increases the potential for wrongful prosecution. However, the majority of defense attorneys conceded that the practical effect on their clients was minimal, partly because corroborating evidence was never a common feature of most sexual assault cases and partly because prosecutors in some (primarily southern) jurisdictions were believed to be less willing to prosecute in the absence of corroborating evidence. This suggests that the repeal may be largely symbolic under laws requiring proof of nonconsent and/or that prosecutor discretion may outweigh the law in decision making.

PERCEPTIONS OF IMPACT
OF OTHER REFORM FEATURES

In assessing other rape-law reform features common to the laws of Florida and Michigan only, respondents there were asked to select three features which they saw as having the most significant impact on the criminal prosecution of sexual assault. Florida respondents chose the rape shield provision and redefinition of criminal acts as their first and second choices. Repeal of the corroboration requirement and change in resistance standards tied for third choice. Michigan respondents chose the elimination of the resistance standard, the rape shield provision, and the redefinition of criminal acts as the first, second, and third choices for most significant reform features.

REDEFINITION OF CRIMINAL ACTS   As used in this study, redefinition of criminal acts refers to a new, broadened legal concept of sexual assault. Under the Florida concept, there are four degrees of Sexual Battery graded by the factors of force (whether or not likely to cause serious physical harm) and penetration or contact with a nonconsenting person. Under the Michigan concept, Criminal Sexual Conduct is sexual penetration or contact occurring under circumstances that presume criminal intent and lack of consent. There are four degrees of Criminal Sexual Conduct graded on a precise delineation of those circumstances and the dangerousness of each.

Respondents at both sites agreed that the intent of this reform feature was to make more criminal charges possible, to permit prosecution of a broader range of offenses, and to treat sexual assault more comparably with other felony assaults. The majority of all respondents saw the redefinition of criminal acts as increasing the likelihood that cases would be accepted for prosecution (Fla., 90%; Mich., 93%); and as increasing the likelihood of conviction (Fla., 91%; Mich., 92%). Although Michigan respondents (53%) were more likely than Florida respondents (17%) to see specific advantages in the change it was seen by most respondents at both sites as conceptually improving the administration of criminal justice.

Degree structures were cited as being advantageous for both the prosecution and the defense. Michigan prosecutors saw the greater specificity of the law in delineating criminal acts as allowing them to bring charges more in line with the actual offense committed. In addition, the clarity of Michigan law in specifying, as an aggravating factor, the situation in which an offender is in a position of authority over, is related to, or lives with a minor was seen as enhancing the ability of the system to deal with intrafamily sexual abuse of minors.

The greater clarity of the law in redefining force was seen as advantageous at both sites. Prosecutors across sites saw the degree structures as enhancing their ability to obtain guilty pleas through a better tailoring of charges to each offense. Defense attorneys were also largely inclined to see the new statutory structures as advantageous to their clients in that plea-bargaining opportunities were increased.

CHANGES IN RESISTANCE STANDARDS   Both Florida and Michigan are among the very small number of states that have eliminated case-law resistance standards. It is not necessary for the prosecution to show victim resistance in either state, but Florida courts have assigned responsibility for determining whether the resistance offered is sufficient to demonstrate nonconsent to the jury. Under Michigan law, resistance is irrelevant and explicitly not required by statute.

Despite the different approaches to the issue, assessments of this feature of law reform were similar in many respects across sites. There was, for example, consensus that the change was needed, was fair, and was advantageous to the prosecution. There was general agreement that the intent was to bring the law into conformity with common sense (i.e., "Victims aren't expected to resist other types of crimes.") and to remove an obstacle to prosecution and conviction. The majority of respondents from Florida and Michigan saw such practical benefits as encouraging victims to report (Fla., 72%; Mich., 78%) and to remain in the system (Fla., 83%; Mich., 96%). Similarly, the reform was seen as increasing the likelihood that cases would be accepted for prosecution (Fla., 92%; Mich., 87%).

In assessing the instrumental impact of the reform in Michigan, respondents most often cited the institutionalization of jury instructions regarding resistance. Judges in particular found the instructions helpful in performing their functions and added that the jury instructions were especially useful in cases when force or coercion was nonphysical. Prosecutors found the reform advantageous because it "forces juries to judge the facts and put aside prejudice." They also cited the change as getting more cases into the system and allowing prosecutors to explore the victim's fears and psychological state. Defense attorneys, on the other hand, saw the reform as "shifting the burden of proof" to the defense and disadvantageous because it restricted their ability to attack the prosecution's case on the issues of force and coercion. However, several conceded that their real dissatisfaction was with the new presumption of nonconsent. In their view, nonconsent should be an element of the offense and should be proven by victim resistance.

Although expressing satisfaction with the reform in concept, Florida respondents had less to say about the practical impact of the reform. Assessments were primarily rendered in symbolical or philosophical terms (e.g., "A woman should have never had to prove she submitted to force by showing serious injury. Coercion is equally powerful."). Therefore, it was difficult to determine the instrumental, rather than symbolic, impact of the reform in this state. However, the frequency with which respondents expressed the view that juries still expect victims to resist suggests that the Florida reform may have had less real impact than intended.

SATISFACTION WITH PRESENT AND INTEREST IN FUTURE REFORMS

Predictions of early reform analysts that citizen-inspired and -initiated reform of substantive criminal law would produce unconstitutional law and result in a backlash against victims do not appear to have materialized. No feature of law reform has been found unconstitutional in any of the states in this study. Most appeals in the southern states have not moved beyond the appellate courts; challenges to Michigan's law have gone to the state supreme court where they have been soundly rejected. Thus the legal backlash that would result in "entrenchment of old rape law with new vigor" has simply not occurred.

Neither, it appears, has the criminal-justice system refused to "embrace the reform assumptions" or resisted reform as "too complex" or "too cumbersome." To the contrary, whether or not all reform features in all states were seen as having an instrumental effect on the prosecution of cases, reformed laws were viewed with satisfaction by the majority of respondents in this study.

Across sites, the majority of all respondents (Ga., 70%; Fla., 92%; Mich., 86%) described themselves as satisfied with reformed laws. Dissatisfaction among defense attorneys, particularly in Michigan (50%), reduced satisfaction ratings in all states, but variations were few across other respondent groups. Of the prosecutors, 96% were satisfied with reformed law, as were all (100%) of the judges. Similarly, police (80%) and victim advocates (90%) expressed overall satisfaction with the law reforms.

When asked for opinions regarding the need for further reform, responses varied across sites. Of those seeing a need for further law reform in Florida, 52% recommended abolishing the consent standard, 41% wanted cautionary jury instructions abolished, and 38% saw a need for further change in the legal concept of sexual battery. Mandatory sentences were favored by 29%.

Among Michigan respondents, there was no consensus regarding either the need for further reform or the type of reform needed. The majority of respondents felt that the current law, which covers more fact situations than previous law, had gone about as far as possible in making the criminal-justice system more fair and objective. Of those who recommended further legislative reform, the only consensus was among the 10% who felt spousal exemption should be abolished when couples are living together and the 20% who favored mandatory minimum sentences for all degrees of the crime.

In Georgia there was much more consensus on the need for further rape-law reform. Of those who saw a need for change, the majority (79%) felt the carnal-knowledge concept of rape should be abandoned, and 67% favored gender neutralization of statutory language. Clarification of the law regarding the prosecution of marital rape was seen as needed by 61%, but this was accomplished by the Georgia Supreme Court after the interviews had been completed. A change in jury instructions was favored by 49%, while 48% favored mandatory sentences. In addition, 41% felt that nonconsent should be eliminated as a requisite element of the criminal offense.

Interest in further law reform varied across respondent groups. As in the prereform era, victim advocates were most in favor of further reform, while judges were the least in favor. Police and prosecutors were less likely to see a need but expressed support for certain reforms. Defense attorneys were, with a few exceptions, primarily interested in the recision of current reforms. Specific reform features appealed more to some groups than to others.

Of Georgia respondents seeing a need for further reform, victim advocates (100%), defense attorneys (83%), and to a lesser degree, judges (49%) favored gender neutralization of statutory language more than other respondents. Victim advocates (79%) and prosecutors (79%) agreed on the need for a redefinition of criminal acts (i.e., a broadened legal concept of rape), while police (62%) and victim advocates (79%) were more likely to favor mandatory sentences. Victim advocates alone (43%) saw a need for the elimination of the resistance standard.

Due to the limited numbers of respondents assessing the need for further reform, the policy implications of these findings are also limited. None-theless, they do provide some insight into attitudes toward further law reform. They show that interest in the redefinition of criminal acts remains in states implementing common-law or sexual-battery-law reform models, and they show that some support for mandatory sentencing exists across all law reform models in this study.

CONCLUSIONS

From the perspective of those who implement the reform laws, there was evidence that rape-law reform has had an impact on criminal-justice decision making and on the victim's experience within the justice system. Certain reform features, most notably those lowering the evidentiary standards and changing the legal definition of the crime, were credited with lessening police unfounding of complaints. Those same features and others, such as rape shield laws and changes in resistance standards, were seen as improving victim treatment within the system and increasing victim cooperation with the system. Almost all reform features were seen as advantageous to the prosecution (with degree structures equally advan-tageous to the defense) and as increasing the likelihood that cases would be accepted for prosecution and/or would result in conviction.

There was some evidence that the Michigan criminal-circumstance model is the most effective model in terms of bringing the legal standards for sexual-assault cases more in line with those applied to other crimes. Further, there was some evidence that the comprehensive approaches to law reform adopted by both Michigan and Florida were more satisfactory to the implementers of the law than the selective approach adopted by Georgia. And, in terms of assessing overall impact of law reform on the system, there was clear evidence that the total package of law reform is more significant to case outcomes than individual law-reform features.

While there was some evidence that attitudes have changed within both the criminal-justice and general communities, that evidence is equivocal. Changes in public attitudes were seen as largely superficial in many jurisdictions, with citizens/jurors inclined to view rape still in terms of morality rather than criminality. The fact that this latter perception was expressed across sites would suggest the inability of a law reform to influence public attitudes. However, the fact that it was less expressed in Michigan also suggests that juror bias may be somewhat ameliorated by laws that are less reinforcing of traditional stereotypes of the crime.

As noted earlier, attitudes encountered within the criminal-justice system varied among sites and individuals. Some respondents expressed views resembling those of the early reformers in both tone and substance, while others adhered to traditional views of the crime, including the dichotomy between "real" rape and "innocent" victims and other reported offenses. Nonetheless, there was evidence that the reformed laws, however substantively diverse, are largely being implemented as intended. Their assumptions have been generally embraced by the criminal-justice system, at least insofar as stereotypical (i.e., forcible rape by a stranger) cases are concerned.

With regard to those assumptions, this study suggests that, generally speaking, both legal and individual concepts of sexual assault have changed dramatically over the past decade. For example, the concept that offender coercion or intimidation may be as powerful as physical force in achieving submission is now commonly accepted (qualified only by the relationship, if any, between the parties). The concept that a complainant's past consensual sexual experience does not imply consent is slowly gaining acceptance. The concept of rape as an injurious, if not always physically damaging, act also is gaining acceptance.

In summary, rape-law reform has been both instrumental and symbolic in its impact on the criminal-justice system. Most reform goals, as articulated by the early reformers, have been achieved to some degree. But the findings of this study suggest that rape-law reform remains but a first stop in achieving recognition of the essentially coercive and violent nature of sexual assault, and an incomplete step at that. Despite the new statutory appelations applied to rape by many states today, rape remains the only crime in the United States for which the determination of criminality in most states rests on the proven lack of consent of the victim. Regardless of any "reasonableness" standards now applied, rape remains the only crime that victims are expected by law to resist.

Most important, this study suggests that in most states, social concepts of sexual assault are changing more rapidly than legal concepts. This situation, reflected in the reporting trends noted across sites, may be creating an imbalance in the criminal-justice response to crimes with stereotypical and nonstereotypical case characteristics. Few lawmakers of a decade ago were willing to institutionalize a radical shift in the legal concept of unacceptable behavior. There was, they believed, no way to predict the outcome. Now, however, the Michigan experience with rape-law reform provides evidence that law reform that distills and advances new concepts of unacceptable behavior can work. It suggests that a shift in the burden of proof from the victim's conduct and state of mind to the offender's conduct can be beneficial to the system as well as to the victim. Nonetheless, the impetus for change that characterized the early reform efforts is now missing.

Law reform is no longer thought of as a first step. However inadequate the previous reform efforts, they are now thought of as having been a final solution. In the late-1970 Institute for Social Research study of rape-law reform, Jeanne Marsh and Nathan Caplan warned of a "risk that the passage of the law will be viewed as a solution, will dull social sensibilities to unresolved problems, will slow the impetus for further reform" (Marsh and Caplan 1980). The findings of this study, conducted several years later, suggest that the warning is still relevant.

This study was supported by the National Institute for Justice, U.S. Department of Justice, under grant no. 85–IJ–CX–0006. Points of view or opinions stated are those of the author and do not necessarily represent the official position or policy of the U.S. Department of Justice. At the time the study was conducted, the author was a senior researcher with the Center for Women Policy Studies and served as principal investigator for the study.

REFERENCES AND BIBLIOGRAPHY

BenDor, J.F. 1976. Justice after rape: Legal reform in Michigan. In *Sexual Assault*, ed. M. Walker, S. Brodsky, 149–160. Lexington, Mass.: Lexington Books.

Berger, S. 1977. Man's trial, woman's tribulation: Rape cases in the courtroom. Columbia Law Review, 106.

Bienen, L. 1978. Mistake as to age defense. *Philosophy of Public Affairs*, 224.

——. 1980. Rape IV: National developments in rape reform legislation. *Rutgers Law Review* 6 (3).

Chappell, D., J. Reich, and C. LeGrand. 1976. *Forcible rape: Analysis of legal issues*. Seattle: Battelle Law and Justice Study Center.

Child, B. 1975. Ohio's new rape law: Does it protect complainants at the expense of the accused? *Akron Law Review* 2(9): 337–59.

Corroboration rule and crimes accompanying a rape. 1970. *University of Virginia Law Review*, January.

Dworkin, R.B. 1966. The resistance standard in rape legislation. *Stanford Law Review* 18: 680–87.

Eisenberg, R. 1976. Abolishing cautionary instructions in sex offense cases: People v. Ricon-Pineda. *Criminal Law Bulletin* 1(12): 58–72.

Eisenbud, F. 1978. Limitations on the right to introduce evidence pertaining to the prior sexual history of the complaining witness in cases of forcible rape: Reflections of reality or denial of due process? *Hofstra Law Review* 3: 403–26.

Florida sexual battery statute: Significant reform, but bias against victims still prevails. 1978. *Florida Law Review* 30 .

Forcible and statutory rape: An exploration of the operations and objectives of the consent standard. 1952. *Yale Law Journal* December.

Gager, N., and C. Schurr. 1976. Misogyny and legal reform. In *Sexual assault: Confronting rape in America*, ed. N. Gagner and C. Shurr, 167–201. New York: Grosset & Dunlap.

Giles, L.E. 1975. If she consented once, she consented again—A legal fallacy in forcible rape cases. *Valparaiso University Law Review* 10: 127–67.

——. 1976. The admissibility of a rape complainant's prior sexual conduct: The need for legislative reform. *New England Law Review*, Spring, 127–67.

Haas, C. 1976. Rape: New perspectives and new approaches. *The Prosecutor* 5: 357–59.

Hale, M. 1847. *The history of the pleas of the crown.*

Harris, L.R. Towards a consent standard in the law of rape. *University of Chicago Law Review* 3: 613–45.

Hibey, R.A. 1973. The trial of a rape case: An advocate's analysis of corroboration, consent and character. *American Law Review* 2: 309–34.

Jarrett, T. 1966. Criminal law—Psychiatric examination of the prosecutrix in rape cases. *North Carolina Law Review* 234–40.

Kalven, N., and N. Zeisel. 1966. *The American Jury* 70.

Landau, S. 1974. Rape: The victim as defendant. *Trial* 4: 19–22.

Largen, M.A. 1980. *Sex offenses statutes by state.* Arlington, Va.: New Responses, Inc.

Lear, M.W. If you rape a woman and steal her TV, what can they get you for in New York? Stealing her TV. *New York Times Magazine* 30.

LeGrand, C. 1973. Rape and rape laws: Sexism in society and law. *California Law Review* 3: 919–41.

Marsh, J., and N. Caplan. 1980. Law reform in the prevention and treatment of rape. Institute for Social Research, University of Michigan. Typescript.

Pitler, R. 1972. Rape corroboration requirement: Repeal, not reform. *Yale Law Journal* 7: 1365–91.

———. 1975. "Existentialism" and corroboration of sex crimes in New York: A new attempt to limit "If someone didn't see it, it didn't happen." *Syracuse Law Review* 24: 1–37.

Rawlings, G.E. 1985. Even among friends. *Spokeswoman, PCAR Newsletter,* Fall, 1–3.

Shearer, L. 1985. Date rape—One in five. *Parade,* 22 September, 18.

Walker, P.N. 1985. Georgia's rape shield law: Aiding the accused? *Georgia State University Law Review.*

Wigmore, J.N. 1940. *A treatise on the Anglo-American system of evidence in trials at common law, including the statutes and judicial decisions of all jurisdictions of the United States and Canada,* ed. James M. Chadbourne, Vol. 7, 3d ed. Boston: Little, Brown.

Woods, P.L. 1973. The victim in a forcible rape case: A feminist point of view. *American Criminal Law Review* 2: 335–54.

CHAPTE.
16

THE IMPACT
OF CRIME ON
URBAN WOMEN

STEPHANIE RIGER
Lake Forest College

MARGARET T. GORDON
Northwestern University

Although crime in the United States is so widespread that it affects one-third of the nation's households (U.S. Department of Statistics 1981), this figure still underestimates the true consequences of crime because the social, emotional, and economic costs affect even more people than those directly victimized. Observers for more than a decade have recognized that widespread and increasing fear of crime constitutes a major social problem (e.g., Maltz 1972). Many people suffer from anxiety in anticipation of victimization and modify their lives to avoid crime in ways that cost them lost social and work opportunities (McIntyre 1967; Biderman et al. 1967). The self-imposed isolation of people seeking to prevent victimization also costs their communities in terms of participation in volunteer, leisure, and other activities.

The burden of this fear of crime falls disproportionately on women. In a national poll conducted in 1972, over half the women surveyed, compared with only 20% of the men, said they were afraid to walk alone in their neighborhoods at night (Erskine 1974). Gender is a consistent and powerful predictor of fear in a variety of studies, and it appears to be more important than other sociodemographic predictors such as age, race, and income (Cook et al. 1982).

Reprinted, with changes, from *Social and Psychological Problems of Women: Prevention and Crisis Intervention,* ed. Annette Rickel, Meg Gerrard, and Ira Iscoe (New York: Hemisphere Publishing Corp., Div. McGraw-Hill, 1984), 139–56, by permission of the publisher.

en's high levels of fear of crime seem inconsistent with their ly low rates of victimization. Observers attempting to reconcile pparent paradox have suggested two types of explanations: (1) en's reactions are inappropriate and based on such factors as sociali- n for timidity or (2) women are especially vulnerable because of their of a particularly heinous crime—rape—and their inability to defend mselves against male attackers (see DuBow, McCabe, and Kaplan 79 and Riger, Gordon, and LeBailly 1978, for reviews).

It is our contention that women's reactions to crime are shaped by a number of factors residing both in themselves and in the environments in which they live. It is not simply rates of victimization that generate women's fear, but also the nature and perceived likelihood of that victimization. Further, most women are victimized by men (Dodge, Lentzer, and Shenk 1976), which links criminal encounters to more general patterns of interaction between the sexes. Women are more likely to know their attackers than men and are more often subject to crimes such as rape and wife abuse that affect not only their bodily safety, but also their social identity and emotional well-being (U.S. Department of Justice 1980a, 1980b; Weis and Borges 1973). In addition to women's estimates of their own risk of danger, their perceptions of their physical competence and ties with their neighborhood have an impact on their levels of fear and the extent of precautions they take. Women who perceive their risks as high, who see themselves as slow and weak, and who have marginal ties to the locality are especially fearful, and high fear contributes to frequent use of self-protective, albeit restrictive, behaviors (Riger and Gordon 1981).

Our chapter begins by delineating the unique nature of crime against women and proceeds with a detailed description of women's attitudinal and behavioral reactions to crime. A variety of sociopsychological and community-related factors that affect women's responses to crime are reviewed, and some implications of women's reactions to crime for the quality of their lives are discussed. Feminists have long contended that the threat of crime, especially rape, acts as an instrument of social control over women, encouraging them to restrict their behavior and depend on men for protection (Brownmiller 1975; Griffin 1979). The research findings reviewed here suggest that the restrictive effects of crime do not fall equally on all women; those who appear to have the fewest resources are most affected.

In writing this chapter, we relied primarily on two sources: the U.S. Census Bureau's National Crime Survey reported by Hindelang, Gottfredson, and Garofalo (1978) and others, and our own 1977 study designed to assess the extent and distribution of women's fear of rape and other crimes, to explore major determinants of fear, and to examine strategies that women use to cope with the threat of victimization. We conducted extensive interviews with nearly 300 women in urban neighborhoods in Chicago, Philadelphia, and San Francisco. This chapter reviews the findings of that study in the context of previous research and discusses some implications of those findings. (The methods and results of the study are presented in detail in Gordon and Riger 1978; Gordon et al. 1980; LeBailly 1979; Riger and Lavrakas 1981; and Riger, LeBailly, and Gordon 1981).

VICTIMIZATION OF URBAN WOMEN

Although not without flaws, the National Crime Survey constitutes the best available body of information about victims and their experiences with crime (Skogan 1977). When we compare rates of criminal violence against women with those against men, these data reveal that men are victimized about twice as often as women, with two exceptions: rape and personal larceny with contact (see table 16.1). In 1978, the rate of crimes of violence against men was 45.7 per thousand, while the comparable rate for women was 22.8 per thousand. For crimes of theft, the ratio was closer to unity; men experienced about 20% more victimizations than did women.

In general, more serious crimes occur less often, and murder is the least frequently occurring crime (Skogan and Maxfield 1981). Since victimization survey data are based on self-reports of victims, murder statistics come from police files according to FBI data reported by Bowker (1978) women constitute 24% of all reported murder victims.

Among violent crimes, the most likely to happen to women, as to men, is assault; robbery is the second most likely. Rape is the violent crime that occurs least often to both sexes. Women's rates of theft also parallel men's rates, with personal larceny without contact occurring much more frequently than larceny with contact. The two crimes that women suffer more often than men, rape and personal larceny with contact (primarily purse snatching), are also among the least frequently occurring crimes. In 1978, the rate of rape for women was 1.7 per thousand, while the comparable rate for men (0.2 per thousand) was based on so few cases that the figure is statistically unreliable.

Between 1964 and 1975, crime in the United States rose dramatically. Much of the increase was in violent crime, with rates of assault, robbery, rape, and burglary rising sharply (Skogan 1978b). Since 1975, most victimization rates in cities have remained relatively constant, although the rates for assault increased by about 8% between about 1973 and 1978

TABLE 16.1
VICTIMIZATION RATES IN THE U.S., 1978

Demographic Characteristic	Crimes of Violence	Rape	Robbery	Assault	Crimes of Theft	Petty Larceny With Contact	Petty Larceny Without Contact
Males	45.7	0.2	8.3	37.2	105.6	2.7	102.9
Females	22.8	1.7	3.7	17.2	88.7	3.5	85.1
Race/ethnicity							
White	22.0	1.4	3.4	17.2	90.0	3.1	87.0
Black	29.7	3.8	6.4	19.6	80.2	6.8	73.4
Hispanic	23.0	1.0*	5.3	16.7	92.4	7.5	84.9
Age							
12–15	37.7	2.3	2.7	32.7	126.6	0.7*	125.9
16–19	51.6	4.6	8.3	38.9	139.0	2.0	136.9
20–24	44.4	3.8	7.2	33.4	135.1	5.2	129.8
25–34	25.7	2.0	3.8	19.8	111.1	3.5	107.6
34–49	14.7	0.7	2.9	11.1	88.2	3.2	85.0
50–64	7.8	0.5*	1.5	5.8	52.7	5.1	47.7
65 or more	6.4	0.2*	2.6	3.6	18.6	3.5	15.4
Marital status							
Married	11.7	0.7	2.0	9.0	73.3	2.6	70.7
Widowed	9.1	0.0*	3.9	5.3	37.7	4.0	33.7
Never married	38.7	3.2	5.2	30.3	130.5	3.8	126.7
Separated/ divorced	62.5	5.2	10.0	47.3	125.0	8.5	116.5

Source: U.S. Department of Justice Bureau of Justice Statistics. 1980. *Criminal Victimization in the U.S.: 1973–78 Trends.* Washington, D.C.: U.S. Government Printing Office (Tables 3, 4, and 5).

Note: Rates per 1,000 persons age 12 and over.

*Rate, based on about 10 or fewer sample cases, is statistically unreliable.

and the rate for robbery fell 13% during this time (U.S. Department of Justice 1980a). Violence against men increased by about 3.6% between 1973 and 1978, while the parallel increase against women was 5.5 percent. Rates of rape reported to census takers appear to have remained fairly constant during this time, while police data have shown a sharp increase in rapes since 1933 (Hindelang and Davis 1977).

But data about the prevalence of victimizations do not tell the whole story of crime against women. As table 16.1 shows, black women are more likely than white or Hispanic women to be victims of violent crime, although they are the least likely of these three subgroups to experience theft. Age 24 seems to demarcate risk levels for women, with those younger being in generally greater danger than those older than 24 years.

Women who have never married and those who are separated or divorced have considerably higher rates of victimization of both violence and theft than married or widowed women. Thus, with the exception of age, the heaviest burden of violent crime falls on those women who appear least likely to have the resources for coping with victimization.

The apparent paradox between women's high fear levels and low victimization rates presumes that victimization surveys accurately reflect the actual incidence of crime against women. Is this so? Methodological investigations have been conducted to assess how many crimes reported to police are also reported to survey interviewers. The results indicate that certain classes of crime events sometimes are not reported to survey interviewers, most often rape and nonstranger crime (Skogan 1977). Females are more likely to be victims of rape and to know their attackers than males; about 56% of those victimized by known attackers are female, while about 44% are male (U.S. Department of Justice 1980b). Within the category of marital violence, the sex ratios are even more skewed, with women constituting 94.6% of those victimized by a spouse or former spouse. Thus, the underreporting of violence by known assailants may result in serious underestimation of the extent of violent crime against women.

While many more crimes are reported to survey interviewers than to police, the pattern of distribution of crime is generally similar in both police and survey data (Skogan 1977). However, both police data and victimization surveys include only violent behavior that fairly closely fits legal definitions of crime. In recent years, feminists have called attention to certain kinds of incidents occurring to women, incidents that may be threatening or fear provoking (such as obscene telephone calls, sexual harassment at work, or verbal abuse in the street) but which are not classified as violent crime (Medea and Thompson 1974). Although these incidents could generate fear and leave women feeling victimized, the National Crime Survey does not ask about them, and neither their prevalence nor women's reactions to them have been systematically assessed. In addition, the National Crime Survey does not ask victims directly if they have been raped, but rather asks if assaults that occurred to them were rapes. Thus, it is possible that many rapes are not mentioned by respondents, who are then misclassified as assault victims by the surveyors (McDermott 1979).

In 1979, over 192,000 women reported rapes during the twelve months preceding the victimization surveys (an increase of 47,000, or 24% over the 1976 figures). Many analysts estimate that because many victims do not report their rapes to surveyors or anyone else, these figures may represent only 10–25% of the rapes that actually occur. The figures also indicate that the incidence of rape is much higher in large urban areas in the U.S. than in rural ones. Taken together, these data mean that if a woman lives in a large U.S. city for 25 years, she has a 1 in 12 chance of being raped during that time. (This figure is approximate since rates vary also with age.) If the rates are actually higher, her chances of being raped are still greater.

To summarize, the pattern (although not the magnitude) of criminal violence against women is generally similar to that against men, with certain important exceptions that are likely to have a strong impact on women's reactions to crime. Women are subject to rape and are more likely than men to know their attackers. Among persons assaulted by their spouses, women constitute the majority of victims. In addition, most female victims are attacked by male offenders. Thus, patterns of crime against women strengthen the inequitable gender distribution of power in society by reinforcing male dominance with actual or threatened violence.

We believe that women's greater vulnerability to rape is central to both their fear of and reactions to crime. Apart from murder, rape is the most fear-inducing crime (Brodyaga et al. 1975). Rapes often take place over several hours or days, and there is more opportunity for injury (Stinch-combe et al. 1980). In the National Crime Survey, proportionately more rape victims (48%) reported being otherwise injured than those in any other crime category (Hindelang, Gottfredson, and Garofalo 1978). While most of these injuries are minor (e.g., cuts and bruises), they occur in addition to emotional damage. The National Crime Survey measures only bodily injury, yet a survey of citizens' fear of crime found that 53% of the females and 36% of the males interviewed believed that the worst aspect of a rape was the emotional damage to the victim (Riger, Gordon, and LeBailly 1978). Studies of the after-effects of rape indicate that it is one of the most traumatic of crimes, with many victims developing symptoms of emotional distress that last for several weeks or even years after the attack (Burgess and Holmstrom 1974; Katz and Mazur 1979).

In addition to the damage occurring from the rape itself, attribution of blame to the victim by friends, co-workers, and actors in the criminal-justice system may leave her feeling doubly victimized (Berger 1977; Medea and Thompson 1974). To some extent this may happen to all crime victims, since most people seem to want to believe in a world where people get what they deserve (Lerner 1980). By blaming the victim, we preserve our belief in justice (Ryan 1971). However, researchers have found that such blaming reactions are particularly likely to occur in the case of rape (Feild 1978; Jones and Aronson 1973; Krulewitz 1977). In particular, men are more likely to attribute responsibility to the rape victim than are women (Feild 1978; Selby, Calhoun, and Brock 1977).

Rape may be especially fear-inducing because of widespread beliefs that it is linked with gratuitous violence (in addition to the rape itself) and that it is nearly impossible to resist successfully. In fact, the statistical profile of rape derived from the National Crime Survey indicates that despite the common presence of more than one offender or the use of a weapon, most victims actively resist or attempt to escape (Hindelang and Davis 1977; McDermott 1979). Victims who resist in some manner increase the chances that the rape will not be completed; however, injury (in addition to the rape itself) is more frequent among those who resist (McDermott 1979). Most of the injuries take the form of bruises, cuts, scratches, and black eyes, rather than more severe stabbings or capricious beatings. Since these data are correlational in nature, identification of the causal sequence is impossible. That is, we do not know if these women were injured because they resisted, or if they resisted because they were being injured.

Two recent studies comparing women who were raped with those who managed to deflect an attack found that successful resisters were those who from the moment they realized they might be in danger used a multiplicity of self-protective strategies, such as physical resistance, screaming, and trying to flee (Bart 1981; McIntyre, Myint, and Curtis 1979). Active, forceful fighting at the onset of an attack, rather than passive pleading or screaming, appears to be more successful in warding off attackers (Bart 1981; Sanders 1980). In addition to thwarting the assault, resistance may help some women to preserve their self-esteem and lessen the psychological damage done by rape (Sanders 1980).

In our study, we asked women to estimate their chances of being raped and otherwise assaulted in their neighborhoods. Women who perceived a high risk of rape in their neighborhoods were more fearful than those who thought such risk was low. Surprisingly, *men's* fear levels also were associated with their perceptions of a *woman's* risk of being raped in their neighborhoods. In addition, men's estimates of women's risks of rape were higher than those reported by women themselves (Riger and Gordon 1981).

In short, rape may be a "bellwether crime" against which both men and women judge the general criminal environment in their communities. When rape does occur it may signal that other crimes are likely to happen. The high correlation in the FBI's *Uniform Crime Reports* between the rates of rape and rates of other violent crimes (e.g., for 1976, the Spearman rank-order correlation was 0.68 [Bowker 1978]) indicates this is a reasonable speculation. Women's estimates of their risk of rape are associated with their perceived risk of other violent crimes, and this index of the combined risks of violence is strongly related to fear (Riger, LeBailly, and

Gordon 1981). This suggests that women fear a multiplicity of crimes involving personal confrontations, leading them to experience their environment as a whole as a dangerous place to be.

WOMEN'S RESPONSES TO URBAN CRIME

To what extent is fear of crime commensurate with patterns of victimization? The distribution of the fear of crime by gender and among women and men of varying demographic characteristics is presented in table 16.2, which is based on 1975 National Crime Survey data from the nation's five largest cities—New York, Los Angeles, Chicago, Philadelphia, and Detroit (Garofalo 1977).

About seven out of ten men (68.3%) in this survey reported feeling "very" or "reasonably" safe in response to the question, "How safe do you feel or would you feel when out in your neighborhood alone at night?" In contrast, only about four out of ten of the women (38.9%) interviewed reported feeling safe. Women were almost three times as likely as men to report feeling "very unsafe."

When we look at the distribution of fear by race, marital status, and age, we find that the overall pattern is similar for males and females but that the reported amounts of fear differ sharply. In general, blacks reported more fear than persons of other races or ethnicities; those widowed, separated, or divorced reported more fear than the never or currently married; and older people reported more fear than younger people. Within each of these demographic categories, however, women reported more fear than men. Blacks, whether male or female, appear to be the most fearful of any ethnic or racial subgroup, but about twice as many black females reported high fear as did black males. More of those widowed, separated, or divorced report high fear than the never married or currently married, yet a higher percentage of females than their male counterparts within each of these marital categories fell into the high-fear level.

Gender differences in fear by age are especially pronounced: the lowest proportion of women describing themselves as feeling very unsafe (26.0% of those 20–24 years old) is about the same as the highest proportion of men who feel afraid (26.4% of those age 65 or over). Close to half (49.7%) of the women age 65 or over reported feeling "very unsafe"; these women are the most fearful of any demographic subgroup.

Critics have pointed out a multitude of problems with the way fear is measured in the National Crime Survey (e.g., Baumer 1978; Garofalo 1979). Yet the consistency across a number of surveys of the finding that

TABLE 16.2
FEELINGS OF PERSONAL SAFETY WHEN OUT ALONE
IN NEIGHBORHOOD AT NIGHT (% DISTRIBUTION)

Demographic Characteristic		Very Safe	Reasonably Safe	Somewhat Unsafe	Very Unsafe	N
Gender	Male	21.8	46.5	19.2	12.5	5230
	Female	7.7	31.2	28.1	33.0	6368
Race						
Male	White	24.7	47.5	18.2	9.7	3773
	Black	13.8	43.3	22.2	20.8	1337
	Other	21.5	50.5	17.8	10.2	121
Female	White	8.7	33.3	29.1	28.9	4322
	Black	5.3	26.3	25.6	42.8	1924
	Other	8.5	35.6	32.6	23.3	122
Marital status						
Male	Married	2.0	47.0	19.9	13.1	3252
	Widowed	11.1	35.1	27.0	26.8	182
	Never Married	27.1	48.2	16.7	8.0	1434
	Separated/ Divorced	21.2	41.2	19.6	18.0	344
Female	Married	7.6	32.2	30.1	30.1	3303
	Widowed	6.5	24.9	24.4	44.1	922
	Never Married	8.9	34.6	28.0	28.5	1365
	Separated/ Divorced	6.8	28.9	24.4	39.9	761
Age						
Male	16–19	26.8	49.7	16.2	7.2	553
	20–24	30.1	51.5	13.1	5.3	612
	25–34	27.1	51.2	15.1	6.6	1006
	35–49	21.5	47.3	20.7	10.5	1146
	50–64	17.2	43.1	22.3	17.3	1212
	65 or more	11.4	37.2	25.1	26.4	701
Female	16–19	10.9	35.4	27.5	26.2	607
	20–24	9.3	36.5	28.2	26.0	734
	25–34	7.9	34.5	28.9	28.7	1214
	35–49	8.6	34.6	29.3	27.5	1427
	50–64	6.3	27.2	29.6	36.9	1384
	65 or more	5.0	21.7	23.6	49.7	1003

Source: 1975 national survey, five-city sample.

women fear crime more than men prevents its dismissal as a mere methodological artifact. In addition to indicating greater fear, studies of behavioral reactions to the threat of crime indicate that women employ more precautions than do men (Baumer 1978). In the National Crime Survey, for instance, more females (52%) than males (37%) said they had limited their behavior because of crime (Garofalo 1977).

Feminists have argued that rape and the fear of rape are central to the tendency of women to impose limitations on their own behavior. In *Against Our Will: Men, Women and Rape*, Susan Brownmiller argues that rape is an instrument of social control, "a conscious process of intimidation by which all men keep all women in a state of fear" (1975, 15). While her attribution of conscious collusion in rape by all men has evoked a storm of controversy (see Geis 1977), Brownmiller emphasizes that rape is a crime that affects all women, regardless of whether they are actually victimized. By limiting women's freedom and making them dependent on men for protection, the threat of rape provides support for a social system based on male dominance. Griffin verbalizes what many women experience: "I have never been free of the fear of rape. From a very early age I, like most women, have thought of rape as part of my natural environment—something to be feared and prayed against like fire or lightning" (1979, 3). In addition, Griffith notes that "the fear of rape keeps women off the streets at night. Keeps women at home. Keeps women passive and modest for fear that they may be thought provocative" (1979, 21).

Such fear can induce a continuing state of stress in women and can lead to the use of safety precautions that severely restrict women's freedom, such as not going out alone at night or staying out of certain parts of town. Ironically, taking these precautions does not always provide the protection they promise, since women's own homes are the single most frequent site (about 33%) of rape victimizations (McDermott 1979).

PRECAUTIONARY STRATEGIES

In a discussion of strategies that people use when interacting with their environment, Cobb (1976, 311) distinguishes between adaptation ("changing the self in an attempt to improve person-environment fit") and coping ("manipulation of the environment in the service of self"). This distinction is loosely reflected by DuBow, McCabe, and Kaplan (1979), who discuss avoidance and self-protective behaviors in response to the threat of crime: "Avoiding refers to actions taken to decrease exposure to crime by removing oneself from or increasing the distance from situations in which the risk of criminal victimization is believed to be high" (31). Avoidance behaviors, such as not going out at night or staying out of certain parts of town, limit one's exposure to dangerous situations. In contrast, self-protective behavior, such as self-defense tactics or asking repair persons to show identification, has the goal of minimizing the risk of victimization when in the presence of danger. While avoidance may require changes in one's daily behavior to reduce exposure to risks, self-protection tactics permit the management of risks once they occur (Skogan and Maxfield 1981). The analytical distinction between avoidance and self-protection has been empirically supported through factor analysis of a variety of data sets (Keppler 1976; Lavrakas and Lewis 1980; Riger and Gordon 1979).

Women in our own survey used two basic types of precautionary strategies in response to the threat of crime; we have labeled them *isolation* and *street savvy*. Isolation includes avoidance tactics, designed to prevent victimization by not exposing oneself to risk (e.g., not going out on the street at night). Street savvy, on the other hand, includes tactics intended to reduce risks when exposed to danger, such as wearing shoes that permit one to run or choosing a seat on a bus with an eye to who is sitting nearby.

When we asked women how frequently they used these precautionary strategies, about 41% said they used isolation tactics "all or most of the time" or "fairly often," while about 59% said they "seldom" or "never" did these things (see table 16.3). In contrast, 71% of the men we interviewed

TABLE 16.3
Demographic Distribution of
Frequent Use of Precautionary Behavior

Category	Isolate (% Often)		Street Savvy (% Often)	
	Men	**Women**	**Men**	**Women**
Sample	10.3 (68)	41.5 (299)	29.4 (68)	73.9 (299)
Age				
18–26	5.3 (19)	37.3 (102)	15.8 (19)	74.5 (102)
27–33	5.6 (18)	35.7 (56)	33.3 (18)	75.0 (56)
34–51	16.7 (18)	38.8 (98)	38.9 (18)	75.5 (98)
52–93	15.4 (13)	64.3 (42)	30.8 (13)	66.7 (42)
Race/ethnicity				
Black	9.1 (11)	45.0 (100)	36.4 (11)	78.0 (100)
White	4.9 (41)	33.3 (159)	22.0 (41)	68.6 (159)
Hispanic	11.1 (9)	69.2 (26)	22.2 (9)	80.8 (26)
Income				
< $6,000	14.3 (7)	38.0 (50)	28.6 (7)	84.0 (50)
$6,000–9,999	0.0 (9)	40.7 (54)	33.3 (9)	77.8 (54)
$10,000–14,999	18.8 (16)	52.5 (61)	31.3 (16)	77.0 (61)
$25,000 and over	11.1 (27)	38.7 (106)	33.3 (27)	67.0 (106)
Education				
< High school	15.4 (13)	59.1 (66)	53.8 (13)	71.2 (66)
High school graduate	22.2 (9)	44.3 (88)	33.3 (9)	81.8 (88)
> High school	6.5 (46)	31.7 (145)	21.7 (46)	70.3 (145)

Note: Numbers in parentheses indicate *N*'s.

said they rarely avoided exposure to risk. (Note that since few men were included in the survey, data on men's coping strategies are presented for illustrative purposes only, as statistical tests would be unreliable.) Among demographic subgroups of women, Hispanic (69%) and elderly (64%) women and those with less formal education (59%) relied even more often on isolation tactics. Conversely, the lowest levels of use of isolation prevailed among highly educated women (only 32% used them frequently) and among those white women (33%). As was the case with the distribution of fear, a real effect may be operating: residential segregation of ethnic and racial minorities into high crime neighborhoods could prompt greater use of isolation tactics.

The distribution of the use of street-savvy tactics did not differ significantly among demographic subgroups of women. Overall, about 74% of the women in our sample reported frequent use of street-savvy tactics, while 26% seldom used them. However, 90% of men we interviewed said they rarely used these tactics. Among women, the elderly used street savvy tactics least often (33% responding "seldom" or "never"), while black, Hispanic, and poor women used them frequently.

Although one might expect local crime rates to be the best predictor of the use of these self-protective behaviors, we found fear of crime to be the best predictor of both the use of isolation behaviors and street savvy tactics (Riger, Gordon, and LeBaily 1982). Women who assessed their neighborhoods as unsafe and women who perceived themselves to be less physically competent were especially likely to rely on isolating tactics as a means of protecting themselves. Race and amount of formal education also were significant predictors of isolation. Although differences among age levels were significant in bivariate analyses, age was not related to the use of isolation when the effects of all variables were controlled simultaneously.

Finally, we asked women in our study how frequently they engaged after dark in each of a series of everyday but potentially dangerous activities, such as being home alone, using public transportation, and walking through public parks (Gordon et al. 1980). In every instance, how often our respondents reported doing something was significantly and negatively related to their levels of worry about possible harm when doing those activities. People engaged least often in the activities that worried them most. Especially important for understanding the impact of fear on the quality of women's lives is the finding that activities done least often by women in our sample were those associated with the most choice, such as going out for entertainment alone at night. Activities that seem less discretionary, such as using public transportation to go to work, were avoided less than social or leisure activities.

MITIGATING CIRCUMSTANCES

Following an analysis of data from four Chicago neighborhoods, Lewis and Maxfield (1980) suggest that fear also is a function of the presence of signs associated with danger and social disorder, such as graffiti, abandoned buildings, and teenagers "hanging out" on street corners. Such disturbing (although not necessarily criminal) behavior seems to heighten fear, since perceptions of the frequency of such phenomena were related to increased use of street savvy tactics. Signs of such social disorganization suggest that local mechanisms of social control are not operating, indicating that, in the aggregate, a community is unable to regulate behavior within its boundaries.

Why should such signs of incivility lead women more than men to fear crime? If such signs are cues for danger, then in their presence women may be afraid because of the serious consequences victimization has for them. As noted earlier, women run the risk of rape while men usually do not, and the trauma inflicted by this crime can be severe.

In addition, women may feel less able to defend themselves against attack. We found that 41% of the women we interviewed believed they could successfully defend themselves against attack, in contrast to 54% of the males. We also asked people how strong they thought they were and how fast they thought they could run, compared to the average man and the average women. This index of physical competence was a significant predictor of fear levels. On the average, women believed themselves to be weaker and slower than both men and other women (Gordon and Riger 1978). As Stinchcombe et al. (1980) point out, the physical differences between the sexes are magnified by social conditioning; running fast, fighting, and self-defense are not part of traditional female sex-role socialization.

In our study of women's fear of crime, we found that although signs of incivility or social disorder were associated with fear levels in bivariate analyses, this relationship was not significant in multivariate analyses. However, the perception of signs of local disorder was related to women's use of precautionary behavior.

Other community-related attitudes may have an impact on women's reactions to crime. Women's feelings of attachment to their community are related to their fear levels (Riger, LeBaily, and Gordon 1981). Those who find it easy to distinguish local residents from strangers, who know neighborhood children by name, and who feel a part of their area rather than think of it just as a place to live tend to report less fear. This suggests that some degree of attachment to community may be a prerequisite for perceiving the impact of social control processes. Those who do not feel a part of the neighborhood may incorrectly perceive lack of order, and the presence of neighborhood bonds may permit the exercise of informal social control mechanisms that reduce the frequency of criminal (or noncriminal but deviant) acts that generate or heighten fear.

Discussion or gossip about crime in the neighborhood may also affect women's fear levels. Talk about crime seems to be stimulated by the perception that the local crime problem is serious, and those with strong local ties tend to speak more frequently with neighbors about such problems (Skogan and Maxfield 1981). Stories that circulate about crime tend to concern women and the elderly, although as discussed earlier, these people are the least frequently victimized.

Skogan and Maxfield speculate that such stories about crime become the focus of discussion because they are norm breaking and hence newsworthy. These stories may also indicate greater fear because they may seem to indicate lack of social control in the community. After all, when even those traditionally deemed the recipients of society's protection—women and the elderly—are victimized, then the community's lack of control may be particularly pronounced. In addition, theories about social comparison processes suggest that crime stories tend to generate greater fear in persons who see themselves as similar to victims (Heath, Gordon, and LeBailly 1981). Women and the elderly may hear or read more about victims like themselves and hence be more fearful and have an exaggerated view of the likelihood of victimization (Skogan and Maxfield 1981).

News media reports about crime present a distribution of similar victims (i.e., more women and elderly) and may also contribute to fear (Skogan and Maxfield 1981). In a study of the presentation of rape in major metropolitan newspapers, Heath, Gordon, and LeBailly (1981) found that newspapers reported 13 completed rapes, often with sensational and grisly details, to every 1 rape attempt, although victimization survey data show a ratio of 3 attempts for every completed rape. Such a skewed media presentation of rape may elevate women's fear and risk estimates and lessen their belief that they can successfully resist an attack (see also Gordon and Heath 1981).

While signs of incivility, neighborhood ties, perceptions of risk, and other factors all affect fear levels, they do not necessarily determine who will be victimized. In an extensive analysis of data from the National Crime Survey, Hindelang, Gottfredson, and Garofalo (1978) suggest that victimization is related to lifestyles, since "lifestyles are related to the probability of being in places (streets, parks, and other public places) at times (especially nighttime) when victimizations are known to occur"

(255). Likewise, structural constraints and role obligations dictated by lifestyles circumscribe people's ability to use precautionary tactics, particularly those that involve avoiding dangerous areas. For example, the demands set by occupational schedules may necessitate exposure to risk; indeed employed women report less avoidance behavior than those who do not work outside the home (Furstenberg 1972).

Women may not go out alone at night because of sex-role expectations or child-care obligations or because of fear. Whatever the reason, the result of circumscribing their activities means that women are less exposed to the possibility of being victimized, since it is likely that rate of exposure affects the victimization level. According to Balkin (1979), the actual rate of crime generates fear in people; fear leads people to reduce their exposure to risk, which in turn lowers the frequency of victimization. Our study of women's reactions to crime partially confirms this hypothesis, since we found that fear is the best predictor of women's use of both broad categories of precautionary behaviors (Riger and Gordon 1981).

Since the data in all of these studies are correlational, it is not possible to determine causal directions between attitudes and behaviors. Fear may lead to the use of self-protective behavior, or the use of self-protective behavior may lead to fear (Bem 1970). In the latter case, the employment of precautionary behavior could lead people to infer that they must be afraid. The result of the relationship between fear and precautionary behavior, whatever its causal direction, means that fewer women are exposed to risk and hence are less available as victims of crime. But the relatively high frequency with which women are victimized within the home by known assailants and the fact that more rape attempts that occur within the home are completed (McDermott 1979) raise the question of whether restricting one's movements through public places really keeps women safe. While this may keep women safe from some attacks by strangers, it may not prevent their victimization from other forms of violence.

CRIME AND
QUALITY OF LIFE FOR WOMEN

Feminist analysts of the effect of the threat of rape on women assert that it operates as an instrument of social control, encouraging women to restrict their behavior and keeping them in a state of stress (Brownmiller 1975; Griffin 1979). A sizable proportion of women in our study reported high fear of crime. Those with the fewest resources to cope with victimization—the elderly, blacks, and Hispanics, women with low incomes and less formal education—were those who bore the heaviest burden of fear. Although the pattern of fear among women was similar to that among men, women's fear was significantly greater. Thus, the distribution of fear appears to follow existing social cleavages, delineated by gender, age, race, and social class, that mark status and power inequalities in our society.

Although fear appears disproportionate to the risks women face as measured by victimization and reported crime data, women's fear is proportionate to their own estimates of risk. It is understandable that women perceive themselves to be at risk of rape and that these risk perceptions affect their levels of fear. What is intriguing is that women perceive themselves to be at greater risk of robbery and assault than men, even though all available statistics indicate that men are the most frequent victims of these crimes. A conclusive test of the relationship among fear, victimization, and risk awaits improvements in methods of measuring the "true" amount of crime and some non-self-report ways of measuring fear and precautionary behavior.

It is possible that women's high perceived risk produces fear and consequent precautionary behavior, which in turn leads to low rates of victimization (Balkin 1979). Since estimates of women's risk of robbery and rape are highly correlated, women may perceive a general threat of personal violence from any of a multitude of crimes. The original feminist formulation of rape as a means of controlling women may need to be expanded to include other crimes of violence. Bowker (1978) suggests that wife beating may be a better example than rape of forces of social control that affect women. Since our study focused on street crime, we did not include domestic violence in our calculations of women's fear. Whatever the causes of violence, the effects may be to reinforce constraints already operating on low status victims and, hence, further encourage them to restrict their behavior.

The sizable proportion of women who use isolation tactics regularly gives support to the argument that the impact of the threat of crime on many women is restrictive. Numerous studies have found that women use avoidance behaviors more than men (summarized in DuBow, McCabe, and Kaplan 1979). The social and work opportunities lost to women because of the threat of crime seem likely to reduce the overall quality of their lives. Although the precautionary strategies employed by women may not involve significant monetary expenditures, these strategies are undoubtedly costly in terms of personal freedom.

Hindelang, Gottfredson, and Garofalo (1978) argue that shifts in behavior due to fear of crime are subtle. They assert that people don't change what they do, only how they do it; for example, they might drive instead of walk to their destination. Our findings suggest that for women, the sum of these subtle shifts may exert a considerable toll on their time, effort, budgets, and freedom. When we asked our respondents how often they avoided doing necessary activities such as shopping or errands because of fears for their safety, 78% of the men but only 32% of the women responded "never." Of women in our sample, 34% said they avoided doing these things because of fear for their safety "fairly often" or "most of the time." When we asked about behavior that didn't involve necessary tasks but rather consisted of things they wanted to do, such as visiting friends or going to movies, 75% of males but only 30% of females reported they never let fear deter them. In addition, 36% of females said they often avoided doing such activities because of fear of harm.

As discussed earlier, other data suggest that the price paid by women for safety is greatest in the area of behaviors involving the most discretion, such as visiting friends or going out for evening entertainment (Gordon et al. 1980). High fear seems to shrink the scope of women's choices about their lives by restricting their movement through time and space, giving credence to feminist arguments that the threat of criminal victimization severely limits women's freedom.

The important role of self-assessments of physical competence in determining women's reactions to crimes, both in fearful attitudes and in isolation behavior, raises intriguing questions for future research. What are the socialization and situational factors that induce women to believe that they are less physically powerful not only than men, but also than most women? How do feelings of physical competence affect women's beliefs about potency in other areas of their lives, such as work and family interactions? And are perceptions of physical competence related to women's likelihood of resisting attack? Larwood, O'Neal, and Brennan (1977) suggest that the "social inhibition" that suppresses the expression of physical aggression by females can be disinhibited under certain circumstances. Cohn, Kidder, and Harvey (1978) found that after taking a self-defense training course, women reported feeling stronger, braver, more active, more in control, bigger, safer, and more efficacious in a variety of arenas.

UNDERSTANDING THE IMPACT OF CRIME ON WOMEN

To summarize, victimization rates are an inadequate explanation for women's reactions to crime. Rather, in order to understand women's high fear and frequent use of precautions, it is necessary to look at women in the context in which they live—their perceptions both of themselves and of the world they live in shape their reactions. Women live in a world that is filled with danger, but without resources with which to combat that danger. Out of that world and the constraints imposed by lifestyles, women create ways of coping with the stresses in the environment. The salient factors in understanding women's reactions to crime, then, become women's perceptions of the dangerousness of their neighborhoods and the strength both of their ties to that locality and of themselves. If they perceive that the neighborhood is filled with risks, then women are fearful, and their fear is related to their use of behavioral strategies to cope with danger. Lack of local social control, as perceived through signs of disorder, prompt the use of risk-management tactics (i.e., street savvy) in the face of possible danger. Women who feel that they are slow and weak attempt to enhance their safety by restricting their movements through time and space. In imposing restraints on themselves, women are not simply reacting to crime, but are working actively to shape their environments in order to balance the demands of their lives with the avoidance of danger.

Although the self-protective strategies that women use more than men may not cost money, they do cost time, effort, and freedom. Discretionary activities appear to be most restricted in response to the threat of criminal victimization. Women forego leisure and social opportunities because of the fear of crime, an intangible cost that is hard to measure but that may have a significant impact on the quality of their lives. Hindelang, Gottfredson, and Garofalo (1978) assert that the fear of crime has a subtle impact on behavior and that because of crime people do not change what they do, but rather how they do it. Surveys indicate that women make these changes more than men, and the sum of these changes may be considerable.

The causes of crime against women, as against men, are multiple. Bowker (1978) suggests that rape is the result of several factors: urbanization and the associated geographic mobility, impersonality, anonymity, and bystander apathy; an abundance of available victims; and personal problems in the rapist. He rejects the feminist belief that rape is a means of social control of women, since rapists do not mention this as a motive.

Whatever the causes of rape and other violence against women, a major effect of these crimes on even nonvictims may be self-imposed restrictions. That men are more frequent victims of every violent crime except rape yet do not react by restricting their behavior suggests that something more than crime is implicated. Rarely are men warned not to go out alone at night because they will be victimized, even though they are victimized more often than women. It seems that crime against women, whatever the motivation of the individual criminal, has the cumulative effect of rein-forcing social norms. Women who are victimized, especially by rape, are blamed for that victimization (Feild 1978; Jones and Aronson 1973; Krulewitz 1977). This is not only because of belief in a just world (Lerner 1980) but also because in being victimized women are breaking social norms; blame acts as a cautionary warning to other women not to do likewise.

Perhaps the central question to be answered by research on precaution-ary behavior is whether the use of such restrictive behaviors, does, in fact, keep women safe from crime. There were too few victims in our sample to sufficiently and directly answer this question. Other analyses of nationwide data-sets suggest that it is rates of exposure to crime, rather than degree of precaution, that determine victimization. Hindelang, Gottfredson, and Garofalo (1978) hypothesize that the probability of being in dangerous places at times when crimes are likely to occur is strongly related to victimization rates. Women are often assaulted in their homes, and are more likely than men to know their attacker (Bowker 1978). These findings suggest that while limiting exposure to street crime may keep women safe from some attacks by strangers, it will not prevent their victimization from a myriad of other forms of violence.

What can be done to reduce these restrictions, these indirect effects of crime on women? Since women's fear is not simply a function of crime rates, reducing crime, while a top priority, will be only a partial solution. Two additional alternative approaches are likely to be useful. First, efforts should be made to increase women's sense of themselves as physically powerful and competent. A second strategy would be to increase women's attachments to their neighborhoods. Since those who feel more attached are less fearful, strategies to enhance neighborhood integration may be successful in reducing fear.

But these are individual responses, designed to increase the safety only of those who employ them. If successful, they may simply defer victimi-zation onto others (Cohn, Kidder, and Harvey 1978). Since crime is a problem that affects many women, a more effective strategy would involve collective efforts. In the late 1970s, a new kind of political demonstration occurred in the United States. Throughout the country, women (and men) marched through city streets with chants of "take back the night" accompanied by cries of "stop rape now!" These marches heralded women's refusal to accept the restrictions on their lives advo-cated as protection against the threat of rape and other forms of criminal victimization. Unwilling to go out alone only in daylight, unwilling to hide behind locked and barred windows and doors or to live in a constant state of anxiety over the possible depredations of criminals, women acted to change the situation documented by research—that fear of crime has particularly deleterious effects on the lives of women living in American cities.

Although it is impossible yet to determine if such actions have had an impact on rates of rape and other crimes against women, we suggest they may have increased women's sense of control of their lives. By refusing to live in fear, women are taking control of a situation that has long plagued them. Such active resistance may be critical to maintaining a sense of well-being and self-esteem. Of course crime should be reduced. But as Maltz has said, "unless the public feels safer in proportion to its increased actual safety, the full potential" (1972, 34) of an effective crime control program will not have been reached.

The freedom to walk safely through city streets should be a right enjoyed by every citizen in this country. This freedom is denied to too many women, often through the use of self-imposed behavioral restrictions. The threat of crime, by creating a constant state of apprehension about possible victimization in many women and by leading to the self-imposition of behavioral restrictions, has the effects that feminists decry: it limits women's opportunities to be active participants in public life. It is destructive of the social fabric of our nation. Until the full weight of a range of social institutions can be brought to bear in order to generate the pressures and conditions capable of drastically reducing violent crime, the burden of fear of crime and its consequences will fall disproportionately on women and, among women, on those with the fewest resources for coping with it.

The research on which this chapter is based was conducted at the Center for Urban Affairs and Policy Research at Northwestern University and was partially supported by grant R01 MH-2960 from the National Institute of Mental Health.

REFERENCES

Balkin, S. 1979. Victimization rates, safety and fear of crime. *Social Problems* 26: 343–58.

Bart, P. 1981. Women who were both raped and avoided being raped. *Journal of Social Issues* 37: 123–37.

Baumer, T.L. 1978. Research on fear of crime in the United States. *Victimology: An International Journal* 3: 243–64.

Bem, D.J. 1970. Beliefs, attitudes and human affairs. Monterey, Calif.: Brooks/ Cole.

Berger, V. 1977. Man's trial, woman's tribulation: Rape cases in the courtroom. *Columbia Law Review* 7: 1–103.

Biderman, A.D., et al. 1967. *Report on victimization and attitudes toward law enforcement.* Washington, D.C.: U.S. Government Printing Office.

Bowker, L.H. 1978. *Women, crime, and the criminal justice system.* Lexington, Mass.: D.C. Heath.

Brodyaga, L., et al. 1975. *Rape and its victims: A report for citizens, health facilities and criminal justice agencies.* Washington, D.C.: U.S. Government Printing Office.

Brownmiller, S. 1975. *Against our will: Men, women and rape.* New York: Simon and Schuster.

Burgess, A.W., and L.L. Holmstrom. 1974. *Rape: Victims of crisis.* Bowie, Md.: Brady.

Cobb, S. 1976. Social support as a moderator of life stress. *Psychosomatic Medicine* 38: 300–14.

Cohn, E., L.H. Kidder, and J. Harvey. 1978. Crime prevention vs. victimization prevention: The psychology of two different reactions. *Victimology: An International Journal* 3: 285–96.

Cook, F.L., et al. 1982. *Setting and reformulating policy agendas: The case of criminal victimization of the elderly.* New York: Oxford University Press.

Dodge, R.W., H. Lentzner, and F. Shenk. 1976. Crime in the United States: A report on the National Crime Survey. In *Sample Surveys of the Victims of Crime,* ed. W.G. Skogan. Cambridge, Mass.: Ballinger.

DuBow, R., E. McCabe, and G. Kaplan. 1979. *Reactions to crime: A critical review of the literature.* Washington, D.C.: U.S. Department of Justice.

Erskine, H. 1974. The polls: Fear of crime and violence. *Public Opinion Quarterly* 38: 797–814.

Feild, H.S. 1978. Attitudes toward rape: A comparative analysis of police, rapists, crisis counselors and citizens. *Journal of Personality and Social Psychology* 36: 156–79.

Furstenberg, F.F., Jr. 1972. Fear of crime and its effect on citizen behavior. In *Crime and justice: A symposium,* ed. A. Biderman New York: Nailburg.

Garofalo, J. 1977. *Public opinion about crime: The attitudes of victims and nonvictims in selected cities.* Washington, D.C.: U.S. Government Printing Office.

―――. Victimization and the fear of crime. *Journal of Research in Crime and Delinquency* 16: 80–97.

Geis, G. 1977. Forcible rape: An introduction. In *Forcible rape: The crime, the victim, and the offender*, ed. D. Chappell, R. Geis, and G. Geis, New York: Columbia University Press.

Gordon, M.T., and L. Heath. 1981. The news business, crime and fear. In *Reactions to crime*, ed. D.A. Lewis. Beverly Hills, Calif.: Sage Publications.

Gordon, M.T., and S. Riger. 1978. The fear of rape project. *Victimology: An International Journal* 3: 346–47.

Gordon, M.T., et al. 1980. Crime, women and the quality of urban life. *Signs: Journal of Women in Culture and Society* 5: S144–60.

Griffin, S. 1979. *Rape: The power of consciousness.* San Francisco: Harper and Row.

Heath, L., M.T. Gordon, and R.K. LeBailly. 1981. What newspapers tell us (and don't tell us) about rape. *The Newspaper Research Journal* 2(4): 48–55.

Hindelang, M.J., and B.L. Davis. 1977. Forcible rape in the United States: A statistical profile. In *Forcible rape: The crime, the victim, and the offender*, ed. D. Chappell, R. Geis, and G. Geis, New York: Columbia University Press.

Hindelang, M.J., M.R. Gottfredson, and J. Garofalo. 1978. *Victims of personal crime: An empirical foundation for a theory of personal victimization.* Cambridge, Mass.: Ballinger.

Jones, C., and E. Aronson. 1973. Attribution of fault to a rape victim as a function of responsibility of the victim. *Journal of Personality and Social Psychology* 26: 415–19.

Katz, S., and M.A. Mazur. 1979. *Understanding the rape victim: A synthesis of research findings.* New York: John Wiley and Sons.

Keppler, H. 1976. *Dimensions of reactions to crime: A cluster analysis.* Evanston, Ill.: Center for Urban Affairs and Policy Research, Northwestern University.

Krulewitz, J.E. 1977. Sex differences in rape attributions. Paper presented at annual meeting Midwestern Psychological Association, May, Chicago.

Larwood, J., E. O'Neal, and P. Brennan. 1977. Increasing the physical aggressiveness of women. *Journal of Social Psychology* 101: 97–101.

Lavrakas, P.J., and D.A. Lewis. 1980. The conceptualization and measurement of citizen crime prevention behaviors. *Journal of Research in Crime Delinquency* 17: 154–272.

LeBailly, R.K. 1979. *Method artifacts in telephone and in-person interviews: An examination of bias and consistency.* Evanston, Ill.: Center for Urban Affairs and Policy Research, Northwestern University.

Lerner, M.J. 1980. *The belief in a just world: A fundamental delusion.* New York: Plenum.

Lewis, D.A., and M.G. Maxfield. 1980. Fear in the neighborhoods: An investigation of the impact of crime. *Journal of Research in Crime and Delinquency* 17: 160–89.

Maltz, M.D. 1972. *Evaluation of crime control problems.* Washington, D.C.: Law Enforcement Assistance Administration.

McDermott, J.J. 1979. *Rape victimization in 26 American cities.* Washington, D.C.: U.S. Department of Justice.

McIntyre, J. 1967. Public attitudes toward crime and law enforcement. *Annals of the American Academy of Political and Social Science* 41: 34–36.

McIntyre, J., T. Myint, and L. Curtis. 1979. Sexual assault outcomes: Completed and attempted rapes. Paper presented at annual meeting American Sociological Association, August, San Francisco.

Medea, A. and K. Thompson. 1974. *Against rape.* New York: Farrar, Strauss and Giroux.

Riger, S., and M.T. Gordon. 1979. The structure of rape prevention beliefs. *Personality and Social Psychology Bulletin* 5: 186–90.

Riger, S., and M.T. Gordon. 1981. The fear of rape: A study of social control. *Journal of Social Issues* 37: 71–92.

Riger, S. and P.J. Lavrakas. 1982. Community ties: Patterns of attachment and social interaction in urban neighborhoods. *American Journal of Community Psychology* 9: 55–66.

Riger, S., M.T. Gordon, and R.K. LeBailly. 1978. Women's fear of crime: From blaming to restricting the victim. *Victimology: An International Journal* 3: 274–84.

Riger, S., M.T. Gordon, and R.K. LeBailly. 1982. Coping with urban crime: Women's use of precautionary behaviors. *American Journal of Community Psychology* 10: 369–86.

Riger, S., R.K. LeBailly, and M.T. Gordon. 1981. Community ties and urbanites' fear of crime: An ecological investigation. *American Journal of Community Psychology* 9: 653–65.

Ryan, W. 1981. *Blaming the victim.* New York: Vintage Press.

Sanders, W.B. 1980. *Rape and woman's identity.* Beverly Hills, Calif.: Sage.

Selby, J.W., L.G. Calhoun, and T.A. Brock. 1977. Sex differences in the social perception of rape victims. *Personality and Social Psychology Bulletin* 3: 412–15.

Skogan, W.G. 1977. Dimensions of the dark figure of unreported crime. *Crime and Delinquency* 23: 41–50.

Skogan, W.G.   1978a.   *The Center for Urban Affairs random digit dialing telephone survey.*   Evanston, Ill.: Center   for Urban Affairs and Policy Research, Northwestern University.

————. 1978.   Crime in contemporary America. In *Violence in America*, 2d ed., ed. H. Graham and T.R. Gurr. Beverly Hills, Calif.: Sage Publications.

Skogan, W.G., and M.G. Maxfield. 1981. *Coping with crime: Victimization, fear, and reactions to crime in three American cities.* Beverly Hills, Calif.: Sage.

Stinchcombe, A.L., et al.   1980.   *Crime and punishment-changing attitudes in America.*   San Francisco: Jossey-Bass.

U.S. Department of Justice.   1980a.   *Criminal Victimization in the United States: 1973–78 Trends.*   Washington, D.C.: U.S. Government Printing Office.

U.S. Department of Justice.   1980b.   *Intimate victims: A study of violence among friends and relatives.*   Washington, D.C.: U.S. Government Printing Office.

U.S. Department of Statistics. 1981. *Bulletin*, 0–344–894: QL3, Bureau of Justice Statistics. Washington, D.C.: U.S. Government Printing Office.

Weis, K., and S.S. Borges. 1973. Victimology and rape: The case of the legitimate victim. *Issues in Criminology* 8: 71–115.

CHAPTER
17

AN ANALYSIS OF PORNOGRAPHY RESEARCH

GAIL DINES-LEVY
Wheelock College

In 1970, the U.S. Presidential Commission on Obscenity and Pornography stated that "the commission cannot conclude that exposure to erotic materials is a factor in the causation of sex crimes or sex delinquency" (223). Sixteen years later, however, the Attorney General's Commission on Pornography (1986) came out with a different conclusion: "We are satisfied that the vast majority of depictions of violence in a sexually explicit manner are likely to increase the incidence of sexual violence in this country" (308). These two contradictory statements seem to indicate that crucial changes have taken place in the sixteen years since the first report.

Probably the greatest change has occurred in the nature of the materials under consideration. Although both commissions discussed sexually explicit materials, the later investigation tended to concentrate more on sexually violent depictions, which the commission found to be not only increasingly available, but also more frequently used in the publications that featured them. This finding had been previously reported by Smith (1976) and Malamuth and Spinner (1980).

A second major change has been in the quantity and quality of academic research examining the effects of pornography. Academic interest in pornography increased with the publication of studies by such scholars as Malamuth (1984), Donnerstein (1986), Court (1986), and Eysenck and Nias (1978). Moreover, such studies, which contain reviews of earlier studies, were able to utilize methodological advances in the social sci-ences, such as more sophisticated techniques of statistical analysis. In addition, use of the penile plethysmograph (Malamuth and Check 1980) meant that researchers need no longer rely on self-reports of sexual arousal, a method found to be relatively unreliable (Abel et al. 1977).

The 1986 commission, in keeping with its specific mandate to study the "available empirical evidence on the relationship between exposure to pornographic materials and anti-social behavior" (U.S. Attorney General's Commission on Pornography 1986, 216), presents a thorough and scientific analysis of the major research findings in this field. These findings are summarized as follows:

> In evaluating the results for sexually violent material, it appears that exposure to such materials (1) leads to a greater acceptance of rape myths and violence against women; (2) has more pronounced effects when the victim is shown enjoying the use of force or violence; (3) is arousing for rapists and for some males in the general population; and (4) has resulted in sexual aggression against women in the laboratory. (U.S. Attorney General's Commission on Pornography 1986, 1005)

The commission uses the word "appears" because of the potential methodological problems involved in such research. One such problem, previously stated by Court (1984), is whether the research findings have implications for society at large. This criticism is based largely on the contention that laboratory studies can examine only short-term effects, which provide us with a truncated picture of the mass media experience. In this chapter, the limitations of short-term, limited-exposure studies in examining long-term effects of pornography are discussed, with suggestions provided for alternative methods for studying pornography.

LIMITATIONS OF PORNOGRAPHY STUDIES

Recently, a number of studies have been designed to test the effect of what the commission calls "massive" exposure to pornography, with massive meaning exposure over a duration of one to several weeks. Although such studies more accurately reflect the reality of pornography consumption (several magazines per month over an extended period of time), they are based on subjects receiving a heavy dose of material over a short period (Zillman and Bryant 1984). These studies do not provide us with a theoretical construct, firmly grounded in empirical research, that can address the implications of long-term exposure to pornography.

The difficulty of pornography research becomes more evident when attempts are made at defining pornography. Justice Potter Stewart of the

U.S. Supreme Court has said, "I can't define it, but I know it when I see it" (Longino 1982, 26). Clearly, such a definition is inadequate for legal and scientific purposes, and attempts have been made to clarify the term. One of the most recent and precise definitions was proposed by Mackinnon and Dworkin (1983). They define pornography as the sexually explicit subordination of women, graphically depicted, whether in pictures or words, that also includes the presentation of women in one or more of the following ways:

1. As dehumanized sexual objects, things, or commodities
2. As sexual objects who enjoy pain or humiliation
3. As sexual objects who experience sexual pleasure in being raped
4. As sexual objects tied up, cut up, mutilated, bruised, or physically hurt
5. In postures of sexual submission or sexual servility, including inviting penetration
6. With body parts—including but not limited to vaginas, breasts, and buttocks—exhibited, such that women are reduced to those parts
7. As whores by nature
8. As being penetrated by objects or animals
9. In scenarios of degradation, injury, or torture and shown as filthy or inferior, bleeding, bruised, or hurt in a context that makes these conditions sexual

While such an extensive definition appears to cover all the varied scenarios found in those publications termed pornographic or erotic, research suggests that it extends also into visual depictions contained within mass-circulation publications (Reisman and Dines-Levy 1982). This has been termed the *ripple effect*, meaning that "violent pornography has moved from special hard core magazines and shops to the larger mass media" (Lederer 1982, 4).

One method of evaluating this aspect of pornography is content analysis. The researcher constructs certain categories in relation to media content and then seeks to quantify the occurrence of these categories within the texts under consideration. This method has been attacked on the grounds that it tells only that a certain item occurs frequently or infrequently within a wide range of material. What is missing, it is argued, is any meaningful qualitative analysis (Burgelin 1972).

A more qualitative version of content analysis was adopted by Erving Goffman (1979) in his analysis of gender advertisements. Goffman developed several gender themes and then sought to fit the advertisements into those themes. Although this method does not provide the reader with a rigorous statistical analysis, it does give information about the display of gender in advertisements.

The following example can be used to illustrate this method of analysis. In an advertisement for shoes, two pairs of female legs are photographed from behind. Both women are wearing high-heeled shoes, and the right leg of the first woman is bound by a thin red cord to the left leg of the second woman. The photograph stops at the base of the women's spines; there is a clear view of both women's bare buttocks.

The ad fits into Mackinnon and Dworkin's (1983) definition of pornography in a number of ways. First, because readers do not see the women's faces, they have no sense of who these women are. The women have, in effect, been reduced to their bound legs and bare buttocks, which stand as symbols for the whole woman. Interpretation of the ad continues on a second level. Goffman (1979) argues that "narrative-like action is to be read from what is seen; a before and after are to be inferred and this location in the ongoing stream of activity provides the context. . . ." (16). In the ad, being bound suggests being restrained against one's will, a form of violence against the captive. In addition, the naked buttocks hint of sexual violence.

Preliminary, large-scale content analysis research does suggest that the visual depiction of sexual violence is on the increase. However, given the ubiquitous nature of the print media, short-term, limited-exposure laboratory studies into the effects of pornography will yield findings of limited explanatory value.

AN ALTERNATIVE METHOD
FOR STUDYING PORNOGRAPHY

What is lacking in present-day research of pornography is both a theory and an empirical method of testing that will account for the potential long-term effects of repeated exposure to pornographic themes. This was recognized by Gerbner and Gross (1976) with respect to the effects of repeated exposure to television violence. The main focus of concern is not so much attitude change (although Gerbner and Gross do recognize that it sometimes occurs), but rather the manner in which television cultivates viewers' conceptions of the real world, or how television contributes to the social construction of reality. This is not a short-term effect; rather, it is the result of ongoing, long-term exposure (Gerbner et al. 1976).

Given this theoretical framework, the short-term, laboratory-type study appears unsuitable for empirical investigation. In response, a two-stage research project was developed by Gerbner and colleagues (1976). The first part, message system analysis, requires the recording of week-long samples of network television programs each year in order that a rigorous and detailed content analysis can be performed. This is based on the assumption that "although findings about media content cannot be taken at face value as evidence of impact, representative and reliable observations of content . . . are critical prerequisites to a valid consideration of media influence" (Gerbner et al. 1976, 25).

The second part of the project investigates the degree to which this media reality affects viewers' perceptions. Questions about the "real world" are formulated from the content analysis in order to determine differences between light viewers' and heavy viewers' conceptions of the real world.

Since its conception in 1967, the cultural indicators project has been extended from examining the effects of television violence to other areas, such as sex roles, politics, and aging. In each of these areas, differences were found between light viewers and heavy viewers with similar demographic characteristics. For example, studies on violence showed that "heavy viewers . . . express a greater sense of insecurity and apprehension than do light viewers in the same group" (Gerbner 1984, 7). The findings from the cultural indicators project suggest that the effects of television should not be interpreted solely in terms of the isolated acts of violence it may incite, but also in terms of its dissemination of information regarding inequality, power, and domination—information that has far-reaching consequences.

To understand the long-term effects of pornography, an approach similar to that of Gerbner and Gross (1976) is needed. Although any analysis of pornography must consider rape, the potentially broad effects of violent sexual imagery that portrays women as legitimate victims must be examined. Even though print pornography is not as pervasive as television and its readership tends to be less heterogeneous, it is still a major disseminator of messages regarding female sexuality and sexual relationships. Questions about pornography must include the nature of the facts learned, especially if they are "likely to become the basis of a broader world view" (Gerbner et al. 1976, 28).

Applying the Gerbner-Gross model to a study of pornography is not without problems, among them the difficulty involved in isolating pornographic images. As discussed previously, pornographic images filter into the mass media, and therefore nonreaders of pornography are exposed to some pornographic images. However, all media consumers are exposed to violent sexual imagery in ads, films, and on television. The vast majority of such imagery still is found mainly within those materials defined as sexually explicit. Moreover, only by first understanding the long-term effects of pornography will we be able to conceptualize the contribution that sexually violent media images have made on our social construction of reality.

Research into pornography has yielded important findings regarding the relationship between pornography and violence against women. The studies have also been instrumental in causing the reopening of the pornography debate since the 1970 commission report. However, future research must focus on the long-term effects that pornography is having on our society, and this calls for new methods of assessing the problem.

REFERENCES

Abel, G., et al. 1977. The components of rapists' sexual arousal. *Archives of General Psychiatry* 34: 895–903.

Burgelin, O. 1972. Structural analysis and mass communication. In *Sociology and mass communications*, ed. D. McQuail, 313–38. London: Penguin.

Court, J. 1984. Sex and violence: A ripple effect. In *Pornography and sexual aggression*, ed. N.M. Malamuth and E. Donnerstein, 143–72. New York: Academic Press.

Donnerstein, E. 1984. Pornography: Its effects on violence against women. In *Pornography and sexual aggression,* ed . N.M. Malamuth and E. Donnerstein, 143–72. New York: Academic Press.

Dworkin, A., and C. MacKinnon. 1983. Antipornography law proposed as amendment to Minneapolis, Minn., Code of Ordinances, civil rights title 7, chapters 139, 141. Hearings, 12–13 December.

Eysenck, H.J., and D.K.B Nias. 1978. *Sex, violence and the media.* London: Maurice Temple Smith, Ltd.

Gerbner, G. 1984. Gratuitous violence and exploitive sex: What are the lessons? Prepared for study committee hearing, Communications Commission of the National Council of Churches, 21 September.

Gerbner, G., and L. Gross. 1976. Living with television: The violence profile. *Journal of Communications* 26: 172–99.

Gerbner, G. et al. 1976. Living with television: The dynamics of the cultivation process. In *Perspective on media effects*, ed. J. Bryant and D. Zillman, 17–40. Hillsdale, N.J.: Lawrence Erlbaum Assoc., Inc.

Goffman, E. 1979. *Gender advertisements.* Cambridge, Mass.: Harvard University Press.

Lederer, L., ed. 1982. *Take back the night: Women on pornography.* New York: Bantam Books.

Longino, H. 1982. Pornography, oppression, and freedom: A closer look. In *Take back the night*, ed. L. Lederer. New York, : Bantam Books.

Malamuth, N. 1984. Aggression against women: Cultural and individual causes. In *Pornography and sexual aggression*, ed. N.M. Malamuth and E. Donnerstein, 19–22. New York: Academic Press.

Malamuth, N.M., and J.V.P. Check. 1980. Penile tumescence and perceptual responses to rape as a function of victim's perceived reactions. *Journal of Applied Social Psychology* 10: 528–47.

Malamuth, N., and B. Spinner. 1980. A longitudinal content analysis of sexual violence in the best selling erotic magazines. *The Journal of Sex Research* 16: 226–37.

Reisman, J., and G. Dines-Levy. 1982. An empirical study of Israeli media reality as compared to Israeli social reality. Institute for the Study of Media and the Family, Haifa, and Ministry of Absorption, Israel. Typescript..

Smith, D. 1976. The social content of pornography. *Journal of Communication* 26: 16–33.

U.S. Attorney General's Commission on Pornography. 1986. *Final report.* Washington, D.C.: U.S. Government Printing Office.

U.S. Presidential Commssion on Obscenity and Pornography. 1970. *Report of the Commission on Obscenity and Pornography.* Washington, D.C., U.S. Government Printing Office.

Zillman, D., and J. Bryant. 1984. Effects of massive exposure to pornography. In *Pornography and sexual aggression*, ed. N.M. Malamuth and E. Donnerstein, 115–38. New York: Academic Press.

INDEX

Abbey, A., 202
Abel, G.G., 113, 194, 202
Abramson, P., 197
Abuse
  boys, 92–104
  comparison by gender, 33
  psychiatric illness, 27
Acock, A.C., 213
Adler, N.E., 70
Adolescents
  cues of sex, 252–256
  dating, 256–266
  perceptions, 245–269
Aggression, 114
Albin, R.S., 206, 209
Alcohol
  nurses, 52
  and sexual abuse, 51
Alford, A.C., 203
Allen, S., 211
American Civil Liberties Union, 269, 274
Amir, M., 75
Armenti, N.P., 52, 57
Aronson, E., 76
Astor, G., 112
Atascadero State Hospital, 106
Atkeson, B.D., 170,172
Attitudes
  callous toward victims, 206
  correlates, 212
  impact, 203
  sex role, 230

Balkin, S., 307
Bandura, A., 198
Bard, L., 108
Barnett, N.J., 203
Bart, P., 106
Becker, J., 113, 194, 202
Beckman, L.J., 52, 57
Beliefs
  rape, 203–205
Bell, A., 92
Beneke, T., 201, 209
Benson, D.J., 61, 68
Best, C.L., 171
Bissell, L., 52, 58
Bond, S.B., 206
Borges, S., 200, 202, 205, 207–211, 223, 265
Bowker, L.H., 308, 310
Brannigan, G., 202, 256
Brennan, P., 309
Briere, J., 198
Brodsky, S., 106, 112
Bromberg, W., 113
Broude, G.J., 197
Brown, G.E., 203
Brownmiller, S., 112, 203, 208, 302
Burgess, A.W., 76, 84, 113, 117, 172, 195, 207
Burkhart, B.R., 5, 23, 205
Burt, M., 152, 202, 203, 205, 206, 209–212
Bush, C., 57
Byrne, D., 206

Calhoun, K.S., 170, 172, 205
Calmas, W., 112, 113
Cann, A., 205
Caplan, N., 290
Carmen, E., 51, 57
Carpenter, J.A., 52, 57
Carroll, J.L., 201
Center for Women Policy Studies,
    117
Chappell, D., 105
Check, J., 199, 212
Cherry, F., 208
Classifications of rapists, 110
    compensatory, 111, 122
    displaced anger, 112, 125
    exploitative, 112, 122
    sadistic, 113, 125
Cobb, S., 302
Cohen, F.S., 51
Cohen, J., 98
Cohen, M., 111–113, 118
Cohn, E., 309
College males
    sexually aggressive, 198
Costin, F., 213
Court, J., 317, 318
Covington, S.S., 51, 52
Coyle, E., 113
Crime
    fear of, 294
    impact, 293–312
    mitigating circumstances,
        305–307
    precautionary strategies, 302–304
    quality of life for women,
        307–309
    women's responses, 300–302
Criminal laws, 271
    statutory rape, 271
Criminal justice system
    jury behaviors, 282, 283
    perceptions of charges, 281, 282
Crisis counseling, 172
    supportive, 172, 175, 176
Cultural
    variations of rape, 196

Dating
    adolescent, 256
    behavior, 262
    ethnic differences in, 262
    location, 261
Day, A.E., 64
Dean, C.W., 296, 209, 211
deBruyn-Kopps, M., 206, 209, 211
Decision making
    victim's resistance, 126
Delancey Street Foundation, 78
Deming, M., 204, 207, 209
Densen-Gerber, J., 51
Department of Education, 6, 93
Depression, 169
    Beck inventory, 169, 176
    Hamilton scale, 169
DeSavage, J., 208
Donnerstein, E., 317
Drugs
    dependency, 51–60
    sexual abuse, 52
Dworkin, A., 319, 320
Dykstra, P., 64

Ehrhart, J.K., 204, 206–210
Ellis, E.M., 170
Emslie, G., 42
Eppy, A., 204, 207, 209
Erikson, E., 133
Estep, R.E., 205, 206, 209–211
Ewing, J.A., 53
Eysench, H.J., 317

Farrell, W., 200
Fear, 171
    Wolpe-Lang survey, 171
Fear of rape
    age, 300
    men's, 299
    woman's risk, 299
Federal Bureau of Investigation, 3, 4,
    14
Feild, H.S., 203, 210, 213

Feldman-Summers, S., 76
Ferenczi, S., 144
Feshbach, S., 206
Finkelhor, D., 91, 92, 97, 102, 103
Fisher, G.J., 211, 213
Flintcraft, A., 42
Fogarty, F., 105
Force, 272
Frazier, W., 42
Fremont, J., 201
Freud, S., 133, 134, 136, 142
Fromson, M.E., 198

Garafalo, J., 294, 306, 308, 310, 311
Gebhard, P., 112, 113
Generativity, 137
Genitality, 134, 137
Gerbner, G., 320, 321
Giarrusso, R., 201, 202, 211
Goal Attainment Scale, 173
    treatment, 173
Goffman, E., 319, 320
Gold, E.R., 92
Goodchilds, J., 200, 206, 208, 211
Goodman, H., 212
Goodstein, L., 211, 213
Gordon, M.T., 306
Gottfredson, M.R., 294, 306, 308,
    310, 311
Green, A.H., 28
Greendlinger, V., 206
Greene, S.J., 197
Griffin, S., 209, 210, 302
Gross, L., 320, 321
Groth, A.N., 113, 195, 201, 205, 207
Grunebaum, H., 141
Guttmacker, M., 112, 113

Haber, S., 206
Haberman, P.W., 58
Hale, M., 271
Hariton, E., 206
Harvey, J., 309

Hayashi, H., 197
Heath, L., 306
Hennepin County, 173
Herman, J., 36, 37
Hidden rape, 3–25
Hilberman, E., 36
Hindelang, M.J., 294, 306, 308, 310,
    311
Holmes, K.A., 203, 208, 221
Holmstrom, L.L., 76, 84, 113, 117,
    172, 195, 207
Homosexuality
    and nurses, 57
Hotaling, G., 92
Howell, N., 106
Howells, K., 213
Hyde, S.H., 202

Ireland, N.K., 212

Jaffe, Y., 198
James, J., 77
Janoff-Bulman, R., 152, 153, 164,
    165
Janzen, C., 51
Jaques, E., 137
Johnson, P., 200, 211
Johnson, V., 206
Jones, C., 76
Jury instruction, 272
Juvenille prostitutes, 77

Kanin, E.J., 5, 199, 202, 207, 211
Kanten, J.F., 246
Kaplan, G., 302
Katz, B., 152
Katz, S., 116
Kidder, L.H., 309
Kilpatrick, D.G., 4, 170
Kohen, J., 51
Koss, M.P., 5, 7, 194, 199
Krulewitz, J.E., 212

Laplante, M., 202, 256
L'Armand, K., 209
Larwood, J., 309
Law reform, 271–290
    individual features, 278, 283
    legislative success, 275–278
    origins and goals, 273–275
    rape, 271
LeBailly, R.K., 306
Leonard, K.E., 194
Lester, D., 194
LeVine, R.A., 195
Lewis, C.E., 52
Lewis, D.A., 305
Life-style deviance, 230
Lindner, K., 76
Lottes, I.L., 197, 213

McCabe, E., 302
McConahay, S.A., 212
McCormick, N., 202, 256
MacDonald, J., 76
Macht, L., 141
Mackeller, J., 75
Mackinnon, C., 69, 319, 320
Mahoney, E.R., 198, 211
Makepeace, J.M., 200
Malamuth, N., 196, 198, 204, 206,
    212, 317
Maltz, M.D., 312
Marolla, J., 21, 112, 113, 193, 194,
    203, 207
Marsh, J., 290
Massachusetts Treatment Center,
    108
Maxfield, M.G., 305, 306
Mazur, M., 113
Miller, P.Y., 246
Mills, T., 51
Mosher, D.L., 206
Ms. magazine, 4, 5, 7, 23

Nadelson, C., 85, 143, 172
Nardi, P.M., 52, 57
National Commission on the Causes
    and Prevention of Violence, 209
National Crime Survey, 3, 4, 14, 20,
    294, 297–299, 306
National Survey of Intergender
    Relationships, 95
National Youth Survey, 222
Nias, D.K.B., 317
Notman, M., 85, 172
Nurses
    sexual problems, 55, 56
    sexual trauma, 51–60

O'Brien, P., 106
O'Neal, E., 309

Parrot, A., 211
Payne, E.J., 212
Pepitone, A., 209
Perdue, W.C., 194
Perper, T., 200
Person, E.S., 200
Pines, A., 77, 79, 81
Pornography research, 317
    definition, 320
    limitations, 318
Post, R., 42
Prentky, R., 111, 113, 118
Profile
    sexual aggression, 14
Prostitutes
    juvenile, 77
    rape 76–88
    street, 77
Psychiatric illness, 27, 28
Pugh, M.D., 209

Rada, R., 112
Rader, C.M., 194
Rapaport, K., 5, 198
Rape
  anxiety, 169
  avoiding, 106
  beliefs, 203–205
  depression, 169
  disclosure, 83
  emotional, 82
  etiology, 194
  fear, 169
  hidden, 3–25
  impact, 184
  label, 264
  law reform, 254
  physical impact, 82
  prostitutes, 76–88
  recovery, 151
  resistance, 299
  response strategies, 105–132
  treatment, 172–188
  victim intervention, 83
Rape reporting trends, 278, 279
Rape shield provision, 283
  corroboration, 284
Rape trauma syndrome, 84
Recovery from rape
  self-blame, 151–166
Registered nurses, 53
Reiss, I.L., 197
Resich, P.A., 170, 172
Responsibility
  perceptions, 246
Ressler, R., 113
Rieker, P.P., 51
Roschach, 194
Rose, V.M., 205, 209, 210
Rosenberg Self-Esteem Scale, 159
Rosenfeld, A.A., 28
Rounsaville, B., 28
Rouse, B.A., 53
Russell, D.E.H., 4, 92, 108, 117, 197,
    200, 201, 203–205, 207, 210,
    223
Ryan, W., 210

Sadism, 113
Sanday, P., 197, 221
Sandler, B.R., 204, 207–210
Schiff, A., 117
Schultz, L.G., 208
Schwendinger, J.R., 194, 208
Scully, D., 21, 112, 113, 193, 194,
    203, 204, 207
Seghorn, T., 111–113, 118
Selby, J., 205
Self-blame, 151–166
  behavioral, 153
  characterological, 153
Selkin, J., 117
Server, C.J., 51
Sexual abuse
  boys, 92–104
  classification, 96
  definition, 103
Sexual aggression, 10–20, 23
  child abuse, 91
  incidence, 12
Sexual assault
  adolescent, 227
  definition, 227
  resource services, 188
  uniqueness of victims, 240
  vulnerablity, 221
Sexual dysfunction
  alcoholism, 52
Sexual experiences survey, 8–12
Sexual harassment
  of students, 61–71
Sexual preference
  alcoholism, 52
  male, 52
Sexual socialization, 193–213
  differential sex role, 200
Sexual trauma
  nurses' reports, 52
  sexual problems, 56
Sexuality
  behavioral cues, 253
  cues and signals, 252
  legitimizing force, 254
Sexualized therapy, 133–150

Shiveley, M.D., 198
Shotland, R.C., 211, 213
Silbert, M., 77–79, 81
Simon, W., 246
Singer, J., 206
Sixth Amendment, 276
Skinner, L.J., 194, 202
Skogan, W.G., 306
Smith, D., 317
Spinner, B., 317
Stanton, A.L., 205
Stark, E., 28, 42
Statistical tests
    Armor's *theta*, 160
    Wilkes, 179
Stein, J., 83
Stewart, C.S., 246
Stewart, P., 318
Stinchcombe, A.L., 305
Stock, W., 200, 206
Stockard, J., 61
Stone, A., 148
Storie, K., 64
Strategies for rape resistance,
    119–127
    acquiescence, 121
    escape, 119
    nonconfrontative physical, 121
    nonconfrontative verbal, 120
    physically confrontative, 120
    rapist type, 122–126
    verbally confrontative, 120
Sullivan, E., 52
Symonds, M., 83
Symons, D., 195

Terr, L., 41
Therapist-patient sex, 134
    causes, 134–141
    consequences, 144–146
    consultation, 146
Thomson, G.E., 61, 68
Tieger, T., 198
Traw, M., 198

Underwood, B., 198
Uniform Crime Reports, 299
Urban Institute, 156
U.S. Attorney General's Commis-
    sion on Pornography, 317, 318
U.S. Presidential Commission on
    Obscenity and Pornography,
    317
Utigard, C.N., 213

Verner, A.M., 246
Veronen, L.J., 170, 171
Victim
    domestic, 42
    in-patient, 36, 38
    intervention, 83
    out-patient, 41–49
    and psychiatric illness, 27–39
    response strategies, 105–129
    treatment, 169–188
Victimization
    urban women, 295–300
Volk, K.D., 201
Volpe, R., 64
Vulnerability
    conceptualization, 223
    rape, 222–241

Warr, M., 105
Weihofen, H., 112, 113
Weinberg, M., 92
Weiss, K., 200, 205, 207–211, 223,
    265
Weissman, M.M., 28
Wheeler, J.R., 213
Wigmore, J.H., 271
Williams, J.E., 203, 205, 208, 210,
    213, 221
Wilsnack, S.C., 52, 57
Wolpe-Lang Fear Survey, 171

Zellman, G., 208, 211
Zelnich, M., 246

NOV